BARBED VOICES

The George and Sakaye Aratani Nikkei in the Americas Series

SERIES EDITOR LANE HIRABAYASHI

This series endeavors to capture the best scholarship available illustrating the evolving nature of contemporary Japanese American culture and community. By stretching the boundaries of the field to the limit (whether at a substantive, theoretical, or comparative level) these books aspire to influence future scholarship in this area specifically, and Asian American Studies, more generally.

BARBED VOICES

ORAL HISTORY, RESISTANCE, AND THE WORLD WAR II JAPANESE AMERICAN SOCIAL DISASTER

ARTHUR A. HANSEN

UNIVERSITY PRESS OF COLORADO
Louisville

Published by University Press of Colorado
245 Century Circle, Suite 202
Louisville, Colorado 80027

The University Press of Colorado is a proud member of
the Association of University Presses.

The University Press of Colorado is a cooperative publishing enterprise supported, in part, by Adams State University, Colorado State University, Fort Lewis College, Metropolitan State University of Denver, Regis University, University of Colorado, University of Northern Colorado, Utah State University, and Western State Colorado University.

∞ This paper meets the requirements of the ANSI/NISO Z39.48–1992 (Permanence of Paper).

ISBN: 978-1-60732-811-7 (cloth)
ISBN: 978-1-64642-182-4 (paperback)
ISBN: 978-1-60732-812-4 (ebook)
DOI: https://doi.org/10.5876/9781607328124

Library of Congress Cataloging-in-Publication Data

Names: Hansen, Arthur A., author.
Title: Barbed voices : oral history, resistance, and the World War II Japanese American social disaster / Arthur A. Hansen.
Other titles: George and Sakaye Aratani Nikkei in the Americas series.
Description: Louisville : University Press of Colorado, [2018] | Series: George and Sakaye Aratani Nikkei in the Americas series | Includes bibliographical references and index.
Identifiers: LCCN 2018023680| ISBN 9781607328117 (cloth) | ISBN 9781646421824 (paperback) | ISBN 9781607328124 (ebook)
Subjects: LCSH: Japanese Americans—Evacuation and relocation, 1942-1945. | Japanese Americans—Social conditions—History—20th century. | World War, 1939-1945—Concentration camps—West (U.S.) | Civil disobedience—United States—History—20th century. | World War, 1939-1945—Japanese Americans. | Oral history.
Classification: LCC D769.8.A6 H356 2018 | DDC 940.53/1773089956—dc23
LC record available at https://lccn.loc.gov/2018023680

This publication was made possible, in part, with support from the University of California Los Angeles's Aratani Endowed Chair in Asian American Studies.

Chapter 1 was first published in *The Journal of American History* (© 1995) and is reproduced with permission of the Oxford University Press. Chapter 2 was first published in the *Amerasia Journal* (© 1974) and is reproduced with permission. Chapter 3 is from *Interactive Oral History Interviewing* edited by Eva M. McMahan and Kim Lacy Rogers (© 1994) and reproduced with permission of Taylor and Francis Group, LLC, a division of Informa PLC. Chapter 4 was first published in *Arizona and the West* (© 1985) and is reproduced with permission. Chapter 5 is from *A Matter of Conscience: Essays on the World War II Heart Mountain Draft Resistance Movement* edited by Mike Mackey (© 2002) and reproduced with permission of Mike Mackey. Chapter 6 is from *Guilt by Association: Essays on Japanese Settlement, Internment, and Relocation in the Rocky Mountain West* edited by Mike Mackey (© 2001) and reproduced with permission of Mike Mackey. Chapter 7 is from *Remembering Heart Mountain: Essays on Japanese American Internment in Wyoming* edited by Mike Mackey (© 1998) and reproduced with permission of Mike Mackey. Chapter 8 is from *Nikkei in the Pacific Northwest: Japanese Americans and Japanese Canadians in the Twentieth Century* edited by Louis Fiset and Gail M. Nomura (© 2005) and reprinted with permission of the University of Washington Press.

For three special Nikkei friends:
Kinji Yada, Lloyd Inui, and Kurtis Nakagawa

There is a crack in everything, that's how the light gets in.
Leonard Cohen

CONTENTS

A NOTE ON EDITING

All of the writings in this volume appear as they did when originally published except for minor changes relating to factual errors; typographical, spelling, and grammatical mistakes; unclear or infelicitous narrative constructions; some updated endnotes; and, in the cases of "The Manzanar 'Riot'" (chapter 2) and "A Riot of Voices"(chapter 3), respectively, the transfer of selected endnote content to the text proper and the inclusion of three appendixes. In addition, two overarching alterations have been effected: (1) the vocabulary utilized in relation to the World War II exclusion and detention experience of Japanese Americans has been rendered to reflect the recent terminological shift in the field of Japanese American studies from euphemistic to accurate descriptive language; and (2) all matters of editorial style have been placed in conformity with the guidelines set forth in the 16th edition of *The Chicago Manual of Style*.

Readers of this volume should also be aware of a few unavoidable inconsistencies within the text and the notes owing to historical peculiarities and changes in institutional nomenclature and classification. With respect to the first category, the detention center at Manzanar utilized idiosyncratic designations for its iterations as both an "assembly center" (Owens Valley Reception Center) and a "relocation center" (Manzanar War Relocation Center), while the detention center at Tule Lake was transformed in 1943 from the Tule Lake Relocation Center to the Tule Lake Segregation Center. As to the second category, in 2003 the Oral History Program at California State University, Fullerton, first altered its appellation in 2003 to the Center for Oral and Public History and then again in 2017 to the Lawrence de Graaf Center for Oral and Public History. At the same time, this institution's Japanese American Project, while officially retaining this name, sometimes chose to represent itself as the Japanese American Oral History Project so as to avoid having its title abbreviated with a racist acronym. Then, too, the University of California, Berkeley–sponsored research group that was launched in 1942 under the name of the Evacuation and Resettlement Study (ERS) underwent an evolution in designation to the Japanese Evacuation and Resettlement Study (JERS) and then to the Japanese American Evacuation and Resettlement Study (JERS). In this connection, the collection of documents for this research group housed at UC Berkeley's Bancroft Library was first cataloged in 1958 under the label of the Japanese American Evacuation and Resettlement (JAER) and then re-cataloged in 1996 as the Japanese American Evacuation and Resettlement Records (JAERR). Accordingly, those chapters in this book that were originally published prior to 1996 have been referenced in conformity with JAER categories, while those published after 1996 have been referenced in conformity with JAERR categories.

FOREWORD

LANE RYO HIRABAYASHI

The events surrounding the 1942 beating of Japanese American Citizens League leader Fred Tayama in an American concentration camp for Nikkei (people of Japanese ancestry) are a long-standing mystery. Who were the men who attacked Tayama and why did they do it? Although there were many rumors, no one knew for sure. More than forty years later, Harry Ueno, the alleged ringleader, gave distinguished historian Arthur A. Hansen a sealed envelope containing a "confession" to be publicly divulged at Hansen's discretion, which Hansen then determined to mean well after Ueno's death. The contents of that envelope are revealed for the first time in chapter 3 of this book. Strikingly, Ueno's revelations ultimately tell us more about the power of oral history in the hands of an expert practitioner than they do about criminal responsibility.

Barbed Voices presents eight of Hansen's best essays, but this book is much more than a convenient collection of article-length publications. Each chapter retains the extensive footnotes that mark Hansen's reputation for meticulous detail, but each essay is now accompanied by a new prefatory introduction. By appearing for the first time in this fashion, within the new overarching analysis of the incarceration as a social disaster, this revitalized collection allows readers to appreciate more fully the integrity that has characterized Hansen's research over the course of his long career.

Anyone looking for a social history of Nikkei responses to "incarceration as social disaster" will not be disappointed by Hansen's insights. In eight data-packed chapters Hansen captures the significance of the oppositional politics of Nikkei who refused to accept mistreatment in War Relocation Authority camps like Manzanar (California), Gila (Arizona), and Heart Mountain (Wyoming). At the same time, Hansen demonstrates that Japanese Americans actually responded quite differentially to the question of loyalty during the 1940s. Essays on Harry Ueno, the martyr of Manzanar, Ben Kuroki, the war hero, and James Omura, the veteran Japanese American journalist, bring home the point that loyalty, as defined by Japanese American protagonists, lay at the foundation of the Nikkei's varied responses to the wartime challenges they faced. And it was precisely in the crucible of the 1940s and 1950s that Japanese American ethnicity transformed from a "subconscious core of personal identity" to "the core of JA collective identity," which following the end of the war was decidedly "American" in tone and which indubitably led to the Redress movement in the 1980s.

At this juncture, given the many books now available on Japanese Americans and the war, why is *Barbed Voices* not only a significant but a timely publication? I would argue that this collection is invaluable, since so many current "theoretical" interventions make scant reference to lived experience, thus remaining inexorably ungrounded. But in what fashion does *Barbed Voices* respond to armchair theorists' unfettered abstractions and comparisons?

In Hansen's hands, oral history is not merely a collection of personal narratives, naïvely taken at face value as being "the truth." Rather, such accounts emerge as a remarkably viable way to get at the following:

1. respondents' unfolding consciousness about the sociocultural world;
2. respondents' ideologies, accounting for their contemporaries' motives and actions; and
3. the meanings ascribed to the above.

Drawing from "practice theory" to explain what this means, a researcher's first aim is to track the development of awareness, implying that "consciousness" itself is not fixed but rather that it evolves through time. Consciousness, in turn, exhibits this quality because it is inherently open to interpretation—Hansen's ruminations in chapter 3 on the "truth" of the Manzanar Riot illustrate the virtues of his method in this regard. In terms of ideologies, the historian assumes that subjects are engaged in political arenas wherein struggles of varying intensity occur in the search for power as well as prestige. In this context, ideologies are vernacular assessments that identify the relevant players, what is at stake for them, and what forces may be deployed in the ongoing competition that characterizes struggle in various fields of endeavor. Oral history of this kind is ultimately generative because it offers insight into respondents' lived experience, situating perceptions and practices squarely within respondents' maps of meaning.

By way of conclusion I'd like to note that my own personal sense of identity, as shaped by the Hirabayashi family's legacy, dates back to the 1968 strike at San Francisco State University, where my dad took me to walk the picket line with him. Over the course of the next fifty years, I have pondered what it means to be Nikkei, often under the tutelage of some of the community's best thinkers and activists. In turn I have done my best to contribute to the conversation, but, even so, it is humbling to take a retrospective look at Art Hansen's contributions to our collective discussion.

I commend *Barbed Voices* because it sets a new standard. It exemplifies why Hansen is considered one of the top scholars in his field. Not only is it full of invaluable insights into the Nikkei experience, built from the ground up; it also evidences an irreplaceable data set as well as what is an enduring approach to carrying out social history. In other words, Hansen's corpus presents the most detailed account yet available in terms of Japanese American studies of how to actually carry out social history in a meticulous, insightful, and reflexive (which is to say politically and ethically self-conscious) fashion, And this in a community that because of the way it was "studied" in the 1940s has so many reasons to distrust, if not to reject, anything that smacks of research.

Barbed Voices is thus simultaneously an invitation as well as a primer, rich in both its substantive content and its illustration of methodological, political, and analytic coherence in social research. In *Barbed Voices* we get to see, up close, the research practice of an outstanding scholar. Art has worked tirelessly to comprehend what it was like to be a Japanese American enduring the travails of racial oppression in twentieth-century America. This book is one more resource that helps us understand how he has been able to do just that.

FOR FURTHER CONSIDERATION

For Information on Hansen's family background, his academic training, his professional career at California State University, Fullerton, and his use of oral history vis-à-vis his classes and his undergraduate and graduate students, we are fortunate to have a two-part videotaped interview that can been seen, online, at the Densho Project archives:

Part 1, http://ddr.densho.org/interviews/ddr-densho-1000-295-1/, and
http://ddr.densho.org/interviews/ddr-densho-1000-295-1/
Part 2, http://ddr.densho.org/narrators/165/

Another perspective on Hansen's contributions can be garnered though an examination of his published oral histories, which, as intimated in *Barbed Voices*, are very highly regarded both by his academic peers and by knowledgeable members of the Japanese American community. Exemplary in this regard is the multivolume *Japanese American World War II Evacuation Oral History Project*, definitely one of the most holistic portraits of incarceration yet available, as it is inclusive of those who lived in, studied, and guarded the camps. My own favorite is part 3, *Analysts*, which presents full-length accounts of camp researchers ranging from the Nisei Togo Tanaka to the anthropologist Robert Spencer. The depth and quality of Hansen's oral histories are evident when comparing his questions and the resulting conversations with any similar publications.

ACKNOWLEDGMENTS

During the three-plus decades in which the writings in this volume first appeared in print I became indebted to a veritable legion of people for their timely and useful assistance. In fact, the list of my benefactors is so long as to make it too hazardous to attempt to recount them here. Almost certainly I would overlook inadvertently individuals who fully merit inclusion, which could possibly offend them and thereby leave me to nurse harsh pangs of contrition.

As an alternative to the customary practice, then, I have chosen to acknowledge here only those sociocultural theoreticians, broadly construed, whose writings and other creative productions in the present context both stimulated my creative juices and leavened the loaf of my empirical historical findings. Almost half of these individuals I have known personally, while the others I have encountered only through their work. All served as inspiring and enabling mentors for me, though none should be held accountable for any shortcomings in my representation and/or use of their conceptual formulations.

I would like to thank the following humanistic thinkers, listed alphabetically by surname: Frank Abe, John Bodner, Allan R. Bosworth, Leonard Broom, Jerome Charyn, Frank Chin, Stanley Cohen, Roger Daniels, James C. Davies, Richard Drinnon, John Embree, Gretchen Ehrlich, Kai Erikson, Clifford Geertz, Audrie Girdner, Morton Grodzins, Stephen Fugita, Roger Gottlieb, Ronald Grele, Masumi Hayashi, Sumiko Higashi, James Hirabayashi, Lane Hirabayashi, Eric Hobsbawm, William Hohri, Kathleen Hulser, Samuel Hynes, Yuji Ichioka, Peter Irons, Norman Richard Jackman, Paul Jacobs, Gwenn Jensen, Tetsuden Kashima, Robert Kelley, Lauren Kessler, Charles Kikuchi, Akemi Kikumura, Harry H.L. Kitano, John I. Kitsuse, Yosh Kuromiya, Saul Landau, Christopher Lasch, Alexander Leighton, Lawrence Levine, Anne Loftis, Stanford Lyman, Floyd Matson, Susan McKay, Frank Miyamoto, John Modell, Eric Muller, Carlos Munoz Jr., Kenji Murase, Douglas Nelson, Wendy Ng, Richard Nishimoto, Martha Norkunas, David O'Brien, Raymond Okamura, Steven Okazaki, Gary Okihiro, Chizuko Omori, Emiko Omori, Morris Opler, Richard Pells, Thomas Brewer Rice, Renato Rosaldo, Robert Howard Ross, James Sakoda, Naoko Shibusawa, Tamotsu Shibutani, Matthew Richard Speier, Robert Spencer, Edward Spicer, Paul Spickard, Orin Starn, John Steinbeck, Peter Suzuki, Rae Tajiri, Dana Y. Takagi, Jere Takahashi, Rita Takahashi, Yasuko Takezawa, Janice Tanaka, Togo Tanaka, Studs Terkel, David Thelan, Dorothy Swain Thomas, William Isaac Thomas, Tami Tsuchiyama, Warren Tsuneishi, George Wada, Rosalie Hankey Wax, Michi Nishiura Weglyn, Gene Wise, Toshio Yatsushiro, and David Yoo.

Finally, it has been my great pleasure to receive the encouragement, support, and guidance of the University Press of Colorado staff, most particularly two very special people, former acquisitions editor Jessica d'Arbonne and series editor Lane Ryo Hirabayashi, who also provided the book's luminous foreword. Also, my commendation goes to the two anonymous peer readers of my manuscript, both of whom gave me excellent constructive suggestions for enhancement. In addition, I would like to extend my heartfelt thanks to the following University Press of Colorado staff members—Darrin Pratt, Director; Laura Furney, Assistant Director and Managing Editor; Charlotte Steinhardt, Acquisitions Editor; Daniel Pratt, Production Manager; Alison Tartt, Copyeditor; Beth Svinarich, Sales and Marketing Manager; and Doug Easton, indexer.

BARBED VOICES

INTRODUCTION

This anthology consists of eight articles by me that have previously been published in a variety of books and journals through my career-long passion for and preoccupation with the subject of the World War II exclusion and detention experience of Japanese Americans.[1] All of these writings on that subject intertwine my dual commitment to the historical phenomenon of social resistance and the research method of oral history. Accordingly, the volume as a whole is enriched by the intertextual compatibility of its constituent parts, each of which is informed by my ideological allegiance to employing principled dissent, protest, and struggle to redress oppressive institutional power emanating from whatever source.

In the case of the essays in the volume, the resistance depicted by Japanese American individuals and groups was mounted primarily against an "external" oppressor, the US government, and an "internal" one, the Japanese American Citizens League. Since neither of these two entities was monolithic in nature, it should be assumed that the oppressive power being resisted in both cases was their controlling core leadership, not their inclusive and diverse membership.

DOI: 10.5876/9781607328124.c000

It should be understood, also, that the essays in *Barbed Voices* exemplify and valorize two species of resistance against oppression. Although these are closely related, they are also significantly different. The first type of resistance falls under the classification of *history*, the second of *memory*. In the former instance, the intention has been to document some of the degree and diversity of resistance activity enacted by Nikkei, or Japanese Americans, during the World War II years; in the latter case, the governing purpose has been to draw upon this empirical data both to help develop a new and robust narrative for the Japanese American wartime experience and to provide present and future Nikkei with a usable past upon which to anchor their persisting quest for an enlarged constitutional democracy, comprehensive social justice, and vitalized human dignity.

With respect to the designation of "social disaster" within the study's subtitle to describe the World War II Japanese American experience, I have arrived at it advisedly. Permit me to explain. In comparatively recent times, the older journalistic accounts of disasters have given way to more sophisticated methods of data collection and theorization. Nowadays a special, and rather esoteric, branch of collective behavior, "disaster research" includes a body of findings about the psychosocial impact of disasters.

To date, most research in this field has been focused upon physical disasters—hurricanes, tornadoes, earthquakes, fires, and floods—but increasingly attention has been paid to the impact of man-made disasters such as bombing attacks and industrial accidents. As early as 1972, for example, the British sociologist Stanley Cohen, in *Folk Devils and Moral Panics*, applied disaster research models to explain the reaction of the British public in the 1960s to the Mods and Rockers rebellious youth phenomenon. Therein, Cohen adopted the sequential model used by disaster researchers to describe the phases of a typical disaster: warning, threat, impact, inventory, rescue, remedy, and recovery.

Although mindful that the "moral panics" under investigation by him—the decade-long series of deviant juvenile happenings at British seaside resorts—cannot be considered disasters in the same sense as earthquakes or floods, Cohen still felt both that (1) there are sufficient resemblances between the two categories of events and (2) definitions of "disaster" are broad and inconsistent enough to warrant his extrapolation from existing theory.

Likewise, it is my contention that the events constituting the Nikkei wartime eviction and incarceration experience lend themselves to similar extrapolation. As Cohen observed, although definitions of disaster are characterized by imprecision, an inventory of them reveals agreement on the follow salient elements: "whole or part of a community must be affected, a large segment of the community must be confronted with actual or potential danger, [and] there must be a loss of cherished values and material objects resulting in death or injury or destruction to property."[2]

Given these criteria, it is hardly an exaggeration or a distortion to style what the Japanese American population underwent a disaster. First of all, the mass removal and confinement policy of the US government directly affected almost the entire Japanese American mainland community. Not only healthy adults, but pregnant mothers, hospitalized cases, the extremely aged, and even infants were evicted to makeshift and isolated detention centers.

Second, from the time of Japan's attack on the Pearl Harbor naval base in Hawai'i on December 7, 1941, to the ultimate closing of the ten War Relocation Authority–administered concentration camps, this affected majority of the Nikkei community dwelt in a daily atmosphere colored and confounded by actual and potential danger. If before the Japanese Americans' exclusion and confinement per se it was difficult to distinguish between potential and actual danger, thereafter it became virtually impossible to do so. Who is to say whether living in a horse stall or being surrounded by barbed wire and monitored by armed sentries in watchtowers posed a real or prospective danger to the imprisoned Nikkei. Comparing what the inmates confronted with "famine, flood, drought, disease, or other calamities," Nisei anthropologist Toshio Yatsushiro, a Bureau of Sociological Research staff member at the Poston Relocation Center in southwest Arizona, aptly concluded that "the situation . . . in the center had all the characteristics of a disaster."[3]

Lastly, there is no gainsaying that the third criterion applying to disasters—a loss of cherished values and material objects resulting in death or injury or destruction to property—fits the facts of what the confined wartime Japanese Americans faced. Not only were entire West Coast Japanese American communities uprooted and scuttled by Executive Order 9066,[4] but also the series of actions that this action catalyzed entailed a cataclysmic change in every facet of the victimized population's cultural composition. The fabric of family was stretched and torn, the pattern of leadership disturbed, the economic structure dismantled, and the underlying sense of personal, family, and community identity endangered. Infusing and imparting focus to the assorted socioeconomic losses was the psychological conviction of being a threatened people.

The burden of this anthology is to provide a basis for understanding why, when, where, and how at least some of the 120,000 imprisoned Americans of Japanese ancestry responded with resistance to the perilously threatened status of themselves, their families, their reference groups, and their racial-ethnic community during World War II.

NOTES

1. The bibliographical references for the originally titled eight articles, in the order of their appearance within the volume, are as follows: "Oral History and the Japanese American Evacuation," *Journal of American History* 18 (September 1995): 625–39; "The Manzanar Riot: An Ethnic Perspective," *Amerasia Journal* 2 (Fall 1974): 112–57; "A Riot of Voices: Racial and Ethnic Variables in Interactive Oral History Interviewing," in *Interactive Oral History Interviewing*, ed. Eva M. McMahan and Kim Lacy Rogers, 107–39 (Hillsdale, NJ: Lawrence Erlbaum Associates, 1994); "Cultural Politics in the Gila Relocation Center, 1942–1943," *Arizona and the West* 27 (Winter 1985): 237–62; "Protest-Resistance and the Heart Mountain Experience: The Revitalization of a Robust Nikkei Tradition," in *A Matter of Conscience: Essays on the World War II Heart Mountain Draft Resistance Movement*, ed. Mike Mackey, 81–117 (Powell, WY: Western History Publications, 2002); "Political Ideology and Participant Observation: Nisei Social Scientists in the Japanese Evacuation and Resettlement Study, 1942–1945," in *Guilt by Association: Essays on Japanese Settlement, Internment, and Relocation in the Rocky Mountain West*, ed. Mike Mackey, 119–44 (Powell, WY: Western History Publications, 2001); "Sergeant Ben Kuroki's Perilous 'Home Mission,': Contested Loyalty and Patriotism in the Japanese American Detention Centers" in *Remembering Heart Mountain: Essays on Japanese American Internment in Wyoming*, ed. Mike Mackey, 153–75 (Powell, WY: Western History Publications, 1998); "Peculiar Odyssey: Newsman Jimmie Omura's Removal from and Regeneration within Nikkei Society, History, and Memory," in *Nikkei in the Pacific Northwest: Japanese Americans and Japanese Canadians in the Twentieth Century*, ed. Louis Fiset and Gail Nomura, 271–307 (Seattle: University of Washington Press, 2005).

2. Stanley Cohen, *Folk Devils and Moral Panics: The Creation of the Mods and Rockers* (London: MacGibbon and Kee, 1972), 22. See also the second edition (Oxford, UK: Basil Blackwell, 1987) and third edition (Abingdon, UK: Routledge, 2002) of this work, replete with new introductions. In 2011 Routledge released a new edition of this book in its classics series.

3. Toshio Yatsushiro, "Political and Socio-Cultural Issues at Poston and Manzanar Relocation Centers: A Themal Analysis" (PhD diss., Cornell University, 1953), 393.

4. Signed by President Franklin D. Roosevelt on February 19, 1942, this executive order authorized what was to become the mass forced removal and incarceration of all Japanese Americans on the West Coast.

1

ORAL HISTORY AND THE JAPANESE AMERICAN INCARCERATION

Up until 1972, my primary research and teaching interest centered on American and British intellectual, social, and cultural history. During the first six years of my professorship at California State University, Fullerton, from 1966 to 1972, I was preoccupied simultaneously with the task of developing multiple undergraduate courses for history majors and general education students and completing my doctoral dissertation, under the inspired mentoring of the late Robert Kelley at the University of California, Santa Barbara, on the transnational topic "The British Intellectual and Americanization."[1]

Progress on the completion of my dissertation was painfully slowed owing in part to the inordinately steep course load then required of all California State University system faculty. In addition, the planned two-year-long dissertation research in Britain that I had embarked upon in 1965 was forcibly terminated after only four months by the death of my fifty-three-year-old working-class father in California and the attendant needs of my now-widowed mother in Santa Barbara.

This essay was first published in *The Journal of American History* (© 1995) and is reproduced with permission of the Oxford University Press.

DOI: 10.5876/9781607328124.c001

My initial half-dozen years at Cal State Fullerton, in the late 1960s and early 1970s, were enacted against a backdrop—not only at the national and regional levels, but even within my home campus in the reactionary, conservative southern California climate of Orange County—of dissent, protest, and resistance. Although drawn to the dynamics of near daily campus demonstrations of political and cultural politics challenging established authority governing imperialistic wars, chauvinistic gender arrangements, racist social and economic practices, homophobic sexual pieties, elitist class-rule customs, and paternalistic educational policies, I stopped well short of making the transition from an empathetic observer of these demonstrations into an active participant within them.

But once my dissertation was a matter of record and my academic status secure, I made a couple of consequential changes in my modus operandi. The first of these was in my pedagogical style, which involved scrapping my preference for transmitting congealed knowledge through prepared lectures and adopting a variety of teaching strategies that rendered my classrooms as democratic laboratories for interactive student-centered learning, discovery, and self-realization.

The second major change I made pertained to my principal research topic, which now became the World War II Japanese American exclusion and incarceration experience. Allied to this change was the adoption of a new research method, oral history, and a new research focus within my primary topical area, that of resistance to oppression.

At the time I made these changes, both my elected subject area and my methodology were comparatively undeveloped, while my resistance focus within the context of what befell Japanese Americans during World War II represented practically an innovative development in historical scholarship.

After putting this revised orientation to work for more than two decades in my published scholarship and correlated fieldwork, curriculum offerings, and even my professional activities and community service, I was delighted when Michael Frisch and Linda Shopes, the coeditors of a stimulating oral history series for the Journal of American History, *invited me to reflect upon my experiences in a 1995 essay exploring how the disciplined research activity of oral history contributed to the understanding of the World War II Japanese American experience.*

Most oral histories have been used and will continue to be used to gather information: data about the events of the past. But they can also be used to discover unfolding consciousness, to document the varieties of ideology, the creation of meaning, and the more subjective aspects of historical experience.

—*Ronald J. Grele*

The lines above by noted oral historian Ron Grele of Columbia University both frame and animate the present essay. Since 1972 I have directed the Japanese American Project of the Oral History Program at California State University, Fullerton, which has used oral history to document the World War II Japanese American Incarceration (JAI), the defining historical event for people of Japanese ancestry in the United States. During those decades I have observed a dramatic increase in oral historical activity by academic and community historians on the JAI. Moreover, scholars in this field have lately gone beyond using oral history to fill factual gaps and have begun to tackle extra-empirical questions of the sort Ronald J. Grele delineated.[2]

This essay consists of three sections. The first takes up the documentation of the JAI through interviews by social scientists during World War II. The next discusses and explains the slow emergence in the 1960s and 1970s of oral history scholarship related to the incarceration. The closing section ponders the expansion and reconfiguration of such scholarship since the early 1980s.

BEGINNING AT THE BEGINNING

Perhaps the most valuable source of oral history on the JAI is the one most neglected by researchers, the many interviews in the materials amassed during World War II by social scientists who studied the more than 120,000 Japanese Americans imprisoned in ten concentration camps administered by the War Relocation Authority (WRA). There were three principal groups of social scientists: the WRA's Community Analysis Section (CAS), the Bureau of Sociological Research (BSR) under the aegis of the Office of Indian Affairs, and the Japanese American Evacuation and Resettlement Study (JERS), directed by researchers at the University of California, Berkeley.[3] Although JAI scholars have paid increasing attention to the documentation that these wartime research units produced, their interest has rarely extended to the interviews—done without tape recorders and with extreme discretion to protect informants from being branded "informers"—undergirding the field reports that dominate all three data sets.[4]

I will limit my discussion to a single illuminating example, the documentation collected by the anthropologist Morris Edward Opler while he served as the WRA's community analyst at the Manzanar Relocation Center in eastern California. Opler arrived a couple of months after the Manzanar Riot of December 6, 1942, had claimed the lives of two inmates by military police gunfire. Manzanar was once again aboil as a result of army and WRA questionnaires. The responses given to two key questions would determine whether an individual would remain among "loyals" in a "relocation center" such as Manzanar or be imprisoned in a special segregation center for "disloyals."[5]

The WRA had established the CAS, not to carry on traditional anthropological or sociological research, but to help solve the problems of administering the WRA centers. Opler, a seasoned applied anthropologist with several government agencies, behaved differently from most of his CAS counterparts, who typically deferred to the policy desires of camp directors. Opler consistently adopted an inmate perspective. Not only did Opler elect to live in inmate barracks instead of staff housing, but under the names of the plaintiff's lawyers he penned the brief that challenged the incarceration's constitutionality in *Korematsu vs. U.S.* Indeed, the director of Manzanar attempted, unsuccessfully, to have Opler removed from his post.[6]

Perfervidly, if privately, Opler was opposed to the February 1943 loyalty registration. Convinced that loyalty could not be determined by a calculating machine, he probed deeper for the reasons why many Manzanarians, even those who lacked dual citizenship and had never even traveled to Japan, had refused to answer the loyalty questions, responded negatively, or qualified their responses. (Approximately half of Manzanar's male citizens declined to swear unqualified and exclusive allegiance to the United States, but about half of those respondents "later changed their answers to the affirmative.") Opler attended several hundred hearings for such individuals and took down verbatim much of the proceedings, noting the setting and the attitudes and reactions of board members and detainees. Finally, Opler followed up by interviewing selected individuals.[7]

The qualitative data resulting from Opler's herculean efforts permitted him to write the best-grounded and most luminous CAS reports about the so-called loyalty crisis.[8] The multilayered sources created by Opler and other social scientists represent a gold mine for researchers interested in diverse topics, including family structure, gender relations, community organization, and psychosocial behavior.

THE WAGES OF TRAUMA

In 1974 I coedited *Voices Long Silent*, an anthology that featured edited transcripts of interviews in the CSU, Fullerton, Japanese American Project collection. Our book's title rested on the two assumptions that (1) few interviews had been done with Nikkei (Japanese Americans) about their wartime experience because (2) Issei (aliens) and Nisei (their American-born children, who were US citizens) had been so traumatized by that experience that they were unable or unwilling to communicate their recollections. Those governing assumptions were announced to readers in epigraphs (excerpted below) from project interviews with two Nisei women leaders of a Los Angeles-based group that spearheaded an annual pilgrimage to the Manzanar site.

> Women, if they've been raped, don't go around talking about it. . . . This is exactly the kind of feeling that we as evacuees, victims of circumstances, had at the time of evacuation. A lot of Nisei and Issei are actually ashamed . . . that they were in a concentration camp. (Amy Uno Ishii)

> An NBC reporter asked [Jim Matsuoka], "How many people are buried here in the [Manzanar] cemetery?" and he said, "A whole generation. A whole generation of Japanese who are now so frightened that they will not talk. They're quiet Americans. They're all buried here." (Sue Kunitomi Embrey)[9]

Some oral history activity relative to the JAI began in the 1960s. When Bill Hosokawa, a *Denver Post* associate editor and onetime editor of a detention camp newspaper, was writing *Nisei* in the 1960s, he interviewed many Nisei about their lives before, during, and after their wartime imprisonment. He also exploited the JAI-accented contents of the 307 taped interviews (the majority in the Japanese language) in the Japanese American Research Project (JARP) collection housed at the University of California, Los Angeles (UCLA). These interviews, most with Nikkei, had been done between 1964 and 1969 by Joe Grant Masaoka, a Manzanar detainee who served that camp as a WRA documentary historian, and members of the Japanese American Citizens League (JACL).[10]

Meanwhile, non-Nikkei were conducting and preserving oral histories with JAI participants and observers. Most notably, the Regional Oral History Office (ROHO) at the University of California, Berkeley, interviewed Caucasians connected with the JAI as upper-echelon government officials, WRA administrators, or leaders of fair-play committees. Audrie Girdner and Anne Loftis (daughter of oral history's modern founding father, Allan Nevins of Columbia University) donated to ROHO the numerous interviews they did with Nikkei and non-Nikkei while writing their well-researched popular study of the JAI, *The Great Betrayal*.[11]

For researchers, however, all but the interviews generated by ROHO—which were transcribed, edited, and published—posed problems of access or use. In the tradition of journalists, Hosokawa was silent as to the provenance of his interviews, as were the authors of two other journalistic works—Allan Bosworth's *America's Concentration Camps* and Paul Bailey's *City in the Sun*. The problems of the invaluable JARP interviews became a matter of record in 1974, when Gary Okihiro (then a UCLA graduate student) prepared a survey that bemoaned the lack of a catalogue indicating the tapes' contents, the poor condition of the tapes, the discrepancy in their filing, the difficulties of identifying interview participants, the background noise in recordings, and the interviewers' poor preparation and bias. The Girdner and Loftis tapes were consigned to the Bancroft Library, without transcripts or a detailed finding aid, and preserved under poor storage conditions.[12]

The Japanese American Project at CSU, Fullerton, was unusual in that most of its interviews were focused on the JAI, done with Nikkei participants, fully processed as archival documents, and made readily accessible to researchers. By contrast, in the larger collection of JAI interviews compiled under the direction of Donald Hata, a historian and Gila River Relocation Center survivor, at Fullerton's sister CSU campus in Dominguez Hills, interview summaries and outlines were substituted for transcripts, while the interviews themselves were not widely advertised as research documents. On the other hand, undergraduate student interviewers conducted many of the Fullerton interviews, and so their value for researchers varies dramatically.[13]

The Fullerton collection also privileged Nisei over Issei informants because it depended on non-Japanese-speaking interviewers. Reverend Heihachiro Takarabe, the Japan-born, bilingual pastor of the Parkview Presbyterian Church in Sacramento, California, was not so hampered when he began the Issei Oral History Project in 1969. Advised by historians at CSU, Sacramento, and using the skills of volunteer parishioners, this project had by 1977 taped over 180 interviews. They embraced the experiences of Issei men and women from a variety of backgrounds and many West Coast cities and towns. The project published *Issei Christians*, which contained six transcribed individual interviews plus one group interview. The transcriptions abound with significant stories, told from a Christian perspective, about wartime lives at alien internment and WRA detention centers. The culmination of the project came in 1983, when Eileen Sunada Sarasohn, a Sansei (third-generation Japanese American) born at the Tule Lake camp in California, edited thirty-two project interviews into a polished anthology-cum-narrative, almost half of it devoted to JAI recollections.[14]

BREAKING THE SILENCE

Before the 1980s only a little oral history work had been done on the JAI as a result of individual repression and social amnesia. That small body of work suffered from the absence of methodological or archival sophistication, although historians owe a great debt to those who produced, processed, and safeguarded it for posterity. In retrospect, it is also clear that those producing (and, for that matter, those consuming) oral data on this major event in American history focused on the use of oral history to fill factual gaps at the expense of its capacity to track consciousness, map meaning, and explore ideas, beliefs, and values.

However, a different picture emerged in the 1980s and continues into the 1990s. At the grass roots, as readers of the Nikkei vernacular press are well aware, hardly a month goes by without an announcement of the inauguration, advancement, or completion of an oral history project covering a specific Japanese American community, usually one on the West Coast. Many of the projects represent cooperative ventures with nearby institutions such as universities and colleges, museums, libraries, or community centers. Increasingly, project staff members have ensured that their interviews, documents, and artifacts are systematically organized, properly archived, and used—for example, in curriculum and resource guides, interpretive exhibits, and documentary films.[15]

Over the past fifteen years, oral history of the JAI has also flourished in academe. Readers of the March 1995 *Journal of American History*, for instance, could read reviews of four Japanese American histories by university-based scholars. All the books examined World War II or its consequences and depended heavily upon oral history interviews. In 1993 scholars published two oral history studies centered on the single Nikkei community of Hood River Valley, Oregon, which four years earlier had been the subject of a doctoral dissertation by still another researcher.[16]

If by the mid-1990s the JAI was rapidly becoming one of the best-documented events in American history via oral history interviews, the main reason was indisputably the campaign for redress in Japanese America, which culminated when President Ronald Reagan signed the Civil Liberties Act of 1988. This campaign to obtain an apology and compensation from the US government for its wrongful actions toward Japanese Americans during World War II began institutionally at the 1970 national JACL convention. There JACL renegades sought to extend their work on repealing the Emergency Detention Act of 1950 by introducing a resolution to seek compensatory legislation. That resolution and similar ones proposed at successive JACL conventions provoked resistance from delegates fearful of rocking the boat at a time when Japanese Americans were being lauded as a "model minority." Still, the JACL formed a committee on redress, and in 1979 the organization decided against demanding individual payments for each incarcerated victim and urged instead a government commission to study the matter and recommend remedies.[17]

The creation by Congress in 1980 of the Commission on Wartime Relocation and Internment of Civilians (CWRIC) set the stage for the watershed event in oral history documentation of the JAI: the CWRIC public hearings of 1981. At these hearings, conducted in cities across the United States, the commission heard testimony from over 750 witnesses. Some were former high-ranking civilian and military government officials, non-Nikkei employees at the WRA camps such as teachers, physicians, and social workers, and JAI scholars, journalists, and concerned citizens. But overwhelmingly the witnesses were West Coast Japanese Americans who had experienced incarceration. Roger Daniels, the foremost historian of the JAI and a CWRIC consultant, has described how their passionate oral testimony shattered four decades of self-denial and silence: "Many wept openly, some broke down, and, when at the Los Angeles hearings, Senator [Samuel I.] Hayakawa testified against monetary redress, the audience, largely Japanese American, disrupted the hearing with shouts, boos, and hisses."[18]

That the CWRIC hearings had served Japanese Americans as a community catharsis became evident in the quickened oral history activity on the JAI that followed the commission's 1982 findings (exclusion and detention had resulted, not from military necessity, but from race prejudice, war hysteria, and a failure of political leadership) and 1983 recommendations (the most significant were a congressional apology to all victims and $20,000 tax-free payments to survivors). It was particularly fitting that the first published volume composed almost exclusively of oral histories from former incarcerees at WRA camps, *And Justice for All*, appeared in 1984. Its editor, John Tateishi, had spent his infancy at Manzanar. There his father (to whose memory the book was dedicated) was an outspoken anti-JACL dissident whom camp authorities forcibly removed to an isolation center following the 1942 riot. The younger Tateishi joined the redress movement in the mid-1970s and became the JACL's national redress director.[19]

In the preface to *And Justice for All*, Tateishi explained that, although the people included in his book represented only a small number among the thousands who had suffered "the trauma of false imprisonment," their accounts exemplified what the others had experienced in America's concentration camps. "Up to now," concluded Tateishi, "painful memories have kept Japanese Americans unwilling and unable to talk. But they are silent no more." Those who ruptured the silence included some who had quietly complied with exclusion orders and even volunteered for overseas combat duty and others who had tested the constitutionality of the forced mass incarceration or in other ways challenged government policies and the authority of camp officials.[20]

Two of Tateishi's narrators who fall in the latter category are Harry Ueno, the principal figure in the Manzanar riot, and Jack Tono, a member of the Fair Play Committee at the Heart Mountain camp, where he participated in the only organized draft resistance movement in the WRA camps. Tono was sentenced to three years in a federal penitentiary for refusing to be drafted from behind barbed wire without a prior restoration or clarification of his rights as a US citizen. In the early 1980s, Tono, many of the other eighty-four Fair Play Committee draft resisters, and James Omura, a journalist who was arrested and tried for writing in support of their movement, were interviewed by champions of redress—the Chinese American playwright Frank Chin and two Sansei, the journalist Frank Abe and the poet Lawson Inada. These invaluable interviews, the basis for a forthcoming documentary film on the Heart Mountain draft resistance movement, are available to researchers at Washington State University.[21] As for Ueno, an interview published by Japanese American Project personnel at CSU, Fullerton, in 1986 documents his role as the head of Manzanar's Kitchen Workers Union and his post-Manzanar odyssey through municipal jails, isolation centers, and the Tule Lake Segregation Center.[22]

Unfortunately, the interviews in Tateishi's book were apparently not archived for researcher use. Nor is this an isolated problem. A few years ago, in a session that I chaired at a regional oral history conference, none of the three presenters—an anthropologist, a sociologist, and a historian—had arranged to deposit his/her extensive and seemingly innovative community oral history interviews, many pertaining to the JAI, in a public archive. More recently, when I reviewed four recent JAI-related oral history studies, I was dismayed to discover that one author (a university-based journalist) failed to indicate a repository for her interviews and another (an academic historian) simply listed her interviews in the bibliography as being "in author's possession."

Let us hope that the 1989 American Historical Association guidelines on the use of interviews in scholarly research will help reform this unfortunate practice and thereby broaden and deepen the archival database for students of the JAI.[23] An even more promising step was taken in 1995 when the ably staffed and well-endowed Japanese American National Museum (JANM) in Los Angeles announced its new Life History Program, which is "dedicated to making accessible life history materials documenting the lives of Japanese Americans throughout the United States." The program will act as a central repository for tapes, videos, and transcripts; produce an annotated bibliography of all completed and ongoing oral history works on the Japanese American experience; and establish standards and training for Japanese Americans to collect and preserve their own life histories.[24]

Three fascinating projects give glimpses of the extent and variety of recent oral historical documentation of the JAI. The first encompasses interviews done in 1982–83 by Cornell University students Deborah Gesensway and Mindy Roseman with twenty-five Nikkei artists. The interviews, edited segments of which appear in their remarkable book, *Beyond Words*, deftly explore how the artists' many levels of consciousness were expressed in their paintings, drawings, and sketches of camp life.[25]

The second oral history project documents the horrific experiences of Japanese American victims of the atomic bombings of Hiroshima and Nagasaki. Although most interviews are with Nikkei trapped in Japan at war's outbreak, more relevant here are the few with those A-bomb victims who had been incarcerated in the United States and then opted for repatriation or expatriation to their ancestral land rather than remaining in a country that had distrusted, imprisoned, and profoundly shamed them.[26]

The third is the Japanese Peruvian Oral History Project, begun in 1991 under the aegis of the National Japanese American Historical Society in San Francisco and inspired by conversations its youthful Nikkei coordinator had with her father about his wartime uprooting and internment. The project preserves the painful memories of the 1,800 Japanese Peruvians who were forcibly removed from their country after Pearl Harbor and sent to the United States, interned in Department of Justice camps as a hostage pool for prisoner-of-war exchanges with Japan, and after the war (at least half of them) deported to war-ravaged Japan. Beyond its historical and educational goals, this project seeks to promote dialogue and interaction between the Japanese Peruvians and the broader society in the United States, Peru, and Japan and to provide information for Japanese Peruvians seeking redress and reparations for their wartime mistreatment.[27]

Some of the most exciting recent oral history work on the JAI revolves around the blocked or selective intergenerational transmission of knowledge between Nisei who experienced the incarceration and their Sansei children who did not. The sociologist Wendy Ng, the offspring of a Nisei mother and a Chinese American father, conducted twenty-two interviews in 1987–88 with Nisei and Sansei in Oregon's Hood River Valley. Ng's main interest is "community memory." Communities, she argues, are "created by individuals through interactions with one another, based upon a common history, [and] a part of this creation of community is the . . . memory of the past which individuals bring to the community: a community memory." Ng's interviews persuaded her that the Sansei had learned about their community's past in a patterned way. Many Sansei revealed that their Nisei parents had privatized their time in camp by not discussing it openly, treated it casually as though it had lacked significant meaning for them, or presented either a positive or neutral picture of that portion of their past. Ng also found that the parents' transmission of their wartime past had invariably been accompanied by admonitions to the third generation that they were Americans and should not make a big deal out of being Japanese. "The collective memory of the community," concluded Ng, "transmits, not intentionally, but on a subverted level, a less-than-positive attitude about Japanese ethnicity."[28]

A similarly subjective exploration of the social construction of the JAI as a historical event and a meaningful marker of personal and ethnic identity is found in the oral history–based documentaries produced by the Sansei filmmakers Lise Yasui, Janice Tanaka, and Rea Tajiri. Yasui was brought up in Pennsylvania by a Caucasian-Nikkei couple far removed from other Japanese Americans. When she was ten, her Nisei father (a prewar member of the renowned Yasui clan in Hood River Valley, where Wendy Ng later did her fieldwork) banned her from viewing a 1965 television program about the JAI—"Nisei: The Pride and the Shame." After pursuing this subject independently in high school and college, Yasui resolved, during her graduate film studies at Temple University, to produce a documentary on the JAI as seen through the eyes of her father's family. According to Lauren Kessler, as Yasui "began interviewing her aunts and uncles on tape and found that their versions of the past differed greatly, she realized she had little choice. This would have to be her film, a film not about the past but about her discovery of the past. The pieces would be held together by her perspective and told in her voice." Yasui's probing film, *Family Gathering* (1988), was shown on the PBS series *The American Experience* and nominated for an Academy Award.[29]

Janice Tanaka, like Yasui, was raised largely apart from Japanese Americans. Although incarcerated as an infant with her parents in Manzanar, she knew almost nothing about the JAI until after her mother's death in 1988, when she attempted to reestablish contact with her father, Jack Koto Tanaka. During Janice's childhood, he had divorced her mother, been diagnosed as schizophrenic with paranoid tendencies (manifested in his continuing rage over his detention), and moved back to Los Angeles, his prewar home. There Janice found him living in a halfway house for the mentally ill on skid row. In Los Angeles Janice also reunited with her father's estranged older brother Togo, the prewar editor of the *Rafu Shimpo* (a Los Angeles daily Japanese newspaper), whom I had interviewed in 1973 about his role as a participant in, and a historian of, the Manzanar Riot. A multimillionaire real estate investment broker and much-honored civic leader, Togo Tanaka urged his niece to talk with me about that interview. During our brief telephone conversation, Janice Tanaka confessed that she had never known that dissident Manzanar inmates had vowed to murder her Uncle Togo during the 1942 riot or that the camp's administration had dispatched her, her uncle, her parents, and others who had allegedly collaborated with the government to Death Valley under protective custody. The film that emerged from Janice Tanaka's encounters with her father and uncle, *Who's Going to Pay for These Donuts Anyway?* (1992), uses an interview format and cinema verité style. This documentary, which a reviewer praised as an "investigation of family dynamics and history," powerfully explores Jack Tanaka's victimization through "psychological genocide," movingly captures his reconciliation with his brother Togo (whose overassimilation into American society, the film suggests, exacted a steep price of its own), and simultaneously shows "the effects of the internment on several generations in one family [and] . . . dramatizes the history of visible racial groups whose assimilation will always remain problematic."[30]

The final film, Rea Tajiri's *History and Memory* (1991), has received substantial critical attention from American historians because of the recent historiographical interest in the topic alluded to in its title.[31] As Kathleen Hulser has shrewdly observed, whereas "much documentary work has concentrated on getting the story straight, . . . *History and Memory* attempts to see how distortion and story combine to shape our recollections." In the film, Tajiri shows how she had to construct her image of the JAI by selectively combining distorted official representations with the fragmented stories she gleaned from informal conversations and "interviews" with family survivors. If most of the oral history work on the JAI testifies to what *happened* to Japanese Americans during World War II, Tajiri's half-hour video meditation deals with how memory preserves the experiences of incarceration and its aftermath.[32]

Sumiko Higashi has cogently argued that one problem with *History and Memory* as against Tanaka's *Who's Going to Pay for These Donuts Anyway?* is that the former "succeeds in foregrounding discursive issues that appeal to postmodern critics engaged in textual analyses rather than confronting head-on the disturbing moral issues in question." Neither of those films is nearly as effective as Yasui's far more accessible *A Family Gathering* in going beyond a recognition of the immorality of the JAI to point up how inmates' experience has been translated not only into personal identity and familial bonding but also into ethnic community politics and transformative power. That is the burden and the blessing of Yasuko I. Takezawa's *Breaking the Silence.*[33]

Takezawa came to the United States from her native Japan in 1982, the year following the CWRIC hearings, to enroll in the University of Washington's doctoral studies program in anthropology. A year after her arrival, she commenced doing fieldwork in Seattle's sizable Japanese American community, mostly participant observation at first but increasingly ethnographic interviewing. The main group consisted of sixteen interviews with Nisei and sixteen with Sansei (of both genders). Her Nisei informants had been raised in the Seattle area and had spent most of their lives there; all had been incarcerated during World War II and were in their sixties and seventies at the time of their interviews. The Sansei, none of whom had been incarcerated, ranged in age from the late twenties to the early forties; they too had been Seattle residents for the bulk of their lives.[34]

Takezawa used her open-ended interviews to produce a case study of the redress movement in Seattle. But her deeper concern was what the interviews reveal about the Nisei and Sansei generations' historical experiences of ethnic identity and how those experiences shaped their differing reactions to redress. "Ethnicity," she argues, "is expressed differently over time. It is continually being constructed and reconstructed by interpretation of the past as related to the present."[35]

Before the war the Nisei, who lived simultaneously in the distinct worlds of their ethnic subculture and the mainstream society, experienced both positive and negative ethnic consciousness, but the trauma and shame of their wartime internment inclined them to suppress their ethnic heritage after the war. Without giving up the ethnic pride implanted in them in childhood—and even feeling an upsurge of such pride because of Japan's postwar "economic miracle"—Nisei "made extra efforts to be accepted by the dominate society and tried to Americanize and assimilate."[36]

The Sansei, unlike the Nisei, came of age when mainstream society was receptive to them and circumstances conducive to their upward social mobility. The majority of Sansei were not conscious of their ethnic identity as young children, though they sometimes regarded things Japanese (e.g., language and food) as bad or shameful, and at times they even regretted not being white. But as the Sansei filled the classrooms of colleges and universities in the late 1960s and early 1970s they developed ethnic pride as Japanese Americans and ethnic identity as Asian Americans by taking Asian American studies courses and involving themselves in community agencies and activities. It was at this time that incarceration and redress became common topics of conversation for Sansei and other Asian Americans. "Redress," explains Takezawa, "was a perfect rallying point for the Asian American movement, intent as it was on breaking the image of the quiet Asian, on opposing white 'Americanization' and challenging racism and social injustice."[37] Some Sansei were mad at their parents for not resisting the exclusion order and for not talking to them about their wartime experiences, but many more directed their anger at the governmental injustice and societal racism that caused and sustained the JAI.

The Sansei's refashioned social awareness and ethnic identity precipitated an intergenerational dialogue with their Nisei parents centering on redress. Initially, many Nisei resented their sons and daughters' bringing back bad memories and advised them to forget the past and attend to the present and future. But many more Nisei appreciated the Sansei efforts to exhume the corpse of the JAI and actively to pursue redress. In the fifteen years before the 1988 redress bill, argues Takezawa, "Japanese Americans underwent a transformation in their ethnic identity, feelings about camp, intergenerational relationships, and some of their norms and values."[38]

In planning and executing the interviews and using data from them, Takezawa concerned herself with community, as well as individual, memory. What those data suggest is that, through fighting the battles of the redress campaign together, Nisei and Sansei overcame their divisive generational perspectives and reconfirmed their common ethnic identity. Moreover, she concludes, "in this process, the feeling of shared suffering, which had previously constructed the subconscious core of the *individual* identity, was transformed into the core of the *collective* identity of Japanese Americans."[39] At the same time, since the redress movement was waged as an American issue, using American symbols and acting through American institutions, it strengthened not only the ethnic identity but also the national identity of Japanese Americans.

NOTES

For their invaluable help with this article, I extend my appreciation to Linda Shopes, Michael Frisch, David Thelan, Susan Armeny, and Mary Jane Gormly.

1. See Arthur A. Hansen, "The British Intellectual and Americanization" (PhD diss., University of California, Santa Barbara, 1972). Although an author of major books relating to California history, environmental history, and public history, the most pertinent volume by Robert Lloyd Kelley (1925–93) in the present connection is his classic work *The Transatlantic Persuasion: The Liberal-Democratic Mind in the Age of Gladstone* (New York: Knopf, 1969).

2. Ronald J. Grele, "On Using Oral History Collections: An Introduction," *Journal of American History* 74 (September 1987): 570. On the project's origins and development, see Arthur A. Hansen, "The Japanese American Oral History Project Collection," in *Very Special Collections: Essays on Library Holdings at California State University, Fullerton,* ed. Albert R. Vogeler and Arthur A. Hansen (Fullerton: California State University, Fullerton, 1992), 123–32. For an annotated listing of project interviews, see "Japanese-American History Collection," in *Oral History Collection: California State University, Fullerton,* ed. Shirley E. Stephenson (Fullerton: California State University, Fullerton, 1985), 196–243. For a representative sample of the interviews, see Arthur A. Hansen, ed., *Japanese American World War II Evacuation Oral History Project,* 6 vols. (Westport and Munich: Meckler and K.G. Saur, 1991–95). This work has five parts: *Internees; Administrators; Analysts; Resisters;* and *Guards and Townspeople.* Each of the first four parts forms a volume. Part 5 forms volumes 5 and 6.

3. See, respectively, the following finding aids: Estelle Rebec and Martin Rogin, eds., *Preliminary Inventory of the Records of the War Relocation Authority: Record Group 210* (Washington, DC: NARA, 1955); Deborah Gesensway, Mindy Roseman, and Geri Solomon, eds., *Guide to the Japanese-American Relocation Centers: Records, 1935–1953* (Ithaca, NY: Division of Rare and Manuscript Collections, Cornell University Library, 1981); and Elizabeth Stephens, comp., *Japanese American Evacuation and Resettlement Records* (Berkeley: Bancroft Library, University of California, 1996).

4. See Peter T. Suzuki, "Anthropologists in the Wartime Camps for Japanese Americans," *Dialectical Anthropology* 6 (August 1981): 23–60; and Peter T. Suzuki, "The University of California Japanese Evacuation and Resettlement Study: A Prolegomenon," *Dialectical Anthropology* 10 (April 1986): 189–213; Orin Starn,

"Engineering Internment: Anthropologists and the War Relocation Authority," *American Ethnologist* 13 (November 1986): 700–720; and Yuji Ichioka, ed., *Views from Within: The Japanese American Evacuation and Resettlement Study* (Los Angeles: Asian American Studies Center, University of California at Los Angeles, 1989). For edited transcripts of interviews with JERS social scientists Togo Tanaka, Robert Spencer, and James Sakoda, see Hansen, *Analysts*, pt. 3 of *Japanese American World War II Evacuation Oral History Project*, 149–457.

5. Arthur A. Hansen and David A. Hacker, "The Manzanar Riot: An Ethnic Perspective," *Amerasia Journal* 2 (Fall 1974): 112–57. See Brian Niiya, ed., *Encyclopedia of Japanese American History: An A-to-Z Reference from 1865 to the Present* (New York: Facts on File, 1993), s.v. "loyalty questions"; and Donald E. Collins, *Native American Aliens: Disloyalty and the Renunciation of Citizenship by Japanese Americans during World War II* (Westport, CT: Praeger, 1985).

6. Edward H. Spicer, "The Use of Social Scientists by the War Relocation Authority," *Applied Anthropology* 5 (Spring 1946): 16–36. On his earlier career, see Morris Edward Opler, "Social Science and Democratic Policy," *Applied Anthropology* 4 (Summer 1945): 11. Starn, "Engineering Internment," 710. On the relationship of Opler to the camp director, see Ralph P. Merritt to Dillon S. Myer, August 11, 1944, War Relocation Authority Archive, collection 122, box 12, Department of Special Collections, Charles E. Young Research Library, University of California, Los Angeles; and Morris E. Opler, interview by Arthur A. Hansen and David Hacker, June 4–6, 1978, O.H. 1600, Japanese American Project, Lawrence de Graaf Center for Oral and Public History, California State University, Fullerton. For reports by Opler, see "Annotated Bibliography of the Community Analysis Section, Part IV: Community Analyses Reports from Granada, Minidoka, and Manzanar Relocation Centers," series 16, box 68, Records of the War Relocation Authority, Record Group 210, National Archives, Washington, DC.

7. Dorothy Thomas and Richard Nishimoto, *The Spoilage: Japanese-American Evacuation and Resettlement during World War II* (Berkeley: University of California Press, 1946), 71; Morris E. Opler, "Studies of Segregants at Manzanar," October 28, 1943, 1–2, series 16, box 68, Records of the War Relocation Authority.

8. See, for example, Morris E. Opler, "A Study of Changes of Answer Cases at Manzanar," April 3, 1944, and "The Repatriate-Expatriate Group of Manzanar," August 4, 1944, series 16, box 68, Records of the War Relocation Authority. On the relationship of Opler's reports to the loyalty crisis, see David A. Hacker, "A Culture Resisted, a Culture Revived: The Loyalty Crisis of 1943 at the Manzanar War Relocation Center" (master's thesis, California State University, Fullerton, 1980).

9. Arthur A. Hansen and Betty E. Mitson, eds., *Voices Long Silent: An Oral Inquiry into the Japanese American Evacuation* (Fullerton: California State University,

Fullerton, 1974); Amy Uno Ishii, interview by Betty E. Mitson and Kristen Mitchell, July 9, 20, 1973, O.H. 1342a,b, Japanese American Project; Sue Kunitomi Embrey, interview by Arthur A. Hansen, David A. Hacker, and David J. Bertagnoli, August 24 and November 15, 1973, O.H. 1366a,b, Japanese American Project. For edited transcripts of those interviews, see Hansen, *Internees*, pt. 1 of *Japanese American World War II Evacuation Oral History Project*, 35–187.

10. Bill Hosokawa, *Nisei: The Quiet Americans* (New York: William Morrow, 1969). On these interviews, see Yuji Ichioka, Yasu Sakata, Nobu Tsuchida, and Eri Yasuhara, eds., *A Buried Past: An Annotated Bibliography of the Japanese American Research Project Collection* (Berkeley: University of California Press, 1974), 184–92.

11. See Earl Warren Project, *Japanese American Relocation Reviewed*, 2 vols. (Berkeley: Regional Oral History Office, University of California, Berkeley, 1974); Audrie Girdner and Anne Loftis, *The Great Betrayal: The Evacuation of the Japanese-Americans during World War II* (New York: Macmillian, 1969); and Betty E. Mitson, "Looking Back in Anguish: Oral History and Japanese-American Evacuation," *Oral History Review* 2 (1974): 24.

12. Hosokawa, *Nisei*, ix; Allan Bosworth, *America's Concentration Camps* (New York: Norton, 1967), 258; Paul Bailey, *City in the Sun: The Japanese Concentration Camp at Poston, Arizona* (Los Angeles: Westernlore Press, 1971), v; Gary Y. Okihiro, "The Oral History Tapes of the Japanese American Research Project, Tape Numbers 1–112: A Survey," typescript, June 13, 1974, Japanese American Research Project, Department of Special Collections, University of California, Los Angeles.

13. See Betty E. Mitson, "Look Back in Anguish: Oral History and the Japanese American Evacuation," in *Voices Long Silent*, ed. Hansen and Mitson, 15n4 (this article is a slightly revised version of Mitson's "Looking Back in Anguish."). Eleanor D. Amigo, ed., *Japanese Americans in Orange County: Oral Perspectives* (Fullerton: Japanese American Project, Oral History Program, California State University, Fullerton, 1976).

14. Michiyo Laing et al, eds., *Issei Christians: Selected Interviews from the Issei Oral History Project* (Sacramento: Center for Sacramento History, 1977); Eileen Sunada Sarasohn, *The Issei: Portrait of a Pioneer: An Oral History* (Palo Alto, CA: Pacific Books, 1983).

15. A recent example is the Florin Japanese American Citizens League Oral History Project in Florin, California, started in 1987 in collaboration with the California State University, Sacramento, Library Archives. In March 1995 forty-five completed oral histories were presented to narrators during the Florin Time of Remembrance. Twenty more oral histories were then pending, and the University of California, Davis, plans to purchase the entire set.

16. Stephen S. Fugita, review of *Stubborn Twig*, by Lauren Kessler, *Journal of American History* 81 (March 1995): 1774–75; Lauren Kessler, review of *Farming the*

Home Place, by Valerie J. Matsumoto, *Journal of American History* 81 (March 1995): 1790–91; Arthur A. Hansen, review of *Jewel of the Desert*, by Sandra C. Taylor, *Journal of American History* 81 (March 1995): 1811–12; Roger Daniels, review of *Righting a Wrong*, by Leslie T. Hatamiya, *Journal of American History* 81 (March 1995): 1848–49; Lauren Kessler, *Stubborn Twig: Three Generations in the Life of a Japanese American Family* (New York: Random House, 1993); Linda Tamura, *The Hood River Issei: An Oral History of Japanese Settlers in Oregon's Hood River Valley* (Urbana: University of Illinois Press, 1993); Wendy Lee Ng, "Collective Memory, Social Networks, and Generations: The Japanese American Community in Hood River, Oregon" (PhD diss., University of Oregon, 1989).

17. Yasuko I. Takezawa, *Breaking the Silence: Redress and Japanese American Ethnicity* (Ithaca: Cornell University Press, 1995), 97, 28–59, esp. 42–51.

18. Roger Daniels, *Prisoners without Trial: Japanese Americans in World War II* (New York: Hill and Wang, 1993), 97. At present there is only an expensive and unedited microform edition: *Papers of the Commission on Wartime Relocation and Internment of Civilians*, microfilm, 35 reels (Frederick, MD: University Publications of America, 1984). But a project is underway to publish, in seven volumes, an edited, annotated transcript of the oral testimony presented during the 1981 hearings. See Aiko Herzig-Yoshinaga, "Japanese American Historical Papers Project," National Endowment for the Humanities grant proposal, May 26, 1994, p. 2 (in Aiko Herzig-Yoshinaga's possession).

19. See Herzig-Yoshinaga, "Japanese American Historical Papers Project," 97–98; and *Personal Justice Denied: Report of the Commission on Wartime Relocation and Internment of Civilians* (Washington, DC: GPO, 1983); John Tateishi, *And Justice for All: An Oral History of the Japanese American Detention Camps* (New York: Random House, 1984). Of the thirty first-person narratives in this book, twenty-seven relate the experiences of wartime detainees. John Tateishi, "The Japanese American Citizens League and the Struggle for Redress," in *Japanese Americans: From Relocation to Redress*, ed. Roger Daniels, Sandra C. Taylor, and Harry H. L. Kitano, 191–95 (Salt Lake City: University of Utah Press, 1986).

20. Tateishi, *And Justice for All*, vii–viii. For a similar, if far less refined and balanced, volume of interviews with former inmates, see Roger W. Axford, ed., *Too Long Been Silent: Japanese Americans Speak Out* (New York: Media Publishing and Marketing Inc., 1986).

21. These interviews, some of which are transcribed, were originally housed in the Asian American Studies Program at Washington State University under the supervision of Professors Gail Nomura and Steve Sumida. They are now in the Archives and Manuscript Room, Library, Washington State University, Pullman. Shirley Castelnuovo, a Northeastern Illinois University political scientist, is

compiling interviews for a forthcoming publication (*Soldiers of Conscience: Japanese American Military Resisters in World War II* [Westport, CT: Praeger, 2008]) dealing with Japanese Americans who were resisters within the military during World War II.

22. See Sue Kunitomi Embrey, Arthur A. Hansen, and Betty Kulberg Mitson, eds., *Manzanar Martyr: An Interview with Harry Y. Ueno* (Fullerton: Japanese American Project, Oral History Program, California State University, Fullerton, 1986). For critically edited transcripts of the interview with Harry Ueno and other prominent resistance leaders, see Hansen, *Resisters*, pt. 4 of *Japanese American World War II Evacuation Oral History Project.* For an interview with James Omura, see Hansen, *Resisters*, 131–343. These additional interviews with Omura are available on audiotape in the Archives and Manuscript Room, Washington State University, Pullman: James Omura, interview by Frank Chin, September 10, 1981, James Omura, interview by Frank Chin, Frank Emi, and Lawson Inada, May 15, 20, 1982; Omura, interview by Frank Chin, Lawson Inada, and Glen Hayashi, May 13 and 18, 1982.

23. See David M. Oshinsky, "Oral History, Playing by the Rules," *Journal of American History* 77 (September 1990), 609–14. According to an anonymous peer reviewer of *Barbed Voices* in manuscript, three instructive sites that scholarly researchers should consult regarding the progressive facilitation of employing oral history interviews as sources are as follows: https://www.historians.org/publications-and-directories/perspectives-on-history/february-2008/aha-statement-on-irbs-and-oral-history-research; http://www.oralhistory.org/about/principles-and-practices/; and http://blog.historians.org/2017/01/oral-history-excluded-irb-oversight/. This reviewer's governing rationale is that returning oral history ethical practices to professional oversight instead of university Institutional Research Board (IRB) oversight should make scholars more likely to save and deposit their interviews.

24. For information about the Japanese American National Museum's (JANM) Life History Project holdings, contact the Media Arts Center's director, John Esaki, 369 East First Street, Los Angeles, CA 90012. This program bears the imprint of the life histories that JANM's anthropologist-oral historian-curator has published on her parents: Akemi Kikumura, *Through Harsh Winters: The Life of a Japanese Immigrant Woman* (Novato, CA: Chandler & Sharp, 1981); and Akemi Kikumura, *Promises Kept: The Life of an Issei Man* (Novato, CA: Chandler & Sharp, 1991).

25. Deborah Gesensway and Mindy Roseman, *Beyond Words: Images from America's Concentration Camps* (Ithaca, NY: Cornell University Press, 1987).

26. As of 1992, this collection of interviews with American *hibakusha* (A-bomb survivors) numbered eighteen; more are planned with victims and their children. Plans call for the interviews to be placed in the Bancroft Library at the University of California, Berkeley, and in an archive in the Japanese American community. For

more information, contact Rosalyn Tonai, the executive director of the National Japanese American Historical Society, 1684 Post Street, San Francisco, CA 94115.

27. For information about the Japanese Peruvian Oral History Project, write to its coordinator, Grace Shimizu, PO Box 1384, El Cerrito, CA, 94530. See Harvey C. Gardiner, *Pawns in a Triangle of Hate: The Peruvian Japanese and the United States* (Seattle: University of Washington Press, 1981). For a powerful autobiographical account, see Seiichi Higashide, *Adios to Tears: The Memoirs of a Japanese-Peruvian Internee in U.S. Concentration Camps* (Honolulu, 1993).

28. Ng, "Collective Memory, Social Networks, and Generations"; Wendy L. Ng. "The Collective Memories of Communities," in *Asian Americans: Comparative and Global Perspectives*, ed. Shirley Hune, Hyung-chan Kim, Stephen S. Fugita, and Amy Ling (Pullman: Washington State University Press, 1991), 103–12, esp. 103–9. Ng's two quoted passages appear, respectively, on pages 103 and 109 of her article.

29. Kessler, *Stubborn Twig*, 311, 307–14.

30. For the interview with Togo Tanaka, see Hansen, *Analysts*, 149–74. On his role in the Manzanar Riot and his stay in Death Valley, see Arthur A. Hansen, "A Riot of Voices: Racial and Ethnic Variables in Interactive Oral History Interviewing," in *Interactive Oral History Interviewing*, ed. Eva M. McMahan and Kim Lacy Rogers, 107–39 (Hillsdale, NJ: Erlbaum Associates, 1994); Sumiko Higashi, review of *Who's Going to Pay for These Donuts Anyway?* and three other films, *American Historical Review* 98 (October 1993): 1181–84.

31. See, for example, David Thelan, ed., *Memory and American History* (Blooming-ton: Indiana University Press, 1990); John Bodnar, *Remaking America: Public Memory, Commemoration, and Patriotism in the Twentieth Century* (Princeton, NJ: Princeton University Press, 1992); and Martha Norkunas, *The Politics of Public Memory: Tourism, History, and Ethnicity in Monterey, California* (Albany: State University of New York Press, 1993).

32. Kathleen Hulser, review of *History and Memory* (film), *American Historical Review* 96 (October 1991): 1143, 1142.

33. Higashi, review of *Who's Going to Pay for These Donuts Anyway?*, 1182; Takezawa, *Breaking the Silence.*

34. Takezawa, *Breaking the Silence*, provides no information as to whether or where the transcripts of her interviews are archived.

35. Takezawa, *Breaking the Silence*, 19.

36. Takezawa, *Breaking the Silence*, 126.

37. Takezawa, *Breaking the Silence*, 149.

38. Takezawa, *Breaking the Silence*, 161.

39. Takezawa, *Breaking the Silence*, 190.

2

THE MANZANAR "RIOT"

An Ethnic Perspective

While preparing to teach two sections of historiography (a mandatory course for history majors) during the fall 1972 semester at California State University, Fullerton, I decided to require all forty enrolled students to do their culminating research paper on an aspect of the World War II Japanese American experience. This assignment was met by general student approval save for one female reentry enrollee, Betty Mitson, who felt that fulfilling it would be a redundant exercise for her. This was because in the preceding term she had been obliged in an oral history class to write a research paper focused on the same topic as a precondition to transacting some tape-recorded interviews with southern California survivors of what was then euphemistically styled the Japanese American Evacuation. As an alternative, Mitson asked if she could tape some more similar interviews to add to the growing archive of the university's fledgling Oral History Program. I responded by expressing my serious doubts as to the historical value of oral history. Taken aback by this uncharitable assessment,

---

This essay was first published in the *Amerasia Journal* (© 1974) and is reproduced with permission.

DOI: 10.5876/9781607328124.c002

Mitson then proposed that she be permitted at the next class meeting to play a couple of Japanese American interviews from the collection, after which I could render an informed decision about her substitute class assignment.

Having been surprisingly captivated by the interviews Mitson shared with her classmates and me, I thereupon readily agreed that she should implement her plan. Moreover, she agreed to set up a working archive of relevant primary and secondary source material on the Japanese American Evacuation in the university library so that it could be accessed and used by the other class members in preparing their research papers. In short order, too, Mitson convinced me to launch a Japanese American Project in the Oral History Program, with me serving as director and her as my assistant director, which resulted in the first such oral history project in the country devoted to Japanese American history, society, and culture. In addition, Mitson helped me secure guest lectures by two of the university's community members: a History Department professor, Kinji Yada, who had been an adolescent inmate at the Manzanar Relocation Center in eastern California; and the dean of the School of Humanities and Social Sciences, Hazel Jones, who had been an English teacher at this same wartime detention center. Finally, Mitson took it upon herself to instruct me in how to conduct archival oral history interviews and even floated the idea that in the future we might possibly coedit a book that would marry the research methodology of oral history with the historical subject of the Japanese American Evacuation.

During the subsequent spring 1973 semester, two developments occurred to buttress the mission of the Japanese American Project. Within this interval I taught another section of the historiography class and once again had its students write research papers on a chosen dimension of the Japanese American Evacuation. One student, David Hacker, elected to write his paper on the infamous Manzanar Riot of December 5–6, 1942, in which military police gunfire killed two inmate spectators. I was enthralled by what Hacker's paper communicated to me about the dynamics of this bloody encounter between Manzanar's inmates and guards, especially since they so powerfully resonated with a (thankfully bloodless) campus confrontation I had witnessed three years earlier between Fullerton police and university students and faculty. In critically discussing Hacker's paper with him, we resolved to partner in researching and writing an ambitious account of the Manzanar Riot for presentation at a historical conference and, quite possibly, eventual submission for publication consideration by an appropriate scholarly journal.

Simultaneously, that same semester I arranged to coordinate a ten-part lecture series through the University of California, Irvine's extension program, which was entitled "Japanese American Internment during World War II: A Socio-Historical Inquiry." Another first-of-its-kind event, it attracted a substantial enrollment, mostly of Americans of Japanese ancestry, and featured cutting-edge researchers speaking on various JAI topics. Following this event, I undertook in August of 1973 my very first oral history interviews with two of the lecturers in the series, Sue Kunitomi Embrey and Togo Tanaka; both of these interviews revolved around the riot at Manzanar, a happening that Embrey had experienced indirectly and Tanaka directly during their shared Manzanar incarceration. Concurrently this same summer David Hacker and I researched intensively the abundant source material in the Japanese American Research Project at UCLA and penned a draft of our coauthored paper on the Manzanar Riot for September delivery at the annual meeting of the Western Conference for the Association of Asian Studies in Albuquerque, New Mexico.

Then in the fall of 1973 I attended my first colloquium of the Oral History Association, which was held at the US Military Academy in West Point, New York. There, in early November, I moderated a panel entitled "Taped Interviews and Social History" and drew upon my limited fieldwork interviewing to stress the value of interviews in illuminating social protest movements.[1] While at this conference, I also met with the then editor of the Oral History Review, *Sam Hand, to clarify some questions he had relative to a manuscript submission from Betty Mitson that he had tentatively decided to publish in the forthcoming issue.[2]*

At this juncture, Mitson and I decided to go ahead and put together the book we had previously contemplated doing and to make it available for peer discussion and sale at the 1974 Oral History Association colloquium slated for mid-September at Jackson Lake Lodge in Wyoming's Grand Teton National Park.[3] This volume was anchored by Mitson's article and the paper that Hacker and I had presented the previous September in Albuquerque. Shortly after the Wyoming colloquium, Hacker and I were persuaded to permit the Amerasia Journal, *sponsored by UCLA's Asian American Studies Center, to include a revised version of our piece in its upcoming issue. It is that iteration of our interpretation of the Manzanar Riot, one of the earliest published in-depth case studies of a resistance "incident," which appears below.*

In his recent book, *American Historical Explanations*, Gene Wise reproves American historians for naively assuming that "the real aim of historical scholarship is to discover just what happened in the past; that what happened has been recorded here and there in what historians call 'primary documents'; and that the only true scholarship in the field of history must be based directly on only those primary documents."[4] While granting that this approach has eliminated much flagrant bias and derivativeness, Wise nonetheless maintains that it has led historians into some profound epistemological fallacies. First, it has fostered the scholarly ideal that "objective history"—the whole Truth, nothing but the Truth—can be realized once historians learn to behave as "ideal observers"—i.e., cease viewing reality through existential frames of reference. Second, this approach has promoted the correlative notion that the way for historians to attain this ideal is to devote themselves to an intensive examination of primary sources, for in these documents the original experiences repose in pure and unfiltered wholeness.

To refute these nostrums, Wise explains that "objective" history is impossible precisely because the historian's mind is grounded ineluctably in experience, and therefore s/he observes through selected frames of reference. This same relativism pertains to primary documents since they too are merely commentaries upon original phenomena by similarly bounded minds. Accordingly, Wise suggests an alternative model of historical inquiry—the "perspectivist" model—which he believes more realistic and productive than the "ideal observer" one. This new model would ask different questions of its sources. Because the ideal-observer model is preoccupied with what happened in the past, its questions are designed to untangle the objective truth of history from the snares and delusions of assorted interpreters. On the other hand, since the perspectivist model discounts what happened as its sole or even fundamental concern, it queries its sources in a different manner. Although mindful of what happened, its chief concern, according to Wise, "is with the question, 'How do particular people experience what happened?' And further, 'How do they put form on their experience?' And yet further, 'How do these forms connect into their particular locations in time and place?'"[5]

The present paper utilizes the perspectivist approach in studying one celebrated episode occurring during the incarceration experience of Japanese Americans in World War II, the so-called Manzanar Riot. We have given our study a tripartite division. The first section offers a brief summary of the event itself. The second attempts to delineate and account for the dominant perspective influencing the interpretation of this event in the past. The third and longest section offers a new perspective for interpreting the Manzanar Riot. Although this portion of the study adds considerably to the existing stock of information about the riot (and relies heavily on primary documentation), we feel its major contribution is that it presents a strategy for explaining this information in a significantly different way.

THE MANZANAR RIOT

On the evening of December 5, 1942, some unidentified inmates at the Manzanar War Relocation Center assaulted Fred Tayama, a Nisei who had returned the previous day from Salt Lake City, where he had served as the center's representative at the national convention of the Japanese American Citizens League (JACL). The beating administered to Tayama, formerly a Los Angeles restaurateur and chairman of the Southern District JACL, was severe enough to hospitalize him and prompt the camp authorities to arrest three Kibei (Nisei born in the USA but socialized/educated in Japan before World War II). Two of these suspects were taken into custody at the Manzanar jail and released after questioning, but the remaining one, Harry Ueno, head of the Kitchen Workers Union, was removed from the camp and jailed in nearby Independence, California.

Ueno's arrest aroused widespread hostility and resistance among the inmates. Contrary to the War Relocation Authority (WRA) rationale for this action—that Ueno had been identified positively by Tayama as one of his assailants—many inmates charged that Ueno was innocent and was being victimized due to his recent allegation that certain WRA officials were appropriating meat and sugar intended for the inmates in order to sell them for profit outside the camp.

At 10:00 a.m. on Sunday, December 6, about two hundred inmates assembled in the mess hall of Block 22, Ueno's block, to discuss his arrest and consider ways of effecting his return to the camp. This meeting, consisting of Block 22 inmates and a sprinkling of Kitchen Workers Union members, entertained several plans of action, including the imposition of a center-wide strike of kitchens. After about twenty minutes, the meeting was adjourned, and a second meeting of block managers, mess hall workers, and Kibei groups was arranged for 1:00 p.m. in Block 22.

News of the one o'clock meeting apparently spread throughout the entire camp population, for the crowd that subsequently arrived was so large (estimates place it in excess of 2,000 people) that the gathering had to be moved outside the mess hall to the adjacent firebreak area. Following the delivery of some fiery speeches over a hastily constructed public address system, a Committee of Five was selected to negotiate Ueno's reinstatement with project director Ralph P. Merritt. This committee included two Issei and two Kibei who were associated in some way with the Kitchen Workers Union. Its principal spokesman, however, was Joe Kurihara, a Hawai'i-born Nisei and World War I veteran who, while a friend of Ueno's, was unaffiliated with the union.

Director Merritt, a recent appointee, was so alarmed by police reports of the huge assemblage that he asked the military police to form outside the center's gate in case trouble threatened. To ward off this contingency, he then accompanied the center police chief to the meeting, which was just concluding. In fact, the Committee of Five had already left to confer with Merritt. Accordingly, he returned immediately to the staff area to await them.

Presently the mob arrived in front of the Administration Building, where it was confronted by a massed rank of armed soldiers. When attempts by the authorities to disperse the crowd proved useless, Director Merritt agreed to hear its demands. Urged on by the large throng, the committee informed him that he must immediately obtain release of Ueno from the Independence jail and return him to Manzanar. Merritt refused to capitulate, but he did express his willingness to air this and other grievances with the committee, provided that the crowd disperse and return to its quarters.

The highly volatile mob was determined, however, to stay put until the officials had satisfied its demands. Perhaps sensing that it was no longer in control of the crowd, the committee urged Merritt to concede before matters got completely out of hand. Although the project director publicly reiterated his earlier refusal to this demand, a private conference with the police chief and the commander of the military police convinced him that this concession was necessary in order to avoid bloodshed. Out of the crowd's earshot, Merritt then met with the committee and informed it that Ueno would be returned to the Manzanar jail within one hour after the crowd had returned home if the committee agreed to certain conditions: (1) that Ueno stand trial before Manzanar's Judicial Committee; (2) that no attempt be made to release Ueno from the camp jail; (3) that the Committee of Five would meet with Merritt to decide on any other matters it wished to discuss; (4) that there would be no more mobs or mass meetings of any sort until the center had resumed normalcy; and (5) that the Committee of Five would help maintain law and order in the center and would assist the police in apprehending Tayama's assailants. Merritt also announced that a subsequent statement pertinent to Ueno's return would be issued at six o'clock that evening at Mess Hall 22.

That afternoon Ueno was returned to the camp jail. When the Committee of Five appeared at Mess Hall 22 at six o'clock to affirm this fact, it encountered a crush of 2,000 to 4,000 inmates. Again the meeting was transferred outside. On the grounds that it had accomplished its objective, the Committee attempted to resign. This suggestion was shouted down by the crowd, which felt that the administration had not gone far enough by merely returning Ueno to the Manzanar jail. Ueno should be unconditionally released, even if release required his enforced removal. Moreover, the crowd demanded that inmates like Fred Tayama, whom they suspected of collaborating with the administration and informing to the FBI about pro-Japan activities in camp, should be killed. Having degenerated into an uncontrolled demonstration, the meeting broke up when a hurried plan of action was outlined. The crowd divided itself into two main groups, one to ferret out Tayama in the camp hospital and finish the job begun the night before, and the second to liberate Ueno from jail.

After failing to locate Tayama, the first group broke into splinter groups bent on searching out and killing Tokie Slocum and Togo Tanaka, two other JACL leaders reputed to be stooges. This quest also proved fruitless. By now the second group was approaching the jail. At this point, Director Merritt ordered in the military police, which immediately placed a protective barricade between the crowd and the jail.

From seven o'clock to nine-thirty, the administration attempted to negotiate with the inmate representatives. At first the crowd contented itself with singing Japanese songs and gesturing menacingly at the soldiers. But when some of the inmates began throwing stones and bottles, the military police were ordered to fire tear gas into their midst. Shortly thereafter, for reasons never clearly established, the soldiers opened fire on the crowd, killing a young Nisei and wounding ten other inmates, one of whom died several days later.

During the night, the camp remained in a turbulent state. Kitchen bells tolled continuously, beatings of alleged informers ensued, and military police units patrolled the camp, breaking up numerous inmate gatherings. Those whose names appeared on the inmates' blacklists and death lists were spirited out of camp and placed in protective custody, and the administration began a roundup of those believed responsible for the disruption. Within the next few days, the first group and its families were sent to an abandoned Civilian Conservation Corps (CCC) camp in Death Valley, while the latter group was imprisoned within local jails and then transferred to a temporary isolation center in Moab, Utah.[6]

THE PREVAILING "WRA-JACL" PERSPECTIVE

To date, most of the accounts of the Manzanar Riot have been filtered through what might be labeled the "WRA-JACL" perspective.[7] The appellation is apt because nearly all of the original documentation was prepared by WRA or JACL affiliates and because secondary compilers almost have without exception simply buttressed this official version. This perspective has resulted in uniform meanings being drawn from disparate information. The reasons for this stylization of form inhere within the historical experience of its creators and custodians. But before tracking down these connections, let us first outline the most conspicuous features of the WRA-JACL perspective.

One dimension can be glimpsed through analysis of the language used to describe the event. As a general rule, the primary sources refer to it as an "incident," while the secondary works term it a "riot." Since the former denotes an "occurrence" and the latter signifies a "violent disorder," these designations, at first glance, appear radically different. This impression is reinforced when one encounters statements like the following, which appears in a recent account written from a modified WRA-JACL perspective: "The incident, properly called a riot, at Manzanar early in December, 1942, was handled quite differently from the Poston strike."[8] In perspectivist terms, however, the difference is more apparent than real. What places both words within the WRA-JACL perspective is that each trivializes the event's cultural significance.[9] "Incident" accomplishes this effect by scaling down the affair to commonplace proportions, while "riot" achieves the same by inflating it to melodramatic ones. Because neither term allows for meaningful contextual inquiry, both invite descriptive treatment but discourage explanatory analysis.

A second, closely related feature of this perspective is its tendency to view the "riot" episodically.[10] This myopia has stamped itself upon the literature in various ways. First, it has militated against sustained, in-depth analyses of causation. Most accounts practically ignore the causative factor, and even those aspiring to explain cause have confined their investigation within the parameters of the immediate pre-exclusion, exclusion, and camp experience. Second, it has caused the riot to be misconstrued as a denouement rather than seen as one development along a continuum of inmate resistance. Thus, for example, in direct violation of the available evidence, one account concludes that "the easing of tension, and a return to normal life [at Manzanar] came shortly after Christmas of 1942";[11] another posits that "events which [subsequent to the riot] occasioned conflict in other centers, such as [loyalty] registration, segregation and selective service, occasioned no conflict in Manzanar."[12] Third, it has unduly parochialized the riot; that is, the riot has often been reduced to a purely local phenomenon instead of being related to the meta-pattern of resistance activity within all the detention centers.[13]

Another distinguishing mark of this perspective is its chauvinistic orientation. As a result, the riot has been viewed as a microcosm of World War II. This outlook has hampered seriously an understanding of the event in its own terms. It has, for instance, dramatized the riot as an ideological confrontation between pro-American and pro-Japanese factions. This interpretation can be seen vividly in newspaper accounts of the period like that in the *Los Angeles Times*: "Shouting 'Pearl Harbor, banzai, banzai' an estimated 1,000 pro-Axis Japanese, many of whom are Kibei, adherents of Japan, demonstrated in a firebreak and hooted down Japanese American Nisei . . . who protested their antics."[14] But even the secondary work that dismisses the *Times*'s version as "fanciful or at least exaggerated" prefaces its own description with the similar assertion that "trouble broke out around the first anniversary of Pearl Harbor, between pro-American and pro-Japanese factions."[15] The above quotations reveal two additional by-products of this filiopietistic outlook. First, it has confused the aggressively patriotic posture of the JACL—a small minority—with that of the Nisei as a whole (excepting, of course, the Kibei, who have been represented indiscriminately as "troublemakers"). Second, it has betrayed an inability to understand ethnic identity in terms other than subversive. This fact explains why most accounts of the riot minimize or ignore the massive participation of inmates and instead focus exclusively on the actions of selected groups like the Kibei and colorful personalities like Joe Kurihara.[16]

With this picture in mind, we now must see how the WRA-JACL perspective derives from its promoters. Our task is a dual one. We must account for its origination in the primary sources and explain its survival in the secondary literature. It would be a pointless tautology to say merely because WRA and JACL representatives compiled the original accounts of the riot, they were written from the WRA-JACL perspective. More pertinently, we need to inquire into the connection between their interpretation of the riot and their overall attitude toward incarceration and to relate both to their conception of American society.

Although different in some respects, the WRA and JACL viewpoints on incarceration were fundamentally the same. Roger Daniels has summarized the WRA stance: "Although some of the staff, particularly those in the upper echelons of the WRA, disapproved of the racist policy that brought the camps into being, the majority of the camp personnel . . . shared the contempt of the general population for 'Japs.'"[17]

Attitude, of course, is extremely difficult to evaluate, but the documentation—both written and oral—pertinent to the Manzanar staff suggests that perhaps "contempt" is too strong a word to label their outlook. The staff member most frequently cited by inmates for his contemptuous attitude toward them is Ned Campbell, the assistant project director. For instance, after the Manzanar Riot, Harry Ueno is quoted as remarking, "Every time Ned Campbell speaks he thinks he talks to a slave."[18] When an interviewer asked another inmate, Togo Tanaka, whether he thought Ueno's appraisal of Campbell an accurate one, he replied, "Maybe that was the way he [Ueno] reacted. I just thought he [Campbell] was a loud, obnoxious someone who, you know, in another setting I wouldn't hire, period. But he was a bigshot."[19] Perhaps Campbell himself provides the clearest insight into why his manner may have been construed as contemptuous. The following exchange is drawn from an interview with him:

Had you known Japanese Americans prior to taking this job?
If so, maybe one or two in my lifetime.

You have been criticized by former inmates for not having understood the Japanese psychology. Would you care to comment on that estimate?

Well, that is one hundred percent valid. . . . I went out there a real babe, believe me, a real babe. I went out there with the idea that there here was a job to be done. I shall never forget how distressed I was when, because of being the Assistant Project Director here, I was assigned a big Chrysler— which I liked; everybody likes a big car to drive around. And I felt happy about it. But then to have a boy, a young man, come up one day and say, "You know, you're driving my car." He just wanted to look at it and touch it again. It was the first time I realized just how hard we were stepping on these people's toes. Not only stepping on their toes but rubbing it in their faces. And I think probably that was my first realization that I was dealing with human beings, and this was just not a job to be done with so many bodies out there. Certainly I was very guilty of the fact of going out first with the notion that we have so many people—so many bodies, if you will—and we have a job to do: we've got to feed so many mouths, and we have so many people we have to get into the hospital, and we've got this and that and the other. But they were just numbers to me. And I think probably that instance was the beginning of my realization that I did have a human quotient to deal with.[20]

Similarly, Alexander Leighton has divided the staff into those who were "people-minded" (i.e., regarded the inmates as people first and as Japanese secondarily) and those who were "stereotype-minded" (i.e., regarded the inmates as Japanese first and people secondarily).[21] For our purposes, the distinction is less significant than it appears. Whether or not an individual staff member possessed a humanitarian outlook assuredly did significantly affect his/her day-to-day treatment of the inmates; however, it mattered little with respect to his/her overall perspective, for the decision to affiliate with the detention program implicated one, at least tacitly, in upholding the policy objectives of the WRA.[22] These objectives were concerned with social control and social rehabilitation—that is, with developing protective communities where the evicted Japanese American population could be detained and imbued with American principles and practices. Staff members who resisted these objectives were eliminated. For those who remained, active participation in the camp bureaucracy effectively instilled these corporate goals within them so that ultimately they came to measure their own worth in terms of their fulfillment of the goals.

The JACL posture complemented that of the WRA: while the JACL leadership certainly was not contemptuous of "Japs," its identification with Americanized behavior and attitudes was complete enough to cause disavowal of and dissatisfaction with traditional Japanese customs, social organization, and values. This helps to account for what Douglas Nelson has described as the JACL's policy of "deliberate and calculated compliance" with the detention program. JACL compliance, according to Nelson, began from the outset of that operation. "JACL members assisted the FBI in the initial roundup of suspect Japanese aliens. They were usually among the first volunteers to go to the assembly centers and later to the interior concentration camps, [and] in November 1942, the JACL, meeting at Salt Lake City, resolved to endorse the administrations and goals of the War Relocation Authority."[23]

In return for their cooperation, JACL leaders were accorded a measure of responsibility and influence in the camps. Not infrequently, they were selected for the preferred jobs, chosen to edit the camp newspapers, and granted other social, political, and economic perquisites. As a result of their integration into the WRA administration, however, they too came to evaluate their personal status in terms of the successful realization of WRA objectives.

Behind the WRA's and JACL's shared attitude toward the detention objectives rested a common social ideology. Put simply, both subscribed to a "progressive" view of American history. Central to this persuasion was the idea that the American past made sense only if read as a triumphant progression toward the fulfillment of the nation's democratic potential. This view acknowledged the existence of a long line of reactionary persons and groups who, for selfish ends, had attempted to thwart the advance of democracy. But it took succor from the fact that liberal, humane individuals always had emerged who transcended themselves and rallied the nation into overcoming anti-democratic challenges.[24]

Given these situational and philosophical considerations, we are better able to comprehend the WRA-JACL perspective on the Manzanar Riot. We can now appreciate, for example, why the original accounts chose to describe it innocuously as an "incident." Like all good bureaucrats, the administrators (a term that is used here to embrace the JACLers as well as the WRA staff) intuitively sensed the wisdom of the adage that "no news is good news." For them even to have intimated that what happened on December 6, 1942, was more than slightly out of the ordinary would have been tantamount to admitting that WRA policies were wrong or unsuccessful.

In keeping with this psychological imperative, it followed that causal explanations were largely unwarranted. Interpreting the disturbance as the outgrowth of serious, underlying grievances would have called into question the administration's oft-repeated claim that Manzanar was a "model" American community. That a resistance movement could arise in such a "happy camp" was unthinkable. It made better sense, therefore, to perceive the "incident" as either a transitory release from unanalyzable "frustration" or, as was more often the case, the pernicious work of a small but committed minority of pro-Axis sympathizers.[25]

The latter explanation gained currency among WRA-JACL analysts because they could readily incorporate it into their Manichean view of history. Envisioning themselves as selfless inheritors of America's democratic heritage, they justified their complicity in the detention program by the belief that their efforts furthered the democratic cause. The WRA could argue that the attendant loss of civil liberties was unfortunate, but that perilous times sometimes necessitated short-term undemocratic means to promote long-range democratic ends. The JACL could uphold exclusion and detention by the argument that it would provide Japanese Americans an opportunity to prove their loyalty, thereby paving the way for the enjoyment of democratic liberties in the postwar world. Given that the administration equated the existence of the camps with the cause of democracy, it is hardly surprising that they should interpret the riot as engineered by an anti-democratic faction.

Such an interpretation occasions even less surprise when one considers the Manzanar administration's relative unfamiliarity with all inmate groups except for the JACLers. Robert L. Brown, who as reports officer supervised the substantially JACLer-staffed *Manzanar Free Press*, provides a case in point:

> I might have been isolated by the kids I had working on the newspaper, and the people that were around me. The girls in the office, the Block Leaders, the guy we finally made "mayor" . . . an old Issei.
>
> *You felt, then, that you might have been isolated maybe from what was going on in the population at large, so you couldn't account for, say, the people who were in the*

Kitchen Workers Union; they wouldn't have been people you were in contact with in the camp?

No, I wasn't in contact with that group; I didn't know a damned thing about them.[26]

And Ned Campbell recollects that "the young fellows around the newspaper office were the ones I was more frequently in contact with, and I think they became more friendly to me, and therefore came to me with, not tattle-taling, but forewarning."[27]

Before considering a new perspective for interpreting the riot, we must account for the persistence of the WRA-JACL perspective in the secondary literature. The most obvious reason is documentary in nature: later writers had access to copious materials about the riot, but practically all of them were compiled by WRA-JACL personnel. Nonetheless, this fact does not explain why these writers have not penetrated beyond the existing documentation and staked out different interpretative frameworks. We need, therefore, to explain why their own experiential situations caused them to be receptive to the established perspective.

A caveat needs to be entered at this point: it must not be assumed that, because these writers have extended the WRA-JACL perspective, they have a similar attitude toward the Japanese American Incarceration (JAI) experience. They have not, in other words, acted as outright apologists for the JAI. On the contrary, most have bristled with righteous indignation at what they consider a deplorable and unjustified departure from America's traditional democratic practices. Eschewing the official view that the "relocation centers" were necessary security precautions, almost unanimously they have redefined them as "concentration camps" and attributed their existence to public hysteria, virulent racism, and economic and political opportunism. In light of this condemnatory attitude, it seems paradoxical that these writers have been so obeisant to the entrenched WRA-JACL notion that the riot was inspired by dark, anti-democratic elements.

The paradox can be resolved, however, when we consider another factor. Earlier we noted that the primary accounts of the riot were grounded in the progressivist view of history held by their compilers. This same view, with slight modification, has also informed the secondary writers. While this view was heightened by the overarching wartime distinction between pro- and anti-democratic belligerents, it has continued to thrive in the "Cold War's" atmosphere of emphasizing the ideological juxtaposition of the American-led "free world" and the "communist bloc." One of the liabilities of this persuasion is its criterion that all historical experience emerges as democratic progress. The impossibility of seeing the incarceration of 120,000 Japanese Americans as consonant with the advance of democracy has caused the secondary writers to style the inmates as the unsung torchbearers of the democratic mission. Thus, they have been depicted as 100 percent Americans who set aside their grievances, miraculously transformed their camps into models of democratic life, and contributed to the defeat of fascism by unstinting allegiance to the war effort at home and abroad. Preoccupied with constructing this heroic portrait, secondary writers have been blinded to the existence of inmate resistance. In cases where evidence of resistance is too blatant to be ignored, as with the Manzanar Riot, these writers have seen them either as highly atypical episodes or situations provoked by a handful of subversives.[28]

THE ETHNIC PERSPECTIVE

In contradistinction to the foregoing perspective on the Manzanar Riot, we propose an "Ethnic" perspective. Whereas the WRA-JACL perspective, as we have seen, has interpreted the riot in terms of its ideological meaning within American society, the Ethnic one focuses upon the riot's cultural meaning within the Japanese American community (with particular reference to Manzanar's inmate population). Although ours is a "new" perspective toward the Manzanar Riot, it conforms closely to and draws much sustenance from a small number of general studies—mostly recent and unpublished—on the JAI.[29] We believe it is a perspective which, unlike the WRA-JACL's, promotes analysis and understanding rather than ideological reification.

As a first step in this direction, we replace the word "riot" with "revolt." Terming the event the "Manzanar Revolt" forces us to see it not as an uncaused and inconsequential aberration, but as one intense expression of a continuing resistance movement. This change also credits the participants in the action with a greater degree of purposeful behavior. For while a riot's members are momentarily conjoined because they do not like where they have been, those involved in a revolt have some sense of where they want to go.[30] Overall, then, this redefinition of the collective manifestation encourages us to view it in relation to social change within a larger structural framework, thereby affording a more sociologically meaningful analysis. Instead of dismissing the "riot" as an isolated, spontaneous, and unstructured phenomenon, we now must locate its causes or determinants in the social system.[31]

It will be recalled that while a few accounts written from the WRA-JACL perspective deal with causation, even these restrict their inquiry within the social system to the period bracketed by the immediate pre-exclusion crisis and the "riot." Because the Ethnic perspective is predisposed to see the "revolt" as an expressive moment within a process of cultural development, it is more farsighted. On the one hand, it looks backward to the prewar West Coast Japanese American community in search of explanatory antecedents for the revolt. On the other hand, it looks beyond the revolt to ascertain its connection to subsequent subcultural evolution.

First, we must turn to the prewar community. A heretofore largely ignored study by Toshio Yatsushiro—"Political and Socio-Cultural Issues at Poston and Manzanar Relocation Centers: A Themal Analysis"[32]—is especially useful for our purposes. Its thesis is that prewar Japanese American culture contained a limited number of themes—that is, dynamic affirmations controlling behavior and stimulating activity—which were strengthened by pre-exclusion discriminatory practices, reinforced by the exclusion crisis, and expressed within the concentration camp culture.[33]

Yatsushiro identifies six basic cultural themes that define the prewar community. Each represents an element of traditional Japanese culture, modified by the American setting. The first four themes relate to personal and collective obligation, the governing of human relationships and conduct by precise rules, and the use of go-betweens to avoid possible embarrassment in social relations. The two remaining themes have special relevance to the present study. The first is contained in the following proposition: "Society is an ordered social hierarchy in which status is ascribed largely on the basis of biologically determined factors of sex, age, and generation."[34] This theme was clearly manifest in every aspect of family and community life. In the family, the male Issei wielded near autocratic power; in the community, he controlled political, economic, and social activities by leadership in associations like the Japanese Association and the *kenjinkai* (prefectural organization). The second theme maintains that "the welfare of the group is far more important than that of any single individual."[35] Diametrically opposed to the American cultural strain of individualism, this theme promotes cultural homogeneity by granting the group omnipotence. Thus, the Japanese American community tended to minimize distinctions between personalities and social classes, to attribute all accomplishments to the group, and to seek group aid and advice in all social and economic undertakings.[36]

The importance of these themes lies in their influence on group solidarity. From the time of their arrival in the United States at the end of the nineteenth century, the Issei had experienced a series of attacks—both legal and extralegal—which necessitated the development of self-sufficient "Little Tokyos." Each anti-Japanese attack forced the Issei to retreat further from American cultural values and to depend increasingly on their traditional Japanese culture. This, in turn, reinforced group solidarity. Thus, by the outbreak of World War II, the two most significant characteristics of the Issei-dominated Japanese American community were group solidarity and the predominance of elements of Japanese culture.[37]

These characteristics prevailed less among their children. During the 1930s the Nisei generation was maturing and represented a potential challenge to the group's solidarity and to its cultural orientation. As citizens, Nisei came into greater contact with American society and consequently underwent increased Americanization. Their attendance in public schools led them to emulate activities of the American teen culture, and not uncommonly they resisted their parents' attempts to direct their lives in accordance with traditional Japanese values and practices. Some Nisei, in their anxiety to be accepted as typical Americans, began to resent their parents and to ridicule their Japanese ways. All this conflict served to widen the "social distance" between Issei and Nisei.[38]

On the other hand, the usual picture of Nisei as thoroughly Americanized is far from accurate, for countervailing forces were diminishing the social distance and returning the Nisei to the Japanese American community. One form of pressure emanated from the Issei, who, in addition to asserting ordinary parental influence, mandated Nisei participation in cultural agencies—such as Japanese clubs—which undermined the Americanization process. The result for many Nisei was confusion. Sue Kunitomi Embrey recalls that during her youth in Los Angeles' Little Tokyo, the bilingual instructor in her Japanese language school told her that "he thought that my direction in life was going different from the others, that he didn't think I would be too happy within the Japanese community."[39] Additional pressures came from without. Socially, the Nisei encountered barriers to their assimilation into the larger society and found it necessary to participate in social organizations, residential patterns, and marital arrangements along ethnic lines. Economically, they discovered upon graduation from high school and college that the only available employment opportunities existed within their own communities. Therefore, while the Nisei returned to the community perhaps more from necessity than desire, the result was a partial restoration of their ethnicity and a consequent maintenance of group solidarity.[40]

Because of their influence upon prewar solidarity as well as their later involvement in the Manzanar Revolt, two Nisei subgroups deserve special consideration. The first is the Kibei. Applied literally, the term "Kibei" denoted any Nisei who had gone to Japan, for however short a time, and had returned to America. In some instances it was employed to describe any Nisei, whether s/he had gone to Japan or not, who "spoke Japanese . . . preferably to English and who otherwise behaved in what the Nisei regarded as a 'Japanesy' manner."[41] But its usual meaning was restricted to those whose residence in Japan exceeded two years and who received a portion of their education there.

Many Kibei, especially those whose stay in Japan was brief, experienced little difficulty in adjusting to the American milieu, and their behavior was indistinguishable from that of other Nisei. Other Kibei chose to repress their Japaneseness and exhibited hyperbolic American behavior. But for those who had spent considerable time in Japan, the situation was somewhat different. Although Kibei studies customarily emphasize that those in this category were treated as "pariahs within the larger minority group of the Japanese Americans," this remark is at best a half-truth.[42] True, the more Americanized Nisei often derided and even scorned them for their linguistic and social ineptitude, but by no means were they considered "pariahs" by the Issei. After all, many Issei parents originally had sent them to Japan precisely to allow them to absorb Japanese cultural habits deemed essential for economic and social success within the ethnic community. Their Nisei contemporaries might have found them strange and maladjusted, but on the whole the Issei applauded them as "model" Japanese children. One Nisei, recalling her prewar attitude toward Kibei, offered the following response in an interview:

Were Kibei frowned upon by most of the Nisei?

They were considered odd, and I guess it was mostly because of their language problem. And they really didn't make an adjustment into the community.[43]

These Kibei were mostly nonassimilationists. They formed their own clubs and recreational groups, actively led Buddhist and other cultural organizations, and willingly joined the community business structure; Kibei women married either Kibei or Issei men. For this reason they strengthened group solidarity.[44]

The same cannot be said of the second Nisei subgroup—the JACLers. Properly, this term applied only to Nisei affiliated with the Japanese American Citizens League, an organization formed in 1930 as "a reaction against the Japanese orientation of the Issei leadership."[45] Generally, however, it was applied to Nisei who most fully accepted the attitudes, values, practices, and goals of the American culture. Matthew Richard Speier has observed that while the Issei "retained ethnic perspectives and took account of the dominant society only in the form of a valuation group (i.e., a reference group whose standpoint is not adopted as one's own). . . . Nisei took on Caucasian American society as their reference group . . . and adopted its perspective as their own in the form of an identification group."[46] While this distinction is partly valid for Nisei as a whole, it is more valid with respect to the JACLers. They, to a larger degree, penetrated into the dominant society through social, political, and economic activities. Emotionally, they moved increasingly away from their parents and community. Still, at no time prior to the war did they pose a serious threat to group solidarity. Like other Nisei, the JACLers were young, uninfluential, and almost wholly dependent upon the Issei-dominated Japanese community for their economic livelihood.[47]

With this sketch of the psychosocial makeup of the prewar community in mind, we must now see how it was altered by the combined impact of Pearl Harbor and the subsequent exclusion and incarceration of Japanese Americans. For the Issei, who were subjected to a barrage of restrictions, harassments, and indignities—including the precipitous internment of their leaders in federal detention centers–the effect of Pearl Harbor and its aftermath was a pronounced increase in social solidarity. For them, the repressive measures exercised by the government represented only the latest and most serious of a long series of discriminatory actions, and they responded in their customary manner—with cultural retrenchment.[48]

The Nisei responded ambiguously. In a study centering on this period, Tamotsu Shibutani points out that while "there was increased social solidarity [among Nisei] in the sense that everyone recognized the cleavage between the Japanese and the out-group quite clearly . . . there was increased disunity among the Nisei after the outbreak of the war."[49] In other words, we can summarize their dilemma by stating that the crisis forced them to choose between their identification group—as symbolized by their citizenship—and their ethnic group—as actualized by their families and community. Many were too traumatized by the swirl of events to choose one way or the other, though this attitude was less common among JACLers.

Even before Pearl Harbor, when war with Japan seemed all but inevitable, some JACLers zealously advertised their Americanism. Unfortunately, their patriotic boosterism sometimes included a repudiation of Issei leadership. Togo Tanaka, a national office holder in the JACL and the English-language editor of the Los Angeles–based *Rafu Shimpo*, provides a case in point. As Roger Daniels has related, Tanaka, in a speech early in 1941, "insisted that the Nisei must face . . . 'the question of loyalty' and assumed that since the Issei were 'more or less tumbleweeds with one foot in America and one foot in Japan,' real loyalty to America could be found only in his generation."[50] Moreover, according to a recent study of the *Rafu Shimpo*, during this period Tanaka consistently voiced this sentiment editorially.[51]

Daniels's assertion is not, however, clearly documented. In an effort to clarify this point, the authors, in a telephone conversation with Tanaka on August 29, 1974, queried him about the reputed talk. His response was that, while he had possibly said something of this sort, he very much doubted it and would like to be confronted with evidence to allay his doubt. As to another action attributed to him by Daniels that "On the very evening of Pearl Harbor, editor Togo Tanaka went on station KHTR [*sic*], Los Angeles, and told his fellow Nisei: 'As Americans we now function as counter-espionage. Any act or word prejudicial to the United States committed by any Japanese must be warned and reported to the F.B.I., Naval Intelligence, Sheriff's Office, and local police,'"[52] Tanaka absolutely denies its truth, if for no other reason than the fact that he has never been on radio. On the other hand, Daniels has firm evidential grounds here for his attribution. A perusal of the minutes of the Japanese American Citizens League Anti-Axis Committee for December 8, 1941, reveals that on December 7, 1941, at 11:00 p.m. Tanaka did broadcast such a message over KMTR, although the statement was released on behalf of Joe Masaoka, chairman of the Coordinating Committee for National Defense of the Southern District JACL Council. (By way of foreshadowing their later involvement in the Manzanar Revolt, it is interesting to note that Tanaka was joined on the *Rafu's* editorial board by Fred Tayama and Tokie Slocum.)

Bill Hosokawa, a prominent JACL figure, has written of how JACL leaders were summarily seized and interrogated by federal authorities in the wake of Pearl Harbor. (Tanaka, for instance, was arrested under a presidential warrant and placed in Los Angeles jails for eleven days.)[53] Such persecution, however, only prompted JACLers to redouble their efforts to "prove" their loyalty as American citizens. They fought their campaign on two fronts. On the one hand, they used the limited political influence they possessed to alleviate personal hardship and to exonerate the Japanese American community from irresponsible charges of subversion being leveled against it. More ominously, they cooperated with the authorities as security watchdogs. In this connection, an Anti-Axis Committee was established in Los Angeles, headed first by Fred Tayama and later by Tokie Slocum (and also including Togo Tanaka, Joe Grant Masaoka, and Tad Uyeno—names that would appear on the death list announced on the evening of the Manzanar Revolt—as members), to serve as a liaison with the FBI to help flush out "potentially dangerous" Issei.[54]

However well-intentioned its efforts and helpful its services, the JACL came under heavy fire from the Japanese American community. Issei resented the manner in which JACLers, whom they regarded as young and irresponsible, seemed to arrogate the role of community spokesmen. They were angered further by the JACL's apparent complicity with the FBI in Issei arrests. Nor were the Kibei kindly disposed toward the JACL. The Kibei were disturbed that the JACL apparently had forgotten that they too were citizens. They also believed that JACLers were informing on them as well as on Issei, a suspicion that hardened into conviction after the JACL undertook a Kibei survey in mid-February 1942.[55] There even existed widespread dissatisfaction with the JACL among certain Nisei elements. Leftist groups, for example, "looked upon the J.A.C.L. as a large organization controlled by a small minority of 'reactionary' businessmen who used the body as a means of getting business connections and personal prestige."[56] Other Nisei were disgruntled that the JACL should presume to "represent" the community: in Los Angeles the JACL totaled 650 members out of an eligible community population of 20,000.[57] Whatever their grievances against the JACL, Issei, Kibei, and Nisei generally believed that it was sacrificing the community's welfare for its own aggrandizement.

During the period from President Roosevelt's issuance on February 19, 1942, of Executive Order 9066 (which authorized the secretary of war to establish "military areas" and exclude therefrom "any and all persons") until March 21, when the first contingent of Japanese American voluntary inmates arrived from Los Angeles to the Owens Valley Reception Center, the Japanese American community was rife with rumors about the complicity and duplicity of the JACL. For example:

> The J.A.C.L. was instructed by Naval Intelligence to send questionnaires to all members to report on their parents.
>
> The J.A.C.L. started their survey on the Kibei in order to turn in information to the F.B.I. They are taking this as a protective move to whitewash themselves by blaming others.
>
> The J.A.C.L. is trying to be patriotic and they are supporting the evacuation program. They do not have the welfare of the Japanese people at heart.
>
> The J.A.C.L. is supporting the idea of cooperating with the government and evacuating voluntarily because then they could go in and buy up all the goods in Japanese stores at robbery prices and make a substantial profit.
>
> The J.A.C.L. big shots have their fingers in the graft. They are getting something out of the evacuation.
>
> The J.A.C.L. is charging aliens for information that the aliens could get anywhere.
>
> The J.A.C.L. is planning the evacuation with the officials. They are mixing with high government officials.
>
> All J.A.C.L. leaders are *inu* (dogs; informers).[58]

The content of these rumors is less important (many had little basis in fact; others were clearly apocryphal) than their function. As Tamotsu Shibutani has observed, rumors function as mechanisms of social control (i.e., they keep errant individuals in line) and social definition (i.e., they disseminate a common mood).[59] At a time when governmental actions threatened the very existence of the community and government policies were fraught with ambiguity and inconsistency, the shared belief in rumors about the JACL buttressed group solidarity and provided some certitude within the confusion. Therefore, the community's branding of the JACLers as "deviants" must not be construed as a simple act of censure, but rather as a cultural rite by which the community attempted to define its "social boundaries"—what Kai Erikson has denoted as the symbolic parentheses a community draws around its permissible behavior–vis-à-vis a hostile world, thereby insuring its cultural integrity.[60]

JACLers (i.e., aggressive pro-American Nisei) themselves employed rumors during this critical time, though for contrary purposes. Identifying with the larger American community, they guarded its cultural boundaries by exposing "deviants" in the ethnic community. At times they cast Issei in this role, but more commonly the deviants were Kibei, whom they distrusted as hot-tempered, pro-Japan enthusiasts who were "willing to do almost anything, even at the risk of their lives, for the emperor of Japan."[61] Rumors about the Kibei reflected and underscored this suspicion, as the following reactions illustrate:

> I hear those god damn Kibei bastards botched up our chances in the Army. If those son of a bitches like Japan so much why did they come over here in the first place? I never did like those guys anyway. They came over here with their Japanesy ideas and try to change all America to suit themselves. They don't seem to realize that 130,000,000 people might be right.
>
> I really don't blame the Army for booting the Kibei out. I wouldn't trust those guys either. Some of them are O.K., but a lot of them don't belong in this country. You can't tell what they'd do. They might shoot the guns in the wrong way. But Jesus Christ, they didn't have to wreck everything for us Nisei by burning the [US Army] barracks.
>
> Those Kibei are the guys we have to watch. They're so damned hot-headed they will do anything. Then all the rest of us have to suffer just because they happened to be technically American citizens. It'll get so the *hakujin* (Caucasians) won't trust any Nisei.
>
> I hear those Kibei ran wild after December 7. I'd like to castrate some of those bastards.[62]

Again, like rumors concerning the JACL, many of these were patently untrue. The important point, however, is that if the JACL rumors seemed logical from the community's perspective, these Kibei rumors seemed equally plausible from a JACL perspective.

Having examined the prewar community and charted the changes undergone as a result of the Pearl Harbor and eviction crises, we now must focus upon the situation that unfolded at Manzanar. In keeping with our Ethnic perspective, we need to connect prewar and camp developments and determine their cumulative impact on the inmate population. More specifically, we must ascertain the extent to which, in cultural terms, the Manzanar Revolt represented a logical, even a "necessary," outgrowth of these developments.

First, however, we will relate some basic facts about the Manzanar center. Situated in the Owens Valley of east-central California, Manzanar was the first of the centers to be established. From March 21 to June 1, 1942, it was known as the Owens Valley Reception Center, controlled by the military Wartime Civil Control Administration (WCCA) and administered by a staff drawn predominantly from the Works Progress Administration.[63] After June 1, when it came under the jurisdiction of the WRA, its name was changed officially to the Manzanar War Relocation Center. Its population was chiefly urban in background. Out of an approximate total of 10,000 inmates, 88 percent originated from Los Angeles County, with 72 percent from the city of Los Angeles. Located between the small communities of Lone Pine and Independence, Manzanar's climatological conditions were oppressive and its physical accommodations substandard.[64] Moreover, the administrative personnel were badly splintered, and between the time of the camp's opening and the Manzanar Revolt the camp directorship changed four times.[65]

More pertinent to this study than any of these outward conditions was the internal struggle waged over control of the inmate community. From the outset it was clear that the cultural division that emerged during the exclusion period had carried over into the camp. In line with their decision to accept the JAI as their contribution to the war effort, JACLers readily volunteered to assist in the establishment of the camp. In this enterprise they were joined, actually preceded, by a cadre of left-wing Nisei—and some Kibei—intellectuals who, for ideological and strategic reasons, chose to pursue a similar brand of superpatriotism. Because of their early arrival and their avowed pro-Americanism, the administration rewarded JACLers by granting them the white-collar, supervisory, and generally favored jobs, according them what little power was available to inmates and allowing them a voice in shaping policy. In addition, they were placed in control of the camp newspaper, the *Manzanar Free Press*, which afforded them an opportunity to influence public opinion.[66]

This administration-sponsored JACL hierarchy was deeply resented by Issei and Kibei, who often were relegated to subordinate and menial jobs. It was bad enough to witness the JACLers' usurpation of community authority, but worse to see the purposes for which that authority was used. One can imagine how galling it was for Issei and Kibei to read in the *Free Press* of April 11, 1942, the following "appreciation":

> The citizens of Manzanar wish to express in public their sincere appreciation to General John L. DeWitt and his Chiefs of Staff, Tom C. Clark and Colonel Karl R. Bendetsen, for the expedient way in which they have handled the Manzanar situation.
>
> The evacuees now located at Manzanar are greatly satisfied with the excellent comforts the general and his staff have provided for them. "Can't be better," is the general feeling of the Manzanar *citizens*. "Thank you, General!"[67]

Nor could the JACL's flaunted citizenship and unctuousness toward Caucasian authorities have pleased Nisei. The mass extirpation and confinement in concentration camps permitted Nisei to reflect upon "their past hostility towards the ways of their 'Japanesy' parents . . . the long years of hardships suffered [by Issei] in their behalf . . . [and] they became extremely respectful of the Issei, their judgment, their advice, and their ways."[68] Thus, a growing number of Japanized Nisei increasingly viewed the JACLers' behavior as "patricidal" and "treasonable."[69]

Notwithstanding the JACLers' ostensible authority, the Issei managed quietly to resume the leadership they had occupied within the prewar community. There was, for example, a gradual ascendancy of the Issei-dominated block leaders over the JACL-headed Information Center throughout March, April, May, and June. Initiated at the request of two JACL leaders, Roy Takeno and David Itami, the Information Center emerged in late March in order to answer perplexing questions and supply basic services for new arrivals. It developed branch offices and subsections, eventually numbering fifty-three persons on its roll. In early April the system of block leaders came into existence, whereby each block selected three men, one of whom was appointed block leader by the camp manager. For the most part, those selected were

Issei.[70] It soon became apparent that the inmates preferred to query the block leaders rather than the Information Center, which by the end of June had been displaced by the block leaders. Moreover, it was determined by the camp authorities that now the block leaders should be directly elected instead of being appointed by the administration. At the grass-roots level, then, power was gravitating back into Issei hands.[71]

Just as the Issei were beginning to consolidate their power in the Block Leaders Council in late June, a disquieting directive arrived from Washington declaring that only citizens could elect and serve as block representatives. Naturally, the Issei saw this action as another attempt to undermine their leadership and subordinate them to Nisei. Fortunately, project director Roy Nash, recognizing the Issei's important role in Manzanar's government and fearing the consequences of stripping them of that role, obtained a stay on the ruling. Nonetheless, as community analyst Morris E. Opler pointed out, ". . . considerable damage had been done by the debate and the division which had followed the announcement of the ruling."[72]

The damage was compounded on July 4 by another policy decision from Washington. In a memorandum to Ted Akahoshi, temporary chairman of the block leaders, assistant project director Ned Campbell made the following request: "Will you please get over to all Block Leaders that it is against the policy of the War Relocation Authority to allow meetings to be conducted in Japanese. We have no objection to having meetings held in English interpreted so that all can understand, but we feel that all meetings should be primarily conducted in English."[73] Again the Issei, and many Kibei, interpreted this measure as a device to render them politically impotent. The following week, the Block Leaders Council registered its displeasure by passing a motion that "when a meeting is attended by more Issei then Japanese will be used and brief translation in English be made."[74]

More important, however, was the debate that preceded the motion, for it depicted vividly the evolving Issei-Kibei frame of mind. Chairman Akahoshi, an Issei graduate of Stanford University known for his cooperation with the administration, set the tone with his opening remarks.[75]

> I think this letter [Campbell's memorandum] is very important, because
> majority of those who come to the meetings are Issei and they want to
> conduct the meetings in Japanese. When I saw this letter I told Mr. Campbell

"that the Japanese people are greatest nation in the world for sacrifice"—many of us are day laborers and in spite of low income are able to send our children to university. No nation sacrificed as hard as Japanese. We have, I think, no saboteurs among us, why restriction on Japanese speaking?[76]

Among the following speakers, only two—an Issei and Karl Yoneda, a Kibei Communist who aligned himself with the JACLers, outdoing them in his advocacy of pro-Americanism, approved the policy.[77] The rest, all Issei and Kibei, dissented with emotion!

[AN ISSEI:] I am in favor to conduct meeting in Japanese, because we cannot express ourselves ably in English. (3 or 4 people clapped hands)

[A KIBEI:] I believe all block leaders are very responsible people and they should be trusted by the Administration. You know that once we, the Japanese, decide to carry certain duty, we do accomplish it, that is the nature of us Japanese. (Big applause)

[A KIBEI:] Mr. Yoneda said that he is an American citizen, but he have to give up that right. Same thing true to me too, I am American but I cannot use my citizenship, therefore we must depend on Issei for leadership and certainly I am in favor for Japanese meeting. (Big applause)

[AN ISSEI:] My son is in US Army and when he obtained furlough and came home, he was arrested by the FBI in spite of fact that he is American. (Spoken with tears in his eyes) We are always discriminated against here and only one who protect Nisei is we the Issei. I can speak only Japanese and if it must be English, I must resign as block leader. Don't forget we are Japanese and we are the people who can unite to do anything. (Big applause)

[CHAIRMAN AKAHOSHI:] I think we, the Issei, know what's bad and what's good. Some Nisei have stool-pigeoned on us—some Nisei is boasting that he turned in 175 of us Japanese to the FBI. Other is boasting that he turned in so many and they are boasting each other. I am quite sure that only 2 or 3 out of the 175 are guilty. Roosevelt spoke about national unity—these Nisei are the ones who disrupt national unity and they are the traitors to this country. (Big applause)

[AN ISSEI] Those Nisei are lazy bunch and they are no good. We, the Issei, are doing everything. Look at those janitors. None of the Nisei are cleaning toilets. We Issei have to do all the work.[78]

Equally interesting is that this debate was recorded by Karl Yoneda and offered to the administration in a confidential report. The recommendations that Yoneda appended and his cautionary advice also deserve attention since they reflect an opposing JACL viewpoint:

> . . . may I suggest the following: 1. All meetings in camp must be held in English. 2. Stenographic minutes be made of Block Leaders Council Meetings unless some one of the Administrators attends meeting. 3. Qualification for Block Leader should be that he must understand English and preferably Nisei. (Some Nisei are just as pro-axis as Issei but one can argue with them easier because of their knowledge of American institutions.) 4. The instruction that all meetings are to be conducted in English should be widely publicized.
>
> If we allow another meeting such as was held this morning, the block leaders meetings will be turned into germinating nest for undesirable elements and pro-axis adherents. Crystallization of pro-Axis sentiment is getting stronger every day and if we don't guard against it, eventually there will be a clash between pro-axis and pro-America groups in camp such as occured [sic] at Santa Anita.[79]

This issue was resolved temporarily by the administration's interpretation of the WRA policy as allowing Japanese to be spoken at meetings if followed by an English translation, but a legacy of acrimony and widened division between Issei-Kibei and JACLers resulted.

These feelings were exacerbated by the announcement on July 27 that a new Manzanar Citizens Federation would meet the following evening. The leaders in the meeting were Hiro Neeno, Joe Grant Masaoka, Karl Yoneda, and Togo Tanaka, all closely allied with JACL objectives, who spoke about "improving conditions in camp," "educating citizens for leadership," "participating in the war effort," and "preparing evacuees for postwar conditions."[80] As project director Ralph P. Merritt later observed, the meeting represented "an attempt to organize American citizens into a federation which would aid the administration and which probably would also help the Nisei get more power and political strength in opposition to the Issei."[81]

This strategy ultimately backfired. The meeting itself, packed with pro-American Nisei supporters of the JACL leadership, turned into a rally. Following the general meeting, an open forum took place in which Joe

Kurihara, who would later figure prominently in the Manzanar Revolt, took the floor:

> "I'm an American citizen," he cried. "I served under fire in France. Now I'm in this prison. You're all here, too, with me. I've proved my loyalty by fighting over there. Why doesn't the government trust me?" "If you please, Mr. Chairman," shouted back Tokie Slocum, a self-styled patriot and former Chairman of the JACL's Anti-Axis Committee, "I was a Sergeant-Major in the last war. That was the highest position any Japanese ever attained. Sergeant Alvin York served under me. I was in some of the hottest fighting that took place. For this loyalty the Government gave all of us veterans American citizenship. We're here because of military necessity. I've had three chances to go to other places." "Tokie," challenged Kurihara, "why are you in here? Isn't it because you couldn't go any place? Isn't it because you're a Jap? Isn't it because the government doesn't trust you?" Overriding the Chairman's vain attempts to restore order, Slocum hollered back at Kurihara: "I'll tell you why I'm here. I'm here because my commander-in-chief, the President, ordered me in here."[82]

Shortly thereafter the meeting was adjourned.

Although it is customarily emphasized that this meeting provoked Kurihara into accepting the Issei point of view, its conversion of many other Nisei as well is more significant. Kurihara declared that "he was a Jap and not an American, and . . . [that] he wanted to go . . . to Japan where he belonged."[83] However, other Nisei, "who had had their patriotism dampened by evacuation . . . [grew] cynical over the Federation's petition for a second front and for the drafting of Japanese-Americans."[84]

The following excerpts from an interview with Karl Yoneda shed light both on the purpose of the Manzanar Citizens Federation and the petition drive for a second front and also suggest that the real moving force in both was the leftist faction in the pro-American coalition, not the JACL leaders.

> *You mean the [JACL] didn't have much input into the Block Leaders Council and so they really set up an alternative organization [the Citizens Federation] that would be able to have some policy statements voiced at the camp?*
>
> That's the way, I guess, they started, but when we came in—Jimmy Oda and myself—we turned it around and made it into an entirely different organization altogether, which they didn't like. As soon as we got in, we took over the

leadership—Koji Ariyoshi, Jimmy Oda, and myself. Togo Tanaka, Joe Grant Masaoka [who was the brother of JACL executive secretary Mike Masaoka and, along with Tanaka, the Manzanar documentary historian for the WRA], Kiyoshi Higashi [the inmate police chief], and Fred Tayama, they didn't say "boo."

What were the differences in philosophy with respect to the Citizens Federation? How did the JACL look at its purpose? And how did the people in your group look at its purpose differently?

Our purpose . . . one of the purposes was to push this petition drive [to open a second front]. This was not done in the name of the Federation. But through the Federation we saw that we could muster more support among the evacuees. . . . [We wanted] to open a second front and utilize manpower of the Japanese Americans in the camps. We obtained 218 signatures, among them Fred Tayama, Togo Tanaka, Joe Grant Masaoka and some 40 women.

And what was the JACL's philosophy? How did that differ? What do you think they wanted out of the organization?

Well, the JACL people . . . you know, actually, they didn't know what to do. Many times they asked us, "what do you think?" Because we became the driving force within the Manzanar Citizens Federation. While opening the second front was a Communist Party campaign, it was also our thinking and that of the bulk of the American people's contention (see newspapers of the day), because the US and British governments refused to open such a front (it was finally opened in 1944). This would be a way to help the Russian front, which was being beaten by the Nazis and the Russian people [were] retreating. If opened, then Hitler would have to divert more of his troops toward Europe, and the Soviet Union could recoup.

So you in a sense maneuvered the JACL into certain policies through the Citizens Federation. They really didn't know what they were doing at this point.

Yes. Circulating the petition was a good idea, said Tanaka and Masaoka. And I still think so. Further, they (JACL leaders) were in the same quandary, but we had a better understanding of the true nature of World War II. Of course, one of the driving forces was Koji Ariyoshi, the president of the Citizens Federation, who had been approached by JACLers to head the MCF because of his non-JACL status.[85]

Increasingly, the Issei-Kibei point of view was expanding into an Issei-Kibei-Nisei point of view.[86] From the beginning of August until the revolt in December, the Kibei formed the spearhead of the opposition to the JACLers. Once again, a ruling from Washington galvanized underlying discontent into retaliatory action: Bulletin 22 was issued, which excluded all Kibei from participation in the leave program. This discriminatory measure further reduced the depreciated value of Kibei citizenship and robbed them of an important economic perquisite. When Kibei leader Ben Kishi announced that a meeting of Kibei would be held on August 8, the Nisei secretary of the block leaders voiced the fear that they might "try to find [a] scapegoat among Nisei Leaders and blame them for descriminating [*sic*] against Kibei and [that] this [would] . . . further aggravate sectional strife among Japanese."[87] In response to Kishi's idea that "if the government do not recognize the citizenship right of Kibei and continues to treat them as dangerous element it might as well revoke citizenship of Kibei," the secretary reasoned that "this line of thinking is very dangerous and goes to show that at least some Kibeis are more inclined to forfeit Citizenship and would rather be regarded as aliens."[88]

The proceedings of this famous Kibei meeting were recorded by Fred Tayama in another JACL "confidential" report directed to the administration. In Mess Hall 15 gathered approximately 400 of the camp's Kibei population of over 600, augmented by a large contingent of Issei and roughly seventy Nisei. Five speakers were scheduled. The first was Raymond Hirai, who outlined inmate complaints concerning medical care, educational facilities, food, housing, wages, and self-government. We concern ourselves only with his remarks on the last two subjects:

> Look, for example, [at] the rate of pay for Camouflage workers. Camouflage is a war production. They are using minors: many around the ages of 15 and 16. . . . I demanded many more things of Nash. And Nash told me, "I am the Project Director here and I can do anything the way I want it to be done." So I told Nash, "You are like Hitler and Mussolini combined," and Nash replied, "I am." So I demanded what he had said in writing and immediately Nash turned around and said that he had never said such a thing. That's the type of Director we have here. I got so mad that I told him that I'd get a rock and hit him right on his bald spot (his head). (Laughter and applause from the audience)

We must demand re-election of all Block Leaders. We have people now in control who are unable to say anything and are just taking orders from the Administration. *This is our Camp and the Japanese people should decide for themselves how this Camp should be governed; we should not listen to those prejudiced whites.* (great Applause)[89]

The next speaker, Kiyoshi Hashimoto, entitled his talk "Kibei Nisei *no tachiba*" (The Stand of the Kibei Nisei) but confessed that he was unsure of what he wanted to say. Several persons in the audience shouted *"wakatte-oru"* (we understand). Then Joe Kurihara exclaimed: "I was born in Hawaii. I have never been in Japan but in my veins flows Japanese blood; a blood of *Yamato Damashii* (Japanese Spirit). We citizens have been denied our citizenship; we are 100% Japanese (a roaring applause and stamping of feet)." The third speaker, Bill Kito, directed his commentary to the Manzanar Citizens Federation, charging that certain Nisei had completely disregarded the Issei—a remark that precipitated great applause and provoked someone in the audience to demand that those Nisei ought to be struck down. The fourth speaker, Karl Yoneda, was greeted by sustained booing and cries of "Sit down! Get out! Shut Up!" The last scheduled speaker, Masaji Tanaka, received more sympathy:

I am a Kibei Nisei, but the Kibei Nisei are not Americans; they are Japanese. (big applause) The Kibei are not loyal to the United States and they might as well know about it. (roaring applause) But the Kibei should use their citizenship rights for their own benefit. (everybody looking around the room; no applause) I cannot understand why there are a few Nisei who still talk about their citizenship rights; and about American democracy. I have heard that there are a few who even send reports outside. (boo and down with those rats) Those fools can holler all they want, but in the eyes of the American people they too are Japanese and nothing but Japanese.[90]

Following some extemporaneous speeches from the floor, Chairman Ben Kishi, declaring that he would assume personal responsibility for the meeting, adjourned the gathering by stating, "We may never be able to hold a meeting like this again, and Japanese soldiers will be here soon to liberate all of us."[91]

Several factors about this meeting command notice: the stress of nativistic themes, the aggressive criticism of the camp's administration, the intolerance of dissenting viewpoints, and the heightened determination to punish suspected informers. The circle around the community was drawing tighter.

August witnessed further in-group solidarity. As a result of the Kibei meeting, Director Nash issued an official bulletin reinstating the WRA ban on the use of Japanese in public meetings.[92] This decision revitalized earlier Issei grievances and further aroused the Kibei's anti-administration stand. This month also saw the "enforced" resignation of those block leaders deemed cooperative with administrative policy.[93]

The Issei-Kibei coalition had developed an effective organization. On August 21, when elections were held to select block leaders in those blocks whose incumbents previously had been appointed, JACLers were ousted and supplanted by Issei or Kibei. In Block 4, for example, Karl Yoneda was defeated by an Issei who amassed 93 percent of the votes cast. Yoneda correctly evaluated the reasons behind his defeat in a communication forwarded to the administration, explaining that the Issei-Kibei bloc had criticized him on the following grounds:

1. Circulated petition for Second Front and wanted to send all Japanese American soldiers on front line duty and let the enemy shoot them first.
2. For America's war effort and urged many citizens in the block to work on camouflage nets.
3. That he is a dangerous "red."
4. Married to white woman and does not follow Japanese customs. He washes son's clothes, while wife works on camouflage, let's [sic] wife go to meetings, etc.
5. Stooge for administration and also informer because he has been seen with [Tokie] Slocum on many occasions.
6. Spoke at Kibei meeting against them.
7. Spoke at Citizens Federation meeting for America.
8. Responsible for all meetings, in camp, to be conducted in English.[94]

Viewing himself as a scapegoat for pro-Japan elements, Yoneda believed this opposition to him *politically* significant. The overriding significance, however, is *cultural*; from the perspective of the inmates in his block, Yoneda was a quintessential deviant, representative of all those characteristics the subculture abhorred. A cultural antihero, he symbolized for the inmate population its need of social cohesion.[95]

This need grew urgent when on August 24 the WRA, through Administrative Instruction No. 34, began enforcing the ruling that only citizens could hold office (though aliens might vote and fill appointive posts). The full impact of this ruling occurred in September when the Block Leaders Council learned that it was to be supplanted by a Community Council structured along the above lines. Issei were incensed, arguing that "they had lived long in the United States and that denial of the right to naturalize was unjust [and] to prevent them now from holding office in their own evacuee community was simply to emphasize this injustice."[96] Moreover, they charged that JACLers had inspired the decree and had poisoned the Issei case with the WRA. That is, here was another attempt to diminish their influence. "As a result of evacuation they had lost heavily in property and in prestige. Their places in the old Japanese community were gone. Now they feared that they would be entirely at the mercy of the less sympathetic among the Nisei and of the American government."[97]

Their worst fears materialized, therefore, when the project director appointed a seventeen-man Self-Government Commission composed entirely of Nisei to draft a charter for the new government. Their tolerance disappeared completely on September 25 when the new acting project director, Harvey Coverley, announced that at the end of the month the block leaders would become block managers, exchanging their legislative functions for administrative ones. A rash of resignations followed. Indeed, by mid-October the position of block manager had become so undesirable that the administration could hardly find substitutes for those who had resigned.[98]

Another threat that alarmed Issei was the formation of the Manzanar Work Corps. Designed to include a Representative Assembly and a Fair Practices Committee, it aroused their suspicion because the same JACLers who had formed the detested Citizens Federation also were sponsoring the Work Corps. Thus, when the election of representatives took place in late September, Issei registered little interest in the proceedings.

But it was the Kibei, smarting from their recent exclusion from the Charter Commission, who emerged as the Work Corps' most vociferous opponents. At the first meeting of the Representative Assembly Harry Ueno, a Kibei representing the kitchen workers of Mess Hall 22, clashed with Fred Tayama, chairman of the Work Corps. Upon questioning Tayama regarding the corps' functions, Ueno became convinced that it represented an administrative tool that would not fully protect the interests of kitchen workers. Consequently, Ueno organized the Kitchen Workers Union to "wring concessions from the administration, rather than have the administration wring more work out of the evacuees, as they believed would happen under the Work Corps."[99] Since most Kibei were employed as mess workers and approximately 1,500 of the Manzanar work force of 4,000 were kitchen employees, the Kitchen Workers Union provided Kibei a powerful base for mobilizing community action.[100]

Karl Yoneda's oral historical recollections on Ueno and the Kitchen Workers Union deserve careful attention:

He [Ueno] is such an unknown figure. He talks about organizing Kitchen Workers Union. To me, through my experience of organizing, he just had a handful [of followers] in his kitchen and among the strong pro-Japan kitchen crew in my block, Block 4. . . . Actually, they don't have an organization such as the Kitchen Workers Union; they merely name themselves.

You mean few kitchen workers really identified in any strong sense with the Kitchen Workers Union?

I don't think so, because I was there. If they had such a force, I am sure not only I, but others would have detected it right away.[101]

If the formation of the Kitchen Workers' Union represented one index of rising anti-JACL sentiment, another was the swelling opposition to the JACL-dominated Charter Commission, headed by Togo Tanaka. One form of resistance was passive: few bothered to register for the charter's ratification vote of November 9. When an "educational" meeting on the charter was held, outraged speakers assailed its citizen-alien distinction and cast aspersions upon the commission members. The same evening an ominous message appeared on mess hall bulletin boards:

Attention: We do not recognize any necessity for a self-government system. We should oppose anything like this as it is only drawing a rope around our necks. Let the Army take care of everything. Stop taking action which might bring trouble to our fellow residents.

Blood Brothers Concerned About the People.[102]

The administration, responding to the cumulative pressure, rescheduled the ratification election for November 30. The postponement did not have the desired "cooling" effect, however, for the charter had come to symbolize the deep cultural division between the para-administrative JACLers and, in effect, the rest of the camp population. Using their subsidized press, the charter supporters attempted to mollify the inmates' widespread fears and convince them of the advantages of a speedy ratification. To counter the influence of the *Free Press*'s campaign, the oppositional forces established what Morris Opler has termed the "Manzanar Underground."[103] Soon the community was inundated with posters, bulletins, and other communiqués, variously signed "Manzanar Black Dragon Society," "Southern California Blood Brothers Corps," "Southern California Justice Group," and "Patriotic Suicide Corps." Primary attention was given to undermining the self-government scheme by including intimidating letters to each member of the Charter Commission, but in time the underground branched out to criticize every aspect of Manzanar life.

As the date of the ratification grew closer, it became apparent that the charter was doomed to defeat. Seeking to rid the self-government plan of its JACL stigma, the administration disbanded the Charter Commission and announced that "before the final charter was submitted to the people, a city-wide election was to take place on November 22, and two persons from each block were to be elected to a committee to study the charter and make adjustments."[104] (At the same time, the administration called in two FBI agents to investigate Manzanar's underground, thereby hoping to eliminate a major source of opposition to the charter.) Once again, however, the administration was confronted by passive resistance, for on November 22 the turnout of voters was embarrassingly meager.

Nonetheless, on November 30 the new project director, Ralph P. Merritt, scheduled a meeting of the elected block representatives. This meeting proved even more embarrassing to the cause of the charter. Indeed, only about half of the representatives attended. As a first item of business, the group decided to poll how many opposed the self-government plan. All but one—Togo Tanaka, the JACL head of the commission—raised their hands. This lopsided division was mirrored by the subsequent discussion, which deserves our attention for its representation of the general mood of the camp population:

[HARRY UENO, WHO WAS IN ATTENDANCE AS AN INTERESTED VISITOR:]
In my block we didn't even elect delegates; we see no necessity for such a joke

of a thing, we should organize a strong Japanese Welfare Group in this camp. It will furnish the representation for us. I think it is a plot of the government to use those who can be used when they talk about self-government.

[TOGO TANAKA:] I do not feel that we have anybody capable of speaking in support of 10,000 people. The self-government arrangement would fill that need.

[THE CHAIRMAN, GENJI YAMAGUCHI, AN ISSEI BLOCK LEADER:][105] I wish to differ with Mr. Tanaka. We do have a body capable of speaking for the population and representing them. That is the Block Managers. We can do everything that any Council of Nisei can do. What have you to say to that?

[TANAKA:] The Block Managers have their role to perform. They are important in the scheme of things. But their job is administrative. You do not represent the people so much as you do the Administration, *at least in theory*. The Managers have no power to legislate. That is the difference.

[CHAIRMAN YAMAGUCHI:] There is one question that I would like to put before Mr. Tanaka, if he will be good enough to answer. I don't know whether it's rumor or not, but I have heard that the reason why the W.R.A. decided on the policy of discriminating against the Issei in holding office in the proposed Council is because Mike Masaoka [Executive Secretary] of the National J.A.C.L. got together with Dillon Myer [WRA National Director] and had that discriminatory clause put in. What do you know about that?

[TANAKA:] Now that you tell that to me, I've heard it too. Why don't you write to Washington, D.C. and Mr. Myer and ask him?

[ANOTHER ISSEI:] I would like to ask Mr. Tanaka why it is that the Nisei seem to want to control this camp? Why is it that they are out to persecute the Issei?[106]

Another vote followed on the self-government question—this time with a unanimous negative response.[107] The circle around the community had all but closed.

Two interesting sidelights to this meeting are the role of "spokesman for the people" assumed by Harry Ueno and the attribution to JACL leaders of influence in shaping WRA policy. From the time of his formation of the Kitchen Workers Union two months earlier, Ueno had emerged as a cultural hero. In part, this development stemmed from his style of leadership. A fluent, persuasive, and straightforward speaker in Japanese who customarily spoke in a high-pitched and excitable voice, his actions personified the traditional Japanese cultural theme emphasizing group welfare over personal aggrandizement.

Ueno was not interested in control merely as an end in itself, this he told to all, and his friends were convinced of his sincerity when he said that "everything which I do, I am doing for the sake of the people of Manzanar. I have no selfish motives, and this unselfishness on my part will be recognized by the people."[108]

While his opposition to the Work Corps and the Charter Commission enhanced his reputation in the community, what catapulted Ueno into public stature was his charge that two administrators—assistant project director Ned Campbell and chief steward Joe Winchester—were misappropriating and selling inmate sugar supplies for personal gain. This charge had led to a full-scale investigation by the block managers. Although insufficient evidence was uncovered to implicate the two, the investigation did expose the fact that the inmates were being shortchanged in their sugar allotment.[109] This finding alone guaranteed Ueno's popularity, for it confirmed the inmates' deep-seated conviction that the administrators were capable of the most unscrupulous behavior.

JACL-WRA collusion rumors had been commonplace, but their credibility became intensified by a recent development. While the meeting on self-government was in progress, Fred Tayama and another JACL leader, Kiyoshi Higashi (inmate police chief), were serving as Manzanar's delegates to the JACL National Convention in Salt Lake City. Tayama's departure for that city in mid-November had outraged the inmates, for he, even more than Karl Yoneda, Tokie Slocum, and Togo Tanaka, typified the antithesis of the "Japanese spirit." From the standpoint of the community, "no more unrepresentative person could be chosen to present the views of Manzanar at the convention."[110] Antipathy toward Tayama stretched back to pre-eviction days. As the president of the Los Angeles JACL chapter and chairman of the Southern District Council of JACL, "it was almost axiomatic that [he should have been] the most-criticized Nisei in Los Angeles."[111] But the community's animosity for Tayama was seasoned by other factors as well. At a time when the economic and social fortunes of Japanese Americans were at a low ebb, he was conspicuously prosperous. The proprietor of a chain of restaurants employing thirty-five to fifty workers, Tayama owned a large home, drove around the community in a late-model Buick sedan, "played golf with the Japanese Consul (Tomokazu Hori), and was frequently asked by Nisei clubs to serve, with his wife, as patron and patroness at numerous social functions."[112] Whereas his JACL circle of associates regarded him "as a 'regular guy' who played a stiff hand at poker, traded gusty jokes with the best of 'em and won more than his share of golf trophies," in the pages of *Doho*, a leftist Nisei newspaper, he was accused of "operating [his cafes] under 'sweat shop conditions,' underpaying his help, and of obstructing the unionization of his employees."[113] Nor did his penchant for self-assertiveness and aggressive opportunism endear him to the community. For example, he reputedly announced to his classmates in a public speaking class: "You know, I have been raised to always do my very best and to rise to the very top. I firmly believe that one should always strive to be top. Even if I were to be a bandit, I would expect to be the Chief Bandit."[114]

Tayama's activities during the eviction period further compounded his unpopularity. It was rumored—and generally believed—that in his capacity as a JACL official and as co-owner of the Pacific Service Bureau he exploited Issei, "making exorbitant profits from high charges for services [filing alien travel permits required by the Department of Justice, transferring business licenses, and the like] which could be obtained free" through federal channels.[115] Another damaging rumor circulated to the effect that Tayama had mishandled a relief fund collected for beleaguered Terminal Island fishermen.[116]

Over and beyond these personal endeavors, Tayama was vilified for his "witch hunting" efforts in behalf of the JACL. A vigorous proponent of Americanization and undivided loyalty, Tayama, in March 1941, had been instrumental in the formation of the Southern District's Coordinating Committee for Southern California Defense (CCSCD), whose animating purpose of "making patriotism vital" entailed gathering information on subversive activities (which was turned over directly to Naval Intelligence).[117] After Pearl Harbor, Tayama organized the Anti-Axis Committee to enlarge upon and to step up the work of the CCSCD. His subsequent appointment of Tokie Slocum, a frenetic chauvinist who reportedly accompanied FBI agents on their post–Pearl Harbor sweep of "potentially dangerous" Issei in Los Angeles's Little Tokyo, darkened Tayama's reputation still further. Indignation toward him reached a fever pitch when, following a meeting with army officials and JACL leaders in San Francisco, Tayama broke the news of total exclusion and detention to Southern Californians at a mass meeting at the Maryknoll Catholic Church auditorium, located just outside the heart of Little Tokyo.[118] His actions at Manzanar did nothing to mitigate the community's detestation for him:

> Indeed, if anything, he fell into even greater displeasure. At Manzanar his most unpopular antics were those concerned with his demonstration of his Americanism. As one observer put it, "Tayama was not content to be a 100% American; he was a 350% American." Specifically, Tayama was very loose in his talk about disloyal Americans, openly informing the Administration about manifestations of disloyalty on the part of particular individuals at Manzanar. Tayama is said to have worked off his personal prejudices by accusing those he disliked of being pro-Japanese. He is also said to have informed on the basis of completely inadequate evidence. Tayama did his informing with some secrecy, but the Japanese grapevine kept the community informed of his activity.[119]

Tayama seemed to be accorded special privileges by the camp staff: "Rumors circulated freely about the sugar, canned foods and fine furniture with which his home was filled, and . . . it was assumed that the sugar said to be in his home was a portion of the amount the kitchen workers claimed had mysteriously disappeared."[120] Nor did his role as a leading spirit in both the Citizens Federation and the Work Corps win him anything but more intense hatred. And now he had the audacity to name himself, through political manipulation, Manzanar's "representative" at the Salt Lake City meeting where WRA national leaders would gather and policy decisions would be made. Indeed, word had filtered back to Manzanar that Tayama, in addition to repeating his loose accusations of un-American activities in camp and proposing measures for their elimination, had, along with other JACL delegates, "in the name of the Japanese people in and out of the Centers, asked that Nisei be inducted into combat units of the US Army."[121] The mere mention of his name evoked profound disgust. If anyone endangered the group's existence and threatened its solidarity, it was Fred Tayama.[122]

In the words of Morton Grodzins, "[It] can be said without doubt that the majority of the people at Manzanar did not believe anyone, guilty or not, should be punished for beating Fred Tayama. Tayama was a public nuisance. His assailants were to be praised, not punished." Grodzins cites the following inmate reactions as typical: "It was hard to find a single person at Manzanar who expressed sympathy for Tayama." "Even the highly Americanized and cooperative Nisei were of the opinion that though the approach was unorthodox, Tayama deserved the beating. Since there was no other way of his getting punished, the beating fit the situation perfectly." Grodzin's report, "Manzanar Shooting," is the best account of the social psychology of the Manzanar camp at the time of the revolt. Written immediately after the disturbance, it makes no attempt to judge ideology or morality but merely tries to reflect public opinion. In so doing, it too is written from an Ethnic (i.e., community) perspective.[123]

It will be recollected that Tayama was beaten upon his return to the center, thereby setting in motion the Manzanar "Riot." What must be emphasized is that there is strong reason to believe that the overwhelming majority of inmates fully endorsed this beating. Historians writing from the WRA-JACL perspective may see the attack on Tayama as the unwarranted work of a few pro-Axis Kibei troublemakers, but such an analysis construes the action too restrictively. Even if one concedes pro-Japan terrorism as the basis for the assault and accepts the idea that only a small band of hooligans participated in it, one still has to account for the thousands who protested the arrest of Harry Ueno and who were willing to defy the administration to have him released from jail. Nor did they simply believe him innocent of involvement in Tayama's beating. Indeed, one might say that Ueno was lionized because of his alleged connection with the attack. For the inmates—Issei, Kibei, and Nisei—the time had come when something had to be done to prevent the corrosive effects of the JACLers. Seen through the Ethnic perspective, the beating of Tayama was both necessary and good.

Similarly, what transpired on December 6, 1942, must not be seen in isolation or ascribed solely to ideological motivations. When viewed within the Ethnic (i.e., community) perspective, all of the occurrences of that day—the massive crowds, the membership of the Committee of Five, the composition of the death lists and blacklists, the demands for the dismissal of specified members of the appointed staff, and the character of the inmates' evening demonstration at the jail—assume a definite cultural logic.

While WRA-JACL sources attribute the huge assemblages to the fact that most present were merely curious onlookers, this interpretation stems from narrow wish-fulfillment.[124] It appears to us that a more satisfactory explanation is that the mounting discontent of the inmate population, which heretofore found sporadic expression through grumbling about camp conditions, work slowdowns, strikes against war-related industries and profit-oriented camp enterprises, and pervasive gang activity and "inu" beatings, became crystallized into concerted resistance action through the symbolic juxtaposition of Harry Ueno and Fred Tayama.[125] As Morton Grodzins has perceptively observed:

> The situation was made to order for a popular anti-administration demonstration. The issue cut through political and cultural lines. The question could be put as one involving administrative integrity and fairness to the inmates. Loyalty to America had nothing to do with it. . . . The demonstrations that followed, though in part engineered by the genuine pro-Japanese elements in the camp, were not pro-Japanese demonstrations. Rather, they were simply demonstrations against an administrative policy that according to the trend of thought in the camp, jailed on flimsy evidence one of the community's benefactors.[126]

The cultural significance of the Committee of Five is also noteworthy. In consonance with the Japanese cultural theme mandating that community status be ascribed by factors of sex, age, and generation, the committee was composed largely of mature male Issei. Moreover, all of the members embodied the cultural theme positing the paramount importance of the community's welfare. Four of them were aligned with the Kitchen Workers Union, while the remaining one, Joe Kurihara, was primarily identified by inmates for his attacks on the Citizens Federation and his championship of an alternative organization, the Manzanar Welfare Association.[127]

Likewise, there is a cultural logic informing the death lists and blacklists read off to the crowds by the committee. While the precise membership and order of priority of these lists is somewhat vague, it seems clear that the primary targets were Fred Tayama, Tokie Slocum, Karl Yoneda, Koji Ariyoshi, James Oda, Togo Tanaka, and Joe Masaoka.[128] In addition, the lists included inmates prominently associated with the *Free Press* and the camp internal security force, particularly its special investigative branch.[129] Significantly, all of these individuals were identified with JACL-sponsored organizations and objectives and/or antisubversive activities.

The choice of the particular three members of the administration whose removal was called for by the crowd also made cultural sense. The individual most frequently named, assistant project director Ned Campbell, not only didn't understand the Japanese psychology, but epitomized the *keto* (white man, hairy beast) to the inmates. Loud, stubborn, overbearing, and given to making physical threats against those who disagreed with him, Campbell in his very demeanor evoked the racism undergirding the entire incarceration program.[130] Chief steward Joe Winchester, whom Ueno had accused of being in collusion with Campbell in shorting inmates of their rightful supplies, compounded his culpability in the community's eyes by his penchant for making snap judgments and for treating incarcerees in accordance with simplistic, pejorative stereotypes. For Winchester, inmates were either "good Japs" or "troublemakers." The remaining staff member whose ouster was demanded was Hervey Brown, chief engineer in charge of public works. Like Campbell and Winchester, Brown projected a high-handed manner and appeared to transfer or fire inmate employees for what seemed to them very arbitrary reasons.[131]

Finally, the behavior of the crowd at the evening gathering before the camp jail prior to the shooting—heckling at the military police, speaking almost exclusively in Japanese, and singing the Japanese national anthem and other Japanese songs—is culturally revealing.[132] For the inmates, the jailing of Ueno became a rallying point for their willingness to resist those (like the WRA, the JACL, and the military police) who appeared to threaten their cultural heritage and identity. Thus, in response to their endangered ethnicity, they exhibited heightened ethnic consciousness and behavior.

This was also true with the entire Manzanar Revolt. The events of December 6 were but a logical culmination of developments originating with the administration's decision to bypass the community's natural Issei leadership to deal with its own artificially erected JACL hierarchy and to embark on a program of Americanization at the expense of Japanese ethnicity. When the WRA moved the JACLers out of the camp after the revolt, the Issei took a step toward restoring the dominance they had enjoyed before the JAI, and the entire community served notice that their self-determination and ethnic identity would not be relinquished without a struggle. Through the operation of continuing resistance activity, Manzanar would eventually be transformed into a Little Tokyo of the desert where, as in prewar days, the most salient community characteristics were group solidarity and the predominance of elements of Japanese culture.[133]

NOTES

In addition to thanking my coauthor, David A. Hacker, I would also like to acknowledge the assistance I received for this study from the following individuals: Gary Okihiro, Don Nakanishi, Megumi Dick Osumi, Sue Kunitomi Embrey, Togo Tanaka, George Fukasawa, Frank Chuman, Karl and Elaine Yoneda, Kinji Yada, Robert Brown, Ned Campbell, Betty Mitson, Ronald Larson, and Roberta Johnson Wallace.

1. See George Mazuzan, "In Search of the Recent Past: The Eighth Annual Colloquium of the Oral History Association," *Oral History Review* 2 (Fall 1974): 84.

2. See Betty E. Mitson, "Looking Back in Anguish: Oral History and Japanese-American Evacuation," *Oral History Review* 2 (Fall 1974): 24–51.

3. See Arthur A. Hansen and Betty E. Mitson, eds., *Voices Long Silent: An Oral Inquiry into the Japanese American Evacuation* (Fullerton: Japanese American Project, Oral History Program, California State University, Fullerton, 1974).

4. Gene Wise, *American Historical Explanations: A Strategy for Grounded Inquiry* (Homewood, IL: Dorsey, 1973), vii.

5. Wise, *American Historical Explanations*, 34. Unlike Wise, who derives his inspiration for perspectivist history from the novelistic technique and from recent conceptual breakthroughs in a multiplicity of scientific and humanistic disciplines, we have been led to adopt the perspectivist approach in this study chiefly through our involvement in oral history. This tool of inquiry, with its emphasis on the taped interview, has confirmed our suspicion of "objective" history and directed us to seek answers to the very questions that Wise depicts as central to the perspectivist model of historical explanation.

6. Our account of the Manzanar Riot is drawn from primary materials in the US War Relocation Archive, collection 122, boxes 16 and 17, Special Collections, UCLA Research Library, and Japanese American Evacuation and Resettlement (JAER), Bancroft Library (BL), University of California, Berkeley (UCB), folders E2.332, O7.00, O7.50, O8.10, O10.00, O10.04, O10.12, O10.14, O11.00, R30.00, R30.10, S1.10, and S1.20 A, B, and C. Collection 122 consists of the files collected and maintained by Ralph Palmer Merritt, project director of the Manzanar War Relocation Center. Hereafter cited as WRAA, coll. 122. The Berkeley archives were prepared and indexed in 1958 by Edward N. Barnhart. Hereafter references from this collection will be cited as JAER. We have purposely avoided controversial points of detail in our overview of the events surrounding the riot. On such issues as whether Ueno was one of Tayama's assailants or why the military police fired upon the inmate crowd, there is a plethora of documentation to support conflicting, even contradictory, interpretations. Instead of expending our

energy in historical sleuth work, we have contented ourselves with arriving at a consensual summary of the Manzanar Riot that could serve as a springboard for perspectivist analysis.

7. The primary accounts are contained in WRAA, coll. 122, box 16, and JAER folder O7.00. See also *Pacific Citizen*, December 10, 1942. Secondary treatment of the Manzanar Riot from this perspective includes Allan R. Bosworth, *America's Concentration Camps* (New York: Bantam, 1968), 152–56; Audrie Girdner and Anne Loftis, *The Great Betrayal: The Evacuation of the Japanese-Americans during World War II* (London: Macmillan, 1969), 263–66; Bill Hosokawa, *Nisei: The Quiet Americans* (New York: William Morrow, 1969), 361–62; Norman Richard Jackman, "Collective Protest in Relocation Centers" (PhD diss., University of California, Berkeley, 1955), 170–83, 211–19; Dillon S. Myer, *Uprooted Americans: The Japanese Americans and the War Relocation Authority during World War II* (Tucson: University of Arizona Press, 1971), 63–66; and Thomas Brewer Rice, "The Manzanar War Relocation Center" (master's thesis, University of California, Berkeley, 1947).

8. Girdner and Loftis, *Betrayal*, 263.

9. One primary account of the riot written from the WRA-JACL perspective that reflects an awareness of the event's cultural significance is that authored by Janet Goldberg (under the supervision of Robert L. Brown, Reports Officer, Manzanar War Relocation Center), "The Manzanar 'Incident,' December 5 to December 19," n.d., WRAA, coll. 122, box 16, and JAER, folder O7.00. Still, while this account concludes that one of the two main contributing factors to the uprising was "the inherent conflict between those culturally Japanese and those culturally Americans," nowhere in this thirty-one-page report is there evidence presented that would warrant such a conclusion.

10. For convenience, throughout the discussion of the WRA-JACL perspective, this term will be employed without quotation marks, though the sense should be understood.

11. Rice, "Manzanar," 69.

12. Jackman, "Collective Protest," 183. If anything, the year 1943 was even stormier than the preceding one. Manzanar was the only center, for instance, where over 50 percent of the adult male citizens answered "No" to the question on loyalty, qualified their response, refused to answer, or refused to register at all (by contrast, at Minidoka these groups constituted only 8 percent of the male citizen population). See Morton Grodzins, "Making Un-Americans," *American Journal of Sociology* 60 (May 1955): 577. Moreover, this period saw widespread resistance to the imposition of the draft for Nisei and a mounting number of applications for repatriation and expatriation. See WRAA, coll. 122, boxes 15 and 26, especially the reports prepared by Morris E. Opler, the WRA community analyst at Manzanar. On the

general unrest and inmate resistance during this time, see WRAA, coll. 122, boxes 10, 11, and 31–39, which contain the block managers' reports.

13. By contrast, Gary Y. Okihiro, in "Japanese Resistance in America's Concentration Camps: A Re-evaluation," *Amerasia Journal* 11 (Fall 1973): 20–34, posits a Manzanar Model of Resistance as an explanatory tool for correlating forms of resistance—work slowdowns, struggles for inmate self-determination, lack of cooperation with Americanization programs and war-related industries—which operated within many of the camps.

14. See December 7, 1942. Similar newspaper accounts appearing in various West Coast newspapers, along with official WRA press releases, can be found in WRAA, coll.122, box 17.

15. Girdner and Loftis, *Betrayal*, 263. One account of the riot that shares some of the features of the WRA-JACL perspective, Togo Tanaka's "An Analysis of the Manzanar Incident and Its Aftermath," January 19, 1943, WRAA, coll. 122, box 16, deflates the ideological interpretation: "The impression given in most newspaper accounts of the Manzanar disturbance, that the instigators were all 'pro-Japan' or 'pro-Axis' . . . and that the intended victims of violence were 'pro-American'—all of them—is not necessarily an accurate picture. . . . Undoubtedly, differences in ideology and position on the war played an important part; but these were . . . incidental to the riot itself" (95).

16. The inordinate attention paid Kurihara's role is reflected in the Berkeley collection. See JAER, folders O8.10, R30.00, and R30.10. This preoccupation with Kurihara has been extended further by such secondary accounts as Paul Jacobs and Saul Landau's *To Serve the Devil: Colonials and Sojourners* (New York: Vintage, 1971), 166–270.

17. Roger Daniels, *Concentration Camps USA: Japanese Americans and World War II* (New York: Holt, Rinehart and Winston, 1971), 105.

18. "Harry Yoshio Ueno," Board of Review report, December–January, 1942–43, WRAA, coll. 122, box 16.

19. Togo Tanaka, interview by Arthur A. Hansen, August 30, 1973, O.H. 1271b, Japanese American Project, Lawrence de Graaf Center for Oral and Public History, California State University, Fullerton, 28–29. Hereafter all interviews from this collection will be cited as CSUF O.H.

20. Ned Campbell, interview by Arthur A. Hansen, August 15, 1974, CSUF O.H. 1329. For an uncharacteristically favorable impression of Campbell by an inmate, see Tad Uyeno, *Point of No Return* (Los Angeles: Rafu Shimpo, 1973), 12. Uyeno's story, which focuses upon the post–Manzanar Riot experiences of those "pro-American" inmates sent to the Cow Creek Civilian Conservation Corps camp in Death Valley, was originally serialized in fifty installments in the *Rafu Shimpo* between August 22 and October 20, 1973.

21. Alexander H. Leighton, *The Governing of Men: General Principles and Recommendations Based on Experience at a Japanese Relocation Camp* (Princeton, NJ: Princeton University Press, 1946), 81. Leighton's comments pertain specifically to the Poston staff, though they certainly have general applicability for all of the camps' staffs.

22. Recounting an occasion when he had sided with the inmates against the WRA in a labor dispute, Ned Campbell has confessed that his action "might have been a mistake, a basic mistake in organization. If the boss tells you to do something, you either quit or go ahead and do what the boss tells you to do" (CSUF O.H. 1329). That Campbell did not make many such "basic mistakes" is attested to by one inmate, Koji Ariyoshi, in "Memories of Manzanar," *Honolulu Star-Bulletin*, April 9, 1971.

23. Douglas Nelson, "Heart Mountain: The History of an American Concentration Camp" (master's thesis, University of Wyoming, 1970), 103–4.

24. For a more detailed explanation of how this "progressive" idea has manifested itself within American historiography, see Wise, *American Historical Explanations*, 86–89, 97–100.

25. Cf. Okihiro, "Japanese Resistance." Okihiro's article is central to systematic inquiry into the phenomenon of resistance movements in the camps.

26. Robert L. Brown, interview, Arthur A. Hansen, December 13, 1973, CSUF O.H. 1375, 53.

27. Campbell interview, CSUF O.H. 1329. The experience of Brown and Campbell is especially significant since the latter, in his interview, also explained, "The camp was a two- or three-man operation. I mean, two or three personalities or philosophies [ran the camp]: the police chief, Bob Brown, and me."

28. Okihiro, "Japanese Resistance," 20–21.

29. Three of these works have already been cited: Daniels, *Concentration Camps USA*; Nelson, "Heart Mountain"; and Okihiro, "Japanese Resistance." Three others are unpublished studies: James Minoru Sakoda, "Minidoka: An Analysis of Changing Patterns of Social Interaction" (PhD diss., University of California, Berkeley, 1949); Toshio Yatsushiro, "Political and Socio-Cultural Issues at Poston and Manzanar Relocation Centers: A Themal Analysis" (PhD diss., Cornell University, 1953); and Matthew Richard Speier, "Japanese American Relocation Camp Colonization and Resistance to Resettlement: A Study in the Social Psychology of Ethnic Identity under Stress" (master's thesis, University of California, Berkeley, 1965). A final work is Jerome Charyn's *American Scrapbook* (New York: Viking, 1969), a fictionalized account of the events that has deepened our appreciation for Gene Wise's insight that historians could profit by adopting the novelist's multifaceted view of experience.

30. In their study of the social psychology of the Manzanar Riot's membership, "Riot and Rioters," *Western Political Quarterly* 10 (December 1957): 864, George Wada and James C. Davies provide a definition from which ours is extrapolated.

31. This dynamic conception of collective behavior stems from Speier, "Japanese-American Camp Colonization," 7–8.

32. Yatsushiro, "Political and Socio-Cultural Issues at Poston and Manzanar."

33. Yatsushiro, "Political and Socio-Cultural Issues at Poston and Manzanar," 40.

34. Yatsushiro, "Political and Socio-Cultural Issues at Poston and Manzanar," 41.

35. Yatsushiro, "Political and Socio-Cultural Issues at Poston and Manzanar," 41.

36. Yatsushiro, "Political and Socio-Cultural Issues at Poston and Manzanar," 209–95.

37. Yatsushiro, "Political and Socio-Cultural Issues at Poston and Manzanar," 183.

38. "Social distance" means the degree of sympathetic understanding that operates between any two persons. See Robert Howard Ross, "Social Distance as It Exists between the First and Second Generation Japanese in the City of Los Angeles and Vicinity" (master's thesis, University of Southern California, 1939).

39. Sue Kunitomi Embrey, interview by Arthur A. Hansen and David A. Hacker, November 30, 1973, CSUF O.H. 1366a, 10.

40. Ross, "Social Distance," 113–14. Tamotsu Shibutani, in "Rumors in a Crisis Situation" (master's thesis, University of Chicago, 1944), 36, while emphasizing the cultural schism between Issei and Nisei, still acknowledges that as "the Nisei came of age in large numbers, they did not go out into the American community. Rather they developed a society of their own." Togo Tanaka, in "How to Survive Racism in America's Free Society," in *Voices Long Silent*, ed. Hansen and Mitson, 89, encapsulates the Nisei's prewar plight: "From 1936 [upon graduating summa cum laude from UCLA] to 1942, I immersed myself behind the walls of Little Tokyo, venturing forth into the wider community only as an advocate of equal rights or civil liberty and of the proposition that, although we may look Japanese, look harder and you'll find a good American."

41. WRA, Community Analysis Section, "Japanese Americans Educated in Japan," Community Analysis Report No. 8, January 28, 1944, 2, WRAA, coll. 122, box 16, folder 1.

42. WRA, "Japanese Americans Educated in Japan," 8.

43. On the other hand, another Nisei interviewee maintained that "Kibei more or less looked down on us because they enjoyed the privileges of American citizenship plus they were fluent in the Japanese language; so they could wear both hats and be comfortable in both societies, where many of us were just Americans, period." George Fukasawa, interview by Arthur A. Hansen, August 12, 1974, CSUF O.H. 1336, 16.

44. WRA, "Japanese Americans Educated in Japan," 7. Although the data are drawn from this source, we have placed an entirely different construction upon

them than that intended. To our knowledge, there exists no "sympathetic" study of Kibei; in fact, there seem to be very few Kibei studies of whatever persuasion.

45. John H. Burma, "Current Leadership Problems among Japanese Americans," *Sociology and Social Research* 37 (January 1953): 158.

46. Speier, "Japanese-American Camp Colonization," 4, 43. A Hawaiian Nisei, Koji Ariyoshi, explains in "Memories of Manzanar" that Nisei in Hawaii "disapproved of Mainland Niseis' obsession, particularly among middle-class and college-educated ones, to be like a middle or upper-class Caucasian." "They wanted," writes Ariyoshi, "to crash the white community and be accepted. Failing this, they were frustrated."

47. For an amplification of the prewar JACL and its relationship to the larger Japanese American community, see Togo Tanaka, "JACL," JAER, folder O10.16.

48. See, for example, the case study of one family during the period prior to their incarceration at Manzanar in Leonard Broom and John I. Kitsuse, *The Managed Casualty: The Japanese-American Family in World War II* (Berkeley: University of California Press, 1974), 64.

49. Shibutani, "Rumors," 114.

50. Daniels, *Concentration Camps USA*, 26.

51. Daniels, *Concentration Camps USA*, 27; Patricia Courteau, "*Rafu Shimpo*: A Look at Japanese American Press Reaction, 1941–2," student seminar paper, January 11, 1973, California State University, Fullerton. See John Anson Ford Papers, box 64, Huntington Library, San Marino, California. Courteau's evaluation of Tanaka's editorial policy is also open to some question, especially since she mentions that on December 31, 1941, the *Rafu Shimpo* ran an article entitled "What of Our Issei?," which covered half the width and the entire length of a page and was printed in capital letters. In her own words, this article "disclaimed the American feeling that legally those people [Issei] were 'enemy aliens' and . . . spoke out for them as true Americans . . . [and argued that] the great tragedy was in assuming all were enemies." Japanese American Project files, Lawrence de Graaf Center for Oral and Public History, California State University, Fullerton.

52. Daniels, *Concentration Camps USA*, 41.

53. Hosokawa, *Nisei*, 223–41. For Tanaka's arrest, see Tanaka, "How to Survive Racism," 93.

54. On December 13, 1941, Chairman Fred Tayama of the Anti-Axis Committee issued the following statement: "The United States is at war with the Axis. We shall do all in our power to help wipe out vicious totalitarian enemies. Every man is either friend or foe. We shall investigate and turn over to authorities all who by word or act consort with the enemies." (From an Anti-Axis Committee circular given to the authors by Karl Yoneda.)

Tokie Slocum's anti-subversive activities were pursued with such vigor that even his JACL allies were offended. See Togo Tanaka, interview by Betty E. Mitson and David A. Hacker, May 19, 1973, CSUF O.H. 1271a, 46–47, and Tanaka interview, CSUF O.H. 1271b, 2–7.

One interviewee, who served simultaneously as the vice president of the Santa Monica JACL chapter and a member of the Santa Monica auxiliary police during the pre-exclusion period, maintained that the two roles of assisting the community and aiding the FBI and the military intelligence agencies were not mutually exclusive but compatible. Indeed, in the latter role he averred that he was able to exonerate many Issei from flagrantly irresponsible charges and spare them from being apprehended and sent to detention centers. (CSUF O.H. 1336.) See endnote 43 above for this information.

55. *Nichibei Times*, February 15 and 20, 1942; Shibutani, "Rumors," 109–10. For information about Kibei chapters of the JACL and their policy differences relative to the pre-eviction and detention period, see CSUF O.H. 1336 (see endnote 43 above for this information); and Karl Yoneda, interview by Ronald C. Larson and Arthur A. Hansen, March 3, 1974, CSUF O.H.1376b.

56. Shibutani, "Rumors," 114–15.

57. Goldberg (WRA), "The Manzanar 'Incident,'" 2. Both the unrepresentativeness and the unpopularity of the JACL in Los Angeles are apparent in the following remarks of one Nisei: "The record of the Los Angeles Citizen's League is such that your stomach would turn when looking into it. To say it represented the Nisei would be silly; out of thousands of eligible citizens the LA branch could number about one hundred members. . . . Among the Nisei in Los Angeles the League was considered a malignant cancer; if the evacuation had not taken place it should surely have been cut out and a truly representative group would have taken its place. To most Nisei the League is as distasteful as the pro-axis label." Sachio Saito, Block 33-4-5, Manzanar, California, to Ralph P. Merritt, Project Director, Manzanar War Relocation Center, December 20, 1942. WRAA, coll. 122, box 7. For an analysis and overview of anti-JACL sentiment in prewar Los Angeles, see Togo Tanaka, "A Report on the Manzanar Riot of Sunday, December 6, 1942," JAER, Bancroft, folder O10.12, 13–15; "Addenda," 40–49.

58. All of the rumors derive from Shibutani, "Rumors," 115–16.

59. Shibutani, "Rumors," 162–66.

60. Kai T. Erikson, *Wayward Puritans: A Study in the Sociology of Deviance* (New York: Wiley, 1966), 3–29.

61. Shibutani, "Rumors," 66. The collective indictment of the Kibei and the reasons behind it are implicit in the following remark by one JACL official: "We had most of our opposition [to the JACL strategy of cooperating with government

officials in the exclusion and detention] from a group who called themselves Kibei, that were educated in Japan and who, of course, were indoctrinated in Japanese propaganda and culture through their formative years over there." (CSUF O.H. 1336, 15). See endnote 43 above for details.

62. The preceding four rumors are drawn from Shibutani, "Rumors," 66–67. Shibutani does not attribute these rumors specifically to JACLer sources, though internal evidence strongly suggests that the rumors did indeed originate there. Our imputation here, therefore, represents merely historical inference, not factual information.

63. Morton Grodzins, in "Making Un-Americans," 577, describes Manzanar's WCCA leadership as "a generally unfriendly staff." For a sharply contrasting estimate, see Robert L. Brown's observations in CSUF O.H. 1375. Brown's recollection is confirmed by his diary entries during the March–June 1942 WCCA tenure at Manzanar. Brown's 1942 diary is available in the Faculty Archives and Special Collections Department at California State University, Fullerton.

64. The residents of these two communities expressed considerable hostility toward the inmates, thereby compounding the problem of camp administration and inmate morale. David J. Bertagnoli and Arthur A. Hansen have interviewed extensively among residents of the Owens Valley communities and attempted to assess their reaction to the camp and its inmate population. See CSUF O.H. 1343, 1344, 1345, 1346, 1347, 1378, 1379, 1384, 1385, 1393, 1394, 1395, 1396, 1398, 1399, 1401 (which is reproduced in its entirety in Hansen and Mitson, Voices Long Silent, 143–60), and 1402. In addition, a local businessman and politician, Rudie Henderson, in Robert L. Brown, comp., "Final Report: Manzanar Relocation Center," volume 1: Project Director's Report, Part II, Section 1, Appendix 26, WRAA, coll. 122, describes the reaction of his fellow Owens Valley residents as one of "almost unanimous . . . resentment and open hostility." Henderson also describes a vituperative petition, signed by 500 local merchants and citizens, designed to prevent inmates from shopping in nearby Lone Pine.

65. Rice, Manzanar, 25–28; Yatsushiro, "Themal Analysis," 342–43; Ariyoshi, "Memories of Manzanar," and Kiyotoshi Iwamoto, "Economic Aspects of the Japanese Relocation Centers in the United States" (master's thesis, Stanford University, 1946), 13.

66. Broom and Kitsuse, Managed Casualty, 40, is explicit on the favored role accorded JACLers in all of the camps: "One of the first administrative policies was to assign preferential status to the Nisei. The Administration systematically encouraged the emancipation of the Nisei from Issei control. Special recognition was accorded to the leadership of the JACL, which was committed to cooperation with the Administration. The preferential treatment toward the Nisei extended

into all aspects of center life: community organization, employment, leisure, and relocation."

Whereas a few scholars, such as Daniels, *Concentration Camps USA*, 79, have alluded to the role of the Japanese American left within the JAI experience, this subject has yet to be pursued in a systematic or comprehensive way. John Modell, ed., *The Kikuchi Diary: Chronicle from an American Concentration Camp* (Urbana: University of Illinois Press, 1973), provides a starting point for such an inquiry. Additional understanding of this topic can be gleaned from an examination of the newspaper *Doho*, Japanese American Research Project (JARP), Special Collections, UCLA Research Library, and two unpublished studies focusing upon the policies and personalities of this Los Angeles-based "progressive" journal: Tanaka, "Report on the Manzanar Riot: Addenda," 8–18, and Ronald C. Larson and Arthur A. Hansen, "*Doho*: The Japanese-American 'Communist' Press, 1937–1942," Japanese American files, Lawrence de Graaf Center for Oral and Public History, California State University, Fullerton.

While, for the purpose of convenient analysis, this study treats the JACL leadership and the left-wing intellectuals at Manzanar under the generic label of "JACLers," it should be noted that there were marked differences in overall background and philosophy between these two groups. Indeed, the contrast, in spite of their shared views on exclusion and detention, camp objectives, and the war, was so extreme that Togo Tanaka, in "An Analysis of the Manzanar Incident," and Tanaka interview, CSUF O.H. 1271b, 14–20, designates leftists like Karl Yoneda, Koji Ariyoshi, Chiye Mori, James Oda, Joe Blamey, and Tom Yamazaki as the "Anti-JACL" group. "It should be recalled," writes Tanaka in "An Analysis of the Manzanar Incident," "that members of Group II [left-wingers] arrived at Manzanar as inmates before Group I [JACL]. This was true almost without exception. Group II members established themselves at the relocation center first. When Group I members arrived a month or so later, they generally discovered that Group II 'had laid the mines and torpedoes in advance of our coming; they prepared the Administration—and volunteer inmates—for a hostile reception for us; they kept up the vicious rumors to perpetuate themselves in their petty little jobs, continuing jealousies and frictions of pre-war and pre-evacuation days'" (94). Group II's influence was particularly notable both in the English and Japanese editions of the *Manzanar Free Press*, which was heavily staffed by its members.

Unlike the JACL, who supported the exclusion and detention program primarily for patriotic reasons—to uphold American principles and to safeguard citizenship rights—leftist support stemmed from their internationalist convictions: "We were," reflects Karl Yoneda, in "Manzanar: Another View," *Rafu Shimpo*, December 19, 1973 (supplement), "at war with the most vicious, brutal racists—Hitler's fascist butchers,

Mussolini's musclemen, and the Japanese imperial rapists of Nanking. We had no choice but to accept the US as it was at that time, and fight on the side of the Allies. Although we were guilty in not speaking out against the Evacuation Order and acquiesced fully, we have NO GUILT OR SHAME regarding our efforts to defeat the fascist Axis. We were sure there would be ovens in Manzanar and other camps if the Mein Kampers won the war and that all of us, including all non-white and white anti-fascists would end up in those ovens." A similar outlook is expressed by Koji Ariyoshi in "Memories of Manzanar."

67. *Manzanar Free Press*, April 11, 1942, emphasis added. Robert L. Brown said that this editorial was a gambit designed to circumvent possible resistance by DeWitt to a camp newspaper. According to Brown, "Larry Benedict [a public relations man employed by the WCCA] said [to Brown], 'I don't want to ask, because I know that the old general won't let us do a newspaper, so why don't you just print a newspaper anyway? And on the front page, in a little editorial, why don't you put a little thing thanking the general for allowing you to do it, and he won't remember whether he allowed you to do it or not, and that will make him feel good.' So we did that. We put a little box and thanked General DeWitt for permission to print the paper, because it was such a necessary item. And I remember the old general was tickled to death. He said, 'That's fine. That's fine. That's what they need to do over there; they have to have communication.'" Brown interview, CSUF O.H. 1375, 19–20. While this anecdote explains the origin of the item, it must nonetheless have rankled the Issei and Kibei—and no doubt many Nisei—who read it.

68. Yatsushiro, "Themal Analysis," 310, 356.

69. The growing Japanization of Manzanar's Nisei population occasioned particular concern among JACLers, who communicated this development to the administration. See Tom Yamazaki's personal and confidential report dated August 1942, WRAA, coll. 122, box 9, and Togo Tanaka and Joe Masaoka, "Historical Documentation: Project Report No. 35," August 12, 1942, and "Project Report No. 76," December 1, 1942, WRAA, coll. 122, box 9. The steady evolution of this trend is best grasped through reading the complete collection of project reports submitted by Tanaka and Masaoka between June and December 1942. See JAER, folders O10.06 and O10.08.

70. See Yamazaki, "Report: August 1, 1942," 10.

71. Morris E. Opler, "A History of Internal Government at Manzanar, March 1942 to December 6, 1942," WRAA, coll. 122, box 12, folder 1, 4–30. Although this report issued from a WRA source, it was consistently critical of the WRA-JACL perspective and adopted a line of analysis closely conforming to what we have termed an ethnic perspective. This situation did not endear Opler to the Manzanar administration. When a copy of this report was forwarded to the head of the Community

Management Division in Washington by the Manzanar representative of this division, she felt obliged to append the following message:

> Mr. Merritt [the project director] has read it and has some question in his mind about the material. He feels that the presentation is one-sided in that it criticizes but does not attempt to explain WRA policies and the action of WRA personnel, while, at all points, it attempts to vindicate evacuee attitudes and actions. He feels that some of the events are capable of interpretations which are not suggested by Dr. Opler. . . . I don't have the same questions . . . but I realize, after talking with Mr. Merritt, that the impression given to an outsider might be very one-sided. Mr. Merritt has asked Mr. [Dillon] Myer [WRA director] to look over the material and let us know whether he thinks it is desirable to continue with this type of interpretive, historical study. (Lucy Adams [for Ralph P. Merritt] to Dr. John Provinse, July 26, 1944, WRAA, coll. 122, box 12, folder 1).

72. Opler, "History of Internal Government," 30.

73. Ned Campbell, Assistant Project Director, to Ted Akahoshi, July 4, 1942, memorandum regarding meetings conducted in the Manzanar Relocation Area, WRAA, coll. 122, box 9.

74. Karl G. Yoneda, Block 4 Leader, 4-2-2, Manzanar, California, to Roy Nash, Project Director, and Ned Campbell, Assistant Project Director, Manzanar Relocation Center, Manzanar, California, July 10, 1942, WRAA, coll. 122, box 9.

75. For confirmation of Akahoshi's cooperative stance, see "Board of Review Reports, Dec.-Jan. 1942–43: Ted Ichiji Akahoshi," WRAA, coll. 122, box 16, and J. Y. Kurihara, "Murder in Manzanar," JAER, folder O8.10, 17.

76. All of the subsequent statements relative to the block leaders' debate over the Japanese language ban are drawn from Yoneda to Nash and Campbell, July 10, 1942.

77. In an earlier version of this paper, in Hansen and Mitson, *Voices Long Silent*, 66–67, the phrase "Karl Yoneda, a Kibei Communist who aligned himself with the JACLers, outdoing them in his chauvinism" was used. In a letter dated October 1974 to Arthur A. Hansen, Yoneda objected: "This characterization as a blind patriot hardly jibes with my activities, in Japan as a youth, and [in the] US since 1926 to date. My life has been an open struggle against imperialism, exploitation, fascism, racism and for decent working conditions and peace in the world." Our intention was certainly not to discount or to depreciate Yoneda's acknowledged lifelong achievements as a champion of human rights and dignity. Perhaps "chauvinism" was an unhappy term for us to have used in this connection, but it was intended to convey that in the context of the camp Yoneda assumed a higher profile than JACL leaders (with the exception of Tokie Slocum) in regard to American patriotism. We believe this was the case for two reasons: (1) JACL leaders were so stigmatized that they had to muffle their patriotism during the early months at Manzanar; and (2)

Yoneda's ideological strategy encompassed the use of aggressive pro-Americanism as a tactical weapon to mobilize sentiment and manpower against the Axis forces. Possibly a third reason is suggested by Yoneda's fellow leftist, Tom Yamazaki, in "Report: Aug., 1942," 10, when he asserts that "Karl Yoneda and myself are only ones [in the Block Leaders Council] who hold pro-democratic convictions and are working . . . to support the government war efforts." No doubt Yoneda's patriotism was shrilly pitched in part because of his involvement in a body where pro-Japan attitudes were particularly evident and dominant.

78. Yoneda to Nash and Campbell, July 10, 1942.

79. Yoneda to Nash and Campbell, July 10, 1942.

80. Tanaka and Masaoka, "Project Report No. 36," July 29, 1942, WRAA, coll. 122, box 9.

81. Ralph P. Merritt, Project Director, Manzanar War Relocation Center, Manzanar, California, to M. M. Tozier, Chief, Reports Division, WRA, Barr Bldg., Washington, DC, January 7, 1946, WRAA, coll. 122, box 16, folder 8. Since the JACLers were not "electable" as block leaders because of their general unpopularity among the inmates, the Citizens Federation was conceived as a counter organization to mobilize support for their objectives. For a comprehensive analysis of this group's aims and organizational development, see "Addenda" to Tanaka, "Report on the Manzanar Riot: Addenda," JAER, folder O10, 10–27.

82. Tanaka and Masaoka, "Project Report No. 36." For a description of this meeting by a principal participant, Karl Yoneda, see Yoneda interview, CSUF O.H. 1376b. Another account is offered by George Fukasawa in Fukasawa interview, CSUF O.H. 1336. Fukasawa, second-ranking member of the inmate police force, attended the meeting to provide internal security. Because Tokie Slocum was "targeted for elimination," Fukasawa accompanied him to his quarters after the gathering. Fukasawa describes Slocum, a special officer in the inmate intelligence agency, as "a superpatriot type of person. . . . He was very vocal . . . he'd get up at these meetings and he was quite an orator. I think he was the type of person that would engender a lot of hatred from anybody who would be opposed to his views" (27).

83. Merritt to Tozier.

84. Opler, "History of Internal Government," 40.

85. Karl Yoneda, interview by Ronald C. Larson and Arthur A. Hansen, March 3, 1974, CSUF O.H.1376b. For a copy of the second front petition alluded to by Yoneda, see JARP, box152, folder 4, which also includes other important documents bearing on Yoneda's activities at Manzanar. Ariyoshi's role in and attitude toward the Citizens Federation is discussed by him in "Memories of Manzanar."

86. Tanaka and Masaoka, "Project Report No. 35," August 11, 1942, includes the following cautionary note: "A large proportion of the English-speaking,

American-educated population, composed largely of younger persons, appear to be confused, bewildered, in many cases bitter; they listen readily to pro-Japan elders and Japan-educated & indoctrinated citizens."

87. WRA, "Information Regarding Kibeis taken from Block Reports, Activities of Town Hall, and Special Meetings, August 4–8, 1942," WRAA, coll. 122, box 16, folder 8.

88. WRA, "Information Regarding Kibeis."

89. Fred Tayama, "Brief Report of the Kibei Meeting held at Mess Hall 15, Manzanar Relocation Center, August 8, 1942," WRAA, coll. 122, box 17, folder 1, emphasis added. A copy of this report, which was sent to the FBI, was apparently given to Joe Kurihara. Since it recounted his part in the meeting, Kurihara was determined to kill Tayama. See Emily Brown, "Story of Joe Kurihara," 30, JAER, folder E2.332, and Merritt to Tozier. Ironically, Tayama's report seems to have been passed along to Kurihara by Tokie Slocum, who aimed to distract attention away from his own reputed "stool-pigeoning" activities and concentrate all the blame on Tayama. Brown, "Story of Joe Kurihara," 29–30.

90. Brown, "Story of Joe Kurihara," 29–30.

91. Brown, "Story of Joe Kurihara," 29–30. Karl Yoneda has provided a graphic profile of Ben Kishi (Yoneda interview, CSUF O.H. 1376b):

Who was Ben Kishi exactly?

I describe him as a Meiji samurai type . . . he says something very exciting that the people go for. For instance, when he opened the Kibei meeting, he didn't say, "Men are dying in Asia," but "Men are dying, let's stand up and have a one minute silence." He put it in such a way that everybody, even myself, wondered, "My god, what the hell's this guy trying to prove?" Later I figure out, my gosh, this guy is really pulling this pro-Japan stunt.

Did you think of him as pretty intelligent?

No, he isn't; he's one of those "ghetto-boss" type guys. Oh yeah, he knows how to maneuver: "You follow me. You listen to me. I'll take care of you."

Did you see him as the major leader of any pro-Japan sentiment within the camp? Did you think that Kishi was the leader?

Oh yes, definitely, the leading "open" spokesman from the start.

This portrait of Kishi needs to be set alongside another one offered by John Sonoda, also identified with the JACLer group at Manzanar. Explaining a beating delivered to him in June 1942 by Kishi and five other Kibei for allegedly discriminating against Kibei in his capacity with the Personnel and Employment Division, Sonoda relates that "Ben Kishi was very emotional about it all. When he was telling me about my wrong attitude towards a lot of things, tears were streaming down his face. He said we were all Japanese and we all owed our allegiance to the Emperor of Japan, and all that" (quoted in Tanaka, "Report on the Manzanar Riot," 19).

92. Roy Nash, Project Director, War Relocation Authority, Manzanar, California, Official Bulletin, August 10, 1942, WRAA, coll. 122, box 16, folder 1.

93. In addition, this month saw the wholesale resignation from foremanship jobs and the refusal of administrative cooperationists to accept any positions of responsibility whatsoever. "With the growth of disillusionment over relocation camp conditions, and the rise of the Issei to dominant positions within the Japanese community," explains Morton Grodzins in "The Manzanar Shooting," JAER, folder O10.04, 9, "a prestige job became a marked liability rather than an asset. It subjected its holder to threats of violence or to violence itself." See also Opler, "History of Internal Government," 51–52.

94. Karl G. Yoneda, 4-2-2, Manzanar, to Roy Nash, Project Director, Manzanar, August 24, 1942, report on block leader's election in Block 4, WRAA, coll. 122, box 9, folder 3.

95. The point here is not to contradict Yoneda's assertion, in Yoneda interview, CSUF O.H. 1376b, that while in Manzanar he had "the future of Japanese in America always at heart." Rather, it is merely to suggest that most inmates, at least by the summer of 1942, were inclined to believe the very opposite.

96. Opler, "History of Internal Government," 56–57.

97. Opler, "History of Internal Government," 58.

98. Opler, "History of Internal Government," 71–72.

99. Robert Throckmorton [Project Attorney], "Biographies of Riot Participants in the Lone Pine Jail: Harry Ueno," [January 1943], WRAA, coll. 122, box 17; Opler, "History of Internal Government," 72–73; Rice, "Manzanar Center," 36–37.

On the other hand, Kazuo Suzukawa, a member of the union, claimed that between the time of its organization in September to the time of the Manzanar Revolt its membership grew to consist of the chef and two representatives from each of the thirty-six kitchens. See Throckmorton, "Biographies of Riot Participants in the Lone Pine Jail: Kazuo Suzukawa."

100. Iwamoto, "Economic Aspects," 28. According to Togo Tanaka, in "Report on the Manzanar Riot," 22, Ueno was alleged to have maintained that "the person who controls the mess halls of Manzanar controls the whole relocation center."

101. Yoneda interview, O.H. 1376b.

102. Quoted in Opler, "History of Internal Government," 74–75.

103. Apparently neither the camp internal security nor the FBI, which frequently came into camp for investigations, was able to penetrate the organizational structure of this group. See Fukasawa interview, CSUF O.H. 1336. The clearest insight into the membership of the Manzanar Underground emerges from Karl Yoneda's "Manzanar: Another View." Herein he explains that the membership "consisted of between 25 and 30 members who constantly disrupted things by spreading false rumors and threatening the lives of evacuees, thus keeping the camp in constant turmoil." In Yoneda's opinion, most of the group were "kamikaze type supporters of fascist-militarism," not "truly 'genuine protesters' against evacuation." In his diary entries quoted in this article, there is mention of their pressure tactics as early as June 16, 1942: "Scavenger truck with Kibei crew, bearing Black Dragon flags (skull painted white on black cloth), appears in front of Block Leaders Council and Camouflage Net Garnishing Project telling everyone not to work on nets." An entry of July 22 indicates that pressure had given way to terrorism: "Very hot, 114 degrees. While Tokie Slocum (WWI vet) and I were talking in front of Block 4 office, a Black Dragon truck suddenly charged us at full speed. We managed to jump onto top step. Truck busts lower step and speeds away."

104. Rice, "Manzanar Center," 53.

105. Yamaguchi later served on the Negotiating Committee of Five during the day of the Manzanar Revolt.

106. Tanaka and Masaoka, "Project Report No. 76," ca. early December 1942, emphasis added. This is the documentary source for all of the quoted commentary at this meeting.

107. Prefiguring the action that followed a few days later, the documentary historians, Tanaka and Masaoka, in "Project Report No. 76," observed that small group discussions transpired after the meeting: "Typical comment: 'Why don't the Nisei who think they are Americans get out of the camp. They are disturbing element. If they are willing to throw away their citizenship and become true Japanese, then that's different. We certainly don't need self-government.'" It is also suggestive that this meeting was conducted entirely in Japanese.

108. Quoted in Tanaka, "Report on the Manzanar Riot," 23.

109. Throckmorton, "Biographies: Ueno," 3–10.

110. Grodzins, "Manzanar Shooting," 4.

111. Tanaka, "Report on the Manzanar Riot," 3.

112. Tanaka, "Report on the Manzanar Riot," 2.

113. Tanaka, "Report on the Manzanar Riot," 3–4. For *Doho*'s attacks on Tayama, see the issues of March 1, 1939, July 15, 1941, and August 15, 1941. Prefiguring the later alliance between *Doho* staffers like Karl Yoneda and James Oda and JACL leaders

like Fred Tayama and Tokie Slocum at Manzanar, one should note that Tayama, as chairman of the Anti-Axis Committee, appointed *Doho* editor Shuji Fujii to its subcommittee on publicity. For political reasons, Tayama reluctantly suspended Fujii, though when Slocum succeeded Tayama he reactivated Fujii and expanded his activities to encompass the subcommittee on press control as well. See *Doho*, January 2, 1942, and February 6, 1942.

114. Quoted in Tanaka, "Report on the Manzanar Riot," 5.

115. Tanaka, "Report on the Manzanar Riot," 11.

116. Tanaka, "Report on the Manzanar Riot," 12–13; Grodzins, "Manzanar Shooting," 2–3.

117. Tanaka, "Report on the Manzanar Riot," 8. See also the documentary attachments 8a and 8b.

118. Tanaka, "Report on the Manzanar Riot," 14.

119. Grodzins, "Manzanar Shooting," 3–4.

120. Opler, "History of Internal Government," 124.

121. Opler, "History of Internal Government," 125.

122. Even WRA official sources confirm this fact: "Not one person interviewed in camp following the riots had a good word to say for Tayama. One young Nisei, 24 years old, who holds a most responsible position in camp and knew Tayama prior to evacuation had this to say following December 5: 'Group hatred of Tayama was the general touch off as far as the population was concerned.'" Goldberg (WRA), "The Manzanar 'Incident,'" 1.

123. Grodzins, "Manzanar Shooting," 12.

124. See, for example, Lucy Adams, "Notes on Manzanar Disturbances," JAER, Bancroft, folder O10.00, D6.

125. See the project reports submitted by Tanaka and Masaoka between June and December of 1942. (A series of mostly dated and near-daily reports spanning the time interval indicated.)

126. Grodzins, "Manzanar Shooting," 13.

127. The names of the Committee of Five members, with their generation and age, are as follows: (1) Genji Yamaguchi, Issei, forty; (2) Sakichi Hashimoto, Issei, forty-two; (3) Kazuo Suzukawa, Issei/Kibei, thirty-eight; (4) Shigetoshi Tateishi, Kibei, thirty-five; and (5) Joe Kurihara, Nisei, forty-seven. Although their average age of slightly over forty years is some ten years younger than the average for the Issei generation in camp, nonetheless they were certainly not young men. It is also significant that the two college-educated members of the committee, Yamaguchi and Kurihara, took the leading roles in the negotiation proceedings. See the Board of Review reports for Yamaguchi, Hashimoto, Tateishi, Suzukawa, and Kurihara, December–January, 1942–43, WRAA, coll. 122, box 16. On Kurihara's counter

organization, alternatively called the Manzanar Center Federation, see Henderson (WRA), "Final Report: Manzanar," 1, 27, and Brown, "Story of Joe Kurihara," 24–25.

128. Tanaka, "Report on the Riot," 88–89, 102.

129. Uyeno, *Point of No Return*, 20.

130. See Ariyoshi, "Memories of Manzanar," Yoneda, "Manzanar: Another View," and Kurihara, "Murder in Manzanar," 25.

131. A good insight into the administrative style of Winchester and Brown can be ascertained from reading their comments in the Board of Review reports, WRAA, coll. 122, box 16. The reports suggest that Brown was later dismissed from his position when it was discovered that he had falsified his educational record on his employment application. See especially Ralph P. Merritt, Project Director, Manzanar War Relocation Center, Manzanar, California, to Charles Carr, US District Attorney, US Department of Justice, Los Angeles, California, July 14, 1943, WRAA, coll. 122, box 16.

132. Tanaka, in "Report on the Riot," 105, cites the eyewitness testimony of one inmate: "The mob was raising hell outside [the jail]; they first sang 'Kimigayo' (the Japanese National Anthem); they followed it up with '*Aikoku Koshin Kyoku*' (A Japanese patriotic march), then with '*Kaigun* March' (Navy marching hymn). They even started dancing the ondo. They would get close to the soldiers and taunt them."

133. The restoration of Issei dominance and community ethnicity is a theme taken up in a number of studies dealing with America's concentration camps. The most notable examples include Yatsushiro, "Themal Analysis"; Sakoda, "Minidoka"; and Speier, "Japanese-American Relocation Camp Colonization." The first has special relevance for the Poston center, the second for the Minidoka center, and the third for all of the camps. For a discussion of the patterns of resistance used by the inmate populations in the various centers, see Okihiro, "Japanese Resistance."

3

A RIOT OF VOICES

Racial and Ethnic Variables in Interactive Oral History Interviewing

During the dozen years between 1975 and 1987, although I continued to research, write, and teach about the World War II Japanese American Incarceration, with an emphasis upon dissent, protest, and resistance activity, the bulk of my time and attention was shifted to oral history administration and editorial duties. In 1975, with the resignation of the pioneering director of the California State University, Fullerton, Oral History Program, Gary Shumway, I very reluctantly consented to become his successor. After four years of hard but enjoyable work in this capacity, I submitted my resignation. Subsequently, in 1980, I agreed to serve the Oral History Association as the editor of its journal, the Oral History Review, *then published annually. Fortunately, my wife, Debra Gold Hansen, agreed to be the assistant editor while simultaneously finishing her doctoral history dissertation on American female*

DOI: 10.5876/9781607328124.c003

abolitionism.[1] *Editing the journal of record for oral history in the United States was a demanding though exceedingly rewarding job.*

What interested me most about oral history, no doubt due to my background in intellectual, social, and cultural history, was oral history theory. During the tenure of my editorship at the Oral History Review, *I was blessed to experience the emergence of theory as a significant component of oral history scholarship, not only at Oral History Association conference presentations but increasingly within published articles and books. The two American oral historians whose theoretical contributions to the field most impressed me were Ronald Grele of Columbia University and Michael Frisch of the State University of New York at Buffalo.*[2] *The former was my counterpart during his editorship of the theoretically exacting and exciting* International Journal of Oral History, *while the latter succeeded (and very greatly exceeded) me in 1987 as the editor of the* Oral History Review.

Among a host of other theoretically oriented oral historians were two individuals whom I encountered on a regular basis at Oral History Association–sponsored gatherings and who contributed luminous articles to my edited issues of the Oral History Review, *Eva McMahan and Kim Lacy Rogers. I was deeply moved when they invited me to write a chapter for their 1994 coedited volume,* Interactive Oral History Interviewing, *which, as expressed in their preface, "represents, in the broadest sense, an interpretive perspective of inquiry that has flourished in oral history since the 1970s." In writing my piece for this volume, I kept uppermost in my mind what they had to say about this perspective: that it "considers oral history interviews as subjective, socially constructed, and emergent events—that is, understanding, interpretation, and meaning of lived experience are interactively constructed."*

The truth of objectivism—absolute, universal, and timeless—has lost its monopoly status. It now competes, on more nearly equal terms, with the truths of case studies that are embedded in local contexts, shaped by local interests, and colored by local perceptions.

—*Renato Rosaldo,* Culture and Truth *(1989)*

When invited to write this chapter exploring how race and ethnicity intertwine the relationship between oral history interviewers and narrators, I was delighted yet unnerved. Having transacted interviews for nearly two decades within one racial-ethnic group, Japanese Americans, I naturally was pleased to reflect upon that experience. I found daunting, however, the prospect of extrapolating generic truths about the interviewer-narrator relationship in cross-cultural interviews from my particular interactions with Nikkei (Americans of Japanese ancestry).

Reading the Chicano anthropologist Rosaldo's manifesto for interpretive sociocultural studies, from which my epigraph is taken,[3] had deepened my conviction that the quest for "laws" in the human sciences, although a powerful intellectual prod for gaining knowledge, tends to ignore the changing nature of human facts and to obscure existential truth embedded in meaning and interpretation. In what follows, therefore, I have paid preponderant attention to my own fieldwork encounters with Japanese Americans, specifically those among the Nisei (second-generation Japanese Americans), while consigning generalizations about racial and ethnic variables to a subordinate status. As with Rosaldo and his counterparts in cognate disciplines, my approach is relativist, eclectic, subjective, perspectival, and empirical.

In fall 1987 I attended a conference on the University of California, Berkeley (UCB), campus that was devoted to reevaluating the documentary contribution of those social scientists who, during World War II, had compiled extensive field notes, journals, and reports for the UCB-sponsored Japanese American Evacuation and Resettlement Study (JERS). My responsibility was to critique a revisionist interpretation of two spectacular acts of resistance—a strike and a riot—that had occurred in late 1942 at, respectively, the Poston (Arizona) and Manzanar (California) concentration camps.[4] My concern here is not with the content of that paper. Rather, it is with a trio of Nisei—Harry Ueno, Karl Yoneda, and Togo Tanaka—who were in the audience to hear the paper presented by its Sansei (third-generation Japanese American) author, Brian Hayashi. All three had figured prominently in the Manzanar Riot of December 6, 1942, which culminated in military police gunfire that left two inmates dead and nine others wounded. All, too, were men I had interviewed years before when researching that episode.[5]

During the paper's oral presentation, I glanced, intermittently, at each of my former narrators who had not been together since their common incarceration, along with 10,000 other Nikkei, in the mile-square area constituting the Manzanar War Relocation Center in eastern California.[6] I thought of the traumatic conditions under which, during a five-day span in early December 1942, these men had been spirited out of the Owens Valley camp: Yoneda, on December 2, to enlist in the Military Intelligence Service Language School; Ueno, on December 6, to be confined in a neighboring Inyo County town jail; and Tanaka, also on December 6, to be placed under protective custody at the adjacent military police compound. Seeing them now, forty-five years after the riot, I was struck by how contrasting, even conflicting, their lifestyles and philosophical outlooks had been back then as comparatively young men behind barbed wire and how divergent these had remained ever since.[7]

In this essay, I examine the context of my interview with only one of these three Nisei, Togo Tanaka, as well as another Manzanarian of their generation, Sue Kunitomi Embrey, my very first Japanese American interviewee (i.e., narrator).[8] Even though this scaled-down approach reduces the interviews with Harry Ueno and Karl Yoneda to comparative and illustrative purposes, it simultaneously points up, as we see here, the necessity for interviewers within racial and ethnic populations to be acutely sensitive to the operations of intracultural variation.

Prior to the summer of 1973, when I interviewed both Embrey and Tanaka, I was painfully uninformed about Japanese and Japanese American people, their culture and history, the specific topic of the Japanese American Incarceration (JAI), and the research method of oral history. What scanty knowledge I possessed of Japanese people as a preadolescent in New Jersey had been filtered through the demonic representation of them in wartime Hollywood propaganda films as cunning, immoral, ruthless, and practically inhuman.[9] After moving to southern California in 1949 and forging multiplex peer relationships with Nisei and Sansei through school, athletics, and social organizations, this image was sharply recast. Although I never fully subscribed to the then emergent public stereotype of them as a "model minority," my perception did entail such descriptors for this stereotype as "quiet," "studious," "polite," and "family centered."[10]

Even though I had become conscious of the importance of the JAI in Japanese American history while an undergraduate at the University of California, Santa Barbara, it was not until 1972 that I focused serious attention on it. During a required research seminar offered to history majors at California State University, Fullerton (CSUF), a student affiliated with the CSUF Oral History Program (OHP) asked for my permission to conduct interviews with several Nikkei about their wartime lives. She had me listen to several of the dozen interviews with Japanese Americans already housed in the program's archives. At her urging, I persuaded the Oral History Program to launch a Japanese American project under our joint direction.[11]

The next year I taught several research seminars on the JAI. For background reading, I assigned Harry H.L. Kitano's *Japanese Americans: Evolution of a Subculture* (1969) and Roger Daniels's *Concentration Camps, USA: Japanese Americans and World War II* (1971).[12] A Nisei sociologist who had attended high school in wartime Utah at the Topaz Relocation Center, Kitano adroitly combined *emic* (actor-perceived) and *etic* (investigator-perceived) approaches in his treatment of the history, social structure, and cultural values of the Japanese American community. Daniels's book, on the other hand, represented the first comprehensive study of the JAI by an academic historian. In addition, I led class excursions to the Little Tokyo district of Los Angeles, the cultural and commercial center of the southern California Nikkei community, accompanied by a Nisei colleague/friend, Kinji Ken Yada (who had been raised there before the war and returned to live there after Manzanar's closing in 1945). This same year I began to research the Manzanar Riot, prompting my immersion in the secondary literature inspired by the JAI as well as the primary source material on the Manzanar center archived at the University of California campuses in Los Angeles and Berkeley. Finally, I coordinated a lecture series at the University of California, Irvine, campus that relied mainly on ex-inmates and others from the Nikkei community as speakers and explored Japanese American life from the late-nineteenth-century immigration experience through the contemporary Asian American consciousness movement.

Because two of the series' lecturers, Sue Kunitomi Embrey and Togo Tanaka, had experienced the Manzanar Riot, I decided to make them my first interviewees. From their presentations, I had discovered that both had been employed at Manzanar in news-gathering positions—Embrey as an editor of the *Manzanar Free Press*, the misnamed camp newspaper, and Tanaka as a documentary historian—and so were accustomed to interviewing.

Immediately before interviewing these Nisei in August 1973, I came across two new books that, in tandem, conditioned my approach to and conduct of the interviews. The first, Gene Wise's *American Historical Explanations*, juxtaposed an alternative model of historical inquiry, the "perspectivist" model, against the model then paradigmatic for the discipline, the "ideal-observer" model.[13] At bottom, these models predisposed historians to ask different questions of sources. The ideal-observer model, because it was preoccupied with what happened in the past, urged a line of questioning designed to disentangle the objective truth of history from the snares and delusions of assorted interpreters. The perspectivist model, because it discounted what happened as its sole or even fundamental concern, called for querying sources in quite another manner. In the words of Wise, historians under the sway of this model were concerned primarily "with the question, 'How do particular people experience what happened?' And further, 'How do they put form on their experience?' And yet further, 'How do these forms connect into their particular locations in time and place?'"[14]

The second book was Hilary Conroy and T. Scott Miyakawa's *East across the Pacific*, an anthology containing two essays, Shotaro Frank Miyamoto's "An Immigrant Community in America" and, most especially, Stanford M. Lyman's "Generation and Character: The Case of Japanese-Americans," that afforded me insight into the Nisei interpersonal style.[15]

The main thrust of the selection by Miyamoto, a Nisei sociologist at the University of Washington—who not only had been born, in 1912, and bred within the prewar Japanese American community in Seattle but also had written a classic study about it[16]—is to account for the greater socioeconomic status and degree of cultural and civic assimilation achieved by Japanese Americans relative to other racial-ethnic minorities in the United States. What chiefly interested me, however, was Miyamoto's claim that the foremost normative value instilled in Nisei via parental training had been etiquette. Allowing for distinct family deviations from community norms, this value, according to Miyamoto, had mandated an implicit regard for status. Thus, teachers and other authority figures were to be addressed and otherwise treated with respect, even deference. Moreover, the training Nisei had received in etiquette undergirded other, more nuanced aspects of socialization: "Etiquette requires a regard for others, and [also] a sensitivity for the feeling and attitudes of others. In turn, sensitivity for others induces a coordinate self-awareness and self-control. Although the Nisei, trained and socialized in the direct and informal patterns of America, were by Issei standards lacking finesse in social relations, they nevertheless acquired some basic Japanese features in their habits of interpersonal relations."[17]

Lyman, a sociologist at the New School for Social Research, was born in 1933 to immigrant eastern European Jewish parents and grew up during the Depression and pre–World War II period amid African Americans and Nisei in San Francisco's Western Addition ghetto. After matriculating at the University of California, Berkeley, he became the only non-Nikkei in a club comprising recent Nisei returnees from the wartime camps. Like Miyamoto, then, Lyman's assessment of the social and personal relations of Nisei was rooted in protracted and intensive peer interaction.[18]

After substantiating Miyamoto's claim that Japanese Americans had "outstripped all other 'colored' groups in America in occupational achievement and education," Lyman's "Generation & Character" article considers whether a unique Japanese American character structure might account for the cluster of stereotypical traits attributed to members of this "model minority."[19] That nearly identical traits had been applied but a few years earlier to serve racist evaluations and policies actually enhanced their validity for Lyman and recommended their analytical utility to him.

> What was once caricature is now recognized as character. . . . The existence
> of a correspondence between racist stereotype and culturally-created char-
> acter should not cause great concern. A stereotype survives through time
> and other changes by distorting a kernel of fundamental truth. . . . Progress
> in the social analyses of culture and personality might be enhanced by
> assuming for the sake of research that the worst statements made about a
> people have their origins in some fundamental truth which needs first to be
> abstracted from its pejorative context and then subjected to behavioral and
> cultural analysis.[20]

Guided by a conceptual framework devised by sociological phenomenologist Alfred Schutz and refined by symbolic anthropologist Clifford Geertz, Lyman constructed a characterological typology for comprehending the Nisei personality. According to Lyman, "In every culture and in many subcultures a predominant time-person perspective organizes the relevant temporal and personal categories in order to structure priorities with respect to past, present, and future and to structure orientations with respect to intimacy or impersonality."[21]

Nikkei perceived time and person relative to geographical and generational distance from Japan; thus to them, perspective is geo-generational. Indeed, they are the sole US immigrant group to employ distinct terms (Issei, Nisei, Sansei, etc.) to signify each generation's respective spatiotemporal position and the presumably singular personality corresponding to it. The singularity of generational personality, moreover, is intensified by the subcultural proclivity for simultaneously accentuating contemporaries and downplaying predecessors and successors. Thus, both Issei, who migrated here from Japan between 1885 and 1924, and Sansei, whose maturity is mostly a post–World War II phenomenon, are perceived by the intervening Nisei geo-generation as inhabiting quite separate, albeit shadowy, time and space spheres and possessing profoundly different social and personal orientations from their own.

It is, of course, the personality of the Nisei that Lyman analyzed. Born between 1910 and 1940 but bunched in their late teens on the eve of the JAI,[22] their collective identity is compounded, in its formulation, of a perfervid belief in their objective existence as a unique, time-bounded generational group and the subjective meanings attendant upon group membership. Paradoxically, their identity comforted and distressed Nisei. If their community and generation mitigated the turbulence of mainstream society, they were nonetheless "threatened by both centripetal and centrifugal forces, by individual withdrawal [i.e., through establishing intimate associations in the Nikkei community below and outside the generational level] and acculturative transcendence [i.e., by befriending non-Nikkei peers]."[23]

Phrased in group parlance, what was at risk was "Nisei character," a perfect, if precarious, combination of Japanese and American traits. It was precisely to salvage this vaunted character, proclaimed Lyman, that a Nisei style of interaction distinguished by social distance and personal formalism had evolved to such an extent, in fact, that generational "contemporaries" only rarely were convened to "consociates," whereas virtually all others were denied admittance into the charmed circle of Nisei friendship.

As children of immigrants from late-Victorian Japan, Nisei had been nurtured in a familial-communal context wherein Japanese language was pervasive and Japanese culture paramount. Put more pointedly, their primary socialization had transpired via a linguistic medium whose forms promoted indirection, circumlocution, and politesse and within a cultural milieu that, to quote Lyman, "served the goal of anonymization of persons and immobilization of individual time through its emphasis on etiquette, ceremony, and rigid status deference."[24] Clearly, this socialization process predisposed Nisei toward and deepened their generational style of associational management and emotional control.

Because, as disclosed earlier, I had read Lyman's analysis as I was preparing to interview two Nisei, the most germane section to me was that delineating how conversational discourse inscribed the Nisei personality. Not content with simply echoing Miyamoto's observation as to the ubiquity of etiquette in Nisei deportment, Lyman explained the functional bases for this state of affairs: to conceal genuine feelings from others and to regularize behavior so as to avert unpleasant surprises—and even to emphasize the ways in which etiquette patterns the conversations among Nisei and with non-Nisei.

Lyman suggested that etiquette is embedded in Nisei speech through tonal control, as evidenced by a pervasive flatness of tone and equality of conversational meter. Although this talking style causes little difficulty for those like Miyamoto and Lyman who are intimately familiar with it, those who are not find verbal exchanges with Nisei perplexing, primarily because they cannot readily differentiate important from insignificant items. Moreover, Nisei tonality frequently causes the uninitiated to doubt what is being said to them and, further, to suspect that Nisei conversations often conceal ulterior motives.

Another distinguishing feature of Nisei speech that was traceable to their universal regard for etiquette was to lapse into euphemistic language when touching upon topics considered unseemly or uncomfortable for those with whom they were talking. Lyman explained: "When there is no English euphemism or the use of one is so awkward it could be embarrassing, a Japanese term may be employed. This is especially the case in using nouns to designate racial or ethnic groups."[25]

Aware that race and ethnicity are sensitive, supercharged subjects in this country, Nisei tend to resort to substitute Japanese terms: *hakujin* or *keto* for Caucasians; *kuron-bo* for African Americans; *pake* for Chinese; and *ku-ichi* for Jews.

The use of indirect speech and circumlocutions found in the Japanese language have been imprinted so powerfully upon the Nisei psyche as to be reproduced in a transmuted form in their English-language conversations.

Because propriety requires that the private feelings of both parties in a conversation be respected, Nisei regularly resort to "abstract nouns, noncommittal statements and inferential hints at essential meanings."[26] Projective tests done with Nisei confirm that, when confronted by issues laden with moral or emotional ambiguity, they often take refuge in confabulatory responses. Nor do they come to grips right away with the gist of a given conversation. According to Lyman: "Indeed, conversations among Nisei almost always are an information game between persons who maintain decorum by seemingly mystifying one another. It is the duty of the listener to ascertain the important point from the context and his knowledge of the speaker."[27]

Those attuned to this rhetorical mandate, particularly generational peers, adroitly negotiate conversations with Nisei. It poses a nettlesome problem, however, for "outsiders" or *gaijin*: "Exasperation with the apparent pointlessness, frustration with vain attempts to gauge the meaning of sequential utterances, and the desire to reach a conclusion often lead non-Nisei to ask a pointed question directed at the heart of the matter."[28] This tactic, in turn, is so uncomfortable for Nisei respondents that they respond with rhetorical management: "They may refuse to answer, change the subject, . . . subtly redirect the conversation back to its concentric form [or bury] potentially affective subjects . . . beneath a verbal avalanche of trivia."[29]

The Nisei concern for etiquette surfaced in their conversations in still other ways. There was, for example, their tendency to subordinate content to performative considerations, so discussions involving vital, sometimes controversial issues often got sacrificed to innocuous yet elegant disquisitions about technical, tertiary, or tangential matters. Another way was through the insistent Nisei emphasis upon democratic speech participation, so neither party in a conversation became dominant and threatened the parity of expression. Still another was in the deployment of dissimulation, so Nisei, as ascribed by Lyman, "tended not to volunteer any more information about themselves than they had to . . . some times would not talk about an important event or suggest by style and tone that it was not important at all," or even retreated into obdurate silence.[30]

For Lyman, the manifestations of etiquette found in Nisei conversation were functionally related; all represented linguistic responses to a psychosocial imperative for emotional management. According to Lyman, this imperative became abundantly evident when one heeded paralinguistic forms of

Nisei communication. A prime example was how Nisei set their faces so as to achieve an expressionless countenance, thereby discouraging access by others to their inner selves. "An uncontrolled expression met by the searching gaze of another," remarked Lyman, "may lock two people into a consociative relationship from which [extraction] would be both difficult and embarrassing." Fear of disclosure, moreover, even led some Nisei to "avoid facing others for any length of time or [to] . . . erect barriers to shield them from involvement with another's gaze."[31]

On August 24, 1973, I interviewed Sue Kunitomi Embrey, a fifty-year-old native daughter of Los Angeles who was then employed by UCLA's Asian American Studies Program in a liaison capacity with Los Angeles's large Japanese American population. During the drive to the interview site, I meditated on my two prior meetings with Embrey the past spring. Although I had telephoned her in January to confirm her participation in my lecture series, actual contact was not made until two months before her June presentation.

The day of that encounter, April 14, 1973, marked the fourth annual Manzanar Pilgrimage. It was a particularly significant day both for Embrey and the Nikkei community. At the entrance to the old Manzanar War Relocation Center, Embrey, the Manzanar Committee's founding co-chair, had presided over a dedication ceremony designating the site as a state historical landmark. First, a bronze plaque was cemented into a sentry house by an octogenarian Issei stone mason who, forty years earlier, had built it. Thereafter, Embrey instructed the 1,000-plus "pilgrims"—a large throng of former inmates and their offspring, a small contingent of government officials, and a sprinkling of interested spectators—to assemble inside the camp (proximate to where the Manzanar Riot had been staged) to hear commemorative addresses from Manzanar Committee representatives from America's major metropolitan centers. Embrey then directed the participants to gather around one of the ten raised placards bearing the place-names of the War Relocation Authority detention centers and to weigh the words inscribed upon the plaque:

In the early part of World War II, 110,000 persons of Japanese ancestry were interned in relocation centers by Executive Order 9066, issued on February

19, 1942. Manzanar, the first of ten such concentration camps, was bounded by
barbed wire and guard towers, confining 10,000 persons, the majority being
American citizens. May the injustices and humiliation suffered here as a result
of hysteria, racism and economic exploitation never emerge again.

Because Embrey was preoccupied that day with coordinating the program
and responding to media requests for interviews and background information, I was able to observe her only as a public speaker. To be sure, the customary Nisei attention to etiquette was firmly in place, particularly in the
deference Embrey extended to politicians and the press. But her impassioned
address, which assailed American racism and imperialism and recounted the
struggle the Manzanar Committee and its allies had waged against recalcitrant state bureaucrats to gain the controversial plaque wording, betrayed few
of the telltale traits mentioned by Lyman. Embrey's voice, facial expressions,
and gestures were suitably varied to emphasize her unvarnished message.
She gazed directly at the assembled crowd and spoke directly to us about
unpleasant and, for some perhaps, unpalatable truths. Although comporting
herself with decorum, her vigorous oratorical style implicitly mocked the
title of Bill Hosokawa's recent book about her ethnic generation, *Nisei: The
Quiet Americans.*[32]

My next meeting with Embrey took place on June 5, 1973, after she had lec-
tured about the symbolic meaning of the wartime concentration camp experience for Asian Americans. Following her lecture, she, along with another
Nisei woman from the Manzanar Committee, Amy Uno Ishii, joined me and
my aforementioned Nisei colleague/friend, Kenji Ken Yada, for food, drinks,
and conversation. All three Nisei had been born in the 1920s, grown up in the
Los Angeles Nikkei community, and shared many acquaintances and memories. Although Embrey and my colleague had not met previously, they had
lived in adjacent "blocks" at Manzanar and each knew of the other's family. Because of their enmeshed pasts, it took only minutes for us to fall into
enraptured talk about the prewar and wartime Nisei world. When, several
months later, I reflected upon that evening's conversation through the screen
of Lyman's article, it dawned on me just how large a quotient of our talk had
been expended upon trivia like sports, movies, music, and sheer nostalgia.
However, I could not, in truth, recall that the three Nisei speakers, most particularly the two women, had used the circumlocutions, euphemisms, con-
fabulations, silences, or any other mechanisms of emotional management

mentioned by Lyman. If anything, my recollection of their conversation ran in the opposite direction—toward openness, intimacy, frankness, expressiveness, and subjectivity.

Because of my first meetings with Embrey, I approached our interview from the angle that her personality contradicted Lyman's ideal type. I deduced from Lyman's example that his construct had been based almost exclusively upon conversations with Nisei men. At one point, he even stated explicitly that "the primary concern of a *Nisei male* [emphasis added] is the economical management and control of his emotions."[33] Furthermore, I took seriously the caveat he had entered and then reiterated about ideal types—that because they were mental constructions designed to represent rather than describe reality, which was both messier and more complicated, they did not apply in every aspect to any individual: "No particular Nisei incorporates all the traits described and the typology may also be less applicable to the Nisei who grew up outside the Japanese communities or who associated primarily with non-Nisei peer groups."[34] I learned from our post-lecture conversation that Embrey had grown up within the Nikkei community, but I knew also, as her surname clearly denoted, that she had married exogamously. Moreover, her "performance" at the Manzanar Pilgrimage had made me realize that, although her past associations might have been chiefly intragenerational, her Manzanar Committee involvement meant that her primary interactions of late were likely with activist college-age Sansei. Indeed, several of them had urged me to include her in the lecture series so as to voice *their* perspective on the JAI.

Even before I turned on the tape recorder, Embrey's behavior afforded proof that my approach to our interview was appropriate. Whereas Lyman had portrayed Nisei interactions with colleagues and friends as episodic rather than developmental,[35] Embrey greeted me as a new friend and fondly recalled our previous conversation. Once the interview got underway, her generational "deviance" was registered both by the content and the style of her discourse. Instead of being reticent to explore her roots as the sixth of eight children of Issei parents from the same hamlet in Okayama Prefecture, she eagerly related her family's history. Similarly, she responded with alacrity and detail to my questions about her childhood in the Little Tokyo district (Nihonmachi) of Los Angeles and the inner workings of the prewar Nikkei community there. The following exchange, which occurred early in our interview, illustrates her departure from normative Nisei comportment:

Did you resent going to it [the Japanese language school] like some Nisei?

Well, I went all the way through, almost to the twelfth grade. My mother says I was the only one who seemed to have any interest in the school. . . . But I had a teacher who was bilingual . . . and he said to me that he thought that my direction in life was going different from the others, that he didn't think I would be too happy within the Japanese community. Now where he got this impression, I don't know. But he said to me, "I don't think that you are intellectually tuned in with these kids in this school."[36]

Embrey's plain speaking persisted throughout the interview. When, for instance, the conversation turned to the various political factions at Manzanar, notably the Japanese American Citizens League (JACL) "para-administrators" and the leftist "progressives" who dominated the camp newspaper's editorial staff, Embrey's message and manner of speaking again demonstrated her generational marginality.

What's the name of the woman who was the first editor of the Manzanar Free Press?

Chiye Mori. She was quite active in the Democratic Club [Nisei Young Democrats] before the war, I think. I don't know whether she was active in JACL or not.[37]

About how old was she at the time of the Japanese American Incarceration? Was she a contemporary of yours?

No, I would say she was older than I. I used to watch her, because to me she was a very unusual Nisei. I never had come across anyone who could talk about politics and who damned the leaders of our country like she did; I had never heard such talk before! And she had some very liberal ideas which I had never come across, and I used to listen to her a lot.

[Aside from Chiye Mori] can you think of specific individuals in the left-of-center group [at Manzanar]?

Yes. There was Koji Ariyoshi, who lives in Honolulu now, and Karl Yoneda. And let's see, who were some of the others?

Would they be part of the group you would have described as "Red" prior to the war?

I guess the people considered them that way. I don't know how active they were. I know that both Karl and Koji were very active in labor unions before the war, trying to get labor unions opened up to minority groups. And I think their ideology was based on the thought that they had to fight Fascism first, and they went along with the JAI as just one of the minor things that had to happen during a war.

Would you say they were equally as detested by the Japanese community at Manzanar as the JACL faction?

I think so. Yes, because I think some of them were also victims of beatings as well as those who were connected with JACL. But I think that they were not doing anything that was out of line with what they'd been doing before the war.[38]

It was not until my second taping session with Embrey, four months later, that I was exposed to the full extent of her variance from the conventional behavior of her generation and made privy to the reasons precipitating her postwar transformation from a relatively quiet Nisei to a clamorous advocate for civil rights and human justice.

In the meantime, however, I capitalized upon the information she had supplied me about the Manzanar Riot in our initial session to schedule an interview on that topic with Togo Tanaka. Tanaka had been the English-language editor of the *Rafu Shimpo* (a Los Angeles daily Japanese newspaper) between 1936 and 1942. He had graduated from UCLA in the mid-1930s with Phi Beta Kappa status and was an accomplished orator whose skill had been honed during a lifetime of making public addresses. He had also been one of the most influential Nisei leaders in the prewar Los Angeles Nikkei community and had held important JACL offices. During the war he had been employed by both the War Relocation Authority (WRA) and the UCB-sponsored Japanese American Evacuation and Resettlement Study to produce social-scientific reports. Tanaka had been one of the key persons in the Manzanar Riot and could discuss that event from the perspective of someone who just barely had escaped being murdered by the "rioters."

During his April 1973 presentation in my lecture series, Tanaka's style was urbane, professorial, and direct. By the time that I reviewed a transcript of that lecture, however, I had become acquainted with Lyman's analysis of Nisei character and therefore was sensitized to previously ignored communicative subtleties. I now noticed, for example, how Tanaka's prefatory comments illustrated what Lyman had observed about the Nisei propensity for masking stage fright in potentially embarrassing social situations. To lessen accountability for his address, Tanaka explained at the outset that while he was out of the country, his daughter had accepted the invitation for him to speak because "she felt that there might be some purpose in my doing this." He then further reduced his culpability by declaring: "I find myself somewhat at a handicap here, however, because it has been some three decades since I have had occasion to do anything like this." Finally, having divested himself, at least partially, of the psychological burdens of egoism and personal responsibility, Tanaka segued with consummate humility into his speech proper by entreating his audience to permit him "to start off with some biographical information."[39]

Tanaka's discussion of his family life and upbringing in the Hollywood area resonated with Lyman's and Miyamoto's characterization of the typical Nisei experience as a hybridized one. On the one hand, Tanaka's parents, particularly his father, had transmitted traditional Japanese family and community values to him, thereby preserving and reinforcing a sense of Japanese identity. Upon entering Tanaka in public school at the age of six, his father, "who was proud of his race and of his samurai heritage," deposited him at the classroom door and directed him to "Honor and respect your teachers." Up to this point, Tanaka's only language was Japanese, which his father, "a self-taught Confucian scholar," continued to urge upon him because "he disdained the English language as a means of communication for the white man." Moreover, it was in his native language that his father instructed Tanaka in "*Shushin*, the Japanese code of ethics, and . . . the values of honor, loyalty, service, and obligation that had been taught to him by his forebears in Japan."[40]

On the other hand, a competing set of values was being instilled in Tanaka through his participation in mainstream American institutions. Instead of being raised in the Buddhist religion of his parents, Tanaka was sent by his mother to worship at a Christian Sunday school. Whereas his father had taught him to "challenge and correct anyone calling me a Jap," Christian teaching admonished him to turn the other cheek when "the outrageous slings of racism struck." Then, too, until he matriculated at UCLA in 1932, Tanaka attended schools where "it was usually 99 percent white, 1 percent yellow, and there were neither red nor black." By junior high school, his "Americanization" had become so pronounced as to provoke his chauvinistic father, set on a career for his son in Japan's diplomatic service, into caustic rebuke: "You are beginning to think and talk like the enemy." At Hollywood High School, in spite of domestic pressure to "deliberately conspire to achieve every scholastic award in sight," Tanaka so immersed himself in school and extracurricular activities that he experienced "a growing estrangement from the long-held ideals and objectives" of his father.[41]

In the balance of his speech, Tanaka discussed his undergraduate years as a UCLA political science major amid escalating international and racial hostility, his successive journalistic stints with Los Angeles's two leading Japanese vernacular newspapers, the *Kashu Mainichi* (California Daily News) and the *Rafu Shimpo*, his establishment of the Nisei Business Bureau and its unsuccessful campaign to develop a subdivision where Nisei could obtain housing unfettered by racial restrictions, and his immediate pre– and post–Pearl Harbor encounters with municipal, state, and national officials, including being apprehended by the FBI on December 8, 1941, and held incommunicado in three different Los Angeles jails for eleven days.

In relating this information, Tanaka's communicative style—or so it seemed to me when studying the text of his talk—contrasted noticeably with certain Nisei norms for social interaction that my reading had impressed upon me. I recalled, for example, something that Harry Kitano, himself a highly successful Nisei scholar, had observed in his earlier noted influential treatment of Japanese American life—that is, that although normal for Japanese Americans to be competitive, especially with others of their subculture, it was deemed deviant for them to flaunt their successes. "It is important to be a winner," wrote Kitano, "but equally important that the winner be humble, modest, and self-deprecating."[42] I therefore thought it curious that Tanaka, while suffusing his commentary with a self-effacing tone, should also stud it with references to prominent personalities (e.g., William Randolph Hearst, Eleanor Roosevelt, US attorney general Francis Biddle, and California governor Culbert Olsen) whose paths he had crossed. I was initially puzzled and slightly put off by this affectation. Eventually, however, I realized that Tanaka was not name-dropping. It was merely that he, unlike the "typical" Nisei, did not feel impelled to purge the names of celebrities from his narrative, especially if censorship of this stripe diminished its veracity or vividness.

Tanaka's departure from Nisei behavioral norms was most blatant, however, during the audience participation period. Instead of skirting unpleasant facts and taking cover in circumlocutions, Tanaka responded freely and frankly to his questioners, most of whom were Sansei activists critical of the role played by Tanaka and other JACL leaders during the JAI, as shown in the following excerpt:

I was wondering if you plan to tell us about your experiences in camp?

Yes, I'd be glad to. My family was evacuated to Manzanar. . . . We were there from April 23 until December 6, 1942. . . . We went on the assumption that they would give us jobs for which we thought we had some experience, but the experience of the mass eviction had made those of us identified with the "Establishment" within the Japanese American community somewhat unpopular. And Joe [Grant] Masaoka and I, who had applied for work on the staff of the *Manzanar Free Press*, were told that we could do two things: either sweep the floor or deliver the papers. So we opted for delivering the papers, and we did so for two months. Then the War Relocation Authority offered the job of becoming "documentary historians," and this was a job that they said would entail writing daily reports about camp activities and turning them over to a gentleman in Washington by the name of Solon Kimball, who headed up, I think, a department called Community Services for the WRA. It was explained to us that it was really a part of a research project inspired by Dr. Robert Redfield from the University of Chicago, an anthropologist, and therefore Joe and I had an opportunity to continue our education. What we didn't realize at the time was that we would soon be identified as informers, spies, and dogs, people who were abusing or invading the privacy of the inmates. As a consequence, when the riot broke out on the eve of the anniversary of Pearl Harbor, both he and I were on the death list—not at the top of the list but about in the middle—and we were removed for our safety and placed in protective custody at an abandoned CCC camp in Death Valley.[43]

Reading the transcript of Tanaka's life history in an interview conducted by two Japanese American Project colleagues a month after his Irvine lecture offered me more evidence of Tanaka's marginality within his generation. As mentioned earlier, his perceived deviancy at Manzanar almost led to his death, as the following dialogue illuminates.

What were your circumstances at the time of the riot itself?

Oh, I was in camp, and we lived in Block 36. On the day of the riot, I was notified by several people that the rioters were going to be going after the people on their various death lists, and that it would be advisable for me not to be in my own barracks at a given time that evening, but to probably be at some other location. . . . So I had dinner in a mess hall in another block, then spent that evening with my brother and people in his barrack when the rioting had broken out. Out of concern for what might be happening to my family, I joined the mob—I guess, the rioters—as they went by the block where I was staying and went to Block 36. So I was there when they tried to find me. . . . It was a very dark night, and we were all dressed alike in these Navy-issue pea coats. It was a cold night. Most people were rather warmly dressed. So I saw much of the moving about, but I saw no actual violence.[44]

When I interviewed Tanaka on August 30, 1973, in Los Angeles at the real estate development and investment company he owned, only a week had elapsed since my taping session with Sue Embrey. I was familiar with the analysis of the Manzanar Riot that Tanaka had prepared in early 1943 for the Japanese American Evacuation and Resettlement Study while holed up in Death Valley. It centered on three inmate factions in the disturbance: Group I–the JACL; Group II–the anti-JACL group; and Group III–the anti-administration, anti-JACL group.[45] Because Embrey had not been enmeshed in these Manzanarian cohort groups, she was unable to provide me with authoritative information about their personnel or posture. Everything I had heard from and about Tanaka convinced me that he possessed this vital information. Accordingly, I pivoted my interview with him on his riot report.

In interviewing Tanaka, as I had Embrey, I tried to implement Gene Wise's aforementioned perspectival mode of historical inquiry, whereby I was less attentive to finding out precisely what had transpired at the Manzanar center and during the riot there than in how this period and event had been experienced (and continued to be re-experienced) by the historical actors.

I began by exploring the perspective of Tanaka's own JACL group. I wanted to determine whether all the JACL leaders occupied a marginal position within their ethnic generation, and perhaps even within their subculture, and whether this marginality was the root cause of their ostracism by the Manzanar community.

Aside from Tanaka himself, three other JACLers whose names had been placed on the death list circulated in the camp at the time of the riot were

Fred Tayama, Joe Grant Masaoka, and Tokie Slocum. All of them were
viewed widely by the camp population as being collaborators and paid intelligence agency informers. My interview with Sue Embrey had sensitized me
to this situation from the perspective of an "outsider." What I sought from
Tanaka, however, was an *emic* perspective on these individuals.

Tanaka left no doubt that he regarded Tayama and Masaoka as intimate
Manzanar consociates. I knew already that some unidentified masked
inmates had brutally beaten Tayama on the night of December 5, 1942, following his return from an all-center JACL-WRA conference in Salt Lake City.
I knew, too, that the assault on Tayama had precipitated Harry Ueno's arrest
and removal from camp and that these actions, in turn, had set in motion the
riotous violence that erupted the following evening.[46] I furthermore knew
that at the time of the enforced mass eviction of Japanese Americans Tayama
had been a Little Tokyo restaurateur and a JACL leader. Because I knew very
little of a personal nature about Tayama and virtually nothing about his relationship with Tanaka, I asked for help:

> *Maybe you could tell us . . . about Tayama's character and what connection you had*
> *with him prior to the war.*

> Well, I knew him as the president of the Los Angeles chapter of the JACL as
> well as chairman of the Southwest District Council; he was also a member
> of our editorial advisory board of the English Section of the *Rafu Shimpo*. I
> found myself meeting with him frequently both in connection with the work
> of the JACL and in writing about him and the JACL in the *Rafu Shimpo* English
> Section. Personally, I liked him very much and agreed with many of the
> things he was advocating at our English Section editorial board meetings. . . .
> He was . . . very close to his father and mother, who were Issei—I knew his
> parents. He had many brothers and sisters; they were a very close family and
> successful in business. I looked up to him because of his leadership in the
> community. I regretted very much what happened to him—his beating on the
> night prior to the riot—in Manzanar; he was a decent person in my book.[47]

Because Tayama was one of the few recognized Nisei leaders in the prewar Japanese American community, explained Tanaka, he had participated,
along with a cadre of other JACL officials (including Tanaka himself) in
negotiations with government officials such as Governor Culbert Olson
of California during the several-month interval between Pearl Harbor and

the issuance of exclusion and detention orders. According to Tanaka, it was Tayama's involvement in these unsuccessful negotiations that had brought the community wrath down upon his head, both literally and figuratively: "He was the number one JACL figure, so naturally he was going to be the target of most of the animosity."[48] Because this explanation fell into the area of conventional wisdom, I tried to prod Tanaka out of his explanatory groove with my line of questioning.

What about rumors concerning Tayama's economic activities?

He and his brothers ran a chain of restaurants on Main Street. There was this local bilingual weekly Japanese paper, the *Doho* (Brotherhood), edited by Shuji Fujii; it was a small paper, and Communist. . . . If you refer to Tayama's economic posture, he was fighting a labor union. There was an effort to organize his workers and he said: "To hell with it!" and he fired them. The *Doho* took up the cudgel for the workers, and Fred was identified as "a goddamned, dirty, stinking capitalist who exploited his workers." I think this had some carryover into the camp. Anything he did do or didn't do, he drew attacks in *Doho*'s columns.[49]

So it was a combination of that reputation as an "exploitive capitalist" and his visibility as a JACL leader?

Right. Also the fact that we consorted with members of the United States Naval Intelligence at dinners, before Pearl Harbor, in an effort to secure the JACL's position with the federal government agency. This didn't help our image once we were behind barbed wire. I think this led to the accusation that we were a bunch of dogs or *inu*, informers.[50]

I knew even less about Joe Grant Masaoka than Fred Tayama. I was aware that a younger brother, Mike, was the JACL's controversial executive secretary, that he had been raised in Utah where the Japanese American population was meager, that in prewar Los Angeles he had achieved success as a businessman and JACL leader, that he had worked with Tanaka as a documentary historian at Manzanar, and that his name had appeared during the riot on various inmate blacklists and death lists.[51] Again, I turned to Tanaka to socially situate Masaoka.

It was true, said Tanaka, that Joe Grant Masaoka had been raised in Salt Lake City, but his birthplace was southern California and "he was very much a fixture in Los Angeles before the war and had almost as high a profile as Fred Tayama." At Manzanar, Masaoka was Tanaka's closest friend along with Tad Uyeno, a JACLer who operated and owned a plant nursery in the Los Angeles suburb of San Gabriel before the war and "wrote a column called 'The Lancer' for the *Rafu Shimpo* . . . expressing a JACL point of view in terms of our citizenship obligations." All three had earned a place on the camp administrators' "shit list" for going over their heads to contact officials in Washington or elsewhere. "Tad never did that," Tanaka explained, "but he encouraged us. The three of us shared a great deal in the seven months we were in there. As a result, when Joe and I were on the death list, Tad was also on the death list. He had to be removed from camp to Death Valley like us."[52]

As for Tokutara (Tokie) Nishimura Slocum, Tanaka stressed their differences instead of their similarities. Slocum had been born in Japan and, after his family's immigration to the United States, had been adopted and brought up by the Slocum family in Minot, North Dakota. After serving in the US Army, he successfully lobbied, in the 1930s, for congressional legislation conferring citizenship upon veterans who, like himself, were aliens otherwise ineligible for naturalization. At this same time, he was appointed to the editorial board of the *Rafu Shimpo*, a position he retained during Tanaka's editorial tenure. "So I had occasion to know his views," explained Tanaka.

> I liked what he stood for. I agreed with the substance of what he believed in, but I couldn't stand his methods or his *style*. He was an extremist in so many ways. He was dogmatic, very assertive, and not very cordial or polite. . . . To me he epitomized . . . the people who wear their flag on their sleeve. You never know . . . the kind of people they really are, and they're often personally obnoxious. Slocum was one of these people. So I didn't like him, personally, that much. . . . He was kind of an oddball in my estimation, because our backgrounds were different. He came from a community where there were no other Japanese.[53]

In our interview, Tanaka took pains to distance himself, along with the rest of the JACL leadership at Manzanar, from Slocum. He did not "think it would be too accurate to identify Slocum as JACL," for his "extremism" made him a "loner." Even prior to Pearl Harbor, he was vociferously superpatriotic, "to the extent of offending most Issei and Nisei by his loud and outspoken manner," and proclaimed that "it was his duty and everybody else's to not only inform on but 'turn in' people." So conspicuous a target was Slocum at Manzanar that "anyone who identified . . . with him immediately became suspect in the eyes of most people." Even after the riot, when the JACLers and their families were held in protective custody in the military police compound next to Manzanar, "whenever Slocum appeared on the scene, the conversation died." And when this contingent was sent to Death Valley, Slocum "was removed elsewhere simply because he didn't fit in with the group, even though in the riot most of the people in Manzanar identified him with us."

Would you say, then, that he [Slocum] was almost persona non grata among the JACL people?

Personally, I had neither any feeling of affection, warmth, or trust for the guy. . . . All of us had parents who were "aliens ineligible for U.S. citizenship," who were technically "enemies of this country"—in wartime—and they were our parents. He was raised by a farm family in the Midwest, the Slocums. His wife was a girl from Texas, and she was different too—that is, his second wife, Sally. See, he didn't have much in common with us to begin with.

Was his wife Caucasian?

His first wife was Caucasian. He was married to her for about ten years. Then he married a girl named Sally Yabumoto, of Japanese descent. They had their circle of friends, but I never regarded myself as belonging to it. I used to feel uncomfortable about being identified with him. . . . There were some old-time JACL people . . . [who] recognized his contributions; he was JACL in that sense. I think in terms of their feelings and affinity for him personally, I always figured they felt they had a bull by the tail—you couldn't control him and he was a self-styled spokesman for everybody, in his own estimation, but really only for himself.[54]

If the JACL group denoted in Tanaka's riot report could embrace "Nisei" personalities so diverse as Tad Uyeno, "rather forthright and very clear-cut . . . [but not] a troublemaker," and Tokie Slocum, an "extremist . . . dogmatic . . . oddball," its analytical utility seemed to me exceedingly limited. My attitude in this regard underwent a transformation, however, once our conversation turned to the other two Manzanarian groups depicted in Tanaka's report. I was especially interested in hearing what Tanaka would say about the anti-JACL group composed of political progressives, since in his report he had not cited particular individuals belonging to it. When I reminded him of this fact, he did provide names of people in this group—Chiye Mori, Tomomasa and Ruth Kurata Yamazaki, and Karl and Elaine Yoneda—but confessed that he did not know them well and that his "anti-JACL" label for them was perhaps not altogether accurate. In interviewing Sue Embrey, seven years Tanaka's junior, the previous week, I had tried to comprehend what Tanaka might have meant by the term anti-JACL to define Karl Yoneda and his consociates at Manzanar. But all she could recollect was that this group "wanted an increase in monthly wages . . . fought to try to get some kind of a citizens' council going . . . were all anti-JACL . . . [and] were quite left of center in terms of the JACL."[55] I therefore pressed Tanaka with the same concern.

> From what I can gather from analyzing relevant documentary materials, this designation does indeed seem to be unsatisfactory. For example, when the Manzanar Citizens Federation was established in camp to carry out the work done in the prewar years by the JACL, the person you selected to head this group was Koji Ariyoshi—a close associate of Karl Yoneda's and others in the reputed anti-JACL group. And there are many other examples of close cooperation between the members of the JACL and the anti-JACL groups. In what sense, then, were those in Group II actually anti-JACL?

So long as the adversary was the "pro-Japan" rioters in the camp, the JACLers were one—the prewar JACL leadership group and the liberal left group that I refer to as "anti-JACL." Once removed from the ideological and physical battleground at Manzanar, the so-called "pro-American" coalition came apart at Death Valley. The JACLers, like the Tayamas, Masaokas, Tanakas, and Uyenos, looked to the JACL headquarters at Salt Lake City for leadership. The "anti-JACL" group like Mori, Yamazaki, and Yoneda looked elsewhere. There was close cooperation within Manzanar. I'm not aware that it survived at all outside that camp. You mentioned Koji Ariyoshi, I didn't know him too well. I remember him as an articulate spokesman at some of the meetings and that he was JACL. I think he would be closer to Karl Yoneda than to Fred Tayama, that's just my observation.[56]

At this point, I was reminded of what Lyman had explained about Nisei "regularly resorting to . . . inferential hints at essential meanings" in their conversations. Although Tanaka was providing me with some useful contextual information about Yoneda's group, he was not directly answering my question as to why in his report he had labeled this group anti-JACL. It was incumbent upon me, therefore, to steer—but not veer—our conversation into a somewhat different course of development.

How did this group function prior to the war? You call them something of an aka group. Could you describe what aka means: does it mean precisely Communist or what?

In the prewar establishment press, the *Rafu Shimpo* being an example, the so-called anti-JACL group was referred to as being sympathetic to the Communist Party and its ideals. *"Aka"* was a term used loosely. It was also a broad brush used to smear the liberal left.

The label might apply to Karl Yoneda, for example?

Right, Karl and Koji Ariyoshi—I understood they were labor organizers.

Other than simply commingling with this so-called anti-JACL group for political reasons, did you have much to do with them at Manzanar otherwise, or was it a clear sort of expedient cooperation?

There was probably none at all, except that we might pass each other along the so-called streets of Manzanar or at some meeting. We greeted one another and recognized each other, but beyond that I can't remember ever socializing with them or spending any time with them at all. There was no closeness.

You mentioned in your . . . report . . . that Group I, the JACL people, almost without exception arrived later at Manzanar than the Group II [anti-JACL] personalities. Do you recall why that was?

I think we had less mobility because most of the people in Group I owned their own homes and had businesses, so it took longer to wind up.[57]

Based on Tanaka's responses, I was beginning to fathom why those encompassed by his Group II category might be viewed, for ideological and class reasons, as being both apart from and at odds with him and his JACL cohorts. But if, from Tanaka's perspective, there was "no closeness" between Group I and Group II, it soon became clear from our conversation that Group III, "the anti-administration, anti-JACL" group, was practically a pure analytical invention of his, one largely devoid of specificity or palpability. This was the group, consisting mostly of Issei and Kibei (Nisei educated and socialized in pre–World War II Japan), that spearheaded the resistance to the rabid

pro-Americanism of the other two groups and pressured the camp administration for greater recognition and rights. Before the riot they had drawn
up the blacklist and death lists featuring Group I and Group II leaders; after
the riot they were arrested on suspicion of having fomented the troubles in
camp and then clamped in surrounding Owens Valley town jails.

I queried Tanaka largely about the three men in this group who loomed
most notoriously in the reports on the riot I had read: Ben Kishi, a twenty-
three-year-old Kibei; Harry Ueno, a thirty-five-year-old Hawai'i Kibei; and
Joe Kurihara, a forty-seven-year-old Hawai'i Nisei.[58]

Because Kishi was alleged by camp authorities to have been the head of a
vocal and violent band of fellow Kibei men who had terrorized otherwise-
minded inmates during the half year prior to the riot as well as on the night
of the riot itself, I was surprised that Tanaka had not mentioned him either
in his lecture or his life-history interview. So in our focused interview I put
the matter to him directly in personal terms.

> *What about people . . . regarded as potential troublemakers who had records before*
> *leaving Manzanar? I'm talking about people like Ben Kishi.*
>
> I know of him, but I never met or recall him at all.
>
> *Some people claim in reports that Kishi—during the time the crowd was looking for*
> *you on the night of the riot and you were standing with the crowd outside the door*
> *of your apartment—was the one who led the crowd that sought to murder you. But*
> *these reports also maintain that he was the one who directed the crowd away from*
> *any beating of your family.*
>
> Yes, I heard that, too. I really wouldn't know if he was the person who said,
> "Leave them alone." I didn't know him at all in camp.[59]

I asked Tanaka, too, about Harry Ueno, the head of Manzanar's Kitchen
Workers' Union. His arrest and off-site jailing for the ostensible beating of
Fred Tayama had led Group III leaders to charge that Ueno was really being
punished for accusing two WRA staffers of having appropriated rationed
inmate mess supplies for sale on the black market, to demand that he be
returned at once to the Manzanar center, and to insist that, following his
return, he be released from the camp jail and exonerated of all charges connected with the Tayama assault. Tanaka's response echoed what he had said
about Kishi.

*What about the popularity of Harry Ueno. Did you know Ueno prior to the
Manzanar Riot?*

I don't ever remember meeting him in camp. I might have heard him speak
once, I don't know. During the riot, I wouldn't have been able to identify him;
he was just a name.[60]

If Kishi and Ueno were near abstractions for Tanaka, I knew from reviewing the transcripts of his lecture and life-history interview that Joe Kurihara
was to him a corporeal being. Following the lecture, one student had asked
Tanaka to amplify upon the causes of the Manzanar Riot. After discussing
psychological, climatological, and political forces, Tanaka enlarged upon
what he believed to be a more potent cause.

When you had an active JACL group telling the young men in the camp, "You
are American citizens, and you owe it to your government to fight for the
United States and to volunteer for armed service," this was not a popular
thing to propose. I know that in the three months before we were driven out
of the camp, Joe [Masaoka] and I made it a point to speak at mess halls . . .
throughout the camp . . . urging young men to volunteer, because this had
been the policy of the JACL in Salt Lake City. I had a prewar friend, Joe
Kurihara, who was convinced that Joe Masaoka and I were out of our minds,
and he felt very deeply about this. He would follow us and, after we had made
our presentations and told the audience, "The only way out of this place
is to . . . go the second mile and prove that we belong here [in the United
States], and we must identify ourselves as Americans," this man . . . would
say, "I served my country, the United States of America, in World War I. I
fought and bled on the battlefields of France, and I know what it means to
sacrifice one's life and be willing to give my life to this country. But since this
government, out of its lack of wisdom, has seen fit to regard me as a "Jap,"
by God, I'm going to be a good Jap, 100 percent! I will never do anything to
fight for the United States. I am going to return to Japan. . . . I've never been
there, but I'm going to go to Japan, and if you listen to these young idiots who
have just preceded me you're going to find yourselves in other camps like this
because there are people in Washington today . . . who have proposed bills in
the Congress of the United States to exclude forever any person of Japanese
descent from American citizenship."[61]

A follow-up student questioner noted that he understood one of Kurihara's complaints to be that Tanaka's and Masaoka's documentary reports had been passed along to the FBI, "perhaps through the naiveness of the reporters," who then used the information to intimidate protesting camp groups, especially the Kibei. "His apprehensions," replied Tanaka,

> were justified. We used to meet with Joe Kurihara, and he would say, "Why don't you and Joe quit writing these damn reports, because they're going to use them in kinds of ways that will be detrimental to us." At the time, we couldn't see it. We said, "Well, you know, we have an obligation here to show our best face to the public because we have a public relations function. If we say we have a camouflage factory or we're growing, whatever, rubber plants, guayule, for the war effort, these facts ought to get out, and the fact that we're chronicling these events in no way hurts us in this camp."[62]

What caught my attention when reading Tanaka's life-history interview was a passage discussing Kurihara in juxtaposition to another World War I veteran, JACLer Tokie Slocum, and the interviewee's transformed relationship to these men as a consequence of their wartime experience.

> *You mentioned Joe Kurihara and Tokie Slocum before in your lecture. I wonder if you could expand on that?*
>
> Well, you know, I had regarded both Kurihara and Slocum as personal friends before World War II. Kurihara, because he was a very pleasant, congenial, friendly and outgoing man who used to visit me at the *Rafu Shimpo*. He was an older Nisei and I always enjoyed talking with people who could give me the benefit of their experiences. I knew he was active in the Commodore Perry Post of the American Legion . . . I liked Kurihara as a human being much more than [Slocum]. But in camp, the views Slocum expressed—by a stroke of irony—represented what Joe Masaoka and I believed in: in this war, we were Americans; we were not Japanese; and, when we had to make the choice, this was where we belonged. Kurihara took the other view. In camp, Kurihara never personally or openly expressed to me a dislike for me to the extent that I should arm myself or be equipped to defend myself against his wanting to have us put away. So this, I think was a surprise. Before Joe Masaoka died [in 1970], he and I were involved in a number of things. One was a business venture here. We used to think back and say, "You know, life

is funny. Joe Kurihara was one of the last people in the world we thought would want to get us knocked off whereas we wouldn't have put it beyond Slocum." . . . So Manzanar was a puzzle to us.[63]

A puzzle indeed, a place where former friends, like Joe Kurihara, became murderous foes and prewar ideological deviants, like Karl Yoneda, were deemed camp comrades. "If there were a line with Joe Kurihara on one side and some of us on the other," explained Tanaka, "Karl was friendly with us."[64] Because I possessed ample biographical information on Kurihara, in my interview with Tanaka I limited myself to questioning him about Group III's leadership and Kurihara's role within it.

> *Who do you think of as leaders in the third group? Kurihara doesn't emerge as much of a leader—precisely speaking, with a following. In fact, he's rather atypical in that he was the only Nisei sent to Moab [a WRA isolation center established in Utah after the Manzanar Riot]. All the rest were Issei and Kibei.*
>
> [A Kibei] man named Shigetoshi Tateishi was outspoken. After one of my appearances at a mess hall to explain the desirability of joining the armed services, he was rather conspicuous by saying, in Japanese, what a stupid idea this was. . . . But Kurihara stands out mostly because I could have a dialogue with him; with the others, it was Japanese coming out of their mouths and English out of mine, so we never met.[65]

On the strength of what I found out from Tanaka, augmented by my interview with Sue Embrey and research into relevant archival and secondary sources, I was able in fall 1973 to offer a preliminary reevaluation of the Manzanar Riot. Still, I was disturbed by my overreliance upon Tanaka's perspective and voice. Before I could submit my interpretation of the riot for publication, I had to extend my documentary investigation and secure interviews with some surviving leaders of Tanaka's three Manzanarian groups.

Because Tanaka had alluded to "Point of No Return," Tad Uyeno's just-published account of the post-Manzanar stay of the JACL and anti-JACL groups' families at the Cow Creek camp in Death Valley National Monument,[66] I turned to it immediately after our interview. Upon the exiled party's arrival in Death Valley, recalled JACLer Uyeno, he had been apprehensive lest "a long confinement [would] . . . result in a clash of personalities, a division of attitudes, jealousies, and struggle for leadership."[67] Although the "clash" and "struggle" never occurred, probably because the tenure of residence lasted only two months, Uyeno depicted an attitudinal division between the "death list members" [Tanaka's JACLers] and the "black list members" [Tanaka's anti-JACLers]. According to Uyeno, these two groups of "like-minded persons" found quarters on opposite sides of the camp, carried out segregated social activities, and responded differently to work assignments suggested by the camp director. "We tolerated each other, true," wrote Uyeno, "but we never got to know each other as well as we should have since we had been thrown together for basically the same reason."[68]

I next read a response to "Point of No Return" by Karl and Elaine Yoneda, which was based on their respective wartime diaries. "Although it is an important Evacuation story," wrote the Yonedas, "it is too heavily centered around JACLers and omits many significant events . . . and contributions [at Manzanar] made by non-JACLers. . . . We would like, therefore, to outline some of the untold aspects of the Manzanar story."[69]

Clearly, Uenyo's Manzanar (and Death Valley) tale had revolved around JACLer efforts to cooperate with WRA officials, sell the Nisei cause through public relations, protect Japanese American citizenship and property rights, and gain speedy clearance from concentration camp life so as to renew the JACL's prewar campaign for assimilation into mainstream America. In sharp contrast, the Yonedas pivoted their story on their commitment, as well as that of their leftist cohorts, to improve camp conditions, promote the war against the fascist Axis powers, and help prepare for a postwar international order free of racism, sexism, militarism, and capitalist imperialism.

Reading the Yonedas' account was the precise catalyst I required for arranging interviews with them on March 2–3, 1974, at their San Francisco home, to which I traveled with two other Japanese American Project members, Betty Mitson and Ron Larson. The first day I interviewed Elaine, while my colleagues interviewed Karl about his pre-and immediate post-Manzanar life; the next day, I joined one of them, Ron Larson, for a conversation with Karl centered on his months at Manzanar.[70]

Before interviewing Karl Yoneda, I asked my associates to brief me about the facts of his life. Karl Yoneda was born in 1906 in Glendale, California. He was later taken to Hiroshima, Japan, where he lived, attended schools, and became involved in the student and labor movements. After high school he became a typesetter and was jailed for participating in strikes and then expelled from Hiroshima. In an outlying village, he began issuing a radical publication in 1926, for which he was arrested. That same year, he was drafted into the Japanese Imperial Army but ran away and returned to California. Joining the American Communist Party in 1927, Yoneda assumed the name Karl Hama and, between then and the outbreak of World War II, was involved in countless strikes, civil rights demonstrations, labor organizing efforts, and radical leftist organizations. During this interval (in 1933), too, he married another Communist activist, Elaine Black, ran for the California State Assembly on the Communist ticket in 1934, became a Bay Area longshoreman in 1936, and in 1939 fathered a son, Thomas Culbert Yoneda. On the day after Pearl Harbor, FBI agents arrested Karl Yoneda on the waterfront and locked him up for three days in the Immigration Detention Center. After his stormy Manzanar stint, he undertook courageous wartime service in India, Burma, and China for the Psychological Warfare Team of the Office of War Information.[71]

Subsequent to our taping sessions with the Yonedas, my associates and I discussed what we had witnessed, both inside and outside of the interviewing context, about the contrasting interpersonal communication styles of Karl and Elaine. We agreed that, although their marriage was companionate and comradely, it was also a profoundly cross-cultural union. Consonant with her background as the oldest child of turn-of-the-century Russian-Jewish immigrants in New York City, Elaine's conversation, whether for the benefit of the tape recorder or not, was animated, extremely fast-paced, assertive, disputatious, uncensored, warm, shrill, and punctuated by overtalking, abrupt corrections, and histrionic body language.[72]

When not being interviewed, Karl came across as "typically" Nisei, but once the tape recorder was turned on his interpersonal manner became suddenly transformed. Consistent with other Kibei-Nisei who had been returned to Japan as youths and both educated and partially enculturated there,[73] Karl spoke in a thickly Japanese-accented English conveyed by a singsong cadence. This outward linguistic difference was more than matched by other deviations from the Nisei interactional style. Although always polite in his responses, he was never deferential. Although sometimes judiciously qualifying his remarks, he rarely resorted to indirection or circumlocution. Although good-humored and congenial, his conversation was innocent of both trivia and confabulation. The Nisei preoccupation with emotional management, which Lyman's analysis had adumbrated and Tanaka's lecture faintly evidenced, seemed altogether absent from Yoneda's communicative repertoire. Instead, his conversational style was reminiscent of what I had encountered during my earlier interviews with Tanaka and Embrey: frank, expressive, exploratory, and forthcoming. Like Tanaka, Yoneda peppered his talk with colorful anecdotes and terms, and like Embrey, he occasionally flared up in anger or spoke in contemporary "Youth Movement" argot (e.g., "blow your mind"). However, unlike Tanaka and Embrey (and in common with his Caucasian wife, although less flamboyantly), Yoneda's conversation was ideologically constrained.[74] Yoneda, leastwise to our right-wing Orange County–conditioned ears, communicated as much, if not more, through his political subculture as he did his ethnic generation.

By the time that Embrey informed me that Harry Ueno was alive and willing to be interviewed by the two of us, my assessment of the Manzanar Riot had been published.[75] Nonetheless, believing Ueno's testimony to be of historical significance, we traveled to his San Jose, California, home in fall 1976 to tape his recollections.[76]

I already knew fragments of Ueno's life at Manzanar and during the balance of World War II, but he told us the details of his pre-Manzanar life and fleshed out the facts of his wartime experiences after the Manzanar Riot. Born in 1907 at a sugar plantation on the island of Hawai'i from parents who had emigrated there as laborers from Hiroshima, Ueno was sent to Japan at eight years old to live with his grandparents in Hiroshima and attend school. At sixteen, he took a job on a ship bound for the United States, where upon arrival in the port of Tacoma, Washington, he jumped ship. Unable to speak English fluently, he worked for several years in a Tacoma lumber mill, then lived briefly with a brother in Milwaukee, Wisconsin, and returned in 1927 to the Northwest. Banned from lumbering work by anti-Japanese sawmill workers' unions, Ueno moved first to northern California, where he was married to an Issei woman, and then to Los Angeles. There, from 1930 until he, his wife Yasu, and three boys were consigned to Manzanar in May 1942, Ueno worked at a fruit stand and several Jewish-run markets, lived away from other Japanese Americans, and stayed aloof from Nikkei organizations.

In the aftermath of the riot, which Ueno observed from inside the Manzanar jail,[77] he was taken out of camp and put behind bars for a month in two nearby Owens Valley jails. At the second of these, where he occupied a small cell with fifteen other allegedly pro-Japan dissidents responsible for the riot, the military police "sometimes got drunk [at night] and shot the [cell] door with a rifle."[78] There Ueno also got into a near-violent row with two other prisoners (the aforementioned Ben Kishi and another twenty-three-year-old Kibei) when they overheard him telling Joe Kurihara that they were untrustworthy "two-timers." On January 9, 1943, Ueno and his other cellmates, without being granted a hearing or given a specific reason for their arrest, were transferred to an abandoned CCC camp in Moab, Utah, that served as a temporary isolation center for inmate "troublemakers" in all the WRA centers. During his four-month stay at Moab, Ueno refused to work because of his unclarified prisoner status, mail censorship, and harsh regulations. He also purportedly headed a gang of former Manzanarians who physically threatened those who did work, was placed in a special isolation barracks, attempted to renounce his US citizenship, and was thrown into the county jail in Moab for his resistance to authority.[79] After a brutal thirteen-hour truck ride, Ueno passed several days in the Winslow, Arizona, town jail and then, on April 28, 1943, was transported to the Leupp Isolation Center, located in a onetime Indian Bureau school on the adjacent Navajo reservation and guarded by military police. There, he cooperated with the camp administration until his transfer to the Tule Lake (California) Segregation Center on December 4, 1943. Rejoined with his family, he stayed clear of the turbulent politics in that camp for presumed "disloyals," established a model record as a maintenance worker, changed his mind about giving up his American citizenship, and was finally released from Tule Lake in March 1946.[80]

Since my interview with Karl Yoneda two and one-half years earlier, I had taped numerous oral histories with Nikkei, including four former Manzanarians: the male Issei head of dental services; a female Kibei elementary school teacher; and two male Nisei, the director of the camp hospital and a member of its internal security force.[81] Of these, both the Kibei teacher and the Nisei policeman were congruent in most respects with the normative Nisei interpersonal style depicted by Lyman, whereas the Issei dentist (who characterized himself as "very different") and the Nisei medical administrator comported themselves more in the fashion of Togo Tanaka. By the time of the interview with Harry Ueno, then, I remained attentive to

Lyman's paradigm but was far less constrained by it than I had been during my interviews with Embrey, Tanaka, and Yoneda.

Ueno was a Kibei who, like Yoneda, had spent part of his developmental years in Japan's Hiroshima Prefecture. Both spoke in Japanized English, but this communicative aspect was positively more pronounced in Ueno than Yoneda. This was no doubt because, as their respective interviews certify, they had moved in exceedingly different social and domestic spheres. For example, whereas before and during World War II Yoneda had enjoyed regular contacts with a multicultural array of political progressives and was married to a Caucasian American woman, Ueno's "few friends were mostly Kibei" and his slightly older wife a native of Japan who had come to the United States when she was nineteen years old.[82] Their intonation pattern was comparable, although the rise and fall in pitch of Ueno's speaking voice, again, was far more conspicuous.

Nonetheless, the interactional styles of these two Kibei men were noticeably similar. If Yoneda, as mentioned earlier, deviated from the model Nisei style in terms of greater spontaneity, intimacy, directness, excitability, and emotional range, so too did Ueno (whose deviation, arguably, was magnified by having spent his early childhood in Hawai'i rather than on the mainland). Indeed, Embrey had barely opened the interview with Ueno when, in response to a question about his early stay in Japan, his effervescent mien metamorphosed into tearful melancholy: "The thing is, you know, to be separated from your father and mother for seven years is . . . I don't know. I think all the Kibei feel the same way. I think I had better explain to you the Kibei's mental status."[83] Listening to Ueno converse with Embrey and myself for the next two and one-half hours (and correlating his discourse with what I had read about Kibei deportment in the wartime camps)[84] made me realize that, had Lyman's early socialization with second-generation Japanese Americans been with Kibei-Nisei rather than Nisei bereft of a prolonged stay in Japan, his essay would have assumed a substantially different complexion. I now appreciated in a more profound sense than before Embrey's observation during our interview that many Kibei, upon their return to the United States, never made the adjustment to Nisei society.[85]

There was one notable point in Ueno's interview, however, when he sounded characteristically Nisei. Because of its centrality both to the Manzanar Riot and Ueno's interpersonal style of communication, it merits our careful attention.

All of a sudden on the night of December 5, 1942, Fred Tayama was beaten by some masked people, and you were accused of being one of them. The attackers had something over their heads. Fred Tayama and his wife identified you. They said they could identify your eyes. Later, Joe Kurihara claimed that he was behind the beating, that he had master-minded it, and did not indicate whether you were included or not. But you were accused of the beating and, on the basis of that accusation, you were picked up and taken out of Manzanar. Now I would like to ask you very pointedly, were you involved in the beating of Fred Tayama?

No, not me. And I don't think Kurihara was either.

He didn't say that he was there.

If he were involved, he probably would have told me—we were so close right after the incident.

Do you know who did beat Tayama up?

No, no. I don't think so.

You didn't hear anything from anybody at the jail, or later at Moab, or at Leupp, any speculation as to who was involved? Was Ben Kishi there?

I don't know.

You didn't hear any speculation from anybody? It seems odd, because rumors would circulate around the camp and people would talk about them.

I know, but I think we felt that we didn't want to discuss it. You know what I mean?

Do you mean that you know who did it, but you're just not saying?

Well, maybe I know and maybe I don't. I think there are a lot of things that we don't want to discuss unless we have proof, you know.[86]

(In connection with Ueno's last statement, see Appendixes A, B, and C. See also the frankly illuminating interview with Harry Yoshio Uneo by Arthur A. Hansen, June 17, 2000, O.H. 1518.3, Japanese American Project, Center for Oral and Public History, California State University, Fullerton.)

Here, it would seem, was a prime example of the indirection, circumlocution, and confabulation in Nisei speech that Lyman had postulated and which projective tests with those in that generation had confirmed. Still, it appears more plausible to infer from this uncommon exchange that Ueno was exercising prudential restraint out of concern for the reputation and security of others and not merely engaging in prototypical rhetorical management. As with Embrey, Tanaka, and Yoneda, Ueno represented an exception that made the rule problematic, at best.

We now need to exploit this case study of the Manzanar Riot involving one racial-ethnic group, Japanese Americans, in the interest of generating useful knowledge about all such groups and, more specifically, of postulating some provisional guidelines for transacting oral-historical fieldwork within racial-ethnic communities in the United States.

Two decades ago British historian Eric Hobsbawm shrewdly observed that studies of social conflict, ranging from revolutions to riots, require more careful assessment than other historical topics because they dramatize crucial aspects of the sociocultural structure.[87] In the case of the Manzanar Riot, our investigation has revealed, minimally, that the racist assumption underpinning the Japanese American Incarceration—"A Jap is a Jap"—was not only pernicious but egregiously false. Among primarily the Nisei generation at one concentration camp alone, we have encountered differences in ideas, values, and behavior so acute as to result in extreme acts like social ostracism and death threats. Moreover, we have seen that even seemingly compact generational coteries at this camp were fractured during pivotal moments when latent disparities in socialization and attendant cultural style were forced to the surface or when the mise-en-scène shifted from the public to the private domain.

Although the sheer "discovery" of intracultural variation among Japanese Americans should hardly be surprising, the considerable degree of heterogeneity disclosed in this racial-ethnic group, especially when one considers their historical legacy and wartime situation, is significant both in itself and for what it suggests about the composition of all such American subcultures. Nonetheless, before pursuing this point I want to set aside, for heuristic purposes, the manifest diversity within the Nikkei population and argue that their plight, at least until after World War II, embodied an extreme-case scenario of the socialization process of other racial-ethnic groups in which normative behavior inordinately molded actual behavior.

As Stephen Fugita and David J. O'Brien showed, structural constraints—stemming both from the cultural legacy that Japanese immigrants (Issei) brought with them to the mainland United States and from the conditions they and their offspring (Nisei) encountered in American society—produced a remarkably uniform personality type as against that found in white immigrant groups from Europe (an observation that I would extend to embrace "persons of color" coming from the rest of the world).[88]

On the one hand, Japan was a very small island nation made up of mostly small agricultural villages inhabited by culturally homogeneous people. According to Fugita and O'Brien, "As early as the seventh century, the Japanese saw themselves as a single people living in a unified nation."[89] Moreover, for two centuries prior to the nineteenth-century Meiji Revolution and the decision to westernize, the ruling Tokugawa Shogunate had permitted neither immigration into or emigration out of Japan. Thus, the Japanese immigrants who came to the United States chiefly in the four decades extending from 1885 to 1924 (when the Immigration Exclusion Act was passed), largely from four southwestern prefectures (Hiroshima, Yamaguichi, Fukuoka, and Kumamoto),[90] were mostly experienced farmers (augmented by a substantial number of students and merchants) seeking to better their economic situation.[91]

On the other hand, once they arrived in the mainland United States, the overwhelming percentage of the always numerically insignificant Japanese immigrant population lived in the western states of Washington, Oregon, and (most especially) California. There, owing to intense discrimination against them in housing and employment, they resided and worked in re-created traditional communities in rural areas and urban centers that insulated them from mainstream American society. Although the Japanese immigrants and their Nisei children "did not experience the kind of complete isolation enforced upon blacks, . . . they did nonetheless live apart from white society in many significant ways . . . and their most intimate relationships and institutional affiliations were found within the ethnic community."[92] In addition, anti-miscegenation laws and community pressure conspired to minimize outmarriage and to strengthen the sense of peoplehood of Japanese America, as did the special character of the ethnic economy revolving around small business enterprises and labor-intensive agriculture.[93] This "concentrated" community existence was exacerbated by the rise of legal and extralegal discrimination against people of Japanese ancestry and culminated in the World War II policy of exclusion and concentration camp detention.

In the late 1950s and early 1960s, when many Americans indulged themselves in a wave of self-congratulatory democratic liberalism, a profusion of articles appeared in mass-circulation magazines announcing that the JAI had been for the Nikkei a "blessing in disguise," for it had broken up their ethnic enclaves, relocated them geographically to other parts of the country, and precipitated not only their assimilation into the larger society but also set them on a course leading to their status as America's "model minority." At the time I did not appreciate the perversity of the logic informing this line of thought and, unwittingly, became a temporary captive of it.

The "blessing in disguise" for me came a decade later when I again took up the topic of the JAI and, by chance, came to study it via the method of oral history and through the madness of the Manzanar Riot. Talking on tape to Japanese American participants in this event forced me to realize an important truth: notwithstanding a historical legacy, socialization process, and public policy that worked to stylize Nikkei thought and behavior, there was still ample scope for subcultural diversity and individual differences (even during a time of extreme crisis when the expectation would be minimal normative deviation). The realization of this truth, in turn, made me appreciate that the same situation would obtain for transacting interviews in any other racial-ethnic community, that the racist myth of homogeneity would have to be supplanted by a strategic, humanistic quest for and appreciation of heterogeneity. Or, put another way, those of us studying such communities would have to attend to chronological, generational, class, gender, and ideological divisions within them if we wanted to gain a more complex sense of past reality and avoid the charge of racism. Furthermore, my early interviewing experiences with Nikkei survivors[94] of the Manzanar Riot, like Togo Tanaka, Karl Yoneda, and Harry Ueno, impressed upon me the fact, too often ignored by scholars and lay people alike, that time is a critical dimension in the study of racial-ethnic communities, as with all others, and that oral historians working in these communities must exorcise the bogeyman of not only homogeneous racial-ethnic communities but that of unchanging ones as well.[95]

APPENDIX A

The December 5, 1942, Fred Tayama Beating at Manzanar

In September 1994, I had an exchange of letters with Harry Ueno about the December 5, 1942, beating of Japanese American Citizens League leader Fred Tayama and Ueno's knowledge of and/or involvement in this event that catalyzed the December 6, 1942, "riot" at the Manzanar Relocation Center in eastern California's Owens Valley. Below are the relevant portions of these two letters, dated respectively September 2, 1994, and September 8, 1994. After I received Harry Ueno's reply to my September 2 letter, I offered him a choice as to when the information contained within it could be made available to researchers at the California State University, Fullerton Oral History Program (now the Lawrence de Graaf Center for Oral and Public History) archives, and he replied "immediately." After consultation with Sue Kunitomi Embrey, who on October 30, 1976, had interviewed Ueno with me at his family home in San Jose, California, it was decided to defer making this historical documentation a matter of public record until a later date. This is now that later date.

September 2, 1994, letter from Arthur A. Hansen to Mr. Harry Y. Ueno: "I wanted to ask you a question about a comment you made in the item you wrote for Jimmie Omura entitled 'Joseph Yoshisuke Kurihara.' You conclude it by writing this line: 'He never tell me his family history. I try to take a blame the Manzanar incident but one of those things. It happen. We are just a Humans, we have many faults.' I don't know exactly what you mean by this sentence, Mr. Ueno. I know that Joe Kurihara, in some of his documents, confesses to masterminding the beating of Fred Tayama, but I don't recall ever reading anything by you, or hearing anything from you, to the effect that you took the blame for the Manzanar Riot. Am I missing something? Please clarify your meaning on this sentence, okay? Thanks. Back in 1976 when Sue Embrey and I interviewed you, I turned off the tape recorder and suggested to you that you *might* want to leave a record for posterity of the secret details of the Manzanar Riot—leastwise as you were privy to them—prior to your passing from this earth. Let me repeat that suggestion here. It may be that, if you do so, you place a, say, fifty-year restriction on the release of this information so as not to place a hardship on still living people and their immediate families. Nobody needs to know about these details now, but it would be nice if at some safe point in the future the historical record could be clarified."

September 8, 1994, letter from Harry Y. Ueno to Dr. Arthur A. Hansen: "Back to Joseph Kurihara. He makes a statement to Mr. [Raymond] Best [project director] at Tule Lake [Segregation Center]. He is responsible for the attack [on] Fred Tayama. I think he make such a statement because he already decide to leave United States [and] therefore he have nothing to loose [*sic*]. Take all the blame for those deaths and injure [*sic*] at Manzanar. I was with him almost 3 years but he never once talk about the attack [on] Tayama. Since almost 52 years is pass[ed] by I might as well clear the whole thing. I swear Kurihara have nothing to do on attack [of] the Tayama. He is never even suggest to such a action to any young people far as I know. He hate these informer[s] much as anyone in Manzanar but not took any step. In early November Koichi Tsuji came to me and he talk about he and several other young his friend[s] try to attack the Karl Yoneda. They were waiting [for] him to come back from visiting someone in the camp. They failed. I guess they are scared or [lack] guts enough to go through [with] it. Now he was talking go after Fred Tayama. I was worry Tayama have a many ally. If you fail you will be in danger. You must be very careful. If you failed first time there is no second chance. Ned Campbell [Manzanar's assistant project director] and office plus his [Fred Tayama's] brothers is danger [and] also [Inmate] Chief of Police Kiyoshi Higashi and his brother is his [Fred Tayama's] protector at his apartment. I don't like to involve but he is getting [on] our nerve. Draft the prisner [*sic*] in camp is [Dillon] Myer [director of the War Relocation Authority] and J.A.C.L. [Japanese American Citizens League] both cordnate [*sic*] plan. We have to be more than careful. I decide to lead them. I plan every move around just little after 6:30 p.m. We get together. I told not to injured [*sic*] to[o] much just let him [Fred Tayama] know we are not going [to] let him control the camp as his will. Knock [on] his door and I said good evening [in] friendly voice. He [Fred Tayama] open the door. I jump in first. He seem just come out from the bed or changing the cloth [*sic*], he didn't have any cloth [*sic*] on. He is kinda big man for Japanese [,] 180 lb. or more. Young people strike him 4 or 5 times. He was crying it hurt. I signal that enough [and] we rush out the door and every one separate different way. It was quick and few minute[s] action. There was no one in his home[;] his protector Higashi brother was not home. Before he call the help we are all gone a different way. In W.R.A.

[War Relocation Authority] document his wife [says she] recognize me. It's a lie. I never met her."

APPENDIX B

Arthur A. Hansen's Introduction to Manzanar Martyr: An Interview with Harry Y. Ueno, *edited by Sue Kunitomi Embrey, Arthur A. Hansen, and Betty Kulberg Mitson (Fullerton: Japanese American Project, Oral History Program, California State University, Fullerton, 1986)*

The preceding introduction by Sue Kunitomi Embrey is written from the perspective of a person who, like Harry Y. Ueno, experienced the World War II Japanese American Incarceration (JAI), at least in part, from behind barbed wire at the Manzanar War Relocation Center in the Owens Valley of California. This introduction, on the other hand, is from the perspective, not of a participant-observer chronicler of the events at Manzanar, but from that of a historian of those events. As a student of the JAI, I have, since the early 1970s, been particularly interested in the varieties of resistance that occurred in the concentration camps established by the US government during World War II for those of Japanese ancestry. The most renowned example of such resistance is the "riot" that erupted at the Manzanar camp in the winter of 1942. Owing to my interest in the Manzanar Riot, I was led, first, to interview Embrey in 1973 and then, three years later, to conduct with Embrey the interview of Ueno that is featured in this volume. Since Embrey describes in some detail the context surrounding the obtaining of the interview with Ueno for the Japanese American Project of the Oral History Program at California State University, Fullerton, and Betty Mitson hereafter describes how that interview was prepared for publication, I will restrict my remarks to a few personal notes before moving on to some historiographical concerns.

At the time of my interview with Embrey, I was engaged in writing an article about the "riot" at Manzanar for the book *Voices Long Silent: An Oral Inquiry into the Japanese American Evacuation* (Fullerton, CA: Japanese American Project, Oral History Program, California State University, Fullerton, 1974), which Mitson and I were jointly compiling; it was based upon the oral history interviews contained within the Japanese American Project, for which I was the director and Mitson the assistant director. While I was mainly interested in interviewing Embrey about her recent activities with the Manzanar Committee, naturally a considerable portion of the interview was devoted to her earlier detention experience, including her recollections of the Manzanar Riot and some of the principals associated with it. I recall asking her then whether or not she knew the whereabouts of Harry Ueno and her reply that, while she did not, she would let me know should something ever turn up in this connection.

Although I had the good fortune in my research to avail myself of an abundance of written and some oral archival material about the Manzanar Riot, I was anxious to talk directly with the two individuals most frequently identified with that event, Fred Tayama and Harry Ueno. I found that talking with the first of these men was out of the question because Tayama had died several years earlier, but I still held out hope that Ueno would prove to be alive and available to interview. So I persisted in seeking out information about him from those who seemed likely sources. Customarily, the responses I received from ones who might know fell into one of three categories: they had not heard of him since the war; they thought he was living somewhere in Japan; or they assumed he had passed away. Accordingly, I reluctantly added his name to the list of other crucial Manzanarians whom I apparently would not be able to query on tape.

By the time Embrey informed me in 1976 that she had not only heard from Dr. Don Hata of California State University, Dominguez Hills, that Ueno was still alive and living in northern California, but also that he would like to be interviewed, my interpretation of the Mazanar Riot was already a matter of published record (Arthur A. Hansen and David A. Hacker, "The Manzanar Riot: An Ethnic Perspective," *Amerasia Journal* 2 [Fall 1974]: 111–57). Still, it was immediately evident that Ueno's testimony was critical. So, after making contact with Ueno and mapping out a strategy for our interviewing session with him, Embrey and I headed north to San Jose. There, in his home on October 30, 1976, he told us his story.

There are those who will say, of course, that Ueno's story of the events at Manzanar does not correspond to the history (objective reality) of what transpired there in 1942, that the remarks of one person do not necessarily constitute historical truth. In addition, others will assert that, because Ueno's testimony seems evasive on the question of who was involved in the beating of Fred Tayama on the evening of December 5, 1942 (the event which

precipitated the arrest and jailing of Ueno and set the stage for an immediate series of confrontations between inmates and governmental authorities,
ending in the deaths of two inmates and the wounding of nine others), his
story, however interesting, is not historically valuable. These are not trivial
concerns, nor do I regard them as such. Precisely because they are concerns
that penetrate to the core of both historical inquiry as a whole and the oral
history approach in particular, they deserve attention here.

Let us consider each of the above concerns, in turn, by illuminating the
conjunction between history, oral history, and Harry Ueno's testimony.
Historians are in general agreement that "history" can be construed both as
"reality" and as "accounts of reality." In the former sense of the word, history
is literally everything that ever happened; in the latter sense, history is an
interpretation of what happened based upon surviving recorded evidence.
Where historians differ, however, is that some, while conceding the latter
to be theoretically valid, remain steadfast in the belief (or at least behave
like they do) that by carefully combing through all of the available source
material they can arrive at an account of some past phenomenon (some
chunk of reality) that is objectively true. This, however, is simply impossible,
not alone because only a limited portion of the past was ever recorded and a
still more limited portion has survived, but also because those sources themselves are usually but accounts of reality. Furthermore, the historian who
interprets them necessarily overlays his own subjective point of view.

Which brings us to oral history. The cross that those who practice it have
had to bear is the charge leveled by believers in "objective history" that oral
historians traffic in tainted sources. Some have said that these sources are
not only distorted by the biases of their informants, but that they are further damaged by the frailty of human memory. Put simply, oral history is
anything but objective and, therefore, unreliable. True! But that makes it a
good deal like any other source of historical documentation, such as letters,
diaries, memoranda, autobiographies, governmental reports, and newspaper
accounts. All are flawed by the ravages of temperament and time.

So where does this leave us? It leaves us with a sense of trying to attain the
unattainable—with a humility that should be the precondition of the historical enterprise. It forces us to recognize that, while objective history is not
fully realizable, historians still must quest for truth through the elimination
of unverifiable and/or implausible interpretations of past happenings. One

way to do this is through applying internal and external checks to historical accounts, whether they exist in the form of primary or secondary documents. Another way to do this is to recognize the special properties of the different documents we employ in the service of historical interpretation.

A case in point is documentation generated by oral history interviews. Instead of dismissing oral testimony, we need to be alert to its usefulness, to appreciate that oral evidence can be used as a corrective and supplement to existing sources, that it can serve as a probe to uncover new problems for consideration, that it can help us to distinguish belief from practice and intention from result, that it can convey how people *felt* about something as well as what they *did*, that it can serve as an antidote to the simplifications and smug certitudes of structural and statistical explanations, and that it can sensitize us to groups and people and issues shielded from our view in more conventional sources. All of these points are taken up with force and clarity by historian Paul Thompson in his magisterial study *Voices of the Past: Oral History* (New York: Oxford University Press, 1974). To quote Thompson: "Oral evidence can achieve something more pervasive, and more fundamental to history. While historians study the actors of history from a distance, their characterizations of their lives, views, and actions will always risk being misdescriptions, projections of the historian's own experience and imagination: a scholarly form of fiction. Oral evidence, by transforming the 'objects' of study into 'subjects,' makes for a history which is not just richer, more vivid and heartrending, but *truer*."

Which brings us full circle to Harry Ueno and his story. I am not prepared to say that everything in his oral memoir is the full truth or that his recollections are free of error. (Who among us can recall every detail of what happened to us thirty years ago and in proper sequence?) But I will say that, on the basis of my understanding of the written and oral sources that I have waded through in my research on the events his interview encompasses, there is precious little he says here that has a false ring to it. Naturally, his memory has faltered in a few instances. Certainly, too, he has placed a construction on events at Manzanar that consistently casts him in a positive role. He could not always see the big picture. But these things are understandable enough. While Ueno may have been regarded by thousands of inmates at Manzanar as the time of the riot (and even now) as a martyr representing their plight, this is the bottom line: he was and is a mortal being.

One reason Ueno's testimony is so valuable, in fact, is that it makes us palpably aware of his mortality. Something my earlier research had disclosed that has been confirmed by Ueno's memoir is that very few people at Manzanar, whether inmates or administrative personnel, knew who he was or had even heard his name until all hell broke loose. Thereafter, his name was on the lips of virtually every person in camp, leastwise until the dust of the disturbance had cleared and relative calm had returned. But even toward the high tide of his recognition, very few were familiar with his features or knew anything about him or his family, even those who clamored to have him set free from the camp jail. He was a charismatic symbol, one who represented something very real and powerful to the community but whose identity was decidedly vague and inchoate. Now, thanks to the textured portrait provided in this interview, he can be seen as a historical actor living in time and space.

Not that he was just an altogether ordinary man while at Manzanar (or afterward, for that matter). His was a heightened ordinariness. He was an inmate, a husband, a father, a cook. But that is not the whole of it. He was also an American citizen unjustifiably detained by his government and incarcerated in a concentration camp holding 10,000 people, US citizens and law-abiding aliens of Japanese ancestry. And, like many others in his situation, he resented, with righteous indignation (justifiably so) his imprisonment and treatment, which he recognized, even then, as racist. Yet what ultimately set him apart from the crowd was that he quietly determined, a few months after his arrival at Manzanar, that he had to take a stand—against the rip-off by Caucasian administrators of duly allocated inmate provisions and against the collaborationist activities of fellow inmates he deemed corrosive to the community's sense of identity and well-being. His determination to stand up for what he considered to be human decency and fair play may well have led him to vigilante action. He says, however, that he did not take part in the attack on Fred Tayama, and I am inclined to believe he is telling the truth. Others who were either at Manzanar at the time or who have traveled through other documents than I have may beg to disagree. So be it.

I mentioned earlier that some readers of Ueno's interview may denigrate its value because of his ambiguous response to the question of who was Fred Tayama's assailant(s). This would be unfortunate. First, it should come as no surprise to anybody that, even if Ueno does have knowledge of who were involved in the beating of Fred Tayama, he would refrain from revealing this information. "Well, maybe I know and maybe I don't. I think there are a lot of things that we don't want to discuss too much, unless we have a proof, you know." This seems an ethical and prudent response, given the possible damage to reputations (and perhaps reprisals) that might follow in the wake of finger-pointing.

Yet another reason why a wholesale rejection of his remarks would be unfortunate is that the reader can reap from Ueno's testimony a rich harvest of information about such matters as the traumatizing experience of a Kibei childhood, the daily rounds of a schoolboy in pre–World War II Hawai'i and Japan, why some people of Japanese ancestry—including American citizens—were driven to take such desperate measures as jumping ship to enter the mainland United States, how Japanese Americans in urban centers like Los Angeles made a living before the JAI uprooted them, and the steep price of wartime survival paid by many inmates. Ueno was first exiled to a desert concentration camp and later forced to endure (bereft of his rights as a US citizen) a maze of isolation camps and segregation centers established for the detention of "troublemakers" in such remote and desolate places as Moab, Utah; Leupp, Arizona; and Tule Lake, California. In other words, even if Ueno had not played a part in the Manzanar uprising, his interview would still abound in value, not only for ethnic historians, but for American social historians and general readers as well.

But Harry Ueno and the Manzanar Riot are practically synonymous. It is precisely because of this fact that most readers will find his story fascinating. Whether they will also find it true is something that I cannot predict, nor would I care to do so. I will say this, though: that when readers judge the veracity of Ueno's testimony, they will also be evaluating the value of oral history as a research tool and source of documentation—at least in this instance. It should be kept in mind that this interview is not an autobiographically produced memoir, but testimony that emerged out of a structured interactive process involving an informant and two interviewers (and that thereafter the interview was transcribed, refined, and interrogated by a historian/editor). While the ultimate accountability as well as the credit for this interview rests with Harry Ueno, the product you will be reading bears a corporate authorship and concomitant responsibility.

APPENDIX C

Retrospective Commentary on Harry Ueno's Admission to His Participation in the December 5, 1942, Beating of Fred Tayama at Manzanar

Upon my sharing of Harry Ueno's confession about his role in the December 5, 1942, assault at Manzanar on JACL leader Fred Tayama with Lane Hirabayashi—the editor of the University Press of Colorado series Asians in the Americas, in which it is now being publicly revealed—he responded with a chain of probing questions. Accordingly, in keeping with the spirit of oral history, let me render the remainder of this appendix in a dialogical format, placing Hirabayashi's questions in italic type and my answers to them in roman type.

Did Ueno's subsequent confession transform at all the observations that you make in your "A Riot of Voices" article about Japanese American narrative/oral communication patterns or style, along the lines of your dialogue with Stanford Lyman's characterizations?

Certainly not. In this article I established that in the 1976 interview Embrey and I did with Ueno he had demonstrated a communication style at variance with what Stanford Lyman had posited for the prototypical Nisei male, save for his one vacillating response to the question I put to him about Tayama's December 5, 1942, beating at Manzanar. Because I sent Ueno a copy of the "A Riot of Voices" article upon its 1994 publication, I suspect that his very reading of it might well have predisposed him later that same year to break his silence to me about his part in that event.

Does Ueno's confession demand revisions of the larger story of the Manzanar riot/revolt?

Not at all. In fact, it strengthens the contention that David Hacker and I made in our 1974 "Manzanar Riot" article that what had occurred at Manzanar in 1942 was not a *riot*, but instead a *revolt*. When Ueno and his accomplices barged into Tayama's barracks apartment and pummeled him, the revolt had moved from dissent and protest to direct action. Their tempered beating of Tayama was akin to the revenge inflicted during World War II upon Quislings in Nazi-occupied European countries by resistance fighters and partisans. Manzanar and the other War Relocation Authority centers may rightly be characterized as American-style concentration camps, but they were nonetheless concentration camps. Their existence meant that, in a certain sense, the Gestapo had come to America, aided and abetted by the Japanese American Citizens League leadership.

Was the fact of Joe Kurihara "taking the blame" for the beating of Fred Tayama just a matter of his having nothing more to lose, since he decided to go "back" to Japan, or were there other motives at play?

My belief is that Kurihara's decision to renounce his US citizenship and go to live in Japan, which he had never even visited before, was the principal reason for his assuming the blame for the Tayama beating. However, as Eileen Tamura has consummately surmised in her outstanding biography of Kurihara—*In Defense of Justice: Joseph Kurihara and the Japanese American Struggle for Equality* (Urbana, IL: University of Illinois Press, 2013), 78–80—this reason assuredly was not the whole story, especially given Kurihara's detestation of Tayama. I am persuaded by Tamura's argument, which she closes with these measured words: "After examining three reports on the [Tayama] beating and none by Kurihara himself, I am left with the conclusion that Kurihara did not actually organize the beating but probably did discuss it with men who were intent on doing so. In this instance, Kurihara was neither hero nor villain, but a person fighting to maintain his dignity and the dignity of other Nikkei caught up in the tangled mesh of the incarceration."

If Fred Tayama's wife had never had contact with Harry Ueno, why would she insist that she "recognized his eyes." It almost seems like she had some pretty strong information that Ueno was party to the attack, and even though she didn't recognize him, she wanted to make sure he was brought to justice and made to pay for his participation.

I cannot provide a concrete response as to why Tayama's wife claimed that she recognized Ueno's eyes. Documentation suggests, although not definitively, that Tayama was alone in the Tayama apartment at the time of Fred Tayama's beating. However, Harry Ueno and Fred Tayama had clashed at public (and possibly private) meetings held at Manzanar prior to the night of the beating, so quite likely the eyes of her husband's fervent accuser left an indelible impression upon Mrs. Tayama's mind. It follows that she would be strongly motivated to suspect Ueno as her husband's assailant and to seek vengeance for his perceived act of violence.

When Ueno decides to "confess" to you, did it signal a shift in your status as a
"historian/insider" to a trusted person, still highly regarded as a scholar and a profes-
sional, but very much as someone who is trusted to pass the real story on to the next
generations. Did something similar pass through your mind?

Trust, of course, is something that eludes precise definition. In some oral
history interviews in which I have been involved, I could sense that it had
either not been gained or only provisionally achieved. However, during the
1976 interview that Sue Kunitomi Embrey and I conducted with Harry Ueno
in 1976, I think that trust was at the heart of the enterprise. It was established
initially by Embrey, who shared the Manzanar experience with Ueno and
who by the time of the interview had established a well-earned reputation as
the chair of the activist Manzanar Committee for seeking hard truths about
the Japanese American Incarceration and communicating those truths in
unadorned terminology like "concentration camps," "racism," and "economic
exploitation." The trust implanted by Embrey was cultivated by me, which
was in large part possible because Ueno had read the 1974 *Amerasia* article I
wrote with David Hacker on the so-called Manzanar "riot," and was privy to
my intimate familiarity with the primary and secondary historical documentation impinging on the pertinent events and developments at Manzanar in 1942
(as well as my perspective on same). I think the accumulated trust gained in
the interview before I raised thorny questions with Ueno about Fred Tayama's
beating is what in fact emboldened me to ask them. But what I think served to
consecrate the trust is when I made the decision to turn off the tape recorder
after the below exchange with him:

Do you mean that you know who did it, but you're just not saying?

Well, maybe I know and maybe I don't. I think there are a lot of things that we
don't want to discuss unless we have proof, you know.

By respecting Ueno's privacy while at the same time reminding him that, at a
time of *his* choosing, he might want to let posterity know what had occurred
on the night of December 5, 1942, at Manzanar, this simultaneously deepened his trust in me and set in motion the chain of events that led to his 1994
confession. In the intervening years between 1974 and 1994 that trust was
nurtured by both an article and a book that Embrey, Betty Mitson, and I had
published that centered on Ueno's World War II experience. In addition, that

trust was watered both by the many times I visited with him at his retirement home in Sunnyvale, California, and on the periodic occasions I enfolded him into public programs for my California State University, Fullerton, students held during the annual Manzanar Pilgrimages spearheaded by Sue Kunitomi Embrey. By the time of his 1994 confession, he not only had a great deal of trust in me, both as a historian and a friend, but also was ready to trust that it was the appropriate and prudent time to let future generations in on what had occurred on that wintry December night in Manzanar.

What does Ueno's confession mean to you, both historically, substantively, but also in terms of the reflexive dimension of your "A Riot of Voices" article (e.g., what it "says" about the diversity of "Nisei character"; what it means in terms of rapport, trust, and the methodological approach entailed in oral history; what it might mean in terms of your own acceptance and regard vis-à-vis crusty old Nisei and Kibei warriors of the "right" and the "left")?

Minimally, what Ueno's confession means to me is that facts are important building blocks to establishing "historical truth." At the same time, however, it signifies to me that the unfolding of this truth-telling is an ongoing process, and that historians, like scrupulously ethical investigative journalists, need at times for various reasons to protect their sources, even if by so doing this results temporarily in an untidy narrative record of historical "reality." I especially feel that conscientious oral historians need to be far more than fact-mongers. While uncovering new and telling facts is an important feature of the work of oral historians, far more important is that they gain the trust and respect of their narrators. This is achieved not merely through how the interviews are conducted, as open-ended interpretive conversational narratives, but also because they are governed by informed consent, which is buttressed by signed agreement forms and typically reinforced by post-interview opportunities for narrators to edit their recorded stories. In the case of my interviews with Japanese Americans and the writings by me that are vitally supported by these interviews, such as "A Riot of Voices," I place a premium upon deconstructing stereotypical representations of Japanese Americans. When I first began my fieldwork and writing vis-à-vis the World War II exclusion and detention of Japanese Americans, I was made aware of the racist epithet by General John DeWitt, the military officer in charge of defending the West Coast after Japan's attack on Pearl Harbor, that epitomized the rationale for incarcerating 120,000 Americans of Japanese ancestry (two-thirds of them US citizens, and the other third law-abiding aliens deemed ineligible for naturalization). Observing that he saw no meaningful difference between Americans of Japanese descent and the enemy population of Japan, DeWitt declared, "A Jap is a Jap." Giving the lie to this gross simplification has been one of the passions guiding my various research endeavors, thus my preoccupation in my interviews with establishing the characterological idiosyncrasies of my informants. It also helps to explain why in "A Riot of Voices" I was prompted to extend and refine Stanford Lyman's brilliant formulation on Nisei interpersonal style.

NOTES

I am indebted to Eva M. McMahan, Kim Lacy Rogers, Lane Hirabayashi, Sue Kunitomi Embrey, Togo Tanaka, Harry Ueno, and Karl and Elaine Yoneda for their contributions to this article.

1. This dissertation was later published. See Debra Gold Hansen, *Strained Sisterhood: Gender and Class in the Boston Female Anti-Slavery Society* (Amherst: University of Massachusetts Press, 1993).

2. See, for example, Ronald J. Grele, ed., *Envelopes of Sound: Six Practitioners Discuss the Method, Theory and Practice of Oral History and Oral Testimony* (Chicago: Precedent, 1975); and Michael Frisch, *A Shared Authority: Essays on the Craft and Meaning of Oral and Public History* (Albany: State University of New York Press, 1990).

3. Renato Rosaldo, *Culture and Truth: The Remaking of Social Analysis* (Boston: Beacon, 1989), 21.

4. The Berkeley conference, "Views from Within: The Japanese American Wartime Internment Experience," was organized by Professor Yuji Ichioka of the Asian American Studies Center at the University of California, Los Angeles, who later edited an anthology based on papers presented there. See Yuji Ichioka, ed., *Views from Within: The Japanese American Evacuation and Resettlement Study* (Los Angeles: Asian American Studies Center, University of California, Los Angeles, 1989).

5. Togo Tanaka, interview by Arthur A. Hansen, August 30, 1973, Oral History 1271b; Karl Yoneda, interview by Ronald L. Larson and Arthur A. Hansen, March 3, 1974, O.H. 1376b; and Harry Y. Ueno, interview by Sue Kunitomi Embrey and Arthur A. Hansen, October 30, 1976, O.H. 1518a. These interviews and others cited in this chapter are housed in the Japanese American Project collection in the Lawrence de Graaf Center for Oral and Public History at California State University, Fullerton, hereafter cited as CSUF O.H. See Shirley E. Stephenson, ed., *Oral History*

Collection: California State University, Fullerton (Fullerton: Oral History Program, California State University, Fullerton, 1985). The Ueno interview has been published in part and in full. See Sue Kunitomi Embrey, Arthur A. Hansen, and Betty E. Mitson, "Dissident Harry Ueno Remembers Manzanar," *California History* 64 (Winter 1985): 16–22; and Sue Kunitomi Embrey, Arthur A. Hansen, and Betty Kulberg Mitson, *Manzanar Martyr: An Interview with Harry Y. Ueno* (Fullerton: Japanese American Project, Oral History Program, California State University, Fullerton, 1986).

6. One of the anonymous two peer reviewers of the *Barbed Voices* manuscript raised the question of what I saw in the reactions of Togo Tanaka, Harry Ueno, and Karl Yoneda to Brian Hayashi's paper. Not knowing this, noted the reviewer, "certainly leaves the reader hanging." To be honest, I was too preoccupied with my own ruminations about the relationships between these three former Manzanarians to observe their reactions to Hayashi's presentation.

7. Arthur A. Hansen and David A. Hacker, "The Manzanar Riot: An Ethnic Perspective," *Amerasia Journal* 2 (Fall 1974): 112–57; Arthur A. Hansen and Betty E. Mitson, eds., *Voices Long Silent: An Oral Inquiry into the Japanese American Evacuation* (Fullerton: Japanese American Project, Oral History Program, California State University, Fullerton, 1974); Vivian McGuckin Raineri, *The Red Angel: The Life and Times of Elaine Black Yoneda, 1906–1988* (New York: International Publishers, 1991); Judy Tachibana, "Indefinite Isolation: The World War II Ordeal of Harry Yoshio Ueno," *Rafu Shimpo*, December 20, 1980; Togo Tanaka, interview by David A. Hacker and Betty E. Mitson, May 19, 1973, O.H. 127la, OHP-CSUF; John Tateishi, *And Justice for All: An Oral History of the Japanese Detention Camps* (New York: Random House, 1884); and Karl G. Yoneda, *Gambatte: Sixty-Year Struggle of a Kibei Worker* (Los Angeles: Asian American Studies Center, University of California, Los Angeles, 1983).

8. Tanaka, interview by Hacker and Mitson; Tanaka, interview by Hansen; Arthur A. Hansen, ed., *Internees*, pt. 1 of *Japanese American World War II Evacuation Project* (Westport, CT: Meckler, 1991); and Hansen and Mitson, *Voices Long Silent*.

9. Dennis Ogawa, *From Jap to Japanese: The Evolution of Japanese American Stereotypes* (Berkeley, CA: McCutchan, 1971).

10. William Peterson, "Success Story, Japanese American Style," in Minako Kurokawa, ed., *Minority Responses* (New York: Random House, 1970); William Peterson, *Japanese Americans* (New York: Random House, 1971).

11. Hansen, *Internees*.

12. Harry H.L. Kitano, *Japanese Americans: The Evolution of a Subculture* (Englewood Cliffs, NJ: Prentice-Hall, 1969); Roger Daniels, *Concentration Camps USA: Japanese Americans and World War II* (New York: Holt, Rinehart and Winston, 1971).

13. Gene Wise, *American Historical Explanations: A Strategy for Grounded Inquiry* (Homewood, IL: Dorsey, 1973).

14. Wise, *American Historical Explanations*, 34.

15. Hilary Conroy and T. Scott Miyakawa, eds., *East across the Pacific: Historical and Sociological Studies of Japanese Immigration and Assimilation* (Santa Barbara, CA: ABC Clio Press, 1972); S. Frank Miyamoto, "An Immigrant Community in America," in *East across the Pacific*, ed. Conroy and Miyakawa, 217–43; and Stanford M. Lyman, "Generation & Character: The Case of Japanese-Americans," in *East across the Pacific*, ed. Conroy and Miyakawa, 279–314.

16. Shotaro Frank Miyamoto, *Social Solidarity among the Japanese in Seattle* (Seattle: University of Washington Press, 1984).

17. Miyamoto, "Immigrant Community," 229.

18. Stanford M. Lyman, "Growing Up among Ghetto Dwellers," in *Personal Sociology*, ed. P. C. Higgins and J. M. Johnson (New York: Praeger, 1988), 51–66.

See the published (and, at times, choleric) exchange over the Nisei interpersonal style between Stanford M. Lyman, "On Nisei Interpersonal Style: A Reply to S. Frank Miyamoto," *Amerasia Journal* 14 (1988): 105–8; and Stanford M. Lyman, "'American' Interpersonal Style and Nikkei Realities: A Rejoinder to S. Frank Miyamoto," *Amerasia Journal* 14 (1988): 115–23; and S. Frank Miyamoto, "Problems of Interpersonal Style among the Nisei," *Amerasia Journal* 13 (1986–87): 29–45; and S. Frank Miyamoto, "Miyamoto Reply to Stanford Lyman," *Amerasia Journal* 14 (1988): 109–13.

19. Although subsequent references to this luminous essay pertain only to direct quotations, my indebtedness to Lyman extends to his entire analysis.

20. Lyman, "Generation & Character," 281–82.

21. Lyman, "Generation & Character," 282.

22. Kitano, *Japanese Americans*. In the words of one authoritative source: "The Nisei generation ranges over a wide span of years and their experiences differ substantially as a result of changing times and different customs in varied locales. There were Nisei among the children whom the San Francisco School Board segregated for a time in 1906. Yet in 1942, at the time of the relocation, the median age of the Nisei was only seventeen. Thus, many of them reached maturity in the postwar years when the social climate was quite different from the prewar period." Robert A. Wilson and Bill Hosokawa, *East to America: A History of the Japanese in the United States* (New York: Morrow, 1982), 163.

23. Lyman, "Generation & Character," 284.

24. Lyman, "Generation & Character," 285.

25. Lyman, "Generation & Character," 286.

26. Lyman, "Generation & Character," 288.

27. Lyman, "Generation & Character," 288.

28. Lyman, "Generation & Character," 288.

29. Lyman, "Generation & Character," 288.

30. Lyman, "Generation & Character," 291.

31. Lyman, "Generation & Character,"290–91.

32. Bill Hosokawa, s (New York: Morrow, 1969); James Hirabayashi, "Nisei: The Quiet American?—A Re-evaluation," *Amerasia Journal* 3 (Summer 1975): 114–29.

33. Lyman, "Generation & Character," 286.

34. Ibid., 282.

35. This observation proved a bone of contention in the exchange between Lyman and Miyamoto, mentioned in an earlier note, regarding the Nisei interpersonal style.

36. Hansen, *Internees*, 103–11.

37. The progressive character of the Nisei Young Democrats within the context of the competing prewar political styles of the Nisei generation has been clarified by Jere Takahashi in "Japanese American Responses to Race Relations: The Formation of Nisei Perspectives," *Amerasia Journal* 9 (Spring/Summer 1982): 42–51.

38. Hansen, *Internees*, 110–11.

39. Togo Tanaka, "How to Survive Racism in America's Free Society," in *Voices Long Silent*, ed. Hansen and Mitson, 84.

40. Tanaka, "How to Survive Racism," 85.

41. Tanaka, "How to Survive Racism," 87.

42. Kitano, *Japanese Americans*, 110.

43. Tanaka, "How to Survive Racism," 96.

44. Tanaka, interview by Hacker and Mitson.

45. Tanaka, interview by Hansen. Both of Tanaka's contemporary treatments of the Manzanar Riot are archived within the Japanese American Evacuation and Resettlement Study collection at the Bancroft Library of the University of California, Berkeley. See Togo Tanaka, "A Report on the Manzanar Riot of Sunday, December 6, 1942," 1942, unpublished manuscript, University of California, Berkeley; and Togo Tanaka, "An Analysis of the Manzanar Incident and Its Aftermath," 1943, unpublished manuscript, University of California, Berkeley. Japanese American Evacuation and Resettlement (JAER), Bancroft Library (BL), University of California, Berkeley (UCB), folders O10.12 and O10.14. Hereafter in this chapter documents in this collection will be cited as JAER.

46. Hansen and Hacker, "Manzanar Riot."

47. Tanaka, interview by Hansen.

48. Tanaka, interview by Hansen.

49. A 1943 report, "Doho," by Togo Tanaka is available in JAER, folder O10.16. This publication has also been discussed in the autobiographical writings of two of its former staff members, Karl Yoneda and James Oda as well as two historians, Ronald C. Larson and Arthur A. Hansen. See Yoneda, *Ganbatte*, 98, 99, 112–14, 117–19,

122; James Oda, *Heroic Struggles of Japanese Americans: Partisan Fighters from America's Concentration Camps* (Los Angeles: privately printed, 1980), 258–65, and Ronald C. Larson and Arthur A. Hansen, "*Doho*: The Japanese-American 'Communist' Press, 1937–1942," 1976, unpublished manuscript, Japanese American Project files, Lawrence de Graaf Center for Oral and Public History, California State University, Fullerton.

50. Tanaka, interview by Hansen.

51. Hansen and Hacker, "Manzanar Riot."

52. Tanaka, interview by Hansen.

53. Tanaka, interview by Hacker and Mitson, emphasis added.

54. Tanaka, interview by Hansen.

55. Hansen, *Internees*, 110.

56. Tanaka, interview by Hansen.

57. Tanaka, interview by Hansen.

58. Embrey, Hansen, and Mitson, *Manzanar Martyr.*

59. Tanaka, interview by Hansen.

60. Tanaka, interview by Hansen.

61. Tanaka, "How to Survive Racism," 98.

62. Tanaka, "How to Survive Racism," 99–100.

63. Tanaka, interview by Hacker and Mitson.

64. Tanaka, interview by Hacker and Mitson.

65. Tanaka, interview by Hansen.

66. Tad Uyeno, "Point of No Return," *Rafu Shimpo*, August 20–October 22, 1973; Ralph P. "Pete" Merritt, *Death Valley–Its Impounded Americans: The Contributions by Americans of Japanese Ancestry during World War II* (Death Valley, CA: Death Valley '49ers, Inc., 1987).

67. Uyeno, "Point of No Return," 20. (This series of articles was later bound together under the same title and paginated collectively. The 20 here corresponds with the bound version's pagination.)

68. Uyeno, "Point of No Return," 20.

69. Karl G. Yoneda and Elaine Black Yoneda, "Manzanar: Another View," *Rafu Shimpo*, December 19, 1973.

70. Elaine Black Yoneda, interview by Arthur A. Hansen, March 2, 1974, O.H. 1377b, OHP-CSUF; Karl G. Yoneda, interview by Ronald L. Larson and Arthur A. Hansen, March 3, 1974, O.H., 1376b, OHP-CSUF.

71. Raineri, *The Red Angel*; Yoneda, *Ganbatte.*

72. I am greatly indebted to a perceptive article by William E. Mitchell about the Jewish American communicative style: "A Goy in the Ghetto: Gentile-Jewish Communication in Fieldwork Research," in *Between Two Worlds: Ethnographic Essays*

on *American Jewry*, ed. Jack Kuglemaas (Ithaca, NY: Cornell University Press, 1988), 225–39.

73. This terminology, although frequently employed inside and out of the Japanese American community, is technically incorrect because Kibei-Nisei were born in the United States, not Japan.

74. Yoneda and Yoneda, "Manzanar."

75. Hansen and Hacker, "Manzanar Riot."

76. Ueno, interview by Embrey and Hansen.

77. Embrey, Hansen, and Mitson, "Dissident Harry Ueno Remembers Manzanar."

78. Embrey, Hansen, and Mitson, *Manzanar Martyr*, 65.

79. Embrey, Hansen, and Mitson, *Manzanar Martyr*.

80. Embrey, Hansen, and Mitson, *Manzanar Martyr*.

81. Frank Chuman, interview by Arthur A. Hansen, January 6, 13, 1975, O.H. 1475a, OHP-CSUF; George Fukasawa, interview by Arthur A. Hansen, August 12, 1974, O.H. 1336, OHP-CSUF; Seiko Ishida, interview by Arthur A. Hansen, O.H. 1338, CSUF-OHP, August 6, 1974; Yoriyuki Kikuchi, interview by Arthur A. Hansen, O.H. 1340, CSUF-OHP, July 29, 1974.

82. Embrey, Hansen, and Mitson, *Manzanar Martyr*.

83. Embrey, Hansen, and Mitson, *Manzanar Martyr*, 2.

84. The War Relocation Authority administration distrusted Kibei as a group and regularly castigated them as "troublemakers" and "disloyals." The wartime situation of the Kibei has been accorded fictionalized representation. See Max Templeman, *Kibei* (Honolulu, HI: Daimax, 1979).

85. Hansen, *Internees*.

86. Embrey, Hansen, and Mitson, *Manzanar Martyr*, 48–49.

87. Eric J. Hobsbawm, "From Social History to the History of Society," in *Historical Studies Today*, ed. Felix Gilbert and Stephen R. Graubard (New York: Norton, 1972), 1–26.

88. Steven Fugita and David J. O'Brien, *The Japanese American Experience* (Bloomington: Indiana University Press, 1991).

89. Fugita and O'Brien, *Japanese American Experience*, 4.

90. The families of Karl Yoneda and Harry Ueno came from Hiroshima Prefecture, whereas Togo Tanaka traced his family roots back to Yamaguichi.

91. Yuji Ichioka, "Recent Japanese Scholarship on the Origins and Causes of Japanese Immigration," *Immigration History Newsletter* 15 (November 1983): 2–7; Yuji Ichioka, *Issei: The World of the First Generation Immigrants, 1885–1924* (New York: Morrow, 1988); Yasuo Wakatsuke, "Japanese Emigration to the United States, 1866–1924: A Monograph," *Perspectives in American History* 12 (1979): 387–514.

92. Fugita and O'Brien, *Japanese American Experience*, 34–35.

93. The short stories by the late Nisei writer Toshio Mori nicely capture life in pre–World War II Japanese America. See Toshio Mori, *Yokohama, California* (Seattle: University of Washington Press, 1985).

94. I employ this term here not in the histrionic, politically correct manner of some JAI scholars, but because it is descriptive of the historical reality experienced by Togo Tanaka, Karl Yoneda, and Harrv Ueno.

95. Recently, a UC Berkeley professor, Lawrence Levine, celebrated for his innovative approach to African American cultural history, capsulized the larger point of this article:

> Contemporary scholars have demonstrated again and again that, in penetrating the culture of a neglected group, historians often find more than they bargained for. What looked like a group becomes an amalgam of groups; what looked like a culture becomes a series of cultures. Americans on the eve of World War II might have seen only a monolith when they looked at Japanese Americans, but historians must see something vastly more complicated: The Issei born in Japan and legally barred from becoming U. S. citizens, the Nisei, born and raised here and thus citizens by birth, the Kibei, born here but raised in Japan and thus legally Americans and culturally Japanese, as well as those who lived in cities and those who lived on farms, those who struggled to maintain the old ways and those who hungered for acculturation. The complexity I speak of is not the complexity of specialized languages or esoteric methodologies but the complexity of people and the cultures they create.

See Lawrence W. Levine, "The Unpredictable Past: Reflections on Recent American Historiography," in *The Unpredictable Past: Explorations in American Cultural History*, ed. Lawrence Levine (New York: Oxford University Press, 1993), 11–12.

4

TAKING IT TO THE LIMIT

Cultural Politics and Community Control in the
Gila River Relocation Center, 1942–1943

During my editorship of the Oral History Review *in the 1980s I regularly taught a course I developed for the American Studies Department at California State University, Fullerton, "American Cultural Radicalism." It placed a premium on the operation of cultural politics, extending from the time of the Puritans in the sixteenth century to the profusion of dissident ideas, events, and styles that became manifest in the mid-1950s and still persisted in the present day.*

Simultaneously in this decade, while I broadened and deepened my study of resistance activity within the World War II Japanese American detention centers, I also paid increasing attention in my archival scholarship and oral history interviewing to the efforts of those wartime Japanese American and non-Japanese American social scientists who served as field researchers at selected War Relocation Authority centers for three different research groups: the WRA-sponsored Community Analysis

This essay was first published in *Arizona and the West* (© 1985) and is reproduced with permission.

DOI: 10.5876/9781607328124.c004

Section; Bureau of Sociological Research, under the Office of Indian Affairs; and the Japanese American Evacuation and Resettlement Study, sponsored by the University of California, Berkeley.

In the early 1980s, when engaged in researching the extent and variety of resistance activity in the WRA camps via the Japanese American Evacuation and Resettlement Study archives housed at Berkeley's Bancroft Library, I stumbled upon a remarkable cache of research data generated primarily by two of the study's researchers based at the Gila River War Relocation Center in south-central Arizona, Robert Spencer and (to a lesser extent) Charles Kikuchi. These data impinged upon a significant event of resistance that first materialized at the Gila camp in late November of 1942, right after a protracted general strike staged earlier that month at another Arizona WRA incarceration facility, Poston, and just before a major "riot" erupted at the WRA's Manzanar concentration camp in early December. I was sufficiently moved by the Gila "incident" to try and make some cultural sense out of it, which I ultimately did in a 1985 article in the University of Arizona Press–sponsored journal Arizona and the West. *It is that article, anchored by the "paradigm drama" theory developed by American studies scholar Gene Wise, which follows this headnote.*

On Tuesday evening, January 5, 1943, invited guests gathered for a sumptuous New Year's banquet in the barracks mess hall of Block 16 in the Canal Camp of the Gila River Relocation Center, located about thirty miles southeast of Phoenix near the town of Rivers in arid south-central Arizona. At the head table sat four administrators of Canal's War Relocation Authority (WRA): Lewis Korn, assistant project director; Morton Gaba, assistant director of community services; W. E. Williamson, director of internal security; and Francis Frederick, an associate director of internal security. Seated next to them were four representatives of the Japanese American incarcerees: Charles Yonezu, captain of the wardens (police); Joseph Omachi, legal counsel; Kenzo Ogasawara, editor of the Japanese section of the *Gila News-Courier*; and Mr. Omai, chairman of Block 16. Sitting at other tables were some 150 elegantly attired inmates (only twenty of whom were women) from the Canal Camp and the neighboring Butte Camp, which together constituted the Gila River Relocation Center. A majority were affiliated with one or more detainee organizations—the Kenkyu-kai (study or investigative group);

the Engeibu (dramatic society); and the Sumo Club. The host for the evening was Kiyoshi Tani, a prominent member of the Kenkyu-kai who held no official place in Gila's chain of command. A graduate of Japan's prestigious Waseda University, Tani was a reporter and distributor for the *Rocky Nippon*, a semiweekly Japanese American newspaper published in Denver, Colorado. He had personally compiled the guest list from among the more than 13,000 inmates at the Gila River center.

At about 7:30 p.m., Tani delivered a welcoming speech in Japanese and was followed by assistant project director Korn, who extended project director Leroy Bennett's apologies for being unable to attend the dinner. At the close of the speechmaking, a special staff of incarcerated cooks, whom Tani had hired for the occasion, served a resplendent meal. As one of the honored guests later recalled: "The main course of the dinner itself was fried chicken, a delicacy which had never been served at any time [before] at this project [while] mock turtle soup, pineapple and cottage cheese salad, vegetables, fruits, apple pie, jello, soda water and coffee supplied the trimmings." These Western dishes were supplemented by an assortment of traditional Japanese ones. Tani also treated the guests to bourbon highballs and had bottles of bourbon and soda water placed on each table for refills. The host personally poured drinks for the head table, remarking with a sly smile: "Have some Japan tea." A mood of revelry and celebration pervaded the evening, with repeated toasts to Chota Hirokane—one of the older Kenkyu-kai members present. The banquet ended at about 11:00 p.m.[1]

The foregoing scene from a World War II concentration camp experience of evicted Japanese Americans abounds in interpretive possibilities. One interpretation is that harmony and goodwill prevailed between WRA administrators and imprisoned Japanese Americans. This is consonant with the idea that, however much Japanese Americans deplored their exclusion and incarceration, they nonetheless appreciated their kindly, liberal keepers in the camps and readily complied with administrative directives. Such an interpretation is soothing to the consciences of those committed to seeing all historical experience in America, however horrendous, emerge as progress. But it does not bear close scrutiny. Nonetheless, precisely this sort of interpretation dominated the literature on the camps through the 1960s.

An alternative interpretation of the banquet—the one advanced here—is that it represented a strategic species of cultural politics mounted by a portion of the confined population against white WRA leaders and their Japanese American accomplices. This interpretation resonates with the resistance historiography that emerged in the early 1970s and has since gained momentum and greater acceptance.[2] The key documentation for this study is an array of unpublished reports written by Robert F. Spencer, a Japanese American and Resettlement Study (JERS) anthropologist stationed at the Gila center and his corps of Japanese American research associates. Working under UC Berkeley sociologist Dorothy Swaine Thomas, this team of inexperienced social science researchers assembled a remarkable documentary record of one of the most turbulent periods in the camp's history, the winter months of 1942–43. While it suffers in ethnographic sophistication, the material is notable for its breadth of coverage and degree of candor. Surprisingly, historians of the Japanese American Incarceration (JAI) have not accorded it systematic attention.[3]

This neglect has not been salutary, as the JERS material permits a detailed reconstruction of colorful events like the Tani banquet. It also enables historians to place these events within the context of resistance activity, not only at the Gila center but at the nine other WRA camps as well. Moreover, it encourages an enlarged understanding of the relationship of resistance activity in the camps to a special brand of cultural politics practiced there—whereby the function of politics was largely moral, psychological, and cultural and wherein to commit oneself politically carried implications for personal and collective salvation.

To capitalize upon this rich sociocultural documentation requires a methodological approach adapted from a recent development in the field of American culture studies. It involves treating the Tani banquet not merely as an interesting historical event, but rather as a "representative paradigm drama." "Paradigm" refers to an exemplary cultural act within a given community, while the "paradigm drama" metaphor is drawn from the theater to point up the dynamic, transactional nature of a cultural act—the continual dialogue between actors and audience. As for "representative paradigm drama," it conveys a cultural act that dramatizes the "inherent possibilities in a cultural situation . . . [and] spotlight[s] changing boundaries of what is possible for a person or a group at a particular time and in a particular place and in a particular milieu."[4]

The banquet must be placed in a proper context. A month earlier there had been a brutal beating in the Canal Camp. On the evening of November 30, 1942, inmate Takeo Tada was waylaid and severely battered about the head and left arm with ironwood clubs wielded by five other inmates. Tada identified only one of his assailants, Chota Hirokane, who, upon being questioned by the Internal Security Department, readily acknowledged his guilt. He claimed that he had acted alone but with the full consent of the community and on their behalf. An Issei (first-generation Japanese American) father of seven children, Hirokane hoped to alert the administration to the grievances of the disaffected Issei in the camp. Following a hearing a few days later, acting project director Robert Cozzens pronounced Hirokane guilty of assault and sentenced him to the nearby Pinal County Jail. Released on January 5, 1943, Hirokane returned to the Canal Camp and was toasted as a hero at the Tani dinner.[5]

It seems quite evident as to why Hirokane's avowed complicity in the beating of Tada had elevated him to the status of a cultural hero: the inmate community viewed Tada as a traitor. A Nisei (second-generation Japanese American), he belonged to the group of Japanese Americans who, because they had been sent to Japan by their Issei parents for an education, were classified as Kibei. Unlike most Kibei, however, whose cultural and linguistic background disposed them toward identifying with Issei ideas, beliefs, and values, Tada thought and behaved like a typical Nisei. A prewar graduate of Fresno State College in the agricultural heartland of central California, he was at the time of the JAI's onset employed in Los Angeles as secretary of the Japanese Chamber of Commerce, a position that involved him in constant interaction with representatives of the non-Japanese commercial and civic communities. This is no doubt why, after his arrival at the Turlock (California) Assembly Center on May 17, 1942, he was appointed by the Wartime Civilian Control Administration (WCCA) as one of the four members on the Turlock Center Council, which acted as a liaison between the camp administration and inmates.[6]

Interestingly enough, another member of the Center Council was Joseph Omachi, who would later occupy a seat at the head table during the Tani dinner. A Nisei graduate of the University of California, Berkeley, and its Hastings College of Law, Omachi had been a practicing attorney at Stockton before his detention. At Turlock he coupled his duties on the Center Council with being chairman of the Public Welfare and Sanitation Department. There he came into contact with Takeo Tada, who was assigned to the department as a foreman to develop and execute clothing allowance policies. While serving in this capacity, Tada's troubles began.

Tada became a victim of circumstances during the chaotic summer of 1942. At that time most of the Turlock population was transferred to the Canal Camp in Arizona, and the reins of administrative leadership passed from the WCCA (a military agency) to the WRA (a civilian agency). During the transition, many transferees failed to receive expected clothing issues. Because Tada was responsible for clothing requisitions, they blamed him for being denied allotments that, as they later discovered at the Gila center, had been received by transfers from other assembly centers. He also had shared the blame for a shortage of coupon books for purchases at the Turlock store. The situation especially affected the large contingent of Issei and Kibei bachelors housed in the single men's barracks. When the Turlock project director gave Tada the thankless task of translating into Japanese the grim news that the coupon supply had been exhausted and no more were forthcoming, the angry incarcerees reacted violently, overturning the small booth used to issue coupon books and threatening the administration building.[7]

This community hatred followed Tada to the Canal Camp in late July of 1942. Former Turlock detainees made up approximately 60 percent of Canal's population of some 5,000 Japanese Americans. For a few months Tada was spared the full fury of his accusers, while the community adjusted to the desert heat and struggled with a severe housing shortage. This situation changed when the camp became settled, and before long it was rumored that Tada and others had profited from their positions of authority. By September detainees were demanding that Tada explain his activities at Turlock. To prove his innocence of wrongdoing, he enlisted the aid of former associates like Joseph Omachi. The scorn for Tada was so great, however, that not only were his explanations turned aside with a deaf ear, but those such as Omachi, who insisted that Tada was not culpable, "were regarded with contempt and . . . branded as being in conspiracy to the alleged wrong."[8]

Tada's activities at the Canal Camp generated additional animosity. A case in point was his appointment to the post of chief detainee assistant in the Community Activities Section (CAS) of the Community Services Division. In this position, Tada had the primary responsibility for supervising entertainment and organizing clubs among the inmates. An acute lack of equipment and supplies quickly complicated his work. Had it not been for Tada's troubles with clothing and coupon books at Turlock, however, this shortage might have been construed by those at Canal as falling outside his control. But a perspective once formed, especially in the crucible of communal passion, is extremely difficult to revise. Thus, the Canal community tarred Tada with the Turlockian brush and assigned blame for the shortage to favoritism, neglect of duty, and probable malfeasance on his part.[9]

Tada was held most accountable for the sin of favoritism. A prime example was his supposed favoring of the University Club over the Kibei Club. While the CAS officially recognized and provided a recreation hall for the University Club, it denied recognition and a meeting place to the Kibei Club. The decision in the matter rested with Tada's two Caucasian superiors, Luther Hoffman (who presided over community services for the two camps) and Morton Gaba, his deputy at Canal. However, it was Tada who had to communicate and defend their policy decision to the Kibei Club petitioners. In fact, on the very evening of his beating, Tada had gone to a gathering of the Kibei Club to explain what steps were required before their petition for formal recognition would be honored. They had to (1) accept an administratively appointed executive secretary to coordinate their affairs and (2) conduct their proceedings in English rather than in the Japanese language.

The Canal community, perhaps with some justification, believed that Tada was not merely the transmitter of administrative policy but rather the individual who, through his suggestions, had been instrumental in its conception. It was certainly consistent with his general outlook that he should favor a group like the University Club and hamstring the operations of one like the Kibei Club. After all, the University Club had a membership of some thirty-five to forty Nisei, most of whom were university graduates like Tada himself. Moreover, the orientation of the membership tended, like his own, to be aggressively American, as seen through the club's active promotion of such causes in camp as the Americanization program, the camouflage net factory (a war industry with employment restricted to citizen workers), and enlistment in the army's Military Intelligence Service Language School (whereby volunteers would be trained to place their sharpened Japanese language skills at the service of the American war effort against Japan). Still further, many of the men and women in the University Club had held pre-war membership in the Japanese American Citizens League (JACL), a group that during the JAI had come to be reviled by the inmates for allegedly hav-ing gone so far in their accommodation with government authorities as to supply them with the names of those in the community, particularly Issei and Kibei, whom they regarded as subversive or potentially subversive to the American cause. So great, in fact, was the animosity toward the JACL by the time of the community's incarceration in "assembly centers" that they tagged many of the leaders with the pernicious label of *inu* (dog, informer) and threatened and/or victimized them with beatings. Accordingly, the WCCA administration prudently adopted a policy disallowing formal orga-nization of JACL chapters.[10]

In contrast, the Kibei Club, boasting a membership of between 200 and 500 men and women, was dedicated to the promotion of Japanese cultural heritage. Owing to their limited English language skills and relative unfamil-iarity with American political and social processes, the Kibei were relegated to a second-class status at the camp. This was especially true for those who had returned to the United States from Japan just prior to the war. Frustrated and resentful over being spurned and placed on the defensive, the Kibei Club championed things identifiable with the Japanese way of life—language, lit-erature, customs, communal practices, and cultural arts. Disgruntled with the general disinterest by many Nisei (and "renegade Kibei" like Takeo Tada) in their Japanese heritage, Kibei members forged a close alliance with their Issei parents. They placed Issei on their club advisory board and enthusias-tically supported activities favored by Issei groups such as the Sumo Club, the Engeibu, and the Kenkyu-kai. Significantly, these Kibei-Issei groups later supplied most of the guests at the Tani dinner.[11]

Takeo Tada's reputation also was tarnished by his membership on the Temporary Community Council, a body created in October of 1942 that contributed to the emergence of the Kenkyu-kai. According to WRA policy, this council was to be one of the first steps toward forming a democratic government in each camp. At Canal the council was elected from each of the camp's twenty-seven blocks. All inmates over age sixteen could vote, but only those with citizen status could hold council seats. Under US law, Issei were regarded as aliens ineligible for citizenship. Thus, the Nisei and Kibei controlled the community council.

Nevertheless, Issei became involved in the council both as advisers and appointees to committees. In addition, a small number of intensely patriotic Issei had won American citizenship as a result of their participation in World War I and thus were eligible for council membership. These war veterans, however, were unpopular with most of the Issei and were ignored by most Nisei. As a rule, these war veterans became less involved with council matters than with advocating assorted chauvinistic causes. Forming themselves into the Ex-Servicemen's Club, these proud members of the American Legion and the JACL who had in prewar days sponsored Boy Scout troops, organized observances on behalf of national holidays, and presided at flag-raising ceremonies now volunteered themselves at Canal as workers in the camouflage net factory and as teachers for the army language school.[12]

Perhaps because of his bilingual abilities, his experience as a member of the Center Council at the Turlock Assembly Center, and his popularity among the Nisei residents of his block, Takeo Tada was elected as the representative for Block 9 on the Temporary Community Council. Dr. William Furuta, a bacteriologist with a doctorate from the University of Illinois, was selected to chair the camp council. Furuta had been Tada's supervisor at Turlock. Moreover, Tada's defender and fellow councilman at Turlock, Joseph Omachi, was appointed to head a special Constitutional Commission to draw up provisions for a permanent community council. Teizo Yahanda, an Issei graduate of the University of California, Berkeley and an outspoken advocate of the JACL and the Nisei political leadership in the camp, also was active in council affairs and served on Omachi's constitutional commission.[13]

Although the Temporary Community Council was the official representative body at Canal, it was not the most powerful inmate political organization. Months before the council's formation, during the scorching summer days when Canal was taking shape as a settled community, each block (comprising 250 to 300 people) either elected or authorized a delegation to appoint a temporary manager to look after the physical well-being of the residents. Because of Japanese age and gender expectations for people with authority, most of the managers were male Issei. Unlike members of the Temporary Community Council, they were regarded as part of the camp Work Corps and received a small stipend from the government. It was understood that after November of 1942, general elections would be held in the respective blocks to confirm the selection of these managers. In most instances, no elections were held, and the same individuals remained in office.

The WRA and camp administrators hoped to restrict block managers to nonpolitical functions and reserve political power to the representatives on the Temporary Community Council. In practice, however, the block manager became a political force who directed community affairs and executed the details of local government. This came about in two ways: (1) through the activities of block councils and (2) by block managers through the block councils, applying pressure on representatives to the Temporary Community Council.[14]

In each block a group of older Issei men coalesced around the manager to constitute a council. The council became the moving political spirit by controlling decisions at meetings. Nisei participation at these meetings was limited. The deliberations generally were conducted in Japanese, and the younger Nisei were unable to express themselves freely and unabashedly in the mother tongue. Also, the council conducted business in patriarchal Japanese fashion, wherein "the older men" (Issei) voiced their opinions and then looked "with scorn and annoyance on the younger people who tried to make themselves heard."[15]

Although the council set dates for meeting, the block chairman (who frequently was also the block manager) called and presided over the gatherings. Unlike the manager, the chairman received no pay. The two positions were alike, however, in that an older Issei male (e.g., Chota Hirokane, the alleged assailant of Takeo Tada, managed Block 7) usually held the position. The chairman worked closely with the manager, and both were regarded as major political figures in their block.

As the manager, chairman, and other members of the block council elected a citizen representative to the Temporary Community Council for deciding upon matters pertaining to the entire community, they sought to instruct this representative on how to vote. When councilmen resisted guidance by voting independently or in deference to the desires of the camp administration, the Issei leadership in the block resorted to criticism and censure, both directly and indirectly through the neighborhood and the family. A handful resisted the pressure for a while, but ultimately they either complied or tendered their resignation.

Still the existence of the council rankled the Issei leadership. When in September the WRA had announced its projected creation and composition, dissenting Issei had circulated a resolution to extend eligibility on the council to noncitizens. Although twenty-one blocks supported the proposal, the WRA rejected the resolution on several grounds: (1) the government wished to stress that the Nisei's American citizenship was important, and (2) the Nisei, being "more Americanized" than the Issei, were more likely to act in keeping with American institutions and practices.[16]

The general character of the council's action also disturbed the Issei leaders. While they could control the voting behavior of the councilmen, they could not prevent the camp administration from placing before the council issues whose character might be offensive and contrary to the community welfare. One such issue was the proposed camouflage net factory. Issei objected to the factory for several reasons. First, as aliens, they were forbidden under international law to engage in war work. Second, Nisei employed in the factory could earn as much as triple the wages received by other incarcerees under the stringent camp wage structure. Third, the transfer of Nisei workers from places like the block mess halls meant that these physically demanding jobs had to be filled largely by Issei women. And fourth, by working in the net factory, Nisei were aiding in "the killing of their cousins in Japan."

Councilmen were pressured in two directions. While Issei leaders lobbied to reject the net factory, the project director and the Employment Division urged acceptance of the idea. The councilmen could never impress their constituency with the fact that the factory would provide community benefits through a revolving fund made up from monies earned by its Nisei workers. Either the inmates were unwilling to listen, or they believed that allocation of the monies through the Temporary Community Council would mean preferential treatment toward the Nisei. So it went also with other issues foisted upon the council by the administration—such as the recruitment of volunteers for the army language school.[17]

The influence of the council suffered when such proposals were supported by the center's newspaper, the *Gila News-Courier*. The paper was primarily a mouthpiece for WRA and administration policies and for spotlighting Nisei social activities and concerns. A special problem was the editor, Ken Tashiro, who was born in New England. An older Nisei (about thirty-five years of age), he had acquired a speaking knowledge of Japanese only after graduation from high school. More damning in the Issei view, however, was his close association with Larry Tajiri, editor of the JACL's official organ, the *Pacific Citizen*. Moreover, Tashiro was one of the principal leaders of the JACL chapter in Gila's Butte Camp (the first—and only—chartered within any of the ten WRA centers).[18]

Hostility toward Tashiro and the *News-Courier* pointed up a larger problem—the Issei feeling of frustration that "practically all of the key positions at the project under the administration were being manned by the Nisei and Kibei. . . . [and] that the younger element in the community were being given positions of responsibility out of proportion to their ability and experience and that those positions should be filled by more capable Issei workers." The roots of the problem extended back to the "assembly centers." At Turlock, for example, only one of the four members on the community council had been an Issei, and that individual was a woman who tended to view matters from a Nisei perspective. The situation was even more alarming at Canal. Here both the newspaper editor and the inmate heads of such crucial areas as housing, clothing, and recreation were persons holding American citizenship.[19]

This situation often produced unfortunate consequences. A striking example was the administrative selection of two men to be central block managers for the Butte and Canal camps. As these persons had to coordinate with the block managers, they had to be men whom the managers respected and trusted. As it turned out, both appointees were failures. The central block manager at Butte was Henry Miyake, an older Hawai'i-born Nisei who had promoted the establishment of a JACL chapter there. At Canal the appointee was Teizo Yahanda, an Issei whose involvement with the Temporary Community Council and advocacy of cooperation with the camp administration caused him to be ignored by the block managers.[20]

By November of 1942, disaffected Issei leadership decided to take more drastic action. They could easily ignore the central block manager, Yahanda, but numerous problems persisted. Living quarters were inadequate, stoves had not arrived, the food lacked quality, clothing allowances were short, and toilet and washing facilities were abominable. Issei leaders believed that these problems should be receiving the attention of the Temporary Community Council and the camp newspaper rather than such divisive and inflammatory items as the camouflage net factory, the army language school, and the

JACL. The Issei blamed camp conditions on a system whereby the government, army, WRA, and camp authorities had ignored the natural leaders of the Japanese American community and leaned on artificial "leadership" of inexperienced, incompetent, and misguided citizen appointees like Takeo Tada and his crowd.[21]

To this point, the Issei had sought political solutions for what were primarily cultural problems (i.e., the destruction of traditional community arrangements). They now turned to cultural solutions for the overarching political problem of being at the mercy of external forces over which they had little control. To begin with, they blamed the United States for their plight and sought comfort in romanticized recollections of their early lives in the rural villages of Japan. By so doing, they cauterized their wounded feelings and regained a measure of personal inner wholeness. On another level, the Issei set about to create a new sense of community by using the cultural resources at their disposal. As a result of social engineering, they had been victimized by institutional arrangements undermining their personal and collective identities. What was now called for was a brand of cultural politics that refashioned their institutions into recognizable traditional forms and brought about a transformation of identity. Specifically, the Caucasian administration and their inmate accomplices had to be educated to a more humanistic point of view.

To bring this about, the Issei had to employ unattractive means. As one historian has properly observed: "cultural politics is not . . . a completely attractive phenomenon . . . [since] tribalism does things . . . from which it is natural to recoil." But the ends sought in this instance were moral. If the psychological division within the Canal population was to be healed, a more traditional Japanese cultural order had to be ushered in, with communal responsibility exalted over personal aggrandizement. To create such a community, the Issei had to affect consciousness as well as political arrangements, a goal which could be realized more readily through appeals to internalized cultural impulses than to any explicit ideology.[22]

This explains the seemingly spontaneous emergence of the Kenkyu-kai in the Canal Camp during the late fall of 1942. Composed of Issei and Kibei, the organization probably began as a study or investigative group at Turlock at the time of the clothing and coupon book complaints. But it was during a period of crisis at Canal that the Kenkyu-kai achieved its fullest potential as a political/cultural pressure group. Although the exact membership is unknown, some 500 men, mostly Issei family heads, joined its ranks. The numbers, however, are deceptive. Most of the membership was passive, so a few Issei leaders controlled the Kenkyu-kai (much as in block meetings). But in moments of crisis, Kenkyu-kai influence radiated beyond its active nucleus and encompassed a considerable portion—perhaps a majority—of the total camp population.

The preponderant influence of the Kenkyu-kai came about in part because its membership overlapped and interpenetrated a medley of other formal and informal detainee groups emphasizing Japanese cultural forms and practices—e.g., the Engeibu, the Sumo Club, the Bungei-kai (literary society), the Kibei Club, the Zen Buddhists, the Judo Club, the Goh-Shogi organization (chess and checker club), and assorted gambling houses. In addition, the Kenkyu-kai could mobilize the support of the staff of the camp's large mess operations staff, since it was dominated by Issei.[23]

A more powerful reason for the Kenkyu-kai's pervasive influence in Canal was the nature of the camp's population. At neighboring Butte the Japanese Americans were drawn from urban, suburban, and rural backgrounds. Their cultural allegiances were somewhat evenly distributed between traditional Japanese affiliations (Buddhism and *kenjin-kai*, or prefectural organizations) and modern Americanized ties (Christianity and the JACL). At Canal the overwhelming majority of incarcerees came from rural areas in California's Sacramento delta and San Joaquin Valley, where traditional Japanese behavior prevailed not only among the Issei and Kibei, but also the Nisei.

Because of this cultural hegemony, the Kenkyu-kai easily cut across lines of class, gender, generation, and geographical origins.[24] As its leadership was largely sub rosa, it cannot accurately be identified. The best that can be said is that the Kenkyu-kai's most visible spokespersons were three older Issei men. The first of these was a man by the name of Fujimoto, who was not only an adviser to the Kibei Club and head of the Sumo Club but also a person with a reputation for being anti-administration and anti-Nisei leadership. The second was Chota Hirokane, and the third was Kiyoshi Tani, the most avowed and loquacious of the trio.[25]

The purpose of the Kenkyu-kai was to investigate conditions in the Canal Camp and recommend improvements in housing, mess operations, and other areas involving community welfare. To this end, the organization submitted to acting project director Robert Cozzens "a written notice signed by about five hundred Gila residents." They advised that the WRA proposal for limited self-government with a council composed only of US citizens was doomed to fail because of the inexperience of the eligible members. The inmates proposed a plan "under which they would organize a system of government for the center." The moving force behind the notice included Chota Hirokane, along with the most zealous Issei men living in Canal's bachelor barracks.[26]

The Kenkyu-kai also requested permission to launch a newspaper at Canal to balance the Butte-based *News-Courier*. Aware of his considerable prewar journalism experience, the Kenkyu-kai proposed Kiyoshi Tani as editor of the new paper. While their request was pending, the group advised Canal residents to ignore the *News-Courier* and read instead the *Rocky Nippon*.[27]

The Kenkyu-kai took more direct, and less democratic, steps to promote cultural and political solidarity at Canal. According to JERS analyst Joseph Omachi: "Instead of pursuing study and research into matters of community welfare this group began investigating certain individuals among the inmates who were employed in the more important positions at the center, picking out alleged faults and criticism based principally upon unfounded rumors rather than upon confirmed facts." Omachi, however, was hardly a disinterested observer. As chairman of the Constitutional Commission and chief detainee counsel in Canal, he was himself under surveillance by the Kenkyu-kai. What most bothered Omachi were the consequences of this sort of investigative work. In their zeal, he pointed out, the Kenkyu-kai made up "a so-called 'black-list' citing the names of a number of persons to be 'taken care of.'"[28]

The blacklist was very revealing. At the top was Takeo Tada, whose notoriety among the inmates continued to grow. In addition to his presumed administrative failures at Turlock and Canal, his fellow inmates regarded his demeanor as un-Japanese. They complained that Tada "showed off too much" and acted like a "big shot." He flattered alien and citizen detainees alike in order "to gain their conformity to the rules of Canal's Caucasian administration." It was rumored, too, that Tada had tricked a number of Nisei and Kibei into enlisting in the army language school by intimating that he also was volunteering his services. When the students departed and Tada remained behind, he again was accused of bad faith. Actually, Tada had volunteered as a teacher for the school and so was not required to report with the students. Nonetheless, the community grumbled that Tada had deceived and betrayed them.[29]

It was also widely felt that Tada had persistently sought to persuade his CAS superiors to deny formal recognition not only to the Kibei Club but also the Engeibu, the Issei dramatic club. Even after the CAS recognized the Engeibu, Tada used his influence to restrict their meetings to an open-air area of the camp. Given the club's intimate connection with the Kenkyu-kai, Tada's actions furthered blackened his name in Canal.

Immediately following Tada on the Kenkyu-kai blacklist were Teizo Yahanda, the Issei supporter of the JACL and the Temporary Community Council, and Dr. William Furuta, the Nisei chairman of the council. Next came Tada's friend and roommate, Charles Yonezu. Yonezu became unpopular as the recreation head at Turlock. But what really galvanized community opposition was his appointment in early October of 1942 and subsequent activities as Canal Camp's captain of the wardens. What the community questioned was not his ability to discharge his duties but his apparent eagerness to do so.[30]

At the time of Yonezu's appointment, Chief W. E. Williamson was completing a reorganization of internal security at the Gila center. A graduate of the University of California Police School, he instructed the wardens in modern criminology procedures, outfitted them in khaki uniforms, and provided cars and horses to patrol the camp. The appointment of Yonezu to head the sixty-plus wardens constituting Canal's police force nicely complemented Williamson's plans for "a model police organization of a purely impersonal and objective nature." However, the wardens—most were Nisei—strongly resisted Williamson's "grandiose ideas" and felt that he forgot that his wardens had to closely associate and "live with the residents of the community."[31]

Issei, Kibei, and Hawai'i Nisei strongly opposed Williamson's actions. Less Americanized and therefore less attuned to bureaucratic authority structures, these men were unwilling to see themselves socially distanced from the rest of the community. Even Associate Chief Francis Frederick denounced Williamson's innovations. Frederick, who had served as a guard at New York's Dannemora Prison before being employed by the WRA, observed that the new organization "was modeled along metropolitan police lines and [was] not applicable to a community of concentrated population such as a relocation center." Many wardens agreed and supported Frederick in a protracted struggle against Williamson. Charles Yonezu, on the other hand, sided with the chief, and for that reason his name appeared on the Kenkyu-kai blacklist. Like his close associate Tada, Yonezu appeared to the community to be more concerned with self-promotion and social control than with the well-being of the Canal community.[32]

Joseph Omachi, Goro Yamamoto, George Kawahara, and a miscellany of less prominent (largely Nisei) supervisors rounded out the blacklist. Yamamoto was Tada's chief assistant in CAS and, although a Kibei, strongly supported his superior's refusal to recognize the Kibei Club. Kawahara, an older Hawai'i Nisei, was assistant to central block manager Teizo Yahanda, whose name appeared directly below Tada's on the blacklist. Both Yamamoto and Kawahara later would be among the special guests at the Tani dinner (although neither would be seated at the head table).

Apparently, the Kenkyu-kai intended simultaneously to assault all of the individuals included on the blacklist. Chota Hirokane, therefore, probably jumped the gun when he attacked Takeo Tada on the night of November 30, soon after Tada left a meeting of the Engeibu, where he had been criticized for ignoring various demands given him as a staff member of the CAS. The evening after Hirokane's arrest, petitions were circulated condemning his incarceration and demanding the removal of Tada as a camp official. In an impassioned speech before a mass meeting, Kiyoshi Tani stated that, should Hirokane be convicted and severely sentenced, the Kenkyu-kai would conduct more beatings of suspected accommodationists and launch a general strike of the sort recently enacted at Poston, the other WRA center in Arizona. Tani emphasized that Hirokane had acted on behalf of the entire community and had been driven to violence as the only way the Issei and Kibei could force the camp administration to consider their problems.[33] Meanwhile, WRA staff members aired differences of opinion over the investigation of the Tada beating and the hearing scheduled for Hirokane. With Hirokane's confession in hand, acting project director Robert Cozzens, assistant project director Lewis Korn, and project attorney James Terry wanted to halt the investigation, hold a closed hearing, and render a swift decision. However, the Internal Security Department heads—particularly associate director Frederick—urged that the investigation proceed (so that all of Tada's assailants could be apprehended) and that the hearing be an open community forum. The hearing, they argued, was not merely to establish guilt but to illuminate the grievances that had prompted the beating. Neither side scored a total victory. The investigation was quickly closed, but Frederick's plea was heeded. Cozzens—who, under WRA policy, made the sole determination in criminal actions—at first opted for a closed hearing, but changed his mind upon learning that this arrangement was anathema in the Japanese American community and would create more violence.[34]

The hearing was held on December 3 in a small barracks apartment generally used for Temporary Community Council meetings and lasted four hours. The room was packed to capacity. Aside from Cozzens, Hirokane, and project attorney Terry (who handled the prosecution), those in attendance included the members of the Temporary Community Council, Williamson and Frederick from the Department of Internal Security, and about forty inmates. An additional 750 inmates crowded around the barracks, where speakers periodically passed out news of the proceedings as general announcements.

The hearing unfolded in two stages. Testimony during the first half hour described the reasons behind the beating of Tada and emphasized the disgust and anger over his negligence at Turlock. The rest of the hearing focused on dissatisfaction over clothing shortages, crowded housing, inadequate mess supplies (especially sugar and meat), difficulty in traveling between the two camps, and exclusion of Issei from the Temporary Community Council. Outraged Issei stressed how their frustrations contributed to the assault on Tada. Concerned that the proceedings might be misconstrued and lead to a strike or even a riot, Cozzens announced at the close of the hearing that he would hold a general meeting in the Canal Camp's open-air auditorium. Following Frederick's advice, he alerted the military police companies surrounding the camp, and other groups in Phoenix, to the need of enforcing "military law" in the case of a general strike.[35]

That evening approximately 1,000, mostly Issei, men (women of both generations were almost totally absent), gathered in the camp auditorium. Cozzens explained that the WRA (a civilian agency) had been created specifically to reassure the incarcerees that no stringent control of them was intended. The WRA was dedicated to encouraging free speech and to serving the Japanese American community. Although the project director's office was in the Butte Camp, he was equally interested in activities in Canal. His representatives in Canal welcomed requests and were always available to discuss Canal's problems. A general strike, Cozzens warned, would harm the community by increasing the suspicions of those who questioned the loyalty of Japanese Americans. Moreover, a strike was also bound to hurt those Japanese Americans residing outside the camps. And still further, it would damage WRA director Dillon Myer's ambitious relocation plans by retarding the development of external employment for the detainees. As for those wishing to go to Japan, they need only complete the necessary repatriation forms.

Cozzens felt that the hearing had provided valuable insight into the grievances that precipitated the beating of Tada. But he quickly added that further acts of violence could not be tolerated. Canal must be a community of law and order. The wardens and others in the camp hierarchy were there to serve the community and must be respected. They should not be intimidated because most of them were Nisei. "These Issei," Cozzens scolded, "who work against them, who criticize them, and who threaten them, should feel most ashamed of themselves." They were the "older men, the wiser people of the community, and they are the ones who should advise, guide, and control the reins of leadership." Some of them had been "a dissatisfied element among the community, and should be severely censured."

Cozzens then addressed a complaint that had created dissension in the camp for several months and had generated emotion at the Hirokane hearing—the shortage and delay of clothing allotments. He laid some of the blame on the previous WCCA administration and said the WRA could not be held responsible for the mistakes of the military agency. Within the week, he promised, all incarcerees in the Work Corps would receive cash payments to compensate them and their families for clothing allowances outstanding since their arrival at Canal the previous summer.

Finally, the director turned to the item the audience had assembled to hear—the disposition of the Hirokane case. Cozzens had not reached a decision in the matter, but he assured the detainees that it would be based upon a careful consideration of all the facts. It also would be irrevocable. He would not be "high-pressured" by groups or individuals. "[The] Issei are the leaders," concluded Cozzens, "and they should lose the respect of the community at large if they stoop to acts of violence."[36]

Immediate response to the Cozzens address was mixed. The more Americanized Nisei leadership was generally pleased by the acting director's strong stand against intimidation and violence, but they expressed misgivings about the authoritarian tone of his remarks and his emphasis upon Issei leadership. The dissident Issei and Kibei, on the other hand, found Cozzens's tone reassuring; at last they knew where they stood. They also appreciated knowing that the clothing problem would be resolved and that the director was open to suggestions. Most of all, they applauded his recognition of Issei leadership. Still, they were determined not to drop their guard until they heard what sort of sentence Cozzens had in store for Hirokane.

Intense excitement reigned in Canal Camp. The Issei-Kibei contingent announced that if the sentence was harsh they would call a full-scale strike, burn the controversial Community Services canteen, and attack other inmate staffers suspected of currying favor with the administration. At the same time, the Nisei group formulated its own plans for a strike should the sentence be too lenient.

On the day after the hearing, the Temporary Community Council began deliberations on Hirokane's fate. In light of the Tada beating and threats to other councilmen, they refused (as a body) to oppose community opinion. The only councilmen who openly condemned Hirokane and the Kenkyu-kai were the blacklisted pair Dr. Furuta and Teizo Yahanda. Together, they declared that "no amount of pressure" would make them abandon their efforts to act for "what they believed the best interests of the community." Rather than risk reprisals, the majority of the council resigned.[37]

To demonstrate their loyalty to the community, the wardens likewise resigned en masse. Although Chief Williamson refused to accept the resignations, the gesture placated the detainee population. However, one blacklisted warden—Charles Yonezu—refused to back down. Instead, he organized a Nisei vigilante committee and called for "a pitched battle if this were necessary between Issei and Nisei."[38]

On December 5, Cozzens announced Hirokane's sentence—six months in jail, with all but one month to be commuted upon good behavior. Although it fell short of their worst expectations, the news pleased neither faction in the Canal Camp. The Kenkyu-kai felt that the sentence was too stiff and drafted a petition to Cozzens protesting his decision. More menacingly, a large delegation called on the director and urged him to set the verdict aside. When he refused, they threatened a march "of 5,000 persons" from Canal to Butte. Emboldened by radio reports of a riot at the Manzanar camp in eastern California, Kenkyu-kai leaders organized a group of women supporters to go through the Canal Camp collecting (reportedly through "coercive tactics") the signatures of "hundreds of women residents" on a petition to reduce Hirokane's sentence on the grounds "that he had acted for the good of the community." The protest failed, and Hirokane was incarcerated in the Pinal County Jail at Florence.[39]

While Hirokane served out his short sentence, Canal Camp was abuzz with changes. Resignations continued to roll in from representatives to the Temporary Community Council, and there was talk that, to prevent further erosion of the council's prestige, perhaps the members should resign as a group and request new elections. For the time being, the Constitutional Commission shelved plans to bring their proposal for a permanent community council before the residents for ratification. In an unrelated development, a crisis of authority gripped the Department of Internal Security. When the smoke cleared, there had been a large turnover of wardens and a reduction of their status in the Canal community to that of "glorified messenger boys" and "administrative stooges."[40]

Dissatisfaction now spread from Canal to the Butte Camp, where parallel groups took action. The most powerful dissenting groups were the Kyowa-kai (Issei Peace Society) and the Gila Young People's Association (Kibei Club). These two closely connected associations sought to promote the general welfare of the community, but Butte administrators and their inmate associates viewed them with suspicion. Both the Kyowa-kai and the Gila Young People's Association supported a myriad of Japanese cultural practices and activities and repudiated all Western cultural ideals and forms. Moreover, these two organizations were seen as principally responsible for the rash of recent threats and for drawing up a blacklist of Butte individuals (mostly JACL leaders) marked for assault.[41]

In the midst of this tense situation, Leroy Bennett took over as the new project director at the Gila center. During the previous few weeks, two other western WRA centers, Poston in Arizona and Manzanar in California, had experienced, respectively, a protracted strike and a bloody riot. Gila was teetering on the brink of catastrophe, and the Canal Camp, in particular, was nearing a flashpoint. At this critical juncture, Kiyoshi Tani and the *Rocky Nippon* invited a select group of administrators and incarcerees to a New Year's banquet.[42]

Having traveled full circle in a journey of inquiry back to the cultural text—the Tani dinner, which set it in motion—it is now possible to analyze that event as a representative paradigm drama and appreciate its significance as a particularly potent and protean expression of cultural politics.

In a report written less than a month later, Joseph Omachi, one of the inmate guests of honor, attempted to make sense out of why the banquet was staged. "The dinner," he explained, "was apparently meant to be a good-will gesture to forget the past and to cement better relationships with the administrative and evacuee leaders." However, to Omachi the event was primarily "a clever publicity stunt . . . and a move for general community recognition" on the part of Tani and the *Rocky Nippon*. The camp administrators present—Korn, Gaba, Williamson, and Frederick—offered a different interpretation. In their view, the dinner was "a testimonial on the release of Hirokane from prison."[43]

Both explanations overlook the cultural dynamics at work in the Japanese American community. In holding the dinner, Tani and the Kenkyu-kai inaugurated a new set of cultural arrangements for the Canal Camp. Viewed in this context, the explanations of the participants take on added meaning.

The Caucasian administrators correctly perceived that the banquet honored Hirokane, but they missed the point of the testimonial. The toasts paid homage to Hirokane not as an individual but to his embodying the traditional Japanese belief that the welfare of the group "is far more important than that of any single individual." As this principle is diametrically opposed to the American emphasis on individualism, camp administrators mistook the expressions of approval as attempts either to martyr Hirokane or show up the administration. Hirokane was honored for still another reason. As an older Issei, the father of seven children, and a block chairman, he reaffirmed the traditional Japanese cultural principle that "society is an ordered social hierarchy in which status is ascribed largely on the basis of biologically determined factors of sex, age, and generation." Violation of this principle by the administration lay behind the beating of Tada.

Omachi's interpretation of the dinner as an attempt by Tani simultaneously to publicize himself and stimulate sales for the *Rocky Nippon* perhaps reveals more about Omachi's value orientation than Tani's motives. But it also provides a clue as to why Omachi was prominent on the Kenkyu-kai blacklist. It is true that Tani earned a percentage of the revenue from camp sales of the *Rocky Nippon* and that, in the interval between the Tada beating and the banquet, newspaper sales had soared. But Tani had used the profits to subsidize the New Year's dinner. The real significance of the *Rocky Nippon* was neither economic nor personal but cultural. For a long time Tani and the Kenkyu-kai had been agitating for their own newspaper, which would resemble more closely those which the Issei had been accustomed to reading in prewar days—bilingual, but with much larger Japanese-language than English sections. Recently, they had lobbied the administration for an expanded Japanese-language section for the preponderantly English-language *Gila News-Courier*, which explains why the paper's Japanese-language editor, Kenzo Ogasawara, was seated at the head table during the dinner. For Tani and the Kenkyu-kai the media were important, not merely as a means to mold community opinion but also as a mirror of its cultural composition and character.[44]

For their own part, Tani and the Kenkyu-kai promoted the banquet as a "good-will gesture to forget the past and to cement better relationships with the administrative and evacuee leaders." Although Omachi discounted this simple explanation, it has the ring of truth. In the month since the Tada-Hirokane affair, cultural arrangements in the Canal Camp had begun to conform more closely to the pattern cherished by the Issei leadership. This was partly because of the diminished role of the Temporary Community Council. Weakened by resignations, it became virtually leaderless when its chair and dominant member, Dr. William Furuta, who earlier had sought to strengthen the council, decided he lacked the support of the administration and the people and stepped down. Within a short while, his successor also resigned. The council remained crippled when vacant seats could not be filled. This situation strengthened and solidified the already considerable power of the Issei-dominated block councils.[45]

Issei leaders were also pleased with the changes in the Community Activities Section. After his beating, Takeo Tada (who was scheduled to leave shortly for the army language school) removed himself from community fire and resigned his position as incarceree head of CAS. Tada's co-blacklisted chief assistant, Goro Yamamoto, also resigned. Because no second-generation aspirant dared risk community wrath by applying for these vacated positions, Hoffman and Gaba (the heads of CAS) were obliged to appoint Issei replacements. With a greater say in recognizing clubs and organizations, providing facilities, and funding recreation and entertainment, the Issei further tightened their cultural grip on the Japanese American community.

Administrative decisions also played a part in the process. Back clothing allowances were filled, as Cozzens had promised, and attempts were made to rectify problems in housing, transportation, employment, and food—which the Issei had made known at Hirokane's hearing. Bennett, the new director, announced that assistant director Korn would soon be moved from the Butte Camp to Canal and take "full charge of the administration of the colony." The Issei viewed these changes as administrative attempts to heed their advice and recognize their authority.[46]

As things in Canal were going their way, Tani and the Kenkyu-kai membership had a good reason to set aside the camp's unhappy memories and to consecrate a new cultural order by inviting the old guard to "break bread" with them at the banquet. But the motives for the dinner went beyond magnanimity, and Omachi's skepticism about their willingness "to forget about the past" was not entirely misplaced. The Tani dinner was also staged to warn selected guests (certain "administrative and evacuee leaders") that efforts to restore the old camp arrangements must cease or community retaliation would follow.

Most of these efforts involved the Department of Internal Security. This unit had undergone a shakeup since the Tada episode, and the community viewed the changes as unsatisfactory. Chief Williamson had begun removing wardens whom he distrusted (mostly Issei, but also Kibei and Hawai'i Nisei) and retaining those (Nisei) who were fluent in English and whose loyalty he deemed not so questionable. The purge prompted the community to withdraw support for the wardens, and the remaining Nisei began resigning from the department in twos and threes. Williamson replaced them with younger Christian Nisei willing to execute his directives. Given the small percentage of Christians in Canal, the majority of the detainees viewed the policy as "very undesirable."[47]

Inmate leaders regarded Williamson's program of "tracking down alleged subversive and pro-Japan elements" in the community as distressing and dangerous. Associate Chief Francis Frederick, whom the wardens felt was sympathetic to their situation, vigorously opposed the practice. When they petitioned for a separate internal security department at Canal, with Frederick at the helm, Williamson exploded. "He didn't give a damn what they wanted,"

Robert Spencer later reported. "Things were going to stay as they were." In fact, Williamson redoubled his investigatory activities. Although he placed the reluctant Frederick nominally in charge of uncovering subversives, Williamson handed the direction of his witch-hunt to his compliant warden captain, the blacklisted Charles Yonezu.[48]

Having established the rationale for the representative paradigm drama, a consideration of the principal actors is now in order. Chota Hirokane and Kenzo Ogasawara have already been accounted for, and it seems obvious from the above why Williamson, Frederick, and Yonezu were invited to the dinner. But an accounting still needs to be made for the cultural role performed by the other leading players (even though the pertinent information here is skimpy). Lewis Korn, assistant project director at Canal, was likely invited and asked to say a few words so as to lend an air of legitimacy to the transfer of authority from the old to the new order. His participation was particularly important because he had been a strong advocate of Nisei leadership. As expected, he spoke on the recent administrative concessions and emphasized the new spirit of detente at Canal.

Morton Gaba, Canal's community services head, dramatized his department's capitulation to cultural reality. In the past, he and his superior, Luther Hoffman, had placed the fortunes of the incarcerees in the hands of second-generation usurpers of legitimate community authority like Takeo Tada. Recent CAS appointments, however, signaled a step in the right direction. For his part in these appointments, Gaba merited the community's provisional applause.

Joseph Omachi's role in the cultural drama that played out in Block 16 is best understood in relation to that performed by another member of the cast seated near him at the head table, block chairman Omai. As chairman of the Constitutional Commission, Omachi represented the imposition by the US government and the WRA of an unnatural bureaucratic authority on the community. Conversely, Omai (as block chairman) stood for the traditional brand of authority conferred by the community on those whom it considered its natural leaders.

Finally, there was the host, Kiyoshi Tani. A charismatic personality, Tani commanded the limelight because of the part he played in helping heal the psychosocial division within the Japanese American community. By force of his own example, he reminded inmates that attempts to strip them of their cultural dignity and self-determination must be resisted with resolve and resourcefulness. It was for this reason that Tani—who was quite capable of expressing himself in English—chose to deliver his welcoming address in Japanese. By various sanctions, the administration had attempted to make the use of the Japanese language a source of shame; Tani flaunted it as a badge of communal pride.

What about the cultural drama's audience—composed of members of the Kenkyu-kai, the Engeibu, and the Sumo Club? The Sumo Club consisted of 176 members, who were said to be lower class and connected with gambling interests in the camp. As the strong arm for the Kenkyu-kai, several of the members reportedly had been with Hirokane during the Tada beating. Of the camp's various organizations, the Sumo Club was considered by administrators the most dangerously pro-Japan. Its president and several officers had applied for repatriation; and five days earlier, on New Year's morning, at a club-sponsored wrestling match, the contestants and audience (including many Kenkyu-kai) had paused to shout loud "banzais" and sing Japanese national songs. The presence of a large contingent from the club at the Tani dinner, therefore, contributed to the acute discomfort of the honored guests.

The Engeibu, or dramatic society, likewise was considered dangerous, with connections to gambling. Unlike their counterpart in the Butte Camp, which was preoccupied with restoring pure Japanese dramatic art, the Canal Engeibu divided its attention between drama and politics, often employing the former in the service of the latter. Membership included Kibei as well as Issei, many of whom (like Kiyoshi Tani) were leaders in the Canal community. The Engeibu turned out in force for the New Year's banquet. From their perspective, the dinner was a fine species of sociopolitical drama in which the central motif was the restoration of the community's traditional cultural order.[49]

The Kenkyu-kai supplied the remainder of the audience. Although the club enjoyed a substantial membership, it never met en masse but preferred to disperse its efforts through a myriad of informal subgroups. Camp administrators believed that the group, feeling that its mission was accomplished, had disbanded following the Hirokane hearing. Their presence at the Tani dinner served as a warning that they were quite capable of coalescing into a united front should the occasion demand it.

Significantly, the staging of the Tani dinner was formal. The banquet not only commemorated the most ritualized of Japanese holidays but all of the attendant trappings—the elegant dress of the participants, the elaborate entertainment, and the haute cuisine—reflected the so-called "Japanese penchant for formalization." In this case, however, the formality exceeded mere cultural custom and served to publicize not only the arrival of a new year but also the commencement of a new set of power arrangements in the Canal Camp.[50]

The principal props at the dinner—the bottles of bourbon standing on each table—also symbolized the new order. Not long before the banquet, Chief Williamson had conducted an anti-liquor crusade in the pages of the camp newspaper, cautioning the inmates that, as the center was constructed on land leased from the Pima-Maricopa Indian communities, it was a federal offense to possess or transport alcoholic beverages on the premises. The conspicuous display and consumption of "Japan tea" at the dinner, therefore, represented a political statement that said: We will no longer be dealt with like subjugated wards of the government. We are now in control of this camp and we will break with impunity any laws that are not to our liking.[51]

This was no idle boast. In referring to the detainee organizations at the Tani dinner, analyst Robert Spencer noted: "For a time these groups held the balance of power over and against the administration and its Nisei and liberal Issei backers." Consequently, what would appear on the surface to have been a relatively simple event was actually loaded with cultural and political significance. When measured against the definition for a "representative paradigm drama" posed at the outset of this inquiry—an act that spotlights changing boundaries of what is possible for a person or a group at a particular time and in a particular place and in a particular milieu—the Tani banquet qualifies as just such an act. It did indeed dramatize for all those in attendance that the Canal Camp had ceased being run by the WRA and its detained appointees and was now in the command of the authentic inmates. Truly, things at Canal had gone as far as they could go.[52]

EPILOGUE

Although project director Bennett advised his staff not to attend the banquet, some apparently felt the invitation was a command performance. Immediately thereafter, Bennett, aided by Williamson, made plans to remove Canal's dissident leaders, along with their Butte counterparts, from the center at the next sign of resistance. That time came a little over a month later, when the US Army and the WRA began to register internees in all of the camps for the joint purpose of determining their suitability for military service and their fitness for resettlement in American society. This "loyalty" registration met with swift resistance in several centers—including Gila. In Canal the Kenkyu-kai again mushroomed into prominence, while a still more intense demonstration of resistance, spearheaded by the Gila Young People's Association, occurred in Butte. Hastily compiling a list of the principal "troublemakers," the administration contacted the FBI and the US attorney in Phoenix and requested presidential warrants be issued for their arrest. Acting with Director Myer's approval, FBI agents and Internal Security officers, on February 16–17, 1943, swooped down on Gila and, in a matter of minutes, apprehended fifteen aliens and thirteen citizens. Of the eighteen seized at Butte, twelve were Kibei (mostly officers of the Gila Young People's Association, including the Sumo Club president). The rest were Issei, including the leader of the Kyowa-kai. At Canal nine Issei and one Kibei were taken. The Issei included Hirokane, Tani, Fujimoto (Issei adviser to the Kibei Club and head of the Sumo Club), judo leaders Okamoto and Katagawa, Mrs. Matsuda, who had defended Hirokane's assault on Tada, and three unidentified inmates. The sole Kibei arrested was Minoru Okamoto, president of the Kibei Club.[53] The removal temporarily tipped the balance of power back to the WRA authorities. Nevertheless, during the period from the Tada beating through the registration, the formerly anomic and powerless Gila population had rediscovered its cultural identity and wielded it as an instrument for achieving self-determination and community empowerment.

NOTES

In the preparation and revision of this article, I was aided by Nick Polos, Albert Camarillo, Bob Sims, Harwood Hinton, Bruce Dinges, Bob Spencer, Phil Brigandi, and Debra Gold Hansen.

1. The banquet description is from Joseph I. Omachi, "Notes on Spencer's Report of 'Tada Incident,'" February 1, 1943, 7–9, folder K8. 30, and Robert Spencer, "The Rise of Political Pressure Groups in the Gila Community," February 15, 1943, 34–35, 41–42, Japanese American Evacuation and Resettlement (JAER), Bancroft Library (BL), University of California, Berkeley (UCB), folder K8.62. Japanese American Evacuation and Resettlement (JAER), Bancroft Library (BL), University

of California, Berkeley (UCB); hereafter cited as JAER. Because Omachi attended the dinner, I have followed his version where discrepancies exist between the two accounts. Spencer based his rendition of the Tani dinner on information supplied by an eyewitness, Francis Frederick, associate director of internal security.

2. A review of this literature is in Gary Y. Okihiro, "Tule Lake under Martial Law: A Study in Japanese Resistance," *Journal of Ethnic Studies* 5 (Fall 1977), 71–72. See also Gene Wise, *American Historical Explanations: A Strategy for Grounded Inquiry* (Homewood, IL: Dorsey Press, 1973), 86–89, 97–100. Rita Takahashi Cates, "Comparative Administration and Management of Five War Relocation Authority Camps: America's Incarceration of Persons of Japanese Descent" (PhD diss., University of Pittsburgh, 1980); and Richard Drinnon, *Keeper of Concentration Camps: Dillon S. Myer and American Racism* (Berkeley: University of California Press, 1987).

3. Aside from Spencer (a doctoral candidate), most of the reports were written by Charles Kikuchi, a graduate student in the School of Social Welfare at the University of California, Berkeley; Shotaro Hikida, the prewar secretary of the San Francisco Japanese Association; and Y. Okuno, a poet and former high school teacher in Japan. For their problems in conducting fieldwork see the voluminous correspondence (principally between Spencer and Dorothy Swaine Thomas), JAER, folder K8.80C-F. The ethnographic material from the largely anthropologist-staffed JERS project (and that done by the Community Analysis Section of the War Relocation Authority) has produced controversy. See Peter T. Suzuki, "Anthropologists in the Wartime Camps for Japanese Americans: A Documentary Study," *Dialectical Anthropology* 6 (August 1981), 23–60. Norman Richard Jackman, "Collective Protest in Relocation Centers" (PhD diss., University of California, Berkeley, 1955), uses the JERS material but does not explore the events surrounding the Tani dinner.

4. See Gene Wise, " 'Paradigm Dramas' in American Studies: A Cultural and Institutional History of the Movement," *American Quarterly* 31 (Bibliography Issue 1979), 206–7.

5. Documentation for the Tada beating rests mainly on six JERS reports. In addition to the Omachi and Spencer reports cited in note 1, see Spencer's "The Tada Case," December 1, 1943; Omachi's "Tada Case," December 14, 1943; and Omachi's "Supplementary Notes to the 'Report on the Tada Case,'" December 20, 1942, all in JAER, folder K8.65; and Spencer, "Pressure Groups and After," April 28, 1943, JAER, folder K8.54. A conceptual outline of the 1943 reports is in Dorothy Swaine Thomas, "Notes by DST," January 1, 1943, folder K8.30.

6. Additional data on Tada are in Robert F. Spencer, "Administrative Notes on Gila," September 1943, 16n1, JAER, folder K8.66; and James A. Terry, "Narrative Report of Project Attorney," 12–15, in Gila River Relocation Center Final Report,

March 12, 1946, Records of the War Relocation Authority, Record Group 210, National Archives, Washington, DC; hereafter cited as GRRC Final Report.

7. Omachi, "Tada Case," 14.

8. Omachi, "Tada Case," 7. Turlock's former director allegedly had been convicted of bribery and was serving a prison sentence.

9. For an overview of the Community Activities Section and its undertakings, see Robert Spencer, "Recreational Activities in the Gila Community," November 2, 1942; and his "Recreation," n.d., both in JAER, folder K8.56; and Robert Spencer and Charles Kikuchi, "Community Services Division," April 6, 1943, 1–12, in their "Evacuee and Administrative Interrelationships in the Gila Relocation Center," March–April 1943, JAER, folder K8.42, GRC-JERS; and Arthur L. Griswold, "Terminal Report, Community Activities Section," in GRRC Final Report.

10. The composition and activities of the University Club are discussed in Spencer, "Political Pressure Groups," 78–79; and Charles Kikuchi, "Development of Gila JACL," July 1943, 29, JAER, folder K8. 22. The wartime plight of the JACL is described in Arthur A. Hansen and David A. Hacker, "The Manzanar Riot: An Ethnic Perspective," *Amerasia Journal* 2 (Fall 1974), 112–57; Hansen, "Demon Dogs: Cultural Deviance and Community Control in the Japanese-American Evacuation," *Western Conference of the Association for Asian Studies Selected Papers*, n.s., no. 10 (1983): 16–18; and Paul Spickard, "The Nisei Assume Power: The Japanese [American] Citizens League," *Pacific Historical Review* 52 (May 1983): 147–74. For the Gila center JACL, see Spencer, "Political Pressure Groups," 79–85; Kikuchi, "Development of Gila JACL," 1–90; Shotaro Hikida, "Friction between Niseis and Isseis in the Relocation Centers and Fundamental Causes of Such Friction," January 18, 1943, JAER, folder K8.18; and Rosalie Hankey, "Interview with Nobu Kawaii," September 30, 1943, JAER, folder K8.10. Studies discussing the relationship between rumor and the wartime role of the JACL are as follows: Tamotsu Shibutani, "Rumors in a Crisis Situation" (master's thesis, University of Chicago, 1944); Rachel Reese Sady, "The Function of Rumors in Relocation Centers" (PhD diss., University of Chicago, 1947); and Frank Shotaro Miyamoto, "The Career of Intergroup Tensions: A Study of the Collective Adjustments of Evacuees to Crisis at the Tule Lake Relocation Center" (PhD diss., University of Chicago, 1950).

11. Spencer, "Political Pressure Groups," 74–76; Shotaro Hikida, "Comparative Popularity of J.A.C.L. and Gila Young Peoples Ass'n. in the Rivers Community and Relative Standing of Two Groups in Japanese Community in Preevacuation Days," March 15, 1943, folder K8.18, GRC-JERS.

12. Spencer, "Political Pressure Groups," 85–86.

13. Another likely reason for Tada's election to the council was that many Issei did not feel obliged to vote. For information on Furuta, Omachi, and Yahanda, see

Spencer, "Tada Case," 10–34; Omachi, "Supplementary Notes," 1–6; and Omachi, "Notes on Spencer's Report," 5–7.

14. Spencer, "Political Pressure Groups," 18–19. For the Japanese cultural theme governing community authority, see Toshio Yatsushiro, "Political and Socio-Cultural Issues at Poston and Manzanar Relocation Centers: A Themal Analysis" (PhD diss., Cornell University, 1953), 209–28.

15. Spencer, "Political Pressure Groups," 21. Robert Spencer, "The Canal Camp—Block 4," July 1, 1943, 29–37, JAER, folder K8.38. Gordon Brown, "Final Report: War Relocation Authority, Gila River Project, Rivers, Arizona, Community Analysis Section, May 12 to July 7, 1945," *Applied Anthropology* 4 (Fall 1945): 27.

16. John H. Provinse to Ototaro Yamamoto, October 6, 1942, attached to Spencer, "Political Pressure Groups," n.p. Background on this letter and information on Yamamoto is in Robert Spencer, "Preliminary Analysis of Block 61," September 15, 1943, 8–9, 22–23, JAER, folder K8.36.

17. The camouflage net factory controversy is described in Milton T. Madden, "A Physical History of the Japanese Relocation Camp Located at Rivers, Arizona" (master's thesis, University of Arizona, 1969), 54, 99–102; Shotaro Hikida, "Discussion of Camouflage Net Industry at Block Meeting," n.d., JAER, folder K8.18; Shotaro Hikida, James Sakoda, and Robert Spencer, "Block Survey 64," n.d., 6, JAER, folder K8.36; Robert F. Spencer, "Resume: Minutes of the Temporary Community Council of Canal," April 30, 1943, 10–12, JAER, folder K8.60; and Spencer, "Political Pressure Groups," 8. Thomas Reynolds, "Camouflage Net Factory," in GRRC Final Report; *Gila News-Courier*, September 12, October 21 and 24, December 9, 17, and 19, 1942. The army language school issue is discussed in *Gila News-Courier*, October 31 and December 2, 1942. According to Shotaro Hikida, "Recent Enlistment of Niseis to the Army Intelligence Service and General Opinion of Isseis in Gila Center," n.d., 2, JAER, folder K8.18, Nisei enlistment for the school was unpopular among Issei. Of the twenty-nine Gila volunteers, only two came from the Canal Camp. "When there was that recruitment for the language school," Hikida said, "one of the boy[s] from this [Butte Camp] left for Camp Savage. . . . The block manager, one day, proposed a farewell party for this boy and they responded, 'What's the use of having a farewell party for a fellow like that!'" Hikida, Sakoda, and Spencer, "Block Survey 64," 13.

18. For the *Gila News-Courier*, see Madden, "Physical History," 135–42; Ethel A. Flemming, "Final Report of Reports Office," 2–17, in GRRC Final Report; and Charles Kikuchi, "Developments on the Gila Newspaper," November 17, 1942, folder K8.24, GRC-JERS. According to Kikuchi, who served on the JACL board of governors at Gila, Tashiro's editorial policy pushed the Americanization program "as much as possible" and followed the JACL policy of cooperation with the administration." Kikuchi, "Development of Gila JACL," 5, 80–82.

19. Omachi, "Notes on Spencer's Report," 5. According to Shotaro Hikida, "Bon Fires," n.d., 1, JAER, folder K8.18, the delay in installing stoves in the barracks caused the incarcerees to gather around bonfires in the early-morning hours of the late fall and winter of 1942. The Issei first blamed the administration for the lack of heat and then criticized the Nisei supervisors. For the situation at Turlock, see Omachi, "Supplementary Notes," 1.

20. Background on Miyake is in Spencer, "Political Pressure Groups," 53–54, 77–78; and Kikuchi, "Development of Gila JACL," 82–83. For Yahanda, see Spencer, "Canal Camp—Block 4," 20.

21. For an analysis of a similar situation, see Hansen and Hacker, "Manzanar Riot."

22. I have borrowed the opening phrase from Christopher Lasch, as quoted in Richard Pells, *Radical Visions and American Dreams: Culture and Social Thought in the Depression Years* (New York: Harper & Row, 1973), 8. I am also indebted to Pells for my views on cultural radicalism, although I place more stress on the cultural factor of ethnicity. See Robert Kelley, *The Cultural Pattern in American Politics: The First Century* (New York: Alfred A. Knopf, 1979), 27.

23. Further information on the Kenkyu-kai, Engeibu, Sumo Club, and Kibei Club is in Spencer, "Tada Case," 21, 23–30, 34–40; Omachi, "Tada Case," 1, 8, 10–12; Omachi, "Supplementary Notes," 5–7; Omachi, "Notes on Spencer's Report," 1–6, 9–10; Spencer, "Canal Camp—Block 4," 42–43; and Spencer, "Pressure Groups and After," 2, 14. For the connection between these groups, see Spencer, "Political Pressure Groups," 24–76. For more information on gambling, see Spencer, "Pressure Groups and After," 6–15. The mess operations staff is discussed in Spencer, "Canal Camp—Block 4," 21–29; and Brown, "Final Report," 41.

24. Spencer "Political Pressure Groups," 26–27. According to Robert Spencer, "Survey Report: August 15, 1942," 6, 17, JAER, K8.52, Canal inmates were "mainly Nisei but such Nisei as to be considered Issei." "They are," he explains, "subject more to Japanese than American patterns. . . . The lingua franca of the camp is Japanese definitely. Dr. [Nan] Cook [Smith, wife of Gila's first project director, E. R. Smith, and possessor of a Yale PhD in anthropology] stated quite frankly that she believed that only 30% could speak English." Spencer, in an untitled report of August 23, 1942, 16, JAER, folder K8.02, stated that "the situation here is peculiar in its very nipponized atmosphere." The JAI set in motion a marked revitalization of Japanese cultural forms and practices at assembly centers. Robert Spencer, "Case History Number 2: Mariko Y," JAER, folder K8.40.

April 5, 1943, 13, folder K8.40, GRC-JERS. The Japanization process at the block level is discussed in Spencer, "Canal Camp—Block 4." "It is the Issei," explained Spencer, "who have maintained many of the customs of old Japan" (74). A manifestation of cultural revitalization was the custom of "moon walking." According to Shotaro Hikida, artistically inclined individuals and groups in Japan often walked "at the time of the full moon along the sea coast or in the mountains, reciting Haiku and Tanka on the beauties of nature, and serenity of the moonlight" (5). In Arizona, parties were organized for similar walks. The custom was not followed in pre-JAI times. Robert Spencer, "Notes on Administration, Attitudes on Authority, Recreation, Rumors, Etc.," n.d., 5, JAER, folder K8.45; Brown, "Final Report," 13, 35.

25. Spencer, "Political Pressure Groups," 59–60.

26. Omachi, "Tada Case," 12.

27. Omachi, "Notes on Spencer's Report," 5–6. Data on the *Rocky Nippon* are in "The Rocky Shimpo [Nippon], 1941 Larimer St., Denver, Colorado," n.d., JAES, folder S1.20A; and Spencer, "Political Pressure Groups," 59–60, 62. Tamie Tsuchiyama, a JERS researcher at the Poston center, visited Gila and commented in her "Administrative Notes on Gila," September 1943, 30, JAES, folder K8.66, that "the Issei in Gila as in Poston rely almost entirely on the *Utah Nippo* and the *Rocky Shimpo* to keep them informed on current events rather than on the Japanese section of the camp paper. They accept the news in the Japanese papers as biblical truth whereas they take the news in the *Gila News-Courier* with a grain of salt." Little documentation is available on Tani. In addition to the Spencer, Omachi, and "Rocky Shimpo" reports cited above, see Spencer, "Tada Case," 20, 25–26, 28–29, 33; Omachi, "Tada Case," 8; and Spencer, "Pressure Groups and After," 2, 6, 12–13.

28. Omachi, "Notes on Spencer's Report," 5.

29. Omachi, "Tada Case," 7; Spencer, "Tada Case," 36.

30. Yonezu's activities and inmate community opinion of him are described in Omachi, "Supplementary Notes," 6; Spencer, "Tada Case," 10, 32; Spencer, "Political Pressure Groups," 13–15, 34, 47, 56, 61, 65–66; and Spencer, "Pressure Groups and After," 8. W. E. Williamson, Gila's internal security director, heralded Yonezu's appointment: "A fitting and proper man for a man-sized job." *Gila News-Courier*, October 3, 1942.

31. Spencer, "Political Pressure Groups," 12. For more on Williamson's background, see Spencer, "Political Pressure Groups," 13–17, 32, 41–44, 56; and Robert Spencer and Charles Kikuchi, "Internal Security Department," March 29, 1943, 1–10, with Williamson's attached quarterly department report dated January 28, 1943, in "Evacuee and Administrative Interrelationships in Gila," K8.42, GRC-JERS; Omachi, "Notes on Spencer's Report," 7; Spencer, "Pressure Groups and After," 9, 11; Robert Spencer, "Report Number 2-A: Administrative Organization of the Gila River Relocation Center," 18–23, JAER, folder K8.32; Kikuchi, "Development of Gila JACL," 27.

32. Spencer, "Political Pressure Groups," 12. Additional information on Frederick and his subsequent activities at Gila and at the WRA isolation centers at Moab, Utah, and Leupp, Arizona, is in Spencer, "Political Pressure Groups," 13–17, 41–44, 60; Spencer, "Tada Case," 7–10, 18, 21, 21a, 30; Spencer, "Pressure Groups and After," 9; Spencer, "Administrative Organization," 20–23; Omachi, "Notes on Spencer's Report," 7; Robert Spencer to Mr. and Mrs. [Francis S.] Frederick, Memorandum, April 29, 1943, JAER, folder K8.80; Francis S. Frederick, "Personal Narrative Report," March 13, 1946, JAER, folder S1.00; Frances S. Frederick to R. P. Best, Memorandum, April 19, 1943; to Robert Spencer, April 20, 1943; to Paul G. Robertson, August 21, 1943; and [Frederick], "Leupp Isolation Center," n.d., all in JAER, folder S1.10. The twelve case histories on former Gila inmates written by Frederick while chief of internal security at the Leupp Isolation Center are in JAER, folder S1.20A. Also useful is the correspondence in JAER, folder S1.10: between Frederick and Spencer, July 22–December 9, 1943; Robertson to Frederick, December 27, 1943; and Jane Frederick to Spencer, October 25, 1943 [1944].

33. Omachi, "Tada Case," 2, 8; Spencer, "Political Pressure Groups," 37–38; Spencer, "Tada Case," 7, 21–21a, 30–31. For background on Omachi, see Spencer, "Tada Case," 10–34; Omachi, "Supplementary Notes," 1–6; and Omachi, "Notes on Spencer's Report," 5–7. Information on Yamamoto and Kawahara is in Spencer, "Tada Case," 10, 20, 32, 36; Omachi, "Supplementary Notes," 6; Omachi, "Notes on Spencer's Report," 7; Spencer, "Political Pressure Groups." The most concise and precise treatment of Hirokane's arrest and the resulting chain of events is in eight memoranda of Frederick (November 30, 1942; December 1, 2, [3], 3, 4, and 5, 1942) for the Internal Security Department files, all in JAER, folder K8.30. Ninety percent of the camp's adult population allegedly signed petitions protesting Hirokane's arrest and demanding the removal of Tada.

34. Spencer, "Tada Case," 11–12, 17.

35. Spencer, "Tada Case," 12–17.

36. Spencer, "Tada Case," 18–20, 30, 33.

37. Spencer, "Tada Case," 11, reported that immediately following Hirokane's arrest "feeling in the community against any denominations [demonstrations?] of pro-administration tactics became intense . . . [causing] the wardens . . . [to be] boycotted and snubbed." See also Leroy Bennett, "Project Director's Office," 14, in GRRC Final Report; and Spencer, "Political Pressure Groups," 43.

38. Omachi, "Tada Case," 11; Spencer, "Tada Case," 27.

39. Spencer, "Political Pressure Groups," 16.

40. Spencer, "Political Pressure Groups," 6, 31–32. Spencer discusses the activities of the Kyowa-kai (32–33, 55–61) and the Gila Young People's Association (49, 64–70). See also Spencer, "Pressure Groups and After," 1–2; Spencer, "Tada Case," 37–39;

Shotaro Hikida, "Gila Young People's Association," November 19, 1943, JAER, folder K8.06; and Rosalie Hankey, "Notes on Hikida's Report on the G.Y.P.A.," November 25, 1943, JAER, folder K8.06. Gordon Brown, "The Seinenkai," November 25, 1943, JAER, folder 5; Hugo Wolter, "Side Lights No. 3: The G.Y.P.A.–Gila Young People's Society or Seinen Kai," n.d., folder 7, both in box 13, US War Relocation Authority Papers, Special Collections, University of Arizona Library, Tucson; hereafter cited as USWRA Papers.

41. After the resignation in September of 1942 of the Gila center's first director, E. R. Smith, leadership passed through the hands of two acting directors from the WRA regional office in San Francisco, E. R. Fryer and Robert Cozzens. I learned of the reasons for Smith's resignation in a conversation with his widow, Nan Cook Smith, at her home in Santa Fe, New Mexico, during the summer of 1978. For insight into the deplorable physical and psychological conditions at Gila from its opening in late July of 1942 to Smith's resignation two months later, see Survey Reports of August 13 and 15, 1942, JAER, folder K8.52, and August 23/September 13, 1942, folder K8.02; as well as Spencer, "Administrative Organization," especially 56–58, 69–75. The connection between the events at Gila and developments at Poston and Manzanar is explored in Hikida, "Friction between Niseis and Isseis," 1, 5; and Tsuchiyama, "Administrative Notes," 15. For an analysis of the Poston Strike and the Manzanar Riot within the historiographical context of camp resistance studies, see Gary Y. Okihiro, "Japanese Resistance in America's Concentration Camps: A Re-evaluation," *Amerasia Journal* 2 (Fall 1973), 20–34.

42. Omachi, "Notes on Spencer's Report," 9; Spencer, "Political Pressure Groups," 15. William Furuta and Teizo Yahanda declined Tani's invitation, as did Luther Hoffman, chief of the camp's Community Services Division and one of the most vocal supporters of a citizenship requirement for membership on the Temporary Community Council.

43. Yatsushiro, "Political and Socio-Cultural Issues," 209–28, 284–89. Shotaro Hikida, an Issei observer on the JERS research team, explained: "[The] sincere expression of feeling on the part of the individual for his own group and for the people with whom he has lived . . . is the basis of what has been called the Japanese patriotic fanaticism. In spite of the troubles in this community [Gila], the Issei at least are bound by the same ties of proximity and the feeling for national consanguinity. It is the decline of this feeling in the second generation which makes so many Issei heartily resentful of them and causes the disruptions and conflict in the community which took place . . . in the Tada case. . . . When this feeling is broken down . . . group solidarity breaks down as well." Quote is from Robert Spencer's untitled, undated "Family Organization" report, on page 15; see also pages 13–14, JAER, folder K8.15. Hugo Wolter, "Notes on Evacuee Attitudes," April 1944, 4–5,

box 13, folder 5, USWRA Papers, states: "The cultural identification with Japan, together with the sense of social solidarity might suggest that the evacuees are, after all, fundamentally dangerous to this country in time of war. This does not necessarily follow, and the evidence does not indicate potential danger from them. The identification is cultural not political."

44. A useful study of the prewar Japanese American press in Los Angeles is Togo Tanaka, "The Vernacular Newspapers" (January 1943), JAER, folder O10.16 Charles Kikuchi, who neither spoke nor read Japanese, suggested in "Developments on the Gila Newspaper," 9–11, JAER, folder K8.24, that although many Gila administrators felt the Japanese section of the camp newspaper contained a strict interpretation of the English section, this was not the case. The chief opposition to the paper, he noted, came from the Kibei and certain Issei who felt they were being neglected. The Issei yelled for a larger Japanese section; the Kibei wanted to publish their own paper. Flemming, "Final Report of Reports Office," 2–3, said the fear that pro-Japanese material would appear in the Japanese section of the *News-Courier* was unfounded. "Misinformation did appear," according to Flemming, "but almost without exception, it was from a lack of understanding and not intention." Information on Ogasawara is in Tsuchiyama, "Administrative Notes," 17–19, 23–25.

45. Furuta's resignation is discussed in Spencer, "Tada Case," 33. In his "Political Pressure Groups," 5, Spencer claimed that Furuta had resigned as chairman of the council just prior to the Tada beating. I have chosen to follow the first report written at the time of the resignation.

46. Bennett's announcement appeared in the *Gila News-Courier*, December 19, 1942. For CAS changes and the reasons behind them, see Spencer, "Tada Case," 35–37; Spencer, "Political Pressure Groups," 15.

47. Spencer, "Political Pressure Groups," 15.

48. Spencer, "Political Pressure Groups," 14–15.

49. Spencer, "Political Pressure Groups," 61, 72.

50. Spencer, "Pressure Groups and After," 4. Japanese formalization is discussed in Spencer, "Family Organization," 11–14; and Brown, "Final Report," 13–14. The content and meaning of New Year (*Oshogatsu*) within Japanese American culture is explained in Nancy K. Araki and Jane M. Horii, *Matsuri: Festival: Japanese American Celebrations and Activities* (South San Francisco: Heian International Publishing Company, 1978), 17–28. According to the authors, *Oshogatsu* is "the most important celebration of the year." Its dominant theme is "the idea of starting afresh," which is embodied in the payment of all debts and the settlement of disputes and differences, so that the new year can begin with a clean slate. The parallels in form and function with the Tani dinner are striking. Then, too, because Hirokane was in jail during December, the dinner upon his return might be seen as a belated *Bonen-kai*

(year-end party), which Araki and Horii describe as a party "to promote goodwill and to patch up past misunderstandings." For a contemporary description from the Gila center, see Y. Okuno, "The Bonenkai," December 1942, JAER, folder K8.18.

51. On Williamson's anti-liquor crusade, see *Gila News-Courier*, November 7, 1942. Spencer, "Pressure Groups and After," 41, stated: "In view of Williamson's drastic attitude with regard to liquor on the project, the Tani faction must have felt that they gained a definite moral victory."

52. Spencer, "Pressure Groups and After," 5.

53. Spencer, "Army Enlistment and Registration," February 20, 1943, JAER, folder K8.34, and Spencer to Thomas, February 18, 1943, JAER, folder K8.80C-F. Also, Spencer to Thomas, February 12 and 15, 1943, JAER, folder K8.80C-F. John Edgar Hoover to D. S. Myer, February 17, 1943; "Counter Intelligence Topical Study Memorandum B-7-0: Registration of Japanese at Relocation Centers within the Eleventh Naval District," May 10, 1943, JAER, folder K7.00; "Army Registration Summary: Gila River," n.d., JAER, folder K5.12B. William Huso, "The Army Registration," 21–35, in GRRC Final Report.

5

PROTEST-RESISTANCE AND THE HEART MOUNTAIN EXPERIENCE

The Revitalization of a Robust Nikkei Tradition

Assuredly, owing to my reading of Roger Daniels's Concentration Camps USA: Japanese Americans and World War II *and Douglas Nelson's* Heart Mountain: The History of an American Concentration Camp,[1] *I had been well aware since the 1970s of resistance activity by Japanese American inmates at the World War II Heart Mountain Relocation Center in northwestern Wyoming. But it was not until the spring of 1983, when I participated in the International Conference on Relocation and Redress: The Japanese American Experience (held at the University of Utah in Salt Lake City and organized by Daniels with Harry H.L. Kitano and Sandra Taylor), that I became fully engaged in researching and writing about the organized 1944 draft resistance movement enacted at Heart Mountain under the aegis of that camp's Fair Play Committee.[2] This was due to my altogether inadver-*

This essay is from *A Matter of Conscience: Essays on the World War II Heart Mountain Draft Resistance Movement* edited by Mike Mackey (© 2002) and reproduced with permission of Mike Mackey.

DOI: 10.5876/9781607328124.c005

tent yet exceedingly fortuitous meeting at this conference with James Matsumoto Omura. I knew him to be the only Nikkei journalist who, through the Denver, Colorado–based Rocky Shimpo newspaper, supported—on strictly constitutional grounds—the Heart Mountain draft resisters. I also was mindful that Omura's support caused him to be secretly indicted and jailed, along with the Fair Play Committee steering committee members, and tried in a federal court in Cheyenne, Wyoming, on the grounds of unlawful conspiracy to counsel, aid, and abet violations of the military draft.

While at the Utah conference, I arranged with Omura to conduct an interview with him at my family home in Yorba Linda, California. This interview, done for the Japanese American Project of the Oral History Program at California State University, Fullerton, was subsequently held over a period of five days in late August of 1984.[3] This event not only immersed me within the Heart Mountain draft resistance movement story, including its historical context and consequences, but also led to an extensive and enjoyable correspondence with Omura. It resulted, too, in my lending him assistance, along with many other supporters, with the memoir that he had begun preparing for publication in the wake of his testifying in September 1981 at the Seattle hearing of the congressional Commission on Wartime Relocation and Internment of Civilians.

After Omura's death on June 20, 1994, through the urging of his good friend Michi Nishiura Weglyn, the author of the ground-breaking Years of Infamy: The Untold Story of America's Concentration Camps,[4] I was named by the Omura family to edit his nearly completed memoir for publication and provide provisional custody of his collected papers to use in this connection. It was largely for this reason that I was invited to present a paper at a conference funded chiefly by a California Civil Liberties Public Education grant and held in June 2001 in Cheyenne, Wyoming, under the title "Protest and Resistance: An American Tradition." While my paper (the published version of which appears below) did not take up the Heart Mountain draft resistance movement in detail, it did seek to place that landmark event within the historical context of both Japanese American resistance as a whole and the special variant of it experienced at the Heart Mountain Relocation Center prior to the emergence of the 1944 draft resistance movement. The paper also aimed to illuminate its interpretive narrative by reference to a highly useful theory of resistance developed by Roger Gottlieb in relation to the resistance of European Jews during the Holocaust.

In Lane Hirabayashi's luminous essay for Mike Mackey's edited 1998 anthology, *Remembering Heart Mountain*, he cautioned Japanese American Incarceration (JAI) scholars not to overgeneralize about Japanese American "resistance" to oppression within the War Relocation Authority (WRA)–administered camps. But Hirabayashi, a nephew of widely reputed World War II Nisei (citizen-generation Japanese American) resister Gordon Hirabayashi, at once mitigated his warning: "My reading of the archival record confirms, repeatedly, . . . the frequency and tenacity of resistance on multiple occasions and multiple levels."[5]

Having researched the wartime social catastrophe of Nikkei (Japanese Americans) via archival documents and oral history interviews over the past three decades, I find Hirabayashi's trenchant assessment of Japanese American wartime resistance activity to be on target. Moreover, I strongly feel that such resistance to oppression was frequent and tenacious and operated on multiple occasions and levels and not merely during World War II but also prior to and after the war. Indeed, I would argue that resistance within this racial-ethnic community, while never predominant, has always been widespread (and often consequential) and that resistance and protest have been a Japanese American tradition as well as a generic American one.

Before illustrating this contention by specific reference to historical developments, especially during World War II pertinent to events at or associated with the Heart Mountain Relocation Center in northwestern Wyoming, I would like briefly to catechize the concept of resistance. Hopefully, this (albeit schematic) discussion, which borrows liberally from the strikingly original theoretical work of Roger Gottlieb on Jewish resistance during the Holocaust,[6] will provide a broadly suggestive context for the meaningful consumption of my subsequent commentary and examples.

ROGER GOTTLIEB'S CONCEPT OF RESISTANCE

Resistance, according to Roger Gottlieb, necessarily functions within a context of oppression. Styling an action to be one of resistance implicates us in a moral evaluation of a specific set of power relations and places us in a partisan position as regards a given social conflict. For Gottlieb, the term "resistance" categorically has no "neutral" application: we root either for the success or for the failure of the aims expressed in a resistance action. However, even if we favor the outcome of such an action, we may be too cowed, fearful, or indifferent to actually help out the resisters in question.

"A relation of oppression," Gottlieb avers, "is typically based in certain norms."[7] Thus, in the present-day United States, acts of resistance to sexual and racial discrimination characteristically have to do with resistance to the legitimating norms of those forms of oppression. In Nazi-controlled Europe, on the other hand, acts by Jews exhibiting pride and self-respect served as species of resistance to the Nazi campaign to devalue and abase them. Rarely do relations of oppression consist only of physical aggression. Instead, explains Gottlieb, it is customary for an oppressed group to be controlled or assaulted in various ways: "life, property, religion, family, self-respect, culture, and community."[8]

To qualify as authentic acts of resistance, Gottlieb argues, their motivation must be to prevent, restrict, or terminate the oppressor group's exercise of power over the oppressed, not simply to transfer oppression from oneself to another of the oppressed group's members. In short, "the goal of resistance must be to lessen the total quantity of oppression, not just to shift it around. Otherwise one is not resisting, but simply trying to avoid personal suffering."[9]

Intention, theorizes Gottlieb, is indispensable to the concept of resistance. What we need to know is not whether an oppressed group resisted effectively, but rather whether they sought to resist. Stressing intention, though, hardly means that resistance exists whenever someone simply declares to be resisting. Intending to resist oppression ipso facto involves confronting the oppressor's superior power in order to thwart, limit, or end his/her oppressive actions. "The existence and application of this power," Gottlieb argues, "entails that resisters choose among acts, some of which are resistance and some of which are passivity or collaboration. . . . To obstruct the power of an oppressor is to place oneself in jeopardy."[10]

Resisters, in Gottlieb's formulation, must possess two sorts of beliefs. The first concerns their identity: they need to understand implicitly the defining elements of the individual's or group's existence. Beliefs of this type are necessary to the oppressed "recognizing that a part of themselves can be threatened, dominated or destroyed in the relationship of oppression."[11] The second kind of beliefs that resisters must hold relates to the manner in which a given oppressor exercises his/her oppressive actions, about how that particular individual or group is conducting an assault on their identity.

Although the intentions and beliefs manifested through resistance actions may be held in diverse ways and in differing degrees, it is sometimes hard to discern, as with so-called "tacit resistance," whether in fact they are even held. Gottlieb sees the expressed intentions and beliefs in acts of resistance as ranged along a spectrum. At one extreme are found completely formulated political-moral critiques of oppression coupled with a far-reaching determination to overcoming it, such as when an individual or group possesses a plan for overthrowing what one regards as a thoroughgoing domination system. Moving away from this end of the spectrum toward the other end, we find situations wherein an individual or group merely refuses to comply with a discrete order or rule out of a combined feeling of hatred and guilt rather than because of self-righteous conviction. Cases in point are uprisings or "riots" in racial-ethnic enclaves or ghettos, which appear to be prompted by a sense of oppression but which frequently do not flow from an overarching strategy and are bracketed by long periods of passive accommodation to a racist social order. "When a person's beliefs and intentions become too tacit," Gottlieb opines, "a particular refusal or rebelliousness fails to qualify as an act of resistance. Other things being equal, an act is more fully an act of resistance the more fully the agent understands it as such."[12]

Gottlieb posits two other modes of resistance, both of which pose more difficulty respecting placement on a spectrum: "self-deceptive non-resistance" and "unconscious resistance." The first relates to self-proclaimed resisters whose intentions and beliefs cannot be easily or clearly fathomed. To illustrate this brand of "resistance," Gottlieb draws upon his research into the Nazi invasion of Poland and the Nazis' enforced concentration of Jews into urban ghettos. "In each ghetto," he writes,

> [the Nazis] appointed a Judenrat, a council of (usually) influential Jews . . .
> for . . . day-to-day administration. . . . In most cases, the Judenrat administered
> deportations to the death camps; and members . . . often opposed, some-
> times even betrayed, militant resistance groups. Yet . . . the Judenrat generally
> expressed the belief that they were engaged in an . . . effective strategy of
> resistance, that their surface cooperation was part of a larger strategy of
> saving as many Jewish lives as possible. . . . It is clear [however] that in some
> instances Judenrat members were not telling the truth about their intentions.

Sometimes they sought self-protection at the expense of . . . the collective safety of their people. They were not engaged in a resistance effort that was shaped by different beliefs than those possessed by the militants. . . . What they claimed as conscious resistance could be more accurately described as unconscious complicity.[13]

"Unconscious resistance" represents for Gottlieb practically the reverse of "self-deceptive non-resistance." This behavior is associated with an oppressed person or group outwardly complying with an oppressor and foreswearing all intention to resist. Notwithstanding the oppressed party's projection of apprehension, defenselessness, or willing submission, the actions taken can be seen, upon examination, to impede the oppressive intentions and acts of the agent of oppression. The oppressed party may claim that the behavior at issue results from error, timidity, or chance, but it is more likely to constitute either an unacknowledged form of resistance or one to which the party is oblivious. Unconscious resistance is common among oppressed groups. For example, the allegedly "neurotic" behavior of females is, in reality, unconscious resistance to oppressive male domination. Such unconscious resistance behavior, while it thwarts the oppressor from getting the oppressed to fulfill a conventional subservient role on demand, falls well short of actual resistance. Unconscious resistance, after all, is ambivalent resistance. Moreover, because the desire to topple oppression is typically accompanied by fear or acceptance of the oppressor, unconscious resistance is frequently expressed in ways more damaging to the oppressed than to the oppressor. If the oppressing agent does not get what is wanted, the oppressed too often must pay a steep price for refusing to accede to the oppressor. Still, allows Gottlieb, "unconscious resistance behavior may provide direction to and mobilize support for political organizing, the goal of which is to convert unconscious resistance into open rebellion."[14]

PRE–WORLD WAR II JAPANESE AMERICAN PROTEST AND RESISTANCE

With this theoretical framework in place, we are now ready to turn our attention to a historical sketch of Japanese American resistance and to consider, along the way, the nature and degree of the resistance manifested at different times and in different contexts.

Let's begin at the beginning, using the scholarship of Gary Okihiro, the leading historian of Japanese American resistance activity, to guide us on our historical journey.[15] As early as 1868, we find outcroppings of resistance among the 153 members of the party of Japanese laborers who sailed from Yokohama to Hawai'i for employment on the sugar plantations. Okihiro notes that within a month after landing in Hawai'i, this first mass emigration of Japanese overseas, known as the *gannen-mono*, "lodged complaints with the government . . . protesting the withholding of half their $4 monthly wage and the slave-like selling of their contracts between planters . . . [and] even asking for pay for days lost because of foul weather."[16] Well before the termination of their three-year contracts, forty of these *gannen-mono* returned to Japan and, save for one of them, issued a signed public statement charging Hawai'i's planters with malice and multiple violations of the contractual terms.

Whether they went to work in Hawai'i or on the US mainland, Japanese American migrants confronted substantial and seemingly unremitting oppression: legal, paralegal, and extralegal. In Hawai'i the combination of plantation lunas, police, and the courts enforced rules, levied fines, dished out corporal punishment, and jailed laborers viewed as recalcitrant, lazy, or homeless. On the mainland, Japanese Americans were cursed with vicious racist names and beaten by vigilante mobs, severely discriminated against in the workplace, consigned to segregated neighborhoods, schools, and certain public facilities, and sometimes even had their homes and businesses burned by arsonists or got chased by mobs out of their respective places of settlement.

If the majority of immigrant-generation Issei were passive and compliant in the face of such discrimination, some protested their racist exploitation and took steps to redress it through the courts. As early as 1891, one Japanese worker appeared before the Hawaiian Supreme Court to protest against the contract labor system for being tantamount to slavery, while that same year an Issei woman in San Francisco filed a writ of habeus corpus against the immigration commissioner for refusing her entry into that city and making her suffer the indignity of port detainment. "Although both cases were denied," observes Okihiro, "they were heard in the highest courts of the kingdom and nation, and revealed a feisty spirit of resistance from among a people frequently depicted as fatalistic and passive."[17]

Collective action was joined to individual acts of resistance. In 1903, to cite one particularly dramatic example, 500 Japanese and 200 Mexican sugar beet workers in Oxnard, California, coalesced as the Japanese-Mexican Labor Association to attack the contracting/subcontracting system and the policy mandating them to buy solely from designated stores. After this union struck, a settlement was arrived at through negotiations.

On O'ahu, collective action by plantation workers entailed perennial protests against especially punitive lunas over wages and conditions of employment and against irrational regulations and edicts. During 1900 alone, there were officially recorded at least twenty strikes involving nearly 8,000 Japanese plantation laborers. Five years later, workers banded together in the Japanese Reform Association to rescue through concerted action a total of 70,000 Japanese from the combined clutches of the Keihin Bank (which was closed down by Japan's government) and the immigration companies (whose agents met with governmental restriction). In 1909, however, the most significant protest of the period occurred when 7,000 Japanese workers on O'ahu's main plantations struck, collectively, for higher wages. During this four-month-long strike, laborers complained of their wages not keeping pace with inflation and of earning salaries that were below those paid to white laborers doing the same work. Condemned by the planters as well as some from the Hawai'i Japanese community as being inspired by "agitators" and supported by a "criminal organization," the strike was curtailed and the association leaders arrested, imprisoned, and ultimately convicted on conspiracy charges. In Okihiro's considered opinion, this 1909 strike marked the ending of the migrant stage for Japanese Americans.

During the ensuing settlement stage in Japanese American history, which extended to the outbreak of World War II in 1941, resistance activity in response to oppression remained very much in evidence among the Nikkei. As the major site of the mainland anti-Japanese movement, California was the first state, in 1913, to enact an Alien Land Law. This measure prevented ownership of land by "aliens ineligible for citizenship." Since Japanese (along with other Asian immigrants) were prohibited from becoming naturalized US citizens, the law applied chiefly to them. Issei farmers were partially successful on their own in circumventing this law and subsequent ones that reinforced it, while the Japanese Association of America used a number of test cases to challenge the constitutionality of these land laws.

Notwithstanding that the challenges failed, some Issei frustrated their intended consequences by registering land in the names of their US-born citizen Nisei children.

Oppression occurred not only with respect to those Japanese who worked the land in California, but also those who made a living harvesting the sea. In the fourteen-year interval between 1919 and 1933, the California legislature considered seven separate bills aimed at prohibiting the issuance of commercial fishing licenses to Japanese Americans. All such legislation rested upon the use of US citizenship as the basis for receiving a commercial fishing license. Given the Issei's status as "aliens ineligible for citizenship," the legislation was clearly aimed at them. However, Tokunosuke Abe of San Diego, who ran the largest privately managed fishing fleet in southern California during this time, played a leading role in defeating each incarnation of this anti-Japanese legislation. Abe fought his final battle in 1938 when Democratic assemblyman Samuel Yorty of Los Angeles introduced a bill that, if passed, would have practically removed all Issei from the industry. According to historian Donald Estes, "Abe and his allies ultimately defeated the bill, but not without a long and intense battle that saw the state's Japanese American fishermen pitted against Naval Intelligence, the Congress of Industrial Organizations, the US Attorney for Southern California, the American Legion, and the Native Sons of the Golden West, to name only a few."[18] Here, then, was another example, among many, in which protracted Japanese American resistance paid dividends in the war against anti-Japanese oppression.

POST–PEARL HARBOR JAPANESE AMERICAN PROTEST AND RESISTANCE

The most profound oppression directed against Japanese Americans, of course, was set in motion by the aftermath of Pearl Harbor, and this development led to the wartime eviction and incarceration of some 120,000 Nikkei. This story is too detailed and complex to even summarize here. What can be said is that the massive oppression called forth an abundance of resistance activity, resulting in the refurbishment of the Japanese American tradition of protest and dissent. Some of the resistance is well known, particularly the constitutional challenges to the curfew, exclusion, and mass detention mounted by four Nisei—Minoru Yasui, Gordon Hirabayashi, Fred Korematsu, and

Mitsuye Endo—and the spectacular strikes and riots that occurred at the Santa Anita, Poston, Manzanar, and Tule Lake camps.[19]

But there was also informal resistance activity that occurred in comparatively quiet and less dramatic ways. This resistance even preceded the enforced mass movement into their wartime concentration camps, such as the destruction by some Japanese Americans of their possessions rather than to sell them at much reduced prices to avaricious buyers and the transfer by other Nikkei of their farms to friends and neighbors instead of submitting to a takeover by the Farm Security Administration.

But, it may be asked, what about resistance activity by Japanese Americans in the Wartime Civilian Control Administration (WCCA)–run "assembly centers" and the War Relocation Authority (WRA)–operated "relocation centers"? Although this question cries out for systematic and sustained historical treatment, a useful starting point for such an inquiry is Gary Okihiro's unpublished edited anthology, "Resistance in America's Concentration Camps."[20]

As Okihiro's perceptive introduction to this manuscript establishes, the character of WRA camp resistance was shaped by the orientation of the US government and power structure toward those of Japanese ancestry during the interval bracketed by the growing threat of war with Japan in the early 1930s and the immediate post–Pearl Harbor roundup of suspected Japanese American community leaders. Summoning Bob Kumamoto's "The Search for Spies: American Counterintelligence and the Japanese American Community, 1931–1942" as documentary evidence,[21] Okihiro states that during this critical decade the concern for military security was made subordinate to ridding American society of Japanese culture. Instead of seeing Issei patriotism toward Japan as a natural form of ethnic identity and pride (which was especially understandable given that they were barred from becoming naturalized Americans) compatible with the immigrant generation's residential status in America, the US counterintelligence community chose to view it as anti-American. Thus, all Japanese American ethnic distinctions such as language and religion, previously viewed as being merely inferior, were now construed to be potentially subversive and threatening. This racist outlook led during the post–Pearl Harbor roundup of Issei leadership to a concerted assault on all the institutions through which Japanese culture had been transmitted and preserved in Japanese America. "In effect," concludes Okihiro, "by undermining Japanese clubs and civic organizations and by removing the leaders of the cultural community, including Buddhist and Shinto priests, language school teachers, and journalists, they [counterintelligence officials] planned the destruction of the ethnic community and ultimately the elimination of Japanese culture in America."[22]

Because of this pervasive cultural oppression of Japanese Americans, much of their resistance activity in the WRA camps was driven by a desire to preserve their ethnic heritage and to recreate their prewar ethnic institutions, practices, and values in their new "homes." In support of this argument, Okihiro references selections in his anthology wherein the authors, such as David A. Hacker in his study of cultural resistance in Manzanar following the 1942 riot at that camp, emphasize how inmates resisted the "Americanization" campaigns foisted upon them by WRA administrators with reassertions of "Japanization." According to Hacker, explains Okihiro, "cultural resistance [at Manzanar] was successful largely because of the collective group, the family and the wider ethnic community, which sought to channel behavior into acceptable Japanese forms."[23] Okihiro also draws upon one of his own studies in the anthology to show how the revival of traditional Japanese religious beliefs and practices in the camps formed the basis for a wider network of cultural resistance. Here, instead of resistance sentiment being canalized into open rebellion as in the case of the Manzanar Revolt,[24] it was funneled into a revitalization of Buddhism and religious folk beliefs and associated Japanese aesthetic expressions (landscape gardening, flower arrangement, sumo wrestling, music, drama, and poetry) and core Meiji cultural and ethical practices (filial piety and ancestor worship).[25]

As early as 1955, ten years after the end of World War II, sociologist Norman Jackman wrote a study about collective protest in the WRA camps. In it Jackman cataloged and analyzed the myriad protest activity that he uncovered in his research. Characterizing this protest as either "passive resistance and insubordination" or "overt rebellion," he situated his findings relative to extant theoretical and descriptive literature related to imprisoned people.[26] Forty years later, anthropologist Lane Hirabayashi built upon Jackman's stockpile of camp protest incidents in an edited volume of the resistance field reports that participant-observer Richard Nishimoto had compiled at the Poston camp in Arizona for the University of California, Berkeley–sponsored Japanese American Evacuation and Resettlement Study.[27]

In introducing one of Nishimoto's research reports for this volume, which discussed the All Center Conference, held February 16–22, 1945, in Salt Lake City, Utah, Hirabayashi treated it within the context of the "popular resistance" concept adumbrated by Okihiro in his published resistance writings. This conference, explained Hirabayashi, had been called into being in response to the WRA's precipitous unilateral announcement in late 1944 that all WRA camps, save for the segregation center at Tule Lake, would be closed by the end of 1945 (by force if necessary).

At this conference, representatives from seven of the camps made it clear that, while they were certainly not against being returned to mainstream America, they nonetheless resented "that the proposal was yet another instance of the WRA trying to push Japanese Americans around without consulting them and without paying sufficient attention to the needs of specific groups within the overall population."[28] The implied physical coercion exacerbated the representatives' unanimous indignation that such an arbitrary closure date would work an extreme hardship on some Issei and older Nisei who had been pauperized by their eviction and detention experience.

Declaring that such persons, as with the disabled, could not make it on their own within the larger society on the twenty-five dollars and the one-way train ticket back to their point of origin in the country that the WRA promised, the representatives lodged a staunch protest. The government, after all, had been responsible for the mass expulsion and imprisonment of Japanese Americans, and it was therefore incumbent upon the government to ensure their secure and sound return back into American society.

Accordingly, as Hirabayshi depicted, "the All Center representatives hammered out . . . [a] document . . . demanding [governmental] consideration of three key points: (1) monetary reparations for losses and damage, (2) special support for the elderly and needy, and (3) a full guaranty of the rights and safety of individuals."[29] Although such popular resistance action did not deter the WRA from proceeding with their closure policy, it did pay dividends at a future date. Clearly, as Hirabayashi argued, these demands foreshadowed similar ones put forward three decades later within the Redress/Reparations movement, and the result was the passage of the Civil Liberties Act of 1988.

JAPANESE AMERICAN PROTEST AND RESISTANCE WITHIN THE HEART MOUNTAIN RELOCATION CENTER

The Heart Mountain Relocation Center in Wyoming has attracted the critical attention of a substantial number of commentators. Among them have been historians like T. A. Larson, Roger Daniels, Douglas Nelson, Mike Mackey, Louis Fiset, Frank Chin, William Hohri, Eric Muller, Gwenn Jensen, Susan Smith, and Frank Inouye;[30] social scientists such as Aasel Hansen and Rita Takahashi Cates;[31] journalists and journalist historians like Bill Hosokawa and Lauren Kessler;[32] artists such as Estelle Peck Ishigo;[33] photographers like Masumi Hayashi, Hansel Mieth, and Otto Hagel;[34] filmmakers such as Steven Okazaki, Emiko Omori, and Frank Abe;[35] novelists like Gretel Erlich;[36] oral historians like John Tateishi and Susan McKay;[37] archivists such as Eric Bittner;[38] and even firsthand participants and observers like Frank Emi, James Omura, Velma Kessel, and Peter Simpson.[39] With the possible exception of the Tule Lake center, Heart Mountain is probably the best documented of all the wartime Japanese American imprisonment facilities, including so-called assembly centers, relocation centers, segregation centers, isolation centers, and internment camps. Accordingly, it is possible to gain a pretty clear picture of the oppression that existed there as well as the resistance that developed in response to it.

Although Heart Mountain was located outside the Western Defense Command's "Restricted Area," it nonetheless was subject to controls similar to those WRA centers sited within that area, such as Manzanar and Tule Lake in California and Poston and Gila in Arizona. In addition, the same public hostilities were directed at its residents.

In common with those camps in the "Restricted Area," Heart Mountain, as Rita Takahashi Cates has reported, was surrounded by barbed wire fence and watched over by sentry-manned guard towers. The imprisoned population collectively protested these unnecessary indignities. Indeed, a November 1942 petition, signed by half of all the adults in the camp, over 3,000 people, denounced the fence and guard towers as "ridiculous in every respect. . . . a barrier to a full understanding between the Administration and residents" and as "devoid of humanitarian principles . . . [and] an insult to any free human being."[40] The petition was sent to WRA director Dillon Myer charging that the fence proved that Heart Mountain was a "concentration camp" and that inmates were "prisoners of war." Inmates supplemented such written indirect protest against oppression with direct oral resistance to and outright defiance of military authority. As recalled by one noted resistance leader, Nisei Frank Inouye, "on several occasions Nisei men found near the fence . . . were pushed or shoved by guards, and they retaliated with angry cries of 'Go ahead, shoot me.'"[41]

Then, in December 1942, the military policy patrolling the camp boundaries arrested thirty-two persons for security violations. The culprits whom the US Army took into custody on this occasion were all children eleven or under in age, who had been sledding on a hill just outside of camp. Although released later the same day, this callous treatment of children, in the words of Roger Daniels, "understandably inflamed many of the Japanese Americans and sparked a general protest against the whole theory and practice of the evacuation."[42]

This protest extended to the camp authorities' practice of searching outgoing inmate mail and the imposition of a "pass system" for center ingress and egress. This sense of oppression was compounded by the actions of the nearby Park County towns of Powell and Cody, both of which passed resolutions barring inmates.[43] This particular oppression was further exacerbated by Wyoming's governor, Lester Hunt, declaring that these resolutions were well reasoned and in the interest of the inmates' safety and welfare. Heart Mountaineers viewed it as a matter of rank hypocrisy that, while they were not permitted in Cody or Powell, they were permitted, without screening or investigation, to be released from Heart Mountain to harvest crops for beleaguered farmers within the region surrounding the camp. To add to the inmates' sense of being a despised and persecuted people, the major metropolitan newspaper serving the camp population, the *Denver Post*, was stridently anti-Japanese and, in March 1943, leveled flagrant and unfounded charges that Heart Mountain had excessive foodstuffs and that the inmates were guilty of wantonly wasting these supplies.[44]

More oppression emanated from Heart Mountain's appointed staff, a portion of whom referred to their Nikkei charges as "Japs," and both viewed and treated them contemptuously. Some of these Caucasian employees even threatened to resign from their administrative positions if certain demands of theirs were not heeded. Included in a petition signed by them were the following two offenses: (1) "We object to sharing our dorm with the Japs";

and (2) "We ask that a woman janitor be appointed and that the rest of the Japanese be compelled to keep out of our living rooms. They have their own quarters, [and] we feel that we are entitled to ours. WE MEAN IT!"[45]

Another source of inmate oppression included the use at Heart Mountain, as at other WRA camps, of informers. A related problem that contributed to a loss of inmate autonomy was that Heart Mountain authorities strategically placed pro-administration inmates into desired leadership positions so as to enable them to rally support for the actions, programs, and goals of the camp and the WRA administration. A prime case in point, according to Rita Takahashi Cates and Roger Daniels, was the appointment of accommodationist and JACL supporter Bill Hosokawa as *Heart Mountain Sentinel* editor: "During the height of discontent at the camp, Hosokawa's paper 'reacted typically . . . by assuring the Heart Mountaineers that Director Dillon Myer's WRA was doing "everything possible" under the circumstances.'"[46]

Internal factors that influenced inmate perceptions and responses encompassed Heart Mountain's physical conditions, including the provision of basic amenities and support services. In common with other WRA camps, Heart Mountain was beset with problems related to food services. Inmates complained that food intended for them was either not being delivered to them or else was being diverted to some other destination. This led to a series of investigations, some of which were launched by inmate groups. Food supplies ultimately were normalized. However, because some inmates feared that under conditions of heavy snows the camp population could become isolated and starve, camp chefs stowed surplus supplies in the block mess hall storerooms once the all-center warehouses were filled to capacity.

In December 1942, Earl Best, the assistant camp steward and a former army man notorious for his undiplomatic dealings with Japanese Americans, undertook an inventory of Heart Mountain food supplies. When he uncovered a cache of food stored in one block mess hall's attic, he heatedly confronted the chef responsible, a Mr. Haraguchi. Best later formally complained that Haraguchi "had a cleaver in his hand . . . [and] threw a case of applesauce at me when I was leaving."[47] In his solicitude for the people in his block, Haraguchi had become distraught and distempered. Apparently, the situation was even worse than Best had described. Other witnesses divulged that Haraguchi had been wielding a butcher knife and that only the timely intervention of some Japanese women kitchen workers prevented him from killing Best's inmate assistant. Furthermore, Heart Mountain's director of internal security noted in a report on this incident that "all [of the camp] cooks appear to be banded together in some type of union," while a spokesman for the cooks was alleged to have said that if the soldiers tried to prevent a strike, "someone would be killed" and that he "would also kill someone."[48]

Inmates, well beyond this particular incident, continued their anguished concern over camp food service, including the quality and the quantity of the food dished up to them. A January 1943 investigation of the camp's thirty-three mess halls, undertaken by the Block Managers Evacuees Food Committee, reported that menus were unfit for children, unbalanced, too starchy, lacked adequate fruits and vegetables, and included dishes that were far too greasy to be eaten by those on regular diets, to say nothing of those on restricted ones.

As in the other WRA camps, Heart Mountain's housing situation was dismal, especially during the opening phase of the center's existence when the barracks quarters were unfinished and the "apartments" were congested by an overabundance of occupants. If shelter from the elements was a cause for concern, so too was clothing. Despite repeated promises from the camp's administration for the delivery of clothing allowances, none arrived at Heart Mountain until November 1942. In the meantime, the agitated camp population reacted to this oppressive delay by repeated requests, petitions, and even a strike.

A strike also occurred at the Heart Mountain hospital in June 1943. Medical historian Louis Fiset, in a fascinating 1998 article, has covered this incident in compelling detail.[49] In October of 1942 the *Heart Mountain Sentinel* had lauded the hospital, describing the seventeen-wing facility, which was staffed by 150 employees (including nine physicians, ten registered nurses, three graduate nurses, and forty-nine nurses aides), among Wyoming's best hospitals. But the *Sentinel* picture was a misleading one. The hospital's comparative lack of equipment and acutely limited supplies obliged its doctors to move patients to nearby Cody and Powell, or even to transport them as far away as Billings, Montana, for surgeries or special treatments. When supplies that had been ordered failed to arrive, the chief medical officer had to round up basic supplies (e.g., swabs, needles, and drugs) locally.

Of still greater significance, the WRA's tardiness in recruiting a head nurse for the hospital meant that the nonprofessional staff, which would expand to over 300 in number, was deficient in organization, wanting in professionalism, and practically unmanageable. Not only the chief medical officer but also the appointed hospital personnel were culturally obtuse and demonstrated unsound judgment when interacting with the Nikkei medical staff (most of whom were already smarting from having lost much of their lofty pre-war status and being paid insultingly minuscule camp wages for their professional services). Given this overall situation, morale suffered greatly, and eventually resentments built up against the Caucasian personnel in authority to the point where two hospital walkouts occurred in 1943.

Earlier in 1943, dissent at Heart Mountain was precipitated by the WRA's announced plans to convert the government-owned and -operated Community Enterprises stores in the camps into inmate-owned and -operated cooperatives. The seemingly benign purpose for this change was to put inmates at the helm of the camp's largest operation. But rather than embracing this change of affairs with gratitude, the inmates overwhelmingly rejected it. The opposition's most vociferous spokesperson was the fifty-four-year-old, Hawai'i-born Kiyoshi Okamoto.

Okamoto, in the words of fellow camp activist Frank Inouye, "had previously been a sharp critic of the Japanese American Citizens League, which he considered a Quisling organization because of its earlier cooperation and collaboration with the federal authorities during the 1942 removal of West Coast Japanese Americans."[50] Openly denigrating the WRA cooperation plan, Okamoto vented his antipathy at block meetings and in letters to the *Heart Mountain Sentinel*. Through the mechanism of the cooperative plan, reasoned Okamoto, the US government sought to legitimize their unconstitutional eviction and detention of Japanese Americans. Accepting direct responsibility for operating the cooperatives was tantamount to accepting their wartime mistreatment as a valid and necessary move. Precisely because the incarceration was patently illegal, declared Okamoto, "the government and only the government was fully responsible for the welfare of the camp population."[51] Okamoto's viewpoint prevailed at Heart Mountain. The WRA's subsequent abandonment of its plan represented, to quote Frank Inouye once again, "the first in a series of 'victories' by the Heart Mountain internees over the WRA. It gave them a sense of limited control over their circumstances and encouraged later and more far-reaching dissident movements."[52]

Susan McKay's discerning article on the "everyday resistance" of young Nisei women at the Heart Mountain camp divulges a subtle way in which a portion of the inmate population there achieved, in Inouye's formulation, "limited control over their circumstances" and stimulated long-range dissent (not only during the war in camp, but even much later as within the 1970s–1980s movement for redress and reparations). Based upon open-ended, generalized oral history interviews that McKay conducted in the late 1990s with twenty-four former Heart Mountain Nisei women (mostly married mothers while in camp) who were born between 1911 and 1923, this article concludes that these women, in nonpublic ways (what McKay styles "infrapolitics") and largely within the sphere of "informal networks of kin, neighbors, family, and friends," resisted by "speaking up, defying rules, and protesting."[53] Many of their resistance activities typically involved efforts to improve family life, particularly as it affected their children. Others were directed at affronts to their ethnic and social class identity. Still other resistance and protest was directed at improving housing (e.g., demands for separate space) and food conditions (e.g., challenging mess hall managers for disallowing food to be prepared in family barracks for those children reluctant to eat in a communal facility) that related to their family's well-being. Some of the means they used involved risk, such as a hospital nurse defying her Caucasian superior's orders, while others, such as simply acting "normal" in a concentration camp environment (dressing up, wearing cosmetics, and indulging in gossip), opposed their circumstances in less obtrusive yet nonetheless effective ways.

Up until early 1943, notwithstanding what has been described above in the way of protest and resistance activity, some Heart Mountain administrators insisted on characterizing their detention center as a "happy camp." After this point in time, with the emergence of the registration and segregation crisis, dissent became so dramatically manifest as to render such a sanguine label utterly out of whack with the reality at Heart Mountain. With this development, the latent discontents within the camp burst into the open, and the inmate population's opposition to US government, WRA, and center authorities so intensified and ramified that it could justifiably be said that Heart Mountain became, at least for a spell, the least "happy" WRA camp.

The registration program was initiated throughout the Japanese American camps in February 1943 by the issuance of the US Army-WRA "Leave Clearance" questionnaires. At Heart Mountain this program, as aptly phrased by Rita Takahashi Cates, "was implemented with less than 'deliberate speed' and 'desirable results' due to widespread resistance and protest."[54]

Encouraged by the success of the 100th Battalion, rooted in prewar Japanese American volunteers and Hawai'i draftees, the government, in order to create an all-Nisei 442nd Regimental Combat Team, "adjusted" the Selective Service Act barring Nisei enlistees. The military had expected to obtain 1,500 volunteers from Hawai'i, but instead was overwhelmed by over 10,000 of them. On the other hand, the army's belief that an equal number would volunteer for military service from the mainland camps proved embarrassingly wide of the mark. Nevertheless, Secretary of War Henry Stimson, the Cabinet officer who most strongly supported Nikkei exclusion and imprisonment, now became a fugleman for camp volunteerism. To separate the "traitors" or "rotten apples" from the "patriots," he devised a screening system. "It is only by mutual confidence and cooperation," he exclaimed, "that the loyal Japanese American can be restored to their civil rights."[55] The irony of Stimson's exclamation, as Frank Inouye has astutely observed, was not lost on the Nisei at Heart Mountain and the other camps. The "mutual confidence and cooperation" Stimson mentioned would be manifested on their part by their being allowed to die for their country. America's confidence had already been demonstrated in indicting, judging, convicting, sentencing, imprisoning, and dispossessing one-hundred thousand people without evidence or legal formalization.[56]

Because the WRA had been looking for a quick and effective way of distinguishing which of their charges should be permitted to work outside the camps, they capitalized upon a War Department–developed form to be used for recruiting soldiers as the basis for their own questionnaire for leave clearance. The use of these two overlapping documents caused a series of escalating confrontations between the government and the inmates at all of the camps, including Heart Mountain.

Two questions, especially, provoked inmate resentment:

No. 27. Are you willing to serve in the Armed Forces of the United States on combat duty wherever ordered?

No. 28. Will you swear unqualified allegiance to the United States of America?

Adult males and females were obliged to respond to the form. Issei, ineligible to become naturalized US citizens, were indignant because swearing unqualified allegiance to the United States, as question 28 demanded, would mean a repudiation of their Japanese citizenship and would render them stateless people. The Nisei, on the other hand, were upset over this question because it implied that they were foreign nationals seeking US citizenship. In fact, both questions infuriated Nisei males because they saw in them a clever trap. "By signing the questionnaire 'yes/yes,'" explains Frank Inouye, "they could be immediately drafted into the Armed Service as volunteers without further processing or exemptions. They would then be forced to leave their aging Issei parents in camp at the mercy of a government that had already proven its disregard for basic human rights."[57] Nor were Nisei females happy with these questions, since their signing them would indicate a willingness to serve in the military.

The registration crisis was especially acute at Heart Mountain. The responsibility for this state of affairs started at the top with the camp's director, Guy Robertson. Instead of proceeding with deliberation and due caution and collaboration, he threatened the inmates with severe consequences if they did not respond as expected. Feeling that the government expected the camps to produce army recruits in the same abundance as in Hawai'i, he championed the cause of registration in the *Heart Mountain Sentinel* and bullied block leaders to ensure compliance in the process by all of their respective adult denizens.

When the Army Registration Team visited Heart Mountain, they encountered stiff opposition at their first major meeting, on February 6, with inmates (overwhelmingly Nisei men). Led by Frank Inouye, a prewar UCLA senior student, a small group of these Nisei men had been holding advance meetings for the explicit purpose of resisting the registration process. Their intention, plainly, was to "disrupt the meeting by challenging the government's right to recruit volunteers without first clarifying and restoring the Nisei's constitutional rights."[58]

The head of the Army Registration Team began the meeting by reiterating Stimson's line: "Our mission is to return you to a normal way of life. . . . Its fundamental purpose is to put your situation on a plane which is consistent with the dignity of American citizenship. Not all Japanese Americans are loyal to their government . . . and individuals who will not accept any obligation to the land which gives them their opportunity . . . are the disloyal ones."[59] This address called forth, by way of a rejoinder, a Nisei manifesto read by Inouye. He referred to the degradation and discrimination suffered by earlier Nisei draftees in the army, he assailed the US government for the enforced mass eviction and detention of his ethnic community, and he ridiculed the irony of the government now asking these same victims to shed their blood for America. Before requesting the Nisei's military enlistment, Inouye concluded his oration, the government should first acknowledge their rights as American citizens.

This "manifesto" was roundly received among camp Nisei and effectively sabotaged every subsequent attempt by the army team to implement its registration at Heart Mountain. Meanwhile, Inouye called for the creation of an elected central body to explore how best, under the present circumstances, to ensure the best interests of the camp's citizens. And on that very evening each block chose two representatives to serve in the new organization.

On February 11, the group held its first meeting. All of those in attendance were Nisei males, including two who would later become well known the following year as the leaders of the Heart Mountain Fair Play Committee: the aforementioned Kiyoshi Okamoto and Paul Nakadate. Frank Inouye was elected to chair this group, which adopted as its name the Heart Mountain Congress of American Citizens, while Nakadate was chosen to be its secretary. At this meeting, Inouye has recollected, "the delegates submitted fourteen resolutions which were eventually distilled into four main subjects: (1) Clarification of Nisei citizenship status; (2) publicizing of clarification by the US President, the Secretary of War and the Attorney General; (3) Postponement of further registration until clarification was obtained; and (4) implied consent of the Nisei to serve in the armed forces upon clarification of their citizenship status."[60]

The Heart Mountain Congress, as an initial order of business, had to reconcile a paradox associated with the registration. Many camp Nisei were against serving in the armed forces, but at the same time they did not want to lose their US citizenship. The congress resolved, after considerable deliberation, to recommend that Nisei give a "yes" response to question 27. "This," according to Inouye, "was felt to be the most expedient means of attaining the Congress' main goal: clarification of Nisei citizenship status. Unless the men indicated their willingness to serve, they would have little bargaining power with the federal government."[61]

Camp activities during this time came effectively to a halt. Dissident voices were heard, loud and clear, within the community. Frank Emi, destined to be a prominent leader, like Okamoto and Nakadate, within the Fair Play Committee, posted hand-printed copies of his answers to questions 27 and 28 in public places throughout the camp: "Under the present conditions and circumstances, I am unable to answer these questions." Okamoto, who opposed all appeasement of authorities as long as Nisei were illegally detained, spoke out advising Nisei to resist all camp recruiting activities while they were still illegally detained. So alarmed were camp administrators regarding these activities that they tried to prevent the *Sentinel* from covering the congress's activities, while Director Robertson "threatened to invoke the espionage and sedition laws against those seeking to derail the registration process."[62]

Notwithstanding this opposition, the Heart Mountain Congress of American Citizens continued with its campaign. On February 19 it even sent President Franklin Roosevelt a formal petition of protest, plus telegrams to the other nine camps recommending them to act similarly.

Although the registration process eventually proceeded, the Heart Mountain Congress scored an important triumph when the army conceded that inmates could answer questions 27 and 28 with qualified or conditional responses. Moreover, the final tally of registration showed what a bust it had been in all of the WRA camps. Rather than achieving the 1,500 volunteers that the army sought, it received merely 805. The situation at Heart Mountain was still more pathetic: whereas 2,000 volunteers were expected, only 38 signed on, and a scant 19 of these were eventually inducted.

Then, too, the Heart Mountain Congress produced an unexpected—and certainly unwanted—result: 800 Nisei in camp renounced their US citizenship. "The body had been formed to protest the registration process and clarify Nisei rights," Frank Inouye has written. However, what instead emerged, in his opinion "was a massive vote for repatriation to Japan."[63]

While the congress assuredly did not realize its stated demands, it laid down a legacy that was carried on in the early months of 1944 by a group headed by Kiyoshi Okamoto, Paul Nakadate, and Frank Emi. This new group, the Heart Mountain Fair Play Committee, coalesced once the government decided to "honor" the American citizenship rights of the Nisei by reopening the military to them through making them eligible to be drafted into the army.[64]

NOTES

For their respective efforts on behalf of this article, I offer my thanks to Mike Mackey, Carolyn Takeshita, Tak Hoshizaki, James Omura, Lawson Inada, Eric Muller, Frank Abe, William Hohri, Frank Emi, Yosh Kuromiya, and Takashi Fujitani.

1. Roger Daniels, *Concentration Camps USA: Japanese Americans and World War II* (New York: Holt, Rinehart and Winston, 1971); Douglas Nelson, *Heart Mountain: The History of an American Concentration Camp* (Madison: State Historical Society of Wisconsin, 1976).

2. See Roger Daniels, Sandra C. Taylor, and Harry H.L. Kitano, eds., *Japanese Americans: From Relocation to Redress* (Salt Lake City: University of Utah Press, 1986). For my review of this volume, see Arthur A. Hansen, review of *Japanese Americans: From Relocation to Redress*, ed. Roger Daniels, Sandra C. Taylor, and Harry H.L. Kitano, *American Historical Review* 93 (October 1988): 1136–37.

3. See Arthur A. Hansen, "James Matsumoto Omura: An Interview," *Amerasia Journal* 13 (1986–87): 99–113.

4. Michi Nishiura Weglyn, *Years of Infamy: The Untold Story of America's Concentration Camps* (New York: William Morrow, 1976). For my review of this volume, see Arthur A. Hansen, review of *Years of Infamy: The Untold Story of America's Concentration Camps*, *American Historical Review* 82 (June 1977): 765–66.

5. Lane Ryo Hirabayashi, "Re-reading the Archives: The Intersection of Ethnography, Biography, & Autobiography in the Historiography of Japanese Americans during World War II," in *Remembering Heart Mountain: Essays on Japanese American Internment in Wyoming*, ed. Mike Mackey (Powell, WY: Western History Publications, 1998), 208n26.

6. See Roger S. Gottlieb, "The Concept of Resistance: Jewish Resistance during the Holocaust," *Social Theory and Practice* 9 (Spring 1983): 31–49. Unless otherwise specifically noted, the basis for the theoretical portion of this essay derives from Gottlieb's article. I have shaped it to fit the similar but different circumstances of the JAI experience. Although only specific quotations from the Gottlieb piece are referenced here, my indebtedness to the author extends to its entirety.

7. Gottlieb, "Concept of Resistance," 41.

8. Gottlieb, "Concept of Resistance," 42.

9. Gottlieb, "Concept of Resistance," 34.

10. Gottlieb, "Concept of Resistance," 41.

11. Gottlieb, "Concept of Resistance," 34.

12. Gottlieb, "Concept of Resistance," 44.

13. Gottlieb, "Concept of Resistance," 44–45.

14. Gottlieb, "Concept of Resistance," 47.

15. Okihiro's published resistance writings were launched with his seminal "Japanese Resistance in America's Concentration Camps: A Reevaluation," *Amerasia Journal* 2 (Fall 1973): 20–34; they continued through a couple of other stellar journal articles: "Tule Lake under Martial Law: A Study of Japanese Resistance," *Journal of Ethnic Studies* 5 (Fall 1977): 71–86; and "Religion and Resistance in America's Concentration Camps," *Phylon* 45 (September 1985): 220–33; plus a trio of books: (with Timothy J. Lukes) *Japanese Legacy: Farming and Community Life in California's Santa Clara Valley* (Cupertino: California History Center, 1985); *Cane Fires: The Anti-Japanese Movement in Hawai'i, 1865–1945* (Philadelphia: Temple University Press, 1991); and *Whispered Silences: Japanese Americans and World War II* (Seattle: University of Washington Press, 1995). However, the basis for the examples of Japanese American resistance used here is Okihiro's introductory essay, "The Japanese in America," in *Encyclopedia of Japanese American History: An A–Z Reference from 1868 to the Present,* ed. Brian Niiya (Los Angeles: Japanese American National Museum, 2001), 1–23. As with the above citations relating to the article by Roger Gottlieb on the concept of resistance, while only specific quoted passages from Okihiro's essay will be cited, my debt encompasses the author's full work.

16. Okihiro, "The Japanese in America," 2.

17. Okihiro, "The Japanese in America," 4–5.

18. Donald H. Estes, "Abe, Tokunosuke," in *Encyclopedia of Japanese American History,* ed. Niiya, 108.

19. Coverage of these epic events is beyond the scope of this undertaking. For summarized treatment of each of them, along with suggestions for further reading, see the following pertinent entries in Niiya, ed., *Encyclopedia of Japanese American History*; Glen Kitayama, "*Yasui v. United States,*" 422–24; Glen Kitayama, "*Hirabayashi v. United States,*" 194–95; Glen Kitayama, "*Korematsu v. United States,*" 251–52; Glen Kitayama, "*Endo, Ex Parte,*" 159–60; "Assembly Centers" and "Santa Anita Camouflage Net Project," 125, 360–61; "Poston Strike," 338; "Manzanar Incident," 267–68; and "Tule Lake 'Segregation Center,'" 395–97.

20. Okihiro began compiling the contributions for this anthology in the late 1970s and during the 1980s offered it several times, without success, for publication consideration to commercial and university presses. In the late 1980s and early 1990s, I joined editorial forces with Okihiro to revise and resubmit the manuscript for renewed consideration as a book, but this effort never reached fruition.

21. Bob Kumamoto, "The Search for Spies: American Counterintelligence and the Japanese American Community, 1931–1942," *Amerasia Journal* 6 (Fall 1979): 45–75.

22. Unpaginated introduction to Okihiro, "Japanese Resistance in America's Concentration Camps."

23. Okihiro, "Japanese Resistance in America's Concentration Camps," n.p. For an extended treatment of the essay referenced here, see the study from which it derived: David A. Hacker, "A Culture Resisted, A Culture Revived: The Loyalty Crisis of 1943 at the Manzanar War Relocation Center" (master's thesis, California State University, Fullerton, 1980).

24. See Arthur A. Hansen and David A. Hacker, "The Manzanar Riot: An Ethnic Perspective," *Amerasia Journal* 2 (Fall 1974): 112–57.

25. Okihiro, "Religion and Resistance in America's Concentration Camps."

26. Norman Richard Jackman, "Collective Protest in Relocation Centers" (PhD diss., University of California, Berkeley, 1955).

27. See Richard Nishimoto, *Inside an American Concentration Camp: Japanese American Resistance at Poston, Arizona*, ed. Lane Ryo Hirabayashi (Tucson: University of Arizona Press, 1945).

28. Nishimoto, *Inside an American Concentration Camp*, 164.

29. Nishimoto, *Inside an American Concentration Camp*, 165.

30. See T. A. Larson, *Wyoming's War Years 1941–1945* (Stanford, CA: Stanford University Press, 1954), esp. chap. 12, "Heart Mountain," 297–321; Daniels, *Concentration Camps USA*, esp. chap. 6, "A Question of Loyalty," 104–29; Nelson, *Heart Mountain*; Mike Mackey, *Heart Mountain: Life in Wyoming's Concentration Camp* (Powell, WY: Western History Publications, 2000); Mackey, ed., *Remembering Heart Mountain*; Mackey, "The Heart Mountain Relocation Center: Economic Opportunities in Wyoming," in *Remembering Heart Mountain*, ed. Mackey, 51–59; and Mackey's 1998 overview essay entitled "A Brief History of the Heart Mountain Relocation Center and the Japanese American Experience," Heart Mountain Digital Preservation Project, John Taggart Hinckley Library, Northwest College, Powell, Wyoming, available on a CD-ROM or on the project's website at http://chem.nwc.cc.wy.us/HMDP/Homepage.htm. Louis Fiset, "The Heart Mountain Hospital Strike of June 24, 1943," in *Remembering Heart Mountain*, ed. Mackey, 101–18. Frank Chin, "Come All Ye Asian American Writers of the Real and the Fake," in *The Big Aiiieeeee! An Anthology of Chinese American and Japanese American Literature*, ed. Frank Chin, Jeffrey Paul Chan, Lawson Inada, and Shawn Wong (New York: Meridian, 1991), 1–92, esp. 52–82. William Minoru Hohri, ed., *Resistance: Challenging America's Wartime Internment of Japanese-Americans* (Los Angeles: The Epistolarian, 2001). This important volume includes first-person accounts by a leader of the Heart Mountain Fair Play Committee (Frank Seishi Emi) and three draft resisters associated with that Heart Mountain camp organization (Mits Koshiyama, Yosh Kuromiya, and Takashi Hoshizaki). Eric L. Muller, *Free to Die for Their Country: The Story of the Japanese American Draft Resisters in World War II* (Chicago: University of Chicago Press, 2001). Gwenn M. Jensen, "Illuminating the Shadows: Post-Traumatic Flashbacks from Heart Mountain and

Other Camps," in *Remembering Heart Mountain*, ed. Mackey, 217–28. Susan L. Smith, "Caregiving in Camp: Japanese American Women and Community Health in World War II," in *Essays on Japanese Settlement, Internment, and Relocation in the Rocky Mountain West*, ed. Mike Mackey (Powell, WY: Western History Publications, 2001), 187–201. Frank T. Inouye, "Immediate Origins of the Heart Mountain Draft Resistance Movement," in *Remembering Heart Mountain*, ed. Mackey, 121–39; and Inouye's unpublished memoir, "Odyssey of a Nisei: A Voyage of Self-Discovery," Department of Special Collections, Library, University of Cincinnati. Thanks are extended to Professor Roger Daniels for alerting me to the existence of this manuscript and arranging to have it copied and made available to me.

31. Aasel Hansen, "My Two Years at Heart Mountain: The Difficult Role of an Applied Anthropologist," in *Japanese Americans*, ed. Daniels, Taylor, and Kitano, 33–37. Rita Takahashi Cates, "Comparative Administration and Management of Five War Relocation Authority Camps: America's Incarceration of Persons of Japanese Descent during World War II" (PhD diss., University of Pittsburgh, 1980).

32. See, in particular, Bill Hosokawa, "The Sentinel Story," in *Remembering Heart Mountain*, ed. Mackey, 63–73. Lauren Kessler, "Fettered Freedoms: The Journalism of World War II Internment Camps," *Journalism History* 15 (Summer/Autumn 1988): 70–79.

33. Estelle Peck Ishigo, *Lone Heart Mountain* (Los Angeles: Anderson, Ritchie & Simon, 1972).

34. See Masumi Hayashi's website, csuohio.edu, for her American Concentration Camps series of photographs, especially those relating to the Heart Mountain camp: *Blue Room* (1995), *Hospital* (1995), and *Root Cellar* (1996). See Mamoru Inouye and Grace Schaub, *The Heart Mountain Story: Photographs by Hansel Mieth and Otto Hagel of the World War II Internment of Japanese Americans* (Los Gatos, CA: privately printed, 1997). See also Mamoru Inouye, "Heart Mountain High School, 1942–1945," in *Remembering Heart Mountain*, ed. Mackey, 75–100.

35. See Steven Okazaki, producer and director, *Days of Waiting* (1988), a documentary film about Heart Mountain artist Estelle Peck Ishigo, one of the few Caucasian inmates in the camps. Two years earlier, in 1986, KTWO News in Wyoming aired a documentary film on Heart Mountain titled *Winter in My Soul*. See also Emiko Omori, coproducer (with Chizuko Omori) and director, *Rabbit in the Moon* (1999), a documentary film about resistance activity in relation to the Japanese American Incarceration, including extensive footage devoted to such activity in relationship to the Heart Mountain camp; and Frank Abe, producer and director, *Conscience and the Constitution* (2000), a documentary film about the Heart Mountain Fair Play Committee and the draft resistance movement at the Heart Mountain camp.

36. Gretchen Ehrlich, *Heart Mountain* (New York: Viking, 1988).

37. John Tateishi, ed., *And Justice for All: An Oral History of the Japanese American Detention Camps* (New York: Random House, 1984). Susan McKay, "Young Women's Everyday Resistance: Heart Mountain, Wyoming," in *Guilt by Association*, ed. Mackey, 203–16.

38. Eric Bittner, "'Loyalty . . . is a Covenant': Japanese-American Internees and the Selective Service Act," *Prologue* 23 (Fall 1991): 248–334; and Eric Bittner, "Records at the National Archives–Rocky Mountain Region Relating to the Japanese American Internment Experience," in *Remembering Heart Mountain*, ed. Mackey, 209–14.

39. Frank Emi, "Resistance: The Heart Mountain Fair Play Committee's Fight for Justice," *Amerasia Journal* 17 (1991): 47–51; and Frank Seishi Emi, "Draft Resistance at the Heart Mountain Concentration Camp and the Fair Play Committee," in *Frontiers of Asian American Studies: Writing, Research, and Commentary*, ed. Gail M. Nomura, Russell Endo, Stephen H. Sumida, and Russell C. Leong (Pullman: Washington State University Press, 1989), 41–69. James Omura, "Japanese American Journalism during World War II," in *Frontiers of Asian American Studies*, ed. Nomura et al., 71–80. Velma Kessel, "Remembering the Heart Mountain Hospital," in *Remembering Heart Mountain*, ed. Mackey, 187–92. Peter K. Simpson, "Recollections of Heart Mountain," in *Remembering Heart Mountain*, ed. Mackey, 179–85.

40. Quoted in Cates, "Comparative Administration and Management," 190.

41. Inouye, "Immediate Origins," 123.

42. Daniels, *Concentration Camps USA*, 118.

43. See Mike Mackey, "Media Influence on Local Attitudes toward the Heart Mountain Relocation Center," in *Guilt by Association*, ed. Mackey, 239–52, esp. 248. See also Jensen, "Illuminating the Shadows," for evidence that corroborates Mackey's assessment of greater community opposition in Cody than Powell to the Heart Mountain population.

44. On the *Denver Post*'s anti-Japanese and generally racist editorial policies during World War II, see Kumiko Takahara's unpublished manuscript, "The *Denver Post*'s Story of the Japanese American Internment in Colorado." Professor Takahara is a faculty member in the Department of East Asian Languages and Civilizations at the University of Colorado at Boulder. A portion of her book-length manuscript has been published as "Japanese American Women: Guilty by Race and Gender," in *Guilt by Association*, ed. Mackey, 219–38.

45. Quoted in Cates, "Comparative Administration and Management," 199.

46. See Cates, "Comparative Administration and Management," 203, and Daniels, *Concentration Camps USA*, 118.

47. Quoted in Cates, "Comparative Administration and Management," 206.

48. Quoted in Inouye, "Immediate Origins," 122. I have relied very heavily upon Inouye's article for resistance developments at the Heart Mountain camp through 1943, as the many subsequent references to this fine study manifestly testify.

49. Fiset, "Heart Mountain Hospital Strike."

50. Inouye, "Immediate Origins," 123.

51. Inouye, "Immediate Origins," 123.

52. Inouye, "Immediate Origins."

53. McKay, "Young Women's Everyday Resistance," 208.

54. Cates, "Comparative Administration and Management," 485.

55. Quoted in Inouye, "Immediate Origins," 125.

56. Inouye, "Immediate Origins."

57. Inouye, "Immediate Origins."

58. Inouye, "Immediate Origins," 126.

59. Quoted in Inouye, "Immediate Origins," 126.

60. Inouye, "Immediate Origins," 126–27.

61. Inouye, "Immediate Origins," 127.

62. Inouye, "Immediate Origins," 127.

63. Inouye, "Immediate Origins," 127–28.

64. The draft resistance movement at the Heart Mountain Relocation Center, which was rooted in and enacted through that detention center's Fair Play Committee, is too complex to neatly summarize here. It was first dealt with by Daniels, *Concentration Camps USA*, and Nelson, *Heart Mountain*, and recently given full-dress treatment by Muller, *Free to Die for Their Country*. All three of these scholars were connected with the University of Wyoming when developing their respective studies.

6

POLITICAL IDEOLOGY AND PARTICIPANT OBSERVATION

Nisei Social Scientists in the Japanese American Evacuation and Resettlement Study, 1942–1945

Throughout the 1980s, I took frequent research trips to the Bancroft Library at the University of California, Berkeley, with the particular aim of familiarizing myself with the abundant holdings in the Japanese American Evacuation and Resettlement Study. Having done so to my satisfaction, I arranged to conduct an interview in mid-July of 1987 with one of the study's field workers, the anthropologist Robert Spencer, who was then winding down a long academic career at the University of Minnesota. Two months later I participated in a two-day conference at Berkeley titled "Views from Within: The Japanese-American Wartime Internment Experience," the second day of which was devoted to a reassessment of the Japanese American Evacuation and Resettlement Study, a special wartime research project which studied the mass internment of Japanese-Americans. The conference participants included both former JERS staff members and researchers interested in JERS.[1] While at this

This essay is from *Guilt by Association: Essays on Japanese Settlement, Internment, and Relocation in the Rocky Mountain West* edited by Mike Mackey (© 2001) and reproduced with permission of Mike Mackey.

DOI: 10.5876/9781607328124.c006

exciting and enlightening conference, I not only became acquainted with Japanese American JERS staff members but also made plans to interview two of the Nisei staffers, Charles Kikuchi (who conducted field work with Robert Spencer at the Gila River concentration camp) and James Sakoda (whose fieldwork was divided between the Tule Lake and Minidoka detention centers). These interviews, conducted for the Japanese American Project of the Oral History Program at California State University, Fullerton, took place in early August of the following year at their respective Rhode Island residences.

My interviews with Kikuchi and Sakoda, two of the most productive Nikkei associated with the Japanese American Evacuation and Resettlement Study, were both exceedingly memorable. The taping of Kikuchi, a retired New York City social worker, occurred at his family's vacation home on Block Island, which he shared with his wife Yuriko, a renowned dancer affiliated with the Martha Graham Dance Troupe. The interview took place coincident with a Kikuchi family gathering that included the two Kikuchi children, Susan and Lawrence, their spouses, and two grandchildren. My wife and I were honored to be enfolded into this special "reunion." Later that month Charles Kikuchi was scheduled to depart the United States for the Soviet Union to participate as a member of the US contingent in the International March for Peace from Odessa to Kiev. While in the USSR practicing his special variety of people-to-people diplomacy, Kikuchi planned to raise questions with both Russians and Americans about the status of racial minorities in the USSR and the United States. Tragically, Kikuchi was hospitalized in the USSR with terminal cancer, and shortly after being returned to the United States he succumbed.

As for James Sakoda, the interview with this distinguished social psychologist, professor emeritus, and origami artist was transacted both at his Brown University office and at his home in the nearby community of Barrington. This event was concluded on August 10, 1988. Fortuitously, this happened to be the day that President Ronald Reagan signed into law the Civil Liberties Act of 1988, a signal achievement that Sakoda and his wife consecrated with my wife and me at a sumptuous feast, with a champagne toast, held at the Sakodas' elegant riverside home. To mark this occasion for posterity, James Sakoda bestowed upon us the gift of any origami work done by him of our choosing.

In December 1990, at the annual meeting of the American Historical Association, I drew upon my archival knowledge of the Japanese American Evacuation and Resettlement Study and my fieldwork interviews with Charles Kikuchi and James Sakoda to present the paper that became the basis for the published article below, which appeared in the 2001 edited anthology by Mike Mackey entitled Guilt by Association: Essays on Japanese Settlement, Internment, and Relocation in the Rocky Mountain West.

On Independence Day 1942, twenty-six-year-old Charles Kikuchi, an American citizen of Japanese descent confined by his government in the Tanforan Assembly Center south of San Francisco, pondered in his diary the meaning of freedom and democracy. If the country at large was now really feeling "the grim realities of war," these had been acutely apparent to Kikuchi, his family, and his ethnic community from the outset of hostilities between his ancestral and native countries. In the wake of Pearl Harbor, the US government had apprehended and interned a substantial number of resident Japanese aliens, Issei, deemed "potentially dangerous." Ten weeks later, following President Franklin D. Roosevelt's signing of Executive Order 9066 on February 19, 1942, the remaining alien Japanese population and their American-born children, Nisei—all told, some 120,000 people, two-thirds possessing citizenship—were prohibited from living, working, or traveling in specified military zones on the West Coast. This exclusionary policy initially was implemented on a "voluntary" basis, but by late March it had been supplanted by an involuntary uprooting and eviction to fifteen hastily improvised detention centers, built largely within fairgrounds and racetracks (such as Tanforan), that the army operated through its newly created quasi-civilian agency, the Wartime Civil Control Administration (WCCA). As for Kikuchi, in early May he had curtailed his university studies across the bay in Berkeley to join his parents and five younger siblings at Tanforan where, as occupants of converted stable 10, stall 5, they became members of a barbed-wire-girded, military police–guarded "community" that by the Fourth of July totaled 8,000 people. "I get so tired of the flag waving," decried Kikuchi:

> This war must mean more than that. It is supposed to represent a way of
> life to us. We can only hope that it will turn out this way in the post war
> period. . . . The Japanese here are not disloyal. But we may as well be realistic
> about it. How can the democratic victory be applied to all minority groups
> in this country? It certainly won't be any better unless we fight for it now
> since the Caucasian American won't change his attitudes too much. These

questions do prevent many Nisei from not being more positively American. It is difficult to reconcile some things that have happened with true Democracy. Negroes are sent out to Australia to fight for Democracy; at home they don't get a full share of it. Nisei boys serve faithfully in the army; their parents are sent to Tanforan. Our problem is getting it to work better as well as to preserve it in this war. Unless we do this, we risk losing the essence of the whole thing we are defending on the war fronts of the world.[2]

While Kikuchi had accepted with relative equanimity the abrogation of his freedom as a sacrifice in the fight against fascism, he was not prepared to be stripped of his constitutional rights as an American citizen without offering stiff resistance. A case in point was freedom of the press. Remarked Kikuchi, the star reporter for the camp's inmate-staffed newspaper, the *Tanforan Totalizer*: "We . . . had fireworks [today] as far as the paper was concerned." That week's edition—containing three "questionable" submissions by Kikuchi, including one on the Constitution—had been distributed without receiving the mandated double-check by camp authorities. Consequently, staffers were obliged to retrieve all 2,500 copies of the *Totalizer*, editor Taro Katayama was "given hell," and the army clamped a triple-checking approval policy on the paper.

The next week, a Katayama editorial was rejected for quoting a comment from the latest *Pacific Citizen*, the Japanese American Citizens League's newspaper published at the JACL's transplanted wartime office in the "free zone" of Salt Lake City. The offending passage, which the irrepressible Kikuchi advised Katayama to "run anyway," pertained to a recent indignity suffered by a Nisei with the surname of Suzuki:

> What happened to Citizen Suzuki and 70,000 other American-born Japanese in the first year of America's war for world freedom is already a chapter in American history. . . . *The facts are all there. . . . Only the human side of the picture remains to be filled in. . . . Historians need documentation. The men who will write the human picture of the greatest forced movement of people in American history will do so from the personal records of the people themselves. . . . We hope that Citizen Suzuki is keeping a record of his experiences and his times.*[3]

This assault on the freedom of the press incensed Katayama. Before the month was out, he was grumbling to Kikuchi that he didn't "give a damn about the paper because it is so limited and could not have any value as social documentation." Kikuchi, whose "Your Opinion" column was arguably the newspaper's most popular feature, agreed with Katayama, though he opined that the *Totalizer* was not being published "for social documentation but as a service with an eye to raising morale [and giving] some picture of the Nisei to the outsiders that happened to get a hold of the paper."[4] Though not saying so directly, doubtless Kikuchi felt that the University of California–sponsored Japanese American Evacuation and Resettlement Study (JERS), the interdisciplinary project for which he maintained his diary at Tanforan and which had just confirmed his imminent employment as a participant-observer at the newly constructed Gila River Relocation Center in south-central Arizona, would tackle the significant task of social documentation.

The purpose for adducing the foregoing skein of facts has not been to enter the current debate over the nature and degree of censorship exercised against the inmate press in the WCCA assembly centers, such as Tanforan, and the ten semipermanent "relocation centers" administered by the War Relocation Authority (WRA), like Gila, that superseded them.[5] Rather, it has been to provide a point of departure and an analytical context for bringing together and mutually illuminating two late advances in the historiography of Japanese America—the configuring of competing political styles within the Nisei generation and the assessment of the performance of selected Nisei social scientists who, like Charles Kikuchi, were charged with documenting the Japanese American Incarceration (JAI) for JERS. After discussing these two historiographical developments, this paper will argue that the pervasive political approach to social change among the principal Nisei participant observers in JERS was "progressive" (i.e., left-liberal to radical), that this ideological perspective predisposed them toward a policy of "critical" as against "constructive" cooperation with respect to the JAI, and that this predisposition, in turn, manifested itself in the extensive personal-cum-social-scientific data they produced for JERS and, perforce, for future historical interpretation.

NISEI POLITICAL STYLES

Although the motion picture industry in this country continues to depict ethnic minority communities as monolithic enclaves whose members have been incapable of resisting racism through purposeful and consequential self-activity,[6] this baleful situation is being somewhat redressed by practitioners of the new ethnic studies. Much of their scholarship has revolved around questions of conflictual power relations, both of an internal and external variety, and has emphasized the agency of complex and dynamic community institutions and human constituents.[7]

A striking example relative to the Japanese American community is the political sociologist Jerrold Haruo Takahashi's 1980 doctoral dissertation, "Changing Responses to Racial Subordination: An Exploratory Study of Japanese American Political Styles." This study embraces the full sweep of the Japanese American past between the late-nineteenth-century influx into the United States of the immigrant Issei and the maturation of their Sansei grandchildren during the racial consciousness movement of the late 1960s and early 1970s. However, it is only the portion pertaining to the inter-war formation and World War II functioning of Nisei sociopolitical perspectives that requires schematic restatement for the restricted objectives of this piece.[8]

During the two decades prior to World War II, the Nisei combated their subjugated status in America and sought to achieve racial equality and a positive identity through developing three major ideological perspectives or political styles: the cultural bridge; the American ideal; and the progressive. The first of the three emerged during the xenophobic period following World War I. Because it was palliative and not curative for the endemic discrimination confronted by the Nisei, the "cultural bridge" perspective was modified and absorbed into the ideal of Americanization. This political style, which emphasized patriotism at the expense of ethnicity, steadily gained currency throughout the 1920s and into the early 1930s. It was promulgated in West Coast urban centers by a few prominent Nisei businessmen and culminated, institutionally, with the formation of the Japanese American Citizens League (JACL) in 1930.

Within a decade, the JACL became the leading Nisei organization, boasting fifty chapters comprising some 5,600 dues-paying members. Its leadership, both at the national and local levels, consisted chiefly of petty bourgeois, college-educated men. Considerably older than the majority of Nisei, they were commonly bilingual and responsive to the conciliatory temper and concerns of dominant Issei organizations like the Japanese Association. Indeed, the

JACL's "emphasis on legal and legislative change, along with extensive public relations work, paralleled the political style of the Japanese Association," while in matters of foreign policy "the League often became the spokesman for the Issei in defense of Japan's role in the Far East."[9]

Central to the JACL's political style was "a staunch faith in the capacity of American institutions to promote economic and racial progress."[10] Positively, this faith was expressed through an appeal to the Nisei generation to "lower the anchor" into the mainstream culture by pledging unqualified allegiance to their country of birth, exercising their civic duties through voting in local, state, and national elections, upholding the Constitution, and cherishing American political and economic ideals such as individualism, private property, and free enterprise. Negatively, it manifested itself in an aggressive posture toward any group or individual perceived as antithetical to America's capitalistic society or the classical republican virtues underpinning it. JACL leaders campaigned against excessive government regulation of the economy, unions and pro-labor legislation, and radical "agitators," particularly Communists and alleged Communists. In spite of adopting an organizational policy of nonpartisanship, JACL leaders customarily aligned themselves with the Republican Party and its policies.

In the late 1930s, when the Nisei were beset by the Depression and the deteriorating diplomatic relationship between Japan and the United States, a constellation of Nisei liberal and radical groups repudiated the JACL leadership for being preoccupied with material possessions and status mobility on an individual basis and for being "much too conservative in their approach to social change."[11] United under the banner of "progressives," a term used "to circumvent the intense anti-left bias prevalent in the Japanese community,"[12] they fashioned a competing political style. Instead of urging Nisei to lower their anchors, progressives aimed to raise their consciousness through offering a vocal and critical "left perspective on domestic, international and community issues."[13]

Progressive groups like the Los Angeles and Oakland branches of the Nisei Young Democrats consisted of a predominantly working-class membership augmented by some college students and a few card-carrying Communists. Domestically, these economically less privileged and socially more alienated "young bloods" established four priorities: (1) to work on behalf of New Deal slates at the national, state, and local levels; (2) to promote legislation expanding rights and opportunities for racial minority groups, even if to do so required confrontation tactics; (3) to support the demands of unions, like the Congress of Industrial Organizations (CIO), for better wages and working conditions, especially those unions stressing racial equality and solidarity; and (4) to resist "domestic fascism," whether in the form of racism, "red" baiting, or attacks on the labor movement. Internationally, they "clearly opposed the rise of militarism in Japan and Germany and openly voiced their fears about fascist threats to world democracy."[14] Transcending myopic cultural nationalism, they condemned Japan's invasion of China and picketed ships in major West Coast ports loading war materials destined for Japan.

Neither the JACL's ideology and political style nor that of the progressives appealed to the Nisei rank and file, most of whom were still in their teens, lacked political consciousness and experience, and were economically dependent upon their ethnic community. Whereas the former struck them as unsubstantial, snobbish, and insular, the latter appeared to be subversive of democracy and deviant to accepted subcultural norms. That the JACL ultimately prevailed in the intragenerational struggle for dominance with progressive groups like the Nisei Young Democrats was probably due to the combination of the following factors: (1) its orientation was more particularistic (i.e., it stressed ethnic as against class and racial issues); (2) its program, especially at the local level, revolved more around purely social activities; and (3) its approach to social change was more compatible with the cultural values of mainstream America.

When the rapidly eroding relationship between the United States and Japan during 1941 made a war between these two powers probable, the JACL and progressives were drawn into a tenuous alliance. For their part, the JACL disassociated itself from the Japanese Association and ceased its role as an apologist for Japan's incursions into China and Southeast Asia. Concurrently, JACLers suppressed their ethnicity and adopted a chauvinistic Japanese American creed capped by the slogan "Better Americans in a Greater America." As for progressives, they reacted to the deepening crisis by deemphasizing their political differences with the JACL and by muting their critique of American institutions and practices.

Pearl Harbor and the impending exclusion and detention transformed the JACL-progressive alliance into a working consensus. After the imprisonment of Issei leadership, federal and military authorities, responding to the JACL's numerical superiority and greater resonance with the wartime mandate for unambiguous national loyalty, accorded the JACL the role of official representative for the Japanese American community. Although progressive groups continued to be wary of the league's political philosophy, they conceded that, given the intense climate of anti-Japanese sentiment, the JACL was best situated to mobilize community resources and chart a course of action.

After the JACL resolved to cooperate with and not resist the government's exclusion and detention policy, progressives affirmed this position—though they did so "with strikingly different ideological imperatives."[15] As explained by national secretary Mike Masaoka, the league's principal spokesperson during this juncture, the JACL's stance of "constructive cooperation" was a pragmatic one.

> [It] did not waive the unconstitutionality of the evacuation process, nor was it an admission of guilt and disloyalty. Furthermore, cooperation did not mean that Japanese Americans were compromising their rights as American citizens. Rather, the JACL felt that this strategy would improve their rights at a later time. It simply meant a temporary suspension of their rights in order that all their rights could be secured in the future.[16]

Progressives, on the other hand, pursued a policy of "critical cooperation" toward the JAI. This policy was premised on the notion that the fight for democracy and against fascism and militarism, not the JAI, was the primary issue at stake. Their compliance, therefore, was driven by a resolve for national unity. Although progressives pledged their full cooperation in the war effort, they reminded the government that, in times of crisis, it must be solicitous toward the constitutional rights of its citizens as well as the security of the nation. In this spirit, the Nisei Young Democrats of Oakland issued a policy statement proclaiming that the proposed mass exclusion was "inconsistent with the democratic principles in which we believe and for which we fight" and predicting, darkly, that "suspension now of democratic principles for some may mean permanent loss for all."[17] To prevent this development, "many progressives joined the JACL with the intention of moving the League in a more progressive direction."[18]

Significantly, Larry Tajiri, a prominent community journalist and the "godfather" of the Nisei Young Democrats in Oakland and San Francisco, agreed to assume the editorship of the JACL's newspaper, the *Pacific Citizen*, a strategic position from which to promote the progressive philosophy.[19]

JAPANESE AMERICAN EVACUATION AND RESETTLEMENT STUDY

During the interval between Pearl Harbor and the eviction and confinement of Japanese Americans, while the JACL and progressive groups were cementing their coalition, Dorothy Swaine Thomas, a social demographer and professor of rural sociology at the University of California, Berkeley (UCB), was busily engaged in assembling the necessary pieces—scholarly guidance, governmental sanction, operational expenses, and trained personnel—for an ambitious study of the enforced mass migration of the entire West Coast Japanese American population.[20] Aided by her husband, W. I. Thomas, an eminent sociologist and the coauthor of the seminal immigration study *The Polish Peasant*,[21] she gathered together an impressive cadre of interdisciplinary, social-scientific colleagues on the Berkeley campus to conceptualize the contours of her projected study.[22]

Official approval was extended by Milton Eisenhower, the newly appointed director of the WRA, the agency created to administer the planned detention of Japanese Americans.[23] Financial support, ultimately totaling over $100,000, was garnered from foundation grants and university subsidies.[24] As for staff, both in the Berkeley central office and in the field at designated detention camps, it was determined that these were to consist predominantly of selected social science students—graduate and undergraduate, Caucasian and Japanese American—connected with UCB.[25]

Until the 1980s, virtually the only published accounts of this significant endeavor, JERS, were found in the prefaces to the three official and one unofficial project volumes issued in the postwar period. However, during the 1980s, as part of the upsurge in public interest in the wartime experience of Japanese Americans, scholarly attention has been accorded the involvement in the JAI of social scientists, including those affiliated with JERS. One former inmate, the anthropologist Peter Suzuki, was the first scholar to take up both the larger and the more specific dimensions of this topic.[26] In addition to being polemical, Suzuki has not paid substantive attention in his writings to the part played by social scientists of Japanese ancestry, such as those associated with JERS. In contrast, the Nisei historian Yuji Ichioka recently has edited an anthology, *Views from Within: The Japanese American Evacuation and Resettlement Study*, which is both mixed in its assessment of JERS's approach and accomplishments and includes essays by and about the project's Japanese American personnel.[27]

In concluding his cogent introduction to *Views from Within*, Ichioka, almost certainly with the work of Suzuki uppermost in mind, enters this caveat:

> Today, with the benefit of hindsight combined with a political perspective derived from the 1960s, some may condemn JERS out of hand as an unethical research project with no redeeming value. Doubtless, such people would argue that it was carried out solely for the sake of academic professionalism. Those who reaped the benefits were Dorothy Thomas and those JERS staff members who were able to advance professionally as a result of their partic-ipation in JERS. On the other hand, Japanese-Americans, the objects of JERS research, gained nothing—JERS neither improved their condition or status, nor promoted their political interests, either during the wartime years or after. Indeed, some may go so far as to argue that JERS was fundamentally inimical to Japanese-Americans. Detached or divorced from their interests as it were, JERS was necessarily for the benefit of others.[28]

Ichioka then goes on to argue that the fact that JERS was a research project conducted within an academic framework instead of done "in the service of a political cause on behalf of Japanese-Americans" must not be construed to mean that it "has no redeeming value." Indeed, observes Ichioka, "the JERS sources, especially those in the form of daily journals, diaries, life histories, and field reports, expressingly [*sic*] produced at Thomas's insistence upon creating and preserving an empirical record of the internment experience, retain an enduring value because they lend themselves to the writing of a social history of concentration camp life."[29]

NISEI SOCIAL SCIENTISTS IN THE JAPANESE AMERICAN EVACUATION AND RESETTLEMENT STUDY: THE CASE OF JAMES SAKODA

Although a considerable amount of the JERS source material referred to by Ichioka was produced by Caucasian and Issei staffers,[30] most of it was gen-erated by five Nisei participant-observers—Shotaro Frank Miyamoto, Tamie

Tsuchiyama, Tamotsu Shibutani, James Minoru Sakoda, and Charles Kikuchi. On the basis of a preliminary investigation of their staggering wartime output of social-scientific data,[31] their assorted postwar writings,[32] and lengthy, in-depth interviews with Sakoda and Kikuchi,[33] it appears amiss to suggest that these five people transacted their work for JERS "solely for the sake of academic professionalism" and that Japanese Americans "gained nothing" from their efforts. Because prior to the war all of these relatively young Nisei social scientists had adopted a progressive political ideology, albeit to varying degrees, they approached the JAI and their participation in JERS from that perspective. Assuredly, they saw in JERS an opportunity to advance their academic and professional aspirations. At the same time, their political orientation and social consciousness militated against mere status seeking, such as that exhibited by JACLers both before their exclusion and after their arrival at the detention centers. Along with other progressives, they were "concerned about opportunity and mobility, but they looked at them from the standpoint of collective movement among the rank and file in contrast to the quest for individual advancement implicit in the ideology of the JACL."[34] Thus, while there was a convergence of their beliefs and behavior with that of JACL leaders, who were widely reviled among the inmate population for their self-seeking and complicity with the camp administration, this critical philosophical difference shaped their work as social scientists.[35] Certainly they did not establish the overarching framework for the research they did for JERS, but the relevant evidence suggests that JERS director Dorothy Thomas "gave minimal direction to the field research staff."[36] Accordingly, there was greater scope for staffers to select the phenomena they valued for "objective" documentation. Such a situation not only spared the participant-observers some of the pain involved in splitting off questions of knowledge from ones of value, but also served to facilitate the progressivist moral agenda for promoting democratic ideals and constitutional rights.

Due to space constraints, only the experience of James Sakoda will be considered here, and that but suggestively.[37] However restrictive, this strategy commends itself on several scores: (1) in a cohort group characterized by generational marginality, Sakoda represents one extreme of that social condition;[38] (2) his period of service and research productivity matches or exceeds that of the other JERS participant-observers;[39] (3) he served JERS in a multiplicity of research settings;[40] (4) he is the only Nisei participant-observer to be listed as a contributor on two of JERS's authorized postwar publications;[41] (5) of the core JERS Nisei, he was one of only two who officially joined the JACL during the war;[42] and (6) he was among the trio of Nisei participant-observers to base their doctoral dissertations on their JERS fieldwork.[43]

Sakoda, who has characterized himself as a "conservative Nisei," was born in 1916 in Lancaster, California, but at age five moved with his family to the Little Tokyo vicinity of Los Angeles, where he was brought up in strict conformity with traditional Japanese practices and values and largely apart from Americanizing influences. Owing to the Depression, his father, who managed a credit union and money-lending business, was forced to relocate the family to the rural southern boundary of Los Angeles County, where he ran a hog farm. In 1933, when Sakoda had still not completed high school, his father decided to return to Hiroshima, Japan, and was accompanied there by his wife and four children. Ironically, during the next six years, while Sakoda attended a commercial school and studied Japanese and Chinese classics at a university, he became, as he later put it, "more Americanized than I had ever been." As a member of the Hiroshima Nikkei Club, he socialized almost exclusively with Nisei whose situation was similar to his own and enjoyed, as he would afterward recall, "probably the happiest time of my life." So Americanized did he become, in fact, that in 1939 he left his parents in Japan and returned to California to continue his college education.[44]

After a year at Pasadena Junior College, during which he worked as a "schoolboy" and farm laborer, he transferred in the fall of 1940 to UCB as a general education and psychology student. In Berkeley he roomed with Kenny Murase, a Nisei undergraduate who was active in assorted left-wing campus clubs and causes and also belonged to the Nisei Young Democrats of Oakland, which numbered ten or so college students along with a smaller number of Communists, like Mary, Nori, and Kazu Ikeda, and outspoken non-Communists like Michio Kunitani and Haruo Najima, both of whom Dorothy Thomas later employed for JERS. Through the Nisei Young Democrats, too, Murase became friends with members of the Nisei Writers and Artists Mobilization for Democracy (NWAMD).[45] According to a highly romanticized manuscript written by Murase during the spring of 1942, NWAMD was led by a Nisei progressive corps that included the following:

Tomomasa Yamazaki, who once rejected a lucrative position with the Japanese consulate because he did not choose to "sell out to fascism"; Isamu Noguchi, noted sculptor whose works reveal a profound social consciousness; Taro Katayama, a young intellectual; Eddie Shimano, who openly declared himself for China and actively campaigned for its support at the outset of the Japanese aggression; [and] Larry Tajiri, widely respected liberal and pioneer Nisei journalist.[46]

In a matter of months, Yamasaki would be on the editorial staff of the *Manzanar Free Press*, Shimano and the aforementioned Katayama would be editing the papers at two other assembly centers, Santa Anita and Tanforan, while Tajiri, as earlier noted, would be occupying the editorial chair for the JACL-sponsored *Pacific Citizen*.[47]

Although Sakoda never penetrated the periphery of either of these two progressive groups, he was well aware of and influenced by their political orientation.[48] Moreover, through Murase he came into contact with "the more marginal" of the approximately 500 Nisei students on the Berkeley campus, among whom were future JERS coworkers Tom Shibutani and Charles Kikuchi, individuals who, to quote Sakoda, were "both outside of organized Nisei groups and even disliked Nisei groups." Both Kikuchi and his brilliant roommate, Warren Tsuneishi, who was nicknamed "Wang" in tribute to his ostentatious support of China in the Sino-Japanese war,[49] traveled in the same progressive circles as Murase, and they, doubtless, affected Sakoda's politicization. In turn, Sakoda assisted the political education of Murase, Kikuchi, Tsuneishi, and some of the other campus progressives. "Jimmy," explained Murase, "was less a dreamer . . . [and] more of a logician. With six years spent in Japan, Jimmy was in a position to make a comparative estimate of Fascism and democracy; he supplied us with the facts to substantiate what we felt to be the situation under fascist oppression."[50]

Shortly after Pearl Harbor, both Sakoda and Kikuchi were introduced to Dorothy Thomas by Shibutani, one of her students. She needed qualified Nisei to compile social documentation for a projected study on the pending eviction and detention of Japanese Americans. Since the three of them were interested in social science or social work careers and were already collecting data on the unfolding crisis in their ethnic community, it was arranged that they would be put on the JERS payroll.[51]

As it turned out, Shibutani and Kikuchi went to the nearby Tanforan camp, but Sakoda was detained in central California at the Tulare Assembly Center.[52] There he remained for one month, until he was transferred to the Tule Lake Relocation Center on the California-Oregon border in mid-June of 1942. The diary he maintained at Tulare and the few short reports he wrote there reveal his progressive perspective. What most worried him was that the camp administration had permitted JACLers to self-appoint a temporary community council consisting almost exclusively of former JACL chapter presidents, active members, and others "connected with influential Japanese firms." As one diary entry clarifies, Sakoda sparred with one of these former chapter officers who thought it quite "normal" that the council should be formed and dominated by the JACL. Sakoda sharply disagreed: "I told him the advisability of holding an election right away to carry through democratic principles. He asked whether the people weren't disappointed with Democracy. I told him that we were heading for deportation after the war if something weren't done about it, and this seems to have impressed him."[53]

Because Thomas had designated the Tule Lake camp as JERS's major "social laboratory," she sent there not only Sakoda but also Shibutani, Frank Miyamoto, and several other project members.[54] During his fourteen-month tenure at Tule Lake, Sakoda, as his diary and correspondence to Thomas disclose, felt pressured to master social science theory and field research methodology and to transact a series of structural and dynamic reports on camp life, while averting inmate suspicions that he was a government spy or an administrative informer. As Tule Lake was rife with inmate resistance—strikes, work slowdowns, boycotts—Sakoda was preoccupied observing and capturing this activity for JERS, though he did teach a psychology course for the adult education program and, significantly, act as his block's representative to the camp's consumer cooperative.[55] Accordingly, he was, by his own admission, more of an observer than a participant. Privately, some of his acquaintances expressed the opinion that he was "too cold and scientific," that he looked at the detained population "only as specimens to be studied," and that he had "moral integrity, but knew the advantages and disadvantages of situations, too."[56]

The extraordinary pressure Sakoda felt was partly responsible for his conveying this impression; so also was the fact that he and his siblings lived in a block peopled by "strangers" from the rural Sacramento area. Fortunately, his diary indicates the nature of his relatively private—and progressivist— existence in this concentration camp. We discover that his nonprofessional reading consisted of proletarian novels like Steinbeck's *In Dubious Battle* and Dos Passos's *USA* and social reform nonfiction literature like Louis Adamic's *From Many Lands* and Carey McWilliams's *Brothers under the Skin.*[57] We learn, too, that this eligible bachelor ruminated about the sort of woman that he wanted to marry—that she be more of a "companion" and not "too middle class and conventional."[58] We are also told that he was bothered by the "boot-licking" political style of JACL camp leaders who "played the role expected by the Caucasian group with the assumption that this would achieve the greatest amount of rights for the Japanese people." Further, we find that he believed social work harmful "because only enough of it was done to keep the present socioeconomic setup, and kept people from revising the whole system, which was really at fault" and that Nisei, if they wanted to advance, "should join labor unions."[59]

Notwithstanding Sakoda's being impressed with the power of mass political action exerted by the "residents" of Tule Lake to redress injustices stemming from the camp's disproportionate power arrangements, at one point, during the "loyalty" registration crisis of early 1943, he became victimized by such mass action.[60] The public position he took on that occasion—to permit people to decide for themselves whether they wanted to register and that it was crucial for Nisei to protect their citizenship rights—was unpopular, even perilous, and perhaps injudicious, yet it was consistent with his progressive philosophy and commitments. For a number of weeks, he was socially ostracized by his block neighbors, treated like an *inu* (dog, informer), and threatened with bodily harm.[61] So, too, were his JERS coworkers, Shibutani and Miyamoto, who were so intimidated that shortly thereafter they left Tule Lake to work on the resettlement stage of the study in Chicago.[62] During the darkest hour of the crisis, a badly shaken Shibutani paid Sakoda a commiserative visit. "We discussed future possibilities," relates Sakoda in his diary on February 23,

> but we could only come to the conclusion that his study and mine for a PHD thesis had not been in vain. The only thing was that we would not be able to continue it to its logical conclusion. The story of the Japanese people in camps are [sic] going to be written up by someone, and if the Japanese

themselves do not take a hand in it, then the Caucasians are going to write it without being able to get the Japanese side of the story very clearly.[63]

Sakoda weathered the storm. In a few weeks, not only was he able to reconstitute normal relations with his neighbors, but some troubled Nisei even sought his counsel as to the course they should steer with respect to the registration.[64] Moreover, when the WRA announced subsequently that Tule Lake would be converted into a segregation center for those in the ten camps deemed "disloyal" on the basis of their response to the registration and that "loyal" Tuleans would be removed to several other centers, Sakoda assumed an active and constructive role in effecting this transition. Both as an official interviewer and as a behind-the-scenes wire-puller, he helped ensure that the segregation process was transacted humanely and prudently. "In this segregation process," confided Sakoda to his diary in August 1943, "I have been more of a participant that in other incidents. . . . While I could have been satisfied with the role of an observer, just watching how the officials will handle the situation and how the people react, I can't help wanting to point out the mistakes that are being made by the former and the misunderstanding on the part of the latter. This can be based on a desire for leadership and attention, but is probably also due to identification with the interest of the evacuee."[65]

Though Thomas proposed to transfer Sakoda to the JERS "check site" at the Gila River Relocation Center in Arizona, he desired to marry a woman he had met at Tule Lake and to accompany her, her family, and 1,700 other "loyal" Tuleans to the Minidoka Relocation Center in Idaho. His wish was granted. In that camp, from the beginning, Sakoda, although producing a prodigious amount of documentation, was more a participant than an observer.

Heretofore, Minidoka had been a "quiet" camp, characterized by a benevolent administration and an accommodating appointed leadership. To Sakoda and many of the other incoming Tuleans, who had been politicized by their Tule Lake experience, it appeared that the Minidoka administration was becoming increasingly dictatorial and its incarceree leadership more concerned with gaining personal preferments than fighting for the rights of the camp population. Accordingly, although Thomas had cautioned JERS personnel to stay out of camp politics, Sakoda found himself documenting persisting and escalating work walkouts, strikes, and related dissidence as well as working on behalf of establishing a democratically elected camp council.[66]

Moreover, after its establishment, he accepted its labor relations adviser post and investigated labor practices and conflicts (though eventually resigning when his researcher role was threatened).[67]

However, Sakoda continued to take part in a "political clique" whose four-person core of inmates and anti-administration Caucasian personnel dedicated themselves to democratizing Minidoka's system of inequitable governance.[68] He also documented and attempted to mitigate the harsh, unfeeling policy of the Minidoka administration toward inmates during the camp's closure period, not leaving the center until it had been completely vacated in June of 1945.[69]

EPILOGUE

A few months prior to transferring from Tule Lake to Minidoka, Sakoda was sent by Thomas to visit the Arizona WRA centers of Gila and Poston. On his return to California, he stopped off at Salt Lake City. There he bumped into a former progressive friend from his Berkeley days who took him to a discussion session with a group of left-leaning Nisei settlers. They voiced their anti-JACL feelings, probed the possibility of "concerted action with the labor unions," and considered the advisability of political alignment with other oppressed minority groups. "The group," noted Sakoda in his Tule Lake diary, "is rather reminiscent of the Oakland YD [Young Democrats]."[70]

While in Salt Lake City, Sakoda also called at the national JACL office. There he encountered Larry Tajiri and two new progressive assistants, Dyke Miyagawa and Bob Tsuda, on his *Pacific Citizen* staff. Tajiri clearly impressed Sakoda, telling him how he had a free hand in running the newspaper. Flaunting copies of the *Progressive Monthly*, Tajiri proclaimed that Nisei "should not be drafted until their full rights are returned, including the right to return to California," and boasted that the JACL was involved in filing briefs with the Supreme Court in support of the major JAI test cases and contesting anti-Japanese legislation at the state level. "I felt," Sakoda later wrote, "that Larry was different from other JACL leaders. . . . Larry is all right." Before leaving, Sakoda was arm-twisted into joining the JACL, which he did, though with mental reservations. "While there is a possibility of change in the JACL structure," he remarked in his diary, "the Old Guards still seem to be holding firm."[71]

A year later, Sadoka left Minidoka to attend a JERS conference in Salt Lake City. While there, Tajiri invited Sakoda and a few other JERS staffers to attend a dinner party whose guest list included JACL national president Saburo Kido. This experience left Sakoda and his JERS associates cold. No longer did Tajiri strike Sakoda as "quite liberal in view," particularly in regard to the *Pacific Citizen*'s treatment of those Nisei who had protested the Department of War's recent policy to draft them out of the camps into a segregated military unit. Tajiri's "use of the word 'draft-dodger,'" said Sakoda in his Minidoka journal, "especially was distasteful to me because it showed a lack of sympathy [while] to other members of the staff it represented 'flag-waving' and the expression of 120 per cent Americanism." It also shocked Sakoda and the others that Tajiri wanted to have the government suppress the three vernacular newspapers published in Colorado and Utah because they were "distorting the minds of the center residents."[72]

Worse still was the commentary of Kido, an attorney who had been badly beaten by inmates at the Poston center for his aggressive Americanism. In Kido's opinion, Nisei who remained in the centers and refused to relocate "were all hopeless," especially "the 'draft-dodgers.'" Kido, too, "thought it was dangerous to associate with Negroes because of their extreme attitude," citing as an example his experience at a race-relations meeting when a black woman had upbraided him for his attitude toward the jailed Nisei draft resisters, saying, "You shouldn't be against your own people." Finally, Kido, according to Sakoda, flatly stated: "I believe in my country right or wrong." So embarrassing was this statement to Togo Tanaka, a vernacular journalist who was then part of JERS but had barely escaped being murdered for his JACL connections while imprisoned in 1942 at the Manzanar camp, that he "tried to point out to him [Kido] that intelligent persons didn't say things like that."[73]

Upon returning to Minidoka, Sakoda got embroiled in a discussion with the anthropologist Elmer Smith, the camp's community analyst and a member of Sakoda's political clique who was considered very supportive of the inmates. On this occasion, however, he and Sakoda were at swords' points—over the role of the JACL. Whereas Sakoda contended that the JACL lacked the people's support in the camps, Smith felt that its leadership had been correct in exaggerating their patriotism because this was the message Caucasians wanted to hear. The brief account of their exchange in Sakoda's diary, because it so vividly juxtaposes the political styles of the JACL and the progressives, seems a fitting end to this study on the conjunction between political ideology and participant observation within the context of the JERS.

> He [Smith] emphasized over and over again the necessity of winning the support of the CAUCASIANS. That he referred to a certain type of Caucasian became evident when he stated that the Niseis in New York had made the mistake of becoming mixed up with COMMUNISTS!!!, and had lost the support of such persons as Pearl Buck. He also pointed out the danger of being aligned with certain "hotheaded" Negro groups. The JACL had the support of the CAUCASIANS, and therefore it was all right. I tried to point out that it didn't have to exaggerate its behavior to the extent that it was all out of sympathy with its own group. I pointed out, for instance, that it didn't have to worship the WRA blindly, as it seemed to be doing. I kept to my argument. Leaders who did not have the support of the following were not functioning as leaders.[74]

NOTES

Those meriting my gratitude for their role in helping me conceptualize and refine this article include the following: James Sakoda, Charlie Kikuchi, Bob Spencer, Warren Tsuneishi, and Ben Kobashigawa.

1. The proceedings of this conference were edited by Yuji Ichioka and published as *Views from Within: The Japanese American Evacuation and Resettlement Study* (Los Angeles: Asian American Studies Center, University of California, Los Angeles, 1989). The conference, organized and directed by Professor Ichioka, was held at the University of California, Berkeley, on September 19–20, 1987.

2. Charles Kikuchi, Diary, July 4, 1942, Charles Kikuchi Papers, Special Collections, Charles E. Young University Research Library, University of California, Los Angeles. Hereafter cited as CKP.

3. CKP, July 4 and 8, 1942, emphasis added.

4. CKP, July 4 and 8, 1942. For a more accessible, though abridged, version of this episode, see Charles Kikuchi, *The Kikuchi Diary: Chronicle from an American Concentration Camp*, ed. John Modell (Urbana: University of Illinois Press, 1973), 160–68.

5. See Lauren Kessler, "Fettered Freedoms: The Journalism of World War II Japanese Internment Camps," *Journalism History* 15 (Summer/Autumn 1988): 70–79; and Barry Saiki, letter to the editor, *Pacific Citizen*, October 13, 1989, 5. During World War II, Saiki served as one of several editors of the camp newspaper at the

Rohwer War Relocation Center in Arkansas. According to Saiki, among his closest friends while an undergraduate at the University of California, Berkeley, on the eve of the war were three individuals later connected with JERS: Tamotsu Shibutani, James Sakoda, and Charles Kikuchi. See Barry Saiki, "The Uprooting of My Two Communities," in *Japanese Americans: From Relocation to Redress*, ed. Roger Daniels, Sandra C. Taylor, and Harry H.L. Kitano (Salt Lake City: University of Utah Press, 1986), 15–16.

6. See, for example, K. Cha-Jua, "Mississippi Burning: The Burning of Black Self-Activity," *Radical History Review* 45 (Fall 1989): 125–36. The same production team responsible for *Mississippi Burning*, which is centered on the civil rights movement for blacks, has recently completed the shooting of a $15 million companion film relative to the Japanese American Incarceration. This Alan Parker–directed film, entitled *Come See the Paradise*, was released in 1991.

7. For a recent example of this genre pertinent to the Mexican American political experience, see Carlos Munoz Jr., *Youth, Identity, Power: The Chicano Movement* (New York: Routledge, Chapman and Hall, 1989).

8. Jerrold Haruo Takahashi, "Changing Responses to Racial Subordination: An Exploratory Study of Japanese American Political Styles" (PhD diss., University of California, Berkeley, 1980), esp. chaps. 3 and 4 ("The Formation of Competing Political Styles" and "The Internment Experience and the Rising Significance of Americanization"), 110–218. For a slightly revised version of the third chapter of this study, see Jere Takahashi, "Japanese American Responses to Race Relations: The Formation of Nisei Perspectives," *Amerasia Journal* 9 (Spring/Summer 1982): 29–57. The balance of this section of the chapter represents but a digest of the relevant chapters in Takahashi's dissertation plus his article. In mechanically adapting Takahashi's analysis, I have robbed it of its textured, nuanced character and jettisoned his deftly strategic use of Karl Mannheim's concept of "generational unit," Antonio's Gramsci's theory of cultural hegemony, Max Weber's idea of legitimation, and neo-Marxist class analysis.

"The term style," asserts Takahashi in an explanatory note on the first page of his dissertation, "refers to the unique methods and techniques Japanese Americans have devised to deal with the problems of racism and discrimination. It tries to capture not only the influence of distinctive group characteristics but also the impact of larger political and economic realities of the dominant society on this ethnic community. Also, the notion of style seeks to portray members of the community, their leadership and their ideologies as active parts of the socio-historical process."

9. Takahashi, "Japanese American Responses," 38.

10. Takahashi, "Changing Responses," 129.

11. Takahashi, "Japanese American Responses," 41.

12. Takahashi, "Changing Responses," 140.

13. Takahashi, "Changing Responses," 140.

14. Takahashi, "Japanese American Responses," 46.

15. Takahashi, "Changing Responses," 180.

16. Takahashi, "Changing Responses,"162.

17. Quoted in Takahashi, "Changing Responses," 182.

18. Takahashi, "Changing Responses," 151.

19. For Tajiri's critical role in the formation of both the progressivist Japanese American Democratic Club of San Francisco and the Nisei Young Democrats of Oakland, see Takahashi, "Changing Responses," 143. The appellation of "godfather" is attributable to James Matsumoto Omura, the former editor of the prewar Nisei progressivist magazine *Current Life*. See Omura's rejoinder to Takahashi's "Japanese American Responses" as well as my interview with him, respectively, in *Amerasia Journal* 10 (Spring/Summer 1983): 101–4, esp. 103, and *Amerasia Journal* 13 (1986–87): 99–113, esp. 107.

20. See Yuji Ichioka, "JERS Revisited: Introduction," in *Views from Within*, ed. Ichioka, 4–6. See also the obituary for Thomas (1899–1977) in the *Washington Post*, May 3, 1977.

21. For the influence of William Isaac Thomas (1863–1947) and *The Polish Peasant in Europe and America* (the five-volume study he coauthored with Florian Znaniecki between 1918 and 1920) on JERS, see Dana Takagi, "Life History Analysis and JERS: Re-Evaluating the Work of Charles Kikuchi," in *Views from Within*, ed. Ichioka, 198–202. For biographical information on Thomas and the Chicago School of Sociology of which he was a founder and key developer, see "The Polish Peasant in Europe and America: A Landmark of Empirical Sociology," chap. 4 of Martin Bulmer, *The Chicago School of Sociology: Institutionalization, Diversity, and the Rise of Sociological Research* (Chicago: University of Chicago Press, 1984), 45–63; and Lester R. Kurtz, *Evaluating Chicago Sociology: A Guide to the Literature, with an Annotated Bibliography* (Chicago: University of Chicago, 1984), 1–97 esp. 30–34, 84–88, and 89–90.

22. According to Yuji Ichioka, in "JERS Revisited," 6, the University of California colleagues of Dorothy Thomas who were connected at the outset with JERS were "Robert H. Lowie of the Anthropology Department, Milton Chernin of the Social Welfare Department, Frank L. Kidner of the Economics Department, and Charles Aikin of the Political Science Department."

23. Ichioka, "JERS Revisited," 6–7.

24. Ichioka, "JERS Revisited," 6.

25. For a listing of these individuals along with their corresponding academic disciplines, see Ichioka, "JERS Revisited," 7.

26. See Peter T. Suzuki, "Anthropologists in the Wartime Camps for Japanese Americans: A Documentary Study," *Dialectical Anthropology* 6 (1981): 23–60; and Peter T. Suzuki, "The University of California Japanese Evacuation and Resettlement Study: A Prolegomenon," *Dialectical Anthropology* 10 (1986): 189–213. The first of these articles encompasses work transacted by those social scientists affiliated with two other groups that, apart from JERS, conducted research on Japanese Americans during their World War II detention experience: the War Relocation Authority's Community Analysis Section, which was headed up, successively, by the anthropologists John Embree and Edward Spicer and had community analysts stationed at each of the ten WRA centers, and the Bureau of Sociological Research (BSR), which was directed by the anthropologist-psychiatrist Alexander Leighton, restricted to the Poston center in Arizona and run under the aegis of the Bureau of Indian Affairs. Unlike JERS, both of these other projects were applied social-science efforts aimed specifically at improving camp administration. It is Suzuki's contention that many of these applied social scientists served as government intelligence agents or administrative spies. For a recent critical assessment of the WRA community analysts, see Orin Starn, "Engineering Internment: Anthropologists and the War Relocation Authority," *American Ethnologist* 13 (November 1986): 16–36. Both the Community Analysis Section of the WRA and the Poston BSR included Japanese Americans, though to date virtually no attention has been accorded their contributions. Two members of the latter, Richard Nishimoto and Tamie Tsuchiyama, originally were BSR affiliates. For a bibliography of the JERS material, see Elizabeth Stephens, comp., Japanese American Evacuation and Resettlement Records (JAERR), Bancroft Library (BL), University of California, Berkeley (UCB), 1996; hereafter cited as JAERR. This collection also includes most of the work compiled by social scientists in the other two projects. For a complete bibliography of reports issued by the Community Analysis Section, see Estelle Rebec and Martin Rogin, comps., *Records of the War Relocation Authority* (Washington, DC: National Archives, 1955), Record Group 210, Entry 16. Convenient access to the BSR material is available at Cornell University, where it was deposited by Alexander Leighton after the war. See Deborah Gesensway, Mindy Roseman, and Geri Solomon, comps., "Guide to the Japanese-American Relocation Centers Records, 1935–1953" (Ithaca, NY: Department of Manuscripts and University Archives, Cornell University, 1981).

27. Oddly, though the critical assessments of JERS in *Views from Within* are mixed, the promotional statements printed on the back cover by two authorities of the Japanese American wartime experience, Peter Irons and Richard Drinnon, closely correspond to the condemnatory perspective of Suzuki (whose essay "For the Sake of Inter-university Comity: The Attempted Suppression by the University of

California of Morton Grodzins' *Americans Betrayed*," 95–123, is represented in the anthology).

Essays in this volume about Japanese American personnel in JERS are as follows: Lane Ryo Hirabayashi and James Hirabayashi, "The 'Credible' Witness: The Central Role of Richard S. Nishimoto in JERS," 65–94; and Dana Y. Takagi, "Life History Analysis and JERS: Re-evaluating the Work of Charles Kikuchi," 197–216; those by Japanese American personnel are S. Frank Miyamoto, "Dorothy Swaine Thomas as Director of JERS: Some Personal Observations," 31–63; Miyamoto, "Resentment, Distrust, and Insecurity at Tule Lake," 127–40; Miyamoto, "Reminiscences," 141–55; Charles Kikuchi, "Through the JERS Looking Glass: A Personal View from Within," 179–95; James M. Sakoda, "Reminiscences of a Participant Observer," 219–45; and Sakoda, "The ' Residue': The Unsettled Minidokans, 1943–1945," 247–84.

28. Ichioka, "JERS Revisited," 22.

29. Ichioka, "JERS Revisited," 22–23.

30. The major Caucasian field researchers for JERS were the anthropologists Robert F. Spencer and Rosalie Hankey Wax and the sociologist Robert Billigmeier. Their writings are included in JAERR. A retrospective article by Robert Spencer, who was stationed at the Gila center in Arizona, is "Gila in Retrospect," in Ichioka's *Views from Within*, 157–75. Rosalie Hankey Wax, who replaced Spencer at Gila and also did fieldwork at the Tule Lake center in California, has written about her experiences in *Doing Fieldwork: Warnings and Advice* (Chicago: University of Chicago Press, 1971), 59–174. The principal Issei researcher for JERS was Richard Nishimoto at the Poston center in Arizona. For a penetrating assessment of his role, see Hirabayashi and Hirabayashi, "The 'Credible' Witness."

31. For a list of their respective contributions to JERS, see JAERR. For Miyamoto, see esp. 158–59, 162, 170, 176, 181, 186; for Tsuchiyama, 89, 106; for Shibutani, 160–62, 171, 175; for Sakoda, 142–43, 159–60; and for Kikuchi, 104, 172–75.

32. Aside from the essays by Miyamoto, Kikuchi, and Sakoda included in Ichioka's *Views from Within*, a number of other relevant studies by these three men should be consulted. See S. Frank Miyamoto, "The Career of Intergroup Tensions: A Study of the Collective Adjustments of Evacuees to Crises at the Tule Lake Relocation Center" (PhD diss., University of Chicago, 1950); Tamotsu Shibutani, "Rumors in a Crisis Situation" (master's thesis, University of Chicago, 1944), "The Circulation of Rumors as a Form of Collective Behavior" (PhD diss., University of Chicago, 1948), *Improvised News: A Sociological Study of Rumor* (Indianapolis, IN: Bobbs-Merrill, 1966), and *The Derelicts of Company K: A Sociological Study of Demoralization* (Berkeley: University of California Press, 1978); James Sakoda, "Minidoka: An Analysis of Changing Patterns of Social Interaction"

(PhD diss., University of California, Berkeley, 1949); and Kikuchi, *The Kikuchi Diary*.

33. James Sakoda, interview by Arthur A. Hansen, August 9–10, 1988; and Charles Kikuchi, interview by Arthur A. Hansen, August 1–3, 1988, Japanese American Project, Lawrence de Graaf Center for Oral and Public History, California State University, Fullerton. Both of these interviews were transacted in Rhode Island. The verbatim interview transcripts number 276 pages and 390 pages, respectively. Specific quotations from these interviews have not been utilized in this essay since the transcripts need first to be reviewed and released by Sakoda and the widow of the late Kikuchi, Yuriko Amemiya Kikuchi.

34. Takahashi, "Changing Responses," 150.

35. A number of scholars have riveted attention on the widespread antipathy to the JACL in the World War II period. For one comprehensive treatment of this phenomenon, see Rita Takahashi Cates, "Comparative Administration and Management of Five War Relocation Authority Camps: America's Incarceration of Persons of Japanese Descent during World War II" (PhD diss., University of Pittsburgh, 1980). This antipathy was so deep and abiding that it has persisted up to the present. In 1989 the JACL itself appointed an attorney connected with the Asian American Studies Program at the University of California, Berkeley, Deborah Lim, to investigate the policies and actions taken by the JACL during the World War II era of eviction and detention of Japanese Americans. For an online version of the original 1990 Lim Report, see http://www.resisters.com/study/LimTOC.htm. For information about the controversial history of this report, see Brian Niiya's entry on the Lim Report for the *Densho Encyclopedia*, http://encyclopedia.densho.org/Lim_Report/, and chapter 9, "Counterpoint: The Lim Report," in *Resistance: Challenging America's Wartime Internment of Japanese-Americans*, by William Minoru Hohri, with Mits Koshiyama, Yosh Kuromiya, Takashi Hoshizaki, and Frank Seishi Emi (Lomita, CA: The Epistolarian, 2001), 129–56. James Omura, the most vocal and vociferous critic of the JACL's wartime role, is presently completing a volume bearing on this subject that is due for later publication. See Arthur A. Hansen, ed., *Nisei Naysayer: The Memoir of Militant Japanese American Journalist Jimmie Omura* (Stanford, CA: Stanford University Press, 2018).

36. Miyamoto, "Dorothy Swaine Thomas," 39. See also Kikuchi, "Through the JERS Looking Glass," 189; Spencer, "Gila in Retrospect," 160; and Sakoda, "Reminiscences of a Participant Observer," 223.

37. At this point in my research, I have not systematically and exhaustively perused the relevant documentation in JERS respecting Miyamoto, Tsuchiyama, and Shibutani, though all of them, especially Shibutani, appear to have been influenced by the same progressivist ideology and to reflect that outlook in their

JERS writings. Shibutani, like Kikuchi and Sakoda, was a University of California, Berkeley, student who was active in leftist politics on that campus prior to Pearl Harbor. As for the political backgrounds of Tsuchiyama and Miyamoto, both of whom were somewhat older and had passed their doctoral qualifying examinations before the war, these require deeper exploration.

38. Sakoda was the only Kibei (American-born but educated in Japan) participant observer in JERS. As a consequence, his marginality, unlike the other citizen observers, stemmed from his being more "Japanesy" than the typical Nisei. At the other extreme, was Charles Kikuchi, who was raised in an orphanage bereft of any Japanese cultural influences and was thus marginal in relation to his ethnic generation.

39. Sakoda was affiliated with JERS from 1942 to 1945. In addition to his journal, diary, and correspondence, he produced, by his own count, twenty-five interpretive reports totaling over 1,800 pages. See Sakoda, "Reminiscences of a Participant Observer," 232.

40. Sakoda was a participant observer at the Tulare Assembly Center, the Tule Lake Relocation Center, and the Minidoka Relocation Center.

41. See Dorothy Swaine Thomas and Richard S. Nishimoto, *The Spoilage: Japanese-American Evacuation during World War II* (Berkeley: University of California Press, 1946); and Dorothy Swaine Thomas, *The Salvage: Japanese American Evacuation and Resettlement* (Berkeley: University of California Press, 1952). The first of these volumes lists Sakoda, Rosalie A. Hankey, Morton Grodzins, and Frank Miyamoto as contributors, while the latter lists only Sakoda and Charles Kikuchi in this capacity. In addition to these two volumes, there existed a third authorized project publication, Jacobus tenBroek, Edward N. Barnhart, and Floyd W. Matson, *Prejudice, War and the Constitution: Causes and Consequences of the Evacuation of the Japanese Americans in World War II* (Berkeley: University of California Press, 1954); and an unauthorized book, Morton Grodzins's *Americans Betrayed: Politics and the Japanese Evacuation* (Chicago: University of Chicago Press, 1949). For an analysis of the conditions surrounding the publication process connected with these latter two volumes, see Suzuki, "For the Sake of Inter-university Comity."

42. The other Nisei participant-observer in JERS who affiliated with the JACL during the war was Charles Kikuchi, who became both a member and an officer at the Gila center in Arizona. Although his participation in the Gila JACL, the only chapter of the league to emerge in any of the camps, was substantial and spirited, it was enacted within a progressivist ideological perspective. For insight into the Gila JACL and Kikuchi's role in it, see Charles Kikuchi, "Development of Gila JACL," July 1942, JAERR, folder K8.22.

43. The three dissertations, cited above, are Sakoda, "Minidoka"; Miyamoto, "Career of Intergroup Tensions"; and Shibutani, "Circulation of Rumors."

44. See Sakoda, "Reminiscences of a Participant Observer," 220–21.

45. Sakoda, "Reminiscences of a Participant Observer," 220–21. See also the following two unpublished studies: James Sakoda, "As They Await Evacuation: The Impact of the War Between America and Japan on the Values of Different Types of Japanese on the West Coast," April 22, 1942, 42–47, JAERR, folder A17.03; and Kenny Murase, "I Protest," included in Kikuchi Diary, CKP, March 29, 1943. For the part played by the Ikeda sisters in the Nisei Young Democrats of Oakland, see the interview with Kazu (Ikeda) Ijima by Glenn Omatsu, "Always a Rebel: An Interview with Kazu Iijima," in the *Amerasia Journal* 13 (1986–87): 83–98. Kunitani wrote only one report for JERS during his internment at the Tanforan Assembly Center, though this report clearly reveals his progressivist background and the progressive political agenda at Tanforan. See Michio Kunitani, "Tanforan Politics," n.d., JAERR, folder B8.29. For the JERS contribution of Najima, see Tamotsu Shibutani, Haruo Najima, and Tomi Shibutani, "The First Month at the Tanforan Assembly Center for Japanese Evacuees," JAERR, folder B8.31.

46. Murase, "I Protest," 8.

47. Murase, "I Protest," 8.

48. Sakoda, interview by Hansen.

49. Murase, "I Protest," 6. See the tribute written by Tsuneishi, now the chief of the Library of Congress's Asian Division, to the memory of Charles Kikuchi (1916–88) in *Views from Within*, ed. Ichioka, vii.

50. Murase, "I Protest," 6.

51. See Sakoda, "Reminiscences," 221–22.

52. Sakoda, "Reminiscences," 222; Kikuchi, *The Kikuchi Diary*, 68.

53. See James Sakoda, "Report #3," May 24, 1942, and James Sakoda, Journal, May 30, 1942, both in JAERR, folder B12.20.

54. In addition, Thomas sent another Nisei social scientist, Haruo Najima, plus a Caucasian fieldworker, Robert Billigmeier, to Tule Lake. Najima apparently did not write any reports for JERS while at Tule Lake, though the correspondence he carried on from there is available to researchers; see JAERR, folder R21.58. For the diary and various Tule Lake reports authored by Billigmeier, see JAERR, folders R 20.01–R 20.14.

55. See James Sakoda's Tule Lake journal and diary, JAERR, folders R20.81 and R20.82; and Sakoda, "Reminiscences of a Participant Observer," 224–25.

56. Sakoda, Diary, April 10 and January 19, 1943, JAERR, folder R20.81.

57. Sakoda, Diary, March 8 and 10 and March 11–12, 1943, JAERR, folder R20.81.

58. Sakoda, Diary, September 7, 1943, JAERR, folder R.20.81. See also the entries in his Tule Lake diary dated March 11 and 20 March 10, 1943, JAERR, folder R.20.81, in which he comments about one female companion: "M's a fine girl, but our

political ideas do not quite jive since she is a JACL supporter" and "M is a swell, considering girl, although she has a slightly-capitalistic bias and a feeling of superiority toward many of the Niseis."

59. Sakoda, Diary, February 3, 1943, and Sakoda, Journal, December 5, 1942, JAERR, folder R20.81. On Sakoda's attitude toward the JACL while at Tule Lake, see also his diary entries for October 4 and December 25, 1942, and February 10 and 11, 1943, JAERR, folder R.20.81.

60. See Sakoda's recollections about this experience in "Reminiscences of a Participant Observer," 228–29.

61. Sakoda, "Reminiscences of a Participant Observer," 228–29.

62. Sakoda, "Reminiscences of a Participant Observer," 233.

63. Sakoda, Diary, February 23, 1943, JAERR, folder R20.81.

64. Sakoda, Diary, March 9, 1943, JAERR, folder R20.81.

65. Sakoda, Diary, August 19, 1943, JAERR, folder R20.81.

66. See in particular Sakoda's "Pickling Plant Conflict Report," May 24, 1944, and November 26, 1944, and "Warehouse Conflict Report," April 1944, JAERR, folders P8.4, P8.15, and P8.20; and Sakoda, "Reminiscences of a Participant Observer," 229. For a summary of this period at Minidoka, see Sakoda, "The 'Residue,'" 262–63.

67. Sakoda, interview by Hansen.

68. Sakoda, interview by Hansen; Sakoda, "Reminiscences of a Participant Observer," 229–30.

69. See chap. 10, "Eviction," 321–60, in Sakoda, "Minidoka," and his summarization of the same in "The 'Residue,'" 264–67.

70. Sakoda, Diary, June 20, 1943, JAERR, folder R20.81.

71. Sakoda, Diary, June 19, 20, and 22, 1943, JAERR, folder R20.81; quotes from June 19 and 22.

72. Sakoda, Journal, June 16, 1944, JAERR, folder R20.81.

73. Sakoda, Journal, June 16, 1944, JAERR, folder R20.81.

74. Sakoda, Journal, June 29, 1944, JAERR, folder R20.81.

7

SERGEANT BEN KUROKI'S PERILOUS 1944 "HOME MISSION"

Contested Loyalty and Patriotism in the Japanese American Detention Centers

In the summer of 1994 I was invited by Mike Mackey, then a doctoral history student at the University of Wyoming, to present a paper at a symposium he was organizing to be held in late May of the following year at Northwest College in his hometown of Powell, Wyoming, located close by the site of the World War II Heart Mountain Relocation Center. Funded chiefly by a generous grant from the Wyoming Council for the Humanities, the symposium was appropriately titled "Japanese American History: The Heart Mountain Experience." In response to Mackey's request, I told him that I was then working on a manuscript relating to the Nebraskan Nisei Ben Kuroki. Mackey knew, of course, that Kuroki was not only among the very few aerial gunners in the US Army Air Corps during World War II but also someone whose celebrated combat record on both the European and Pacific fronts established him as the war's first Japanese American hero. So I was quick to mention to Mackey that

This essay is from *Remembering Heart Mountain: Essays on Japanese American Internment in Wyoming* edited by Mike Mackey (© 1998) and reproduced with permission of Mike Mackey.

DOI: 10.5876/9781607328124.c007

my work, while it touched on Kuroki's military feats, was focused on a promotional tour he took in the spring of 1944 to three of the intermountain area War Relocation Authority–administered detentions centers for excluded Americans of Japanese ancestry: Heart Mountain, in Wyoming; Minidoka, in Idaho; and Topaz, in Utah. I explained further that my study emphasized the decidedly mixed reception that Kuroki received on this "home mission" to this trio of American concentration camps and that I also explored the intertwined cultural themes of loyalty and patriotism. Mackey assured me that such a presentation was aptly suited to the nature of the Powell symposium.

Prior to that three-day symposium, I discovered that Ben Kuroki was very much alive and living in retirement relatively close to me in the community of Ojai in Ventura County, California, so I arranged to interview him on October 17, 1994, at the home residence that he shared with his wife, Shige. The results of this tape-recorded interview figured prominently in my symposium presentation. It was delivered before a packed auditorium of predominately Nisei who had been wartime Heart Mountain inmates, plus their spouses and offspring. While the majority of the audience consisted of Japanese American Citizens League supporters, there was also a strong representation of onetime draft resisters affiliated with the anti-JACL Heart Mountain Fair Play Committee. The palpable high point of my presentation was an excerpted clip from the Japanese American National Museum film Something Strong Within,[1] *which depicted in Technicolor a rousing victory parade, replete with a Nisei Boy Scout drum and bugle corps, that had been enacted against the backdrop of Heart Mountain's barbed-wire fences, sentry towers, and barracks trappings during Kuroki's week-long visit in April of 1944. What follows is the revised and edited version of this presentation, which appeared in a Mike Mackey-edited 1998 anthology,* Remembering Heart Mountain: Essays on Japanese American Internment in Wyoming.

"The best-known single sentence to come out of America's part of World War II," the writer Samuel Hynes remarked in 1995, "is not from a general's dispatch or a politician's speech. It is three words from a common soldier whose name stood for every soldier: 'Kilroy was here.'"[2] If in the spring of 1944 Hynes, a Marine pilot in America's so-called "good war,"[3] had visited any of the three federal detention centers for evicted West Coast Japanese Americans at Heart Mountain, Wyoming, Minidoka, Idaho, or Topaz, Utah, he might well have heard voiced this very similar declaration: "Kuroki was here."

If asked to explain this utterance, virtually anyone in the imprisoned population likely would have given the same general rejoinder. Technical Sergeant Ben Kuroki was a twenty-five-year-old Nisei, or second-generation Japanese American, who was born and raised in Nebraska. Following Pearl Harbor, he swapped his peacetime life as a potato farmer and truck driver to become, arguably, the first person of Japanese ancestry in the US Army Air Corps. Overcoming massive institutional prejudice, Kuroki served as an aerial gunner on a B-24 Liberator bomber for thirty missions (five more than required) over North Africa and Axis Europe, for which he was decorated with two Distinguished Flying Crosses and an Air Medal. Then shortly after rotating back to the United States in early 1944 and being billeted in Santa Monica, California, Kuroki was denied a scheduled appearance on the popular Ginny Simms radio show. Not long after this rebuff, however, 700 members of the posh Commonwealth Club gave Kuroki a thunderous ten-minute standing ovation after he spoke to them at a luncheon in San Francisco's Palace Hotel. Following this triumph, *Time* magazine lauded Kuroki as an American hero. The same NBC radio program that only a month earlier had denied him airwaves access—because of his ancestry—now welcomed him as its featured guest. When public acclaim for Sergeant Ben Kuroki had peaked, the War Department decided to capitalize on his celebrity by ordering him to go on morale-building, public-relations visits to Heart Mountain, Minidoka, and Topaz, three of the ten Japanese American detention centers administered by the US War Relocation Authority (WRA).

If pressed for details about the Nisei sergeant's reception in the three camps he visited in 1944, the incarcerated Japanese Americans would have told a mixed tale. Many would have narrated accounts resembling those that appeared in the *Heart Mountain Sentinel*, the *Minidoka Irrigator*, and the *Topaz Times*: that Kuroki had been received in a manner befitting Japanese America's first and, at that time, only World War II military hero—regaled in public and private gatherings, wildly cheered and fawned over, and figuratively presented with a key to each camp. Many other inmates, though, would have countered that, official hoopla notwithstanding, Kuroki was widely felt to be a naive "outsider" foisted upon them by the US government, the WRA, and the Japanese American Citizens League (JACL). Ben Kuroki, in the minds of these inmates, had been used as a mouthpiece to combat the resistance to the military draft that had mushroomed within the majority of the ten WRA centers, most dramatically at Heart Mountain, after the War Department reversed its earlier wartime policy of considering Japanese Americans unfit for military induction and reinstituted selective service for Nisei on January 20, 1944.

This article will revisit, review, and reconceptualize Ben Kuroki's so-called "home mission" of 1944, paying particular attention to his week-long tour of Heart Mountain in late April of that year. The emphasis here is not on filling factual gaps in this colorful story but rather in opening up the gaps between the established facts to support a new interpretation of them. I have sought to stake out a view broad enough to embrace and even nurture opposing perspectives. I have also taken pains to resist indulging an analysis that, however viscerally satisfying, is grounded in and sustained by highly selective perceptions and interests.

I first became intrigued by Ben Kuroki's "home mission" tour when preparing for a 1988 interview with Brown University social psychologist James Sakoda,[4] a bilingual Kibei-Nisei who had conducted participant-observation fieldwork at the Minidoka center for the Japanese American Evacuation and Resettlement Study (JERS), sponsored by the University of California, Berkeley.[5] In reading Sakoda's wartime correspondence with the JERS project director, Dorothy Swaine Thomas, I found this captivating reference in a May 2, 1944, letter:

> One . . . item . . . current [at Minidoka] is Ben Kuroki's visit. Thus far it has been highly pathetic because of the lack of response on the part of the people. The Isseis [immigrant-generation Japanese Americans, ineligible for US citizenship] are highly incensed by his statement that he is going to bomb Tokyo, while the Niseis don't dare show too much enthusiasm. I was very much depressed the first day to notice the lack of appreciation of Ben's stand, even though I felt that there were things that he had yet to understand which the people felt deeply.[6]

Sakoda's only other mention of Ben Kuroki and his Minidoka visit, made in a May 15 letter after Kuroki had departed the Idaho center for the Topaz camp in Utah, was still more enticing:

Ben Kuroki was given a poor reception here, and Acre [Acree], the Reports Officer, just about broke his neck trying to make it seem as though Ben received a "roaring" welcome. Ben made a hit with the younger kids, but was being called all sorts of names by the Isseis. I'm afraid the visit here confused him quite a bit, and [I] hope that he doesn't become another [Charles] Lindbergh. . . . Ben Kuroki said that he got a poorer reception here than he did in Heart Mountain. And this was considered the most "loyal" center of them all.[7]

Even though quite removed from my primary research interest at this time on Nisei social scientists in JERS, I duly highlighted the relevant passages about Kuroki's Minidoka visit in the Sakoda-Thomas correspondence and incorporated a query about it into the schedule of questions I prepared for my impending interview with Sakoda. I also consulted several standard volumes on the Japanese American Incarceration (JAI) to add to my small stock of knowledge about Kuroki.

The most useful source was *Nisei: The Quiet Americans*, by Bill Hosokawa, a wartime editor of the *Heart Mountain Sentinel*. First, Hosokawa linked Kuroki with the JACL by describing how Kuroki and his brother Fred, along with some fifty other Rocky Mountain Nisei, had been attending an organizing meeting of a new JACL chapter on the morning of December 7, 1941, in North Platte, Nebraska, when FBI agents burst into the room and arrested the presiding JACL official, Executive Secretary Mike Masaoka. Second, Hosokawa explained how, following that meeting, Kuroki's Issei father had unhesitatingly offered him this advice: "Enlist in the Army, Ben, America is your country. You fight for it." Third, Hosokawa related how, after Kuroki's thirty missions in the European theater, he had waived his eligibility for rotation to a safe job in the United States and "insisted on and received an assignment in the Pacific [where he] flew 28 more combat missions in B-29 bombers, many of them over Tokyo." Finally, Hosokawa alerted me to the existence of a biography on Kuroki: "The story of his heartbreaking efforts to be accepted in the armed forces, to win the right to fight for his country, to overcome the wartime stigma attached to his ancestry, is told vividly by Ralph G. Martin in his book, *Boy from Nebraska*."[8]

I did not, unfortunately, get around to reading Martin's celebratory 1946 biography of Kuroki before recording my interview with Sakoda. As the published transcript of our conversational narrative makes clear, our discussion about Kuroki, though revealing, had been quite brief.

> *I know when Ben Kuroki, who was a flyer, came to Minidoka, he got very cold treatment. You said [in your JERS correspondence with Dorothy Thomas] he even got a worse one [reception] at Minidoka than he did at Heart Mountain.*

Yes.

> *And at Heart Mountain, he got pretty rough treatment, because they had the [organized] anti-draft movement there.*

. . . I talked with Ben Kuroki [when he came to Minidoka] . . . It's very interesting that, because Minidoka had a lot of volunteers [for the army's special combat team that had been organized in early 1943], there were some deaths also. While deaths were announced [at Minidoka] and they had ceremonies for the deceased, I don't think I ever discussed the death of a soldier with anybody. It was as though it was something that nobody wanted to talk about. Maybe the [Issei] parents of the [Nisei] soldiers felt a little guilty about the situation. . . . It would be an interesting topic to pursue, actually, because it was very important for the family.

> *I think another interesting topic for somebody to write on is this Ben Kuroki thing. I think your account of it in your correspondence [for JERS] . . . is real interesting, because he [Kuroki] apparently took a tour around the different camps, and [the reception given him represents] kind of an index of where the [various] camps [he visited stood] at that particular time on a very important issue, the reopening of selective service to the Nisei.*[9]

It was also unfortunate that as part of my preparation for interviewing Sakoda I had not consulted two other books alluding to Kuroki's wartime activities: historian Roger Daniels's *Concentration Camps USA* and redress leader William Hohri's *Repairing America: An Account of the Movement for Japanese-American Redress.*[10] Both books deal with Kuroki in the context of the draft resistance movement at the Heart Mountain camp. Moreover, both discuss the subsequent imprisonment in federal penitentiaries of Heart Mountain Fair Play Committee (FPC) leaders and members for refusing to countenance the drafting of Japanese Americans from behind barbed wire prior to the government's restoring or at least clarifying their constitutional rights as US citizens. Finally, both books connect Kuroki's actions vis-à-vis Heart Mountain in 1944 to the policy initiatives of the "accommodationist" JACL leadership.

In his book Roger Daniels couples Kuroki's 1944 visit to Heart Mountain with a request from the JACL's headquarters that Roger Baldwin, American Civil Liberties Union (ACLU) head, make public his mid-April 1944 letter to FPC head Kiyoshi Okamoto. In that letter Baldwin disassociated himself and the ACLU from the FPC and admonished Okamoto that, while the draft resisters assuredly had a strong moral case, they had no legal case whatsoever. Furthermore, Baldwin warned Okamoto that "men who counsel others to resist military service are not within their rights and must expect severe treatment." The second accommodationist JACL action that Daniels ties in with Kuroki involves the Nisei sergeant essentially echoing the position toward the FPC leadership voiced by the JACLer-dominated *Heart Mountain Sentinel*. First, Daniels notes that, after a federal district judge, in June of 1944, found sixty-three Heart Mountain draft resisters guilty of refusing induction and sentenced them to three-year federal prison terms, the *Sentinel* had "argued that those who encouraged the draft resisters not to report 'deserve penitentiary sentences even more than those convicted.'" Then, having explained that a few months later the seven FPC leaders were declared guilty in the same Cheyenne courtroom for "unlawful conspiracy to counsel, aid, and abet violations of the draft" and handed down two- to four-year prison sentences, Daniels quotes a post-verdict interview that Kuroki, a nontestifying *government* witness at this trial, granted the *Wyoming State Tribune*: "These men are fascists in my estimation and no good to any country. They have torn down [what] all the rest of us have tried to do. I hope that these members of the Fair Play Committee won't form the opinion of America concerning all Japanese-Americans."[11]

William Hohri's narrative in *Repairing America* more pointedly conflates Kuroki's actions toward the FPC with JACL directives. Hohri vivifies this association through citing the testimony that Jack Tono, a former Heart Mountain FPC member and convicted draft resister, presented in 1981 at the New York hearing of the Commission on Wartime Relocation and Internment of Civilians. After telling how, in early April of 1944, the FBI had rounded up the sixty-three Heart Mountain draft resisters and deposited them in an assortment of county jails pending their mass trial, Tono lauds Abraham Lincoln

Wirin, a southern California ACLU lawyer who broke ranks with that organization's national office to represent the resisters at their trial. Tono then draws an invidious distinction between the ACLU and the JACL:

> I shall never forget the Union for their gutsy services. My admiration and esteem for the organization is beyond what I can relate in words. Others have left us high and dry: mainly the Japanese American Citizens League. We were expecting this group to give us their full support, but instead [they] turned their back on us. To this day, I still feel the knife in the back.

Tono's testimony describes how two prominent JACL leaders, Minoru Yasui and Joe Grant Masaoka, visited the resisters in jail shortly before their trial and used scare tactics to try to change their minds about resisting the draft: "If you go to prison, you'll get beat up with a two-by-four." After divulging how the JACL persisted in making life difficult for the resisters even after they had gone to prison, served time, and become eligible for parole, Tono momentarily shifts his wrathful attention to the heralded aerial gunner from Nebraska: "Our great war hero, Kuroki, labeled us 'fascist' in the Wyoming newspaper." Having tossed the JACL and Kuroki into the same trash bag, Tono then scathingly remarks, "For all of these two-faced coins we have the appropriate phase: 'the yellow Uncle Toms.'"[12]

Scrutinizing Daniels's and Hohri's accounts made me bemoan not having been familiar with Kuroki's 1944 camp tour when in 1984 I had interviewed another Nisei, James Matsumoto Omura.[13] Omura had been tried with the seven FPC leaders for conspiring with them to violate the Selective Service Act in his capacity as the English-section editor of the Denver-based *Rocky Shimpo* (a charge for which, in effect, he was ostensibly, though not officially, cleared on grounds of freedom of the press). Minimally, Omura would have been able to shed a great deal of light on Kuroki's attendance at that Cheyenne trial as well as the Nisei war hero's post-trial defamation of the FPC leaders. Moreover, because Omura was a staunch opponent of the JACL's wartime role and was then engaged in writing a memoir centered on that topic,[14] he could have illuminated any connection between Kuroki and the JACL. Sad to say, moreover, I never communicated with Omura about this situation in the decade that separated our interview with his death in June 1994.

However, it was not until after Omura's death that I seriously turned my attention to Kuroki's controversial 1944 junket. As noted earlier, in my 1988 interview with Sakoda I had commented upon how that tour might be an interesting subject for someone, not myself particularly, to research and write up. It seems that, unconsciously, I had been bitten by the Kuroki bug. For when doing research on Sakoda at the Bancroft Library the very next year I reproduced every entry related to Ben Kuroki in the voluminous field-work journal that Sakoda maintained at Minidoka for JERS.

Just prior to Kuroki's arrival at Minidoka, in a journal entry dated April 2, 1944, Sakoda surveyed the camp's Issei population about the situation. One Issei man told Sakoda, "I don't like what he [Kuroki] said [at Heart Mountain] about going to bomb the Japs. You know, he could have just said that he would do his best if he went to the Pacific to fight. After all, he's a Japanese, too." Said one Issei women, rather sarcastically, "It's all right for him to say that he's going to bomb Tokyo because he's an American citizen." More sympathetically, another Issei woman rejoined, "You shouldn't say things like that because if he were in Japan, he would make a good Japanese sol-dier. You should appreciate the fact that he's a splendid soldier." Two other Issei women objected to Kuroki's talking about bombing Japan. One of them remarked that he was being used as a tool by the government, while the other one referred to him as *"baka"* (fool). Another Issei woman, who had sons in the US Army, was more charitable: "You can't help what he says because [coming from Nebraska] he's lived only among Hakujins [Caucasians]."[15]

Sakoda covered Kuroki's arrival at Minidoka in rich detail, but before log-ging his entry he vented his personal views about the Nisei hero's reception: "I feel very sad as I write this, sad for the bitterness that some people feel and their inability to sympathize with the feelings of others. I don't mind Isseis calling Kuroki all sorts of names, but for some Niseis to do the same thing makes me want to cry." Sakoda then turned to describing Kuroki's actual arrival at the Minidoka site. It is sufficiently poignant and significant to war-rant reiteration:

Ben was scheduled to come in through the gate at 10 a.m. I went out to
the Ad[ministration] Area a little before 10, and met [Elmer] Smith, the
Community Analyst, and his staff standing around, too. I stood talking to
them most of the time, looking around to see what was going on. Some of
the Isseis working in the Ad[ministration] Area were poking their heads out
of doors, curious, it seemed, to see what was going on. However, most of the

people who were standing along the main road leading to the gate were Niseis. From the direction of Block 22 some boys and girls were walking up towards the gate. Some Caucasians were intermingled in the crowd. A little after 10 a car drove up to the gate, and Sargeant [sic] Kuroki stepped out, and shook hands with [Harry] Stafford [the project director] and others. He was dark and smiled warmly. The rest of the time he seemed greatly embarrassed, not knowing what to do with himself. He was placed in a jeep. The girls crowded around him noticeably, probably to get a good glimpse of him. A small applause went up, and I clapped, too. Not because he was a hero or anything, but because he was one of us Niseis. He was just as bewildered as the rest of the Niseis by the treatment the Japanese were receiving. His outlook was different from those of most of the people in the center, perhaps, but he was risking his life for what he believed to be our cause. The applause was weak, and there was practically no cheering. One Nisei was saying: "Let's take a look at our hero." He [this same Nisei] also remarked that he was shoved out of the office by his Caucasian supervisor. Some girls were saying: "Gee, he's cute." Another remarked: "He looks sick." The reception was cool. There were only several hundred persons out to greet him, and most of the people only stared at him, dumbly. Some Isseis hung on the fringes of the crowd, looking on rather disinterestedly. It was little wonder that Sergeant Kuroki looked embarrassed. As the parade moved down the main road, music was furnished by the Boy Scout band and a public address system. The jeep on which Ben Kuroki rode was followed by passenger cars with Caucasian and evacuee dignitaries sitting in them. [One staff member] had his car filled with evacuee office workers. On one bus rode the inductees [into the army]. The community analysis staff followed the parade to the high school, where students lined both sides of the road. There were some clapping, but no loud cheering. After the parade went by the students streamed back into their class rooms.[16]

As the welcoming parade serpentined through the Minidoka camp, Sakoda collected additional reactions to Kuroki. One Nisei referred to him as a "baboon." When this Nisei's wife obligingly said, "I don't have to go to see that guy. My husband is just as good as him," the Nisei man quickly retorted, "Don't compare me with that guy, I'm better than him." One Issei dismissed Kuroki as an *inu* (dog), while others referred to him as the *"Chosenjin"* (Korean). Still another Issei said, "He's just being used as a tool by the government. They want to get Niseis to go to the Army."[17]

Reading these journal entries by Sakoda made me extremely curious about the extent to which the ambivalent reception that Kuroki allegedly received at Minidoka had been foreshadowed in his just-completed visit to Heart Mountain, the WRA hotbed of draft resistance. To answer this question, I consulted the following sources: a new study of Heart Mountain; a 1992 interview with the aforementioned outspoken draft resister Jack Tono; particularly relevant issues of the *Heart Mountain Sentinel*; contemporary reports by the camp's director, Guy Robertson, and community analyst Asael Hansen covering Kuroki's visit; and assorted Wyoming newspaper accounts of the FPC trials.[18]

Simultaneously, I wrote letters of inquiries to a number of FPC resisters, including Jack Tono.[19] I also made contact with the Japanese American National Museum in Los Angeles about Ben Kuroki's whereabouts and was informed that he was living in the southern California community of Ojai. After reading Kuroki's biography and entries about him in biographical reference works, I learned that he had graduated in 1936 from Hershey High School and from the University of Nebraska in 1950 and thereafter had pursued a career as a newspaper editor in Nebraska, Michigan, Idaho, and California. The North Platte, Nebraska, librarian confessed to having never heard of Ben Kuroki and furthermore could find nothing in her library relating to him. But from the University of Nebraska's archives I was told that, beyond majoring in journalism at the Lincoln campus, Kuroki had minored in English, philosophy, and political science. From the Nebraska State Historical Society I received a newsletter featuring a transcript of the talk Kuroki had delivered in 1991 at the opening of the Museum of Nebraska's exhibit on Nebraska and World War II.[20] Having mined this document for biographical facts, I then scanned the Heart Mountain, Minidoka, and Topaz camp papers before, during, and after Kuroki's tour for relevant information.

In the summer of 1994 I wrote Ben Kuroki informing him of my research focus and requesting that he permit me to transact a two-day combined life-history and topical interview with him. Several weeks later Kuroki responded by telephone. In a deep yet soft voice, Kuroki said, "I really don't want to do this interview. I was hoping that my 1991 talk at the Museum of Nebraska was my final hurrah." To which I meekly responded, "I really wish you would consent to do this interview with me." Pausing momentarily, Kuroki replied,

"Okay, I'll do it, but it will have to be a one-day interview, not a two-day one like you suggested in your letter." It was then arranged that I would interview him at his Ojai, California, home on October 17, 1994. In a follow-up letter, I asked him to prepare a schematic time line of his life for use by me as an interview guide. I also supplied him with personal and professional facts about myself. Earlier I had told Kuroki that I was a sociocultural historian, not a military historian. Now I supplemented this point: "Owing to a congenital problem with my legs and feet, I was declared 4-F and was even dismissed from otherwise mandatory participation in ROTC during my college years. So I am anything but a war hero like yourself."[21]

In spite of our differences, Ben Kuroki and I really hit it off during our full-day interview. I found him to be one of the most decent men I have ever known: considerate, cooperative, frank, reflective, self-effacing, and conscientious. That day we covered in depth his life both before and after World War II, information that was noticeably absent from the documents I had read about him in preparation for the interview. Owing to my comparative ignorance about military and aviation history, what the interview communicates about Kuroki's experiences as an aerial gunner on B-24s and B-29s is manifestly inadequate. Those who consult this interview will not discover a substantially different Ben Kuroki from that presented in Ralph Martin's biography, but hopefully Kuroki's life will now be seen as possessing greater complexity.

As to Kuroki's "home mission," we had three "dialogues" that I think were quite enlightening and hence merit attention here.

DIALOGUE 1

Now, Heart Mountain's background was that when they had recruited volunteers for the combat team in early 1943, there were very few from Heart Mountain who volunteered to join, and there was some resistance to the recruitment itself. Then, in early 1944, the only organized draft resistance movement in the WRA camps took place at Heart Mountain. I know that when you went there, one of the things you did was to talk to this draft resister group, the Heart Mountain Fair Play Committee. Apparently there was a certain amount of sparks generated by this encounter, leastwise from what I can tell from my research.

Yes. (chuckling)

But I want you to tell me about this, because I've seen things and heard things from other people who were on the other side of the podium at that time. What are your recollections of the Heart Mountain experience?

Well, I [will] never forget one incident. Of course, I was advised that they were a dissident group and that they were also having special guards to avoid any problems there. But I remember getting up and speaking to the group, and one thing that I remember most was that I told them that "If you think Japan's going to win this war, you're crazy." I said, "They're going to get bombed off of the map." And I heard some hissing and booing. (chuckling) I never quite forgot it. But nothing else really happened, no problems.

I guess the situation for the Issei who were in the camp was this: first, that they had been stripped of so many things, and then the idea that they might be stripped of their kids; but also [apparently] there were a lot of Issei who truly felt that Japan was going to win that war, even in 1944 when most people would say it was inevitable that they were going to lose. It didn't take a person like yourself to say that to them. But they still had this power to suspend their disbelief and think that Japan's victory was going to happen.

Oh, very definitely. Yes, I certainly agree with that. I think that some of those dissidents might have even, you know, been disloyal to the US and returned to Japan if they had not been interned. I mean, you can't say for sure. But it was a terrible experience, and in a way I couldn't blame some of them for feeling like they did. I mean, golly, you lose everything that you ever worked for in life, and have it all taken away. And your being a citizen of this country, to have that sort of thing happen, I don't know how I would have reacted in this same situation. It's quite a thing.

DIALOGUE 2

When you were at Heart Mountain, then, the draft resisters baited you a bit, I think, and you responded in kind. Some of them to this day nurture certain grievances against you. One thing you were quoted as saying in a Cheyenne, Wyoming, newspaper was that "These men [the Heart Mountain draft resister leaders] are fascists in my estimation and no good to any country."

(chuckling)

You were very gung-ho at that time, obviously. You re-upped [for five more flights in Europe over the required twenty-five] and then you also fought to go and fight in the Pacific Theater. So, I mean, you had a strong perception about what your role was. And I suspect for the draft resisters it wasn't simply a matter, as their opposition claimed, that they were draft dodgers, but there was a perception, too, that, if you have citizenship rights, one of the ways to honor them is not to put up with having the government put you behind barbed wire and then draft you into a segregated unit in the Army and tell you that "this is a wonderful reward."

Yes.

You've probably thought about these things over the years. I know the Japanese American community has wrestled with who to honor and who to dishonor, and they are finally reaching the conclusion that, you know, we were all involved in this situation together and we responded with our various perceptions of Americanism in different ways and courses of action. Do you feel a bit different now from how you did at the time, or not, towards those Japanese Americans who resisted the draft? I guess my question is this: Do you still continue to see them as draft dodgers rather than draft resisters?

Well, I think in most cases I can sympathize with their viewpoint. However, I believe that not all of them were patriotic. Some were using the loss of rights as an excuse. Some were out and out loyal to Japan—not many of them—and had they not been interned, I think they would have gone back to Japan. Whatever, I'm glad that the draft resisters' position did not prevail at the time the 442nd [Regimental Combat Team] was organized. If theirs was the dominant reaction, the splendid record of the 442nd may have never been. And the Congressional reparations bill and national apology may likewise have never been because I feel that [the] latter would never have reached first base without the achievements of the 442nd and the contributions of the Nisei in the Pacific intelligence units.

DIALOGUE 3

Before you went to the three [WRA] camps . . . you had gone to Salt Lake City for a while, and there you met with some of the leaders of the Japanese American Citizens League.

Yes.

Had you joined the JACL at that time when you were in North Platte, Nebraska, for that fateful recruitment meeting held on December 7, 1941? Or were you still not a JACL member at the time you went to Salt Lake City in 1944 and met with the JACL leaders?

I don't think they ever got the chapter started in North Platte because Mike Masaoka got jailed and nothing was done, as I remember.

So did you become a JACL member afterward? One thing I've read recently said that you'd been a longtime JACL member, but then it didn't go on to say when you joined the organization.

I don't remember where I joined the JACL, but I know I was with the JACL for a long time.

Did you feel that you were coached in any way as to what you should be talking about when you were in these camps [in 1944] by the War Department, the War Relocation Authority, or the Japanese American Citizens League? Because those three groups were intertwined in certain respects.

No, absolutely not. I did not have any instructions from the government, and I don't remember anybody else ever giving me any instructions.

Were you reluctant to undertake your tour of the three camps, or were you anxious to do it? I mean, compared with going on a bombing mission? (chuckling)

Well, a little of each, I guess. I was still a dirt farmer from Nebraska at that time and I wasn't really cut out for something like that.

Right after my interview with Kuroki, I received from Mike Mackey copies of two letters written by high-profile Heart Mountain personalities containing information about Ben Kuroki's wartime visit to that camp. The first was by Bill Hosokawa, the *Heart Mountain Sentinel*'s founding editor and a postwar JACL leader who authored a series of popular histories encompassing the World War II experiences of Japanese Americans.[22]

As for Ben Kuroki, I was gone by the time he visited Heart Mountain, but the *Sentinel*'s stories indicate he was lionized as a hero and he had a tremendous impact on the youngsters in the camp. I met him after the war. I would say he was respected and admired by the overwhelming majority of Nisei. Today, perhaps Sansei and Yonsei [third- and fourth-generation Japanese Americans] would not recognize his name, but Nisei would go out of their way to shake his hand whereas they would have little interest in any of the No-No boys. I would guess, without having made any sort of study or survey, that among many Nisei he is looked on as a greater hero than the individuals who went to court to challenge the evacuation. Ben is living quietly in retirement north of Los Angeles and has avoided the limelight, mainly I would guess, because he is at heart a farm boy who prefers the quiet life.[23]

The second letter was from the late Frank Inouye, an early resistance leader at Heart Mountain and a vocal critic of the WRA, the JACL, and the *Heart Mountain Sentinel*.

When Ben [Kuroki] appeared in [Heart Mountain] camp as part of his tour . . . , I was struck by his "un-military" persona. Altho' he was in uniform and his visit had been preceded by considerable publicity in the "Sentinel," I saw nothing unusual or commanding about his appearance or speech. He appeared to be what he was: a Nebraska farmer's son, in uniform. . . . As the first Nisei war hero, his visit should have elicited enormous pro-volunteer sup- port in camp. That it didn't was due in large measure to the thorough mistrust the camp residents had for anything the WRA and the US military advocated.

Altho' Ben was accorded the full courtesies due a visiting celebrity, includ- ing interviews and speaking engagements, my impression is that, while many Nisei admired him for his heroic missions, few identified with him personally. He was, to most of us, a rather remote and distant figure, more of a manipu- lated robot than "one of us."

One reason for this lack of emotional linkage with Ben is that for all of us in camp, the war was a very distant and barely felt experience. We saw our- selves as its victims and our isolation worked against any personal identifica- tion with it, except in general terms.[24]

Several convicted Heart Mountain draft resisters responded by post to my appeal for assistance. One who did so with alacrity was Mits Koshiyama. Even though he was in jail at the time of Kuroki's Heart Mountain visit, Koshiyama harbored strong feelings both about that occasion and Kuroki himself. "I believe that, from what I hear from those who were there," stated Koshiyama,

that he was well received in Heart Mountain Camp. Imagine, a parade, peo- ple waving the flag, Boy Scouts in uniform in a concentration camp. Could make a good TV drama which could show how a small group (the Japanese American Citizens League) with the help of the War Relocation Authority can control a helpless majority. Also can you imagine a person coming into a camp and be[ing] blind to the fact that these innocent people were incarcerated behind barbed-wire fences, [plus] watch towers with armed guards. He should have protested the treatment his fellow Japanese-Americans were forced to endure. All he thought was that he was such a great war hero that he became blind to the injustices dealt to a group of unfortunate people. I wonder what he went to fight for.[25]

Koshiyama also referred me to another Heart Mountain draft resister, George Nozawa, whom he termed "our historian." So I wrote to Nozawa for help. In my letter I reviewed for him what I had learned from James Sakoda's wartime reports about Kuroki's mixed reception at Minidoka—that the children idolized him, that the teenage girls were captivated by him, but that the Nisei men of draft age and their Issei parents were very cool toward him (both because their sons were being placed at risk and because many of them truly believed that Japan would win the war and punish those who participated in the war effort of the United States). I also relayed the information that, in advance of Kuroki's Minidoka visit, the word apparently had gotten out that in a speech at Heart Mountain Kuroki had declared that "he wanted to bomb the rice out of his dishonorable ancestors in Japan."[26]

In his reply letter, Nozawa expressed general agreement with Sakoda but took exception to his observation that many Issei parents believed Japan would win the war and punish all those who had abetted the US war effort. "The Isseis that objected to the draft," maintained Nozawa, "based [their objection] on the fact that it was insensitive and unfair for the Government to take their sons when the future of the family was in total disarray. Come hell or high water they would be needed to help reestablish the family first and foremost; then talk of drafting."[27]

I also heard from Frank Emi, one of only two surviving members among the seven FPC leaders:

You asked if there was any "relationship" between Ben Kuroki and the [draft] resisters. As far as I know, there wasn't any relationship, communication, or dialogue between the resisters and Ben. The consensus of the resisters was that he was just a Nebraska corn-husker with J.A. features who was completely insensitive to, and without any understanding about the injustices committed to the J.A.s, and was just being "used" by the military for propaganda purposes.

You also mentioned that rumor has it that I "detested" him. I did not "detest" him. I respect the fellow for his military accomplishments, but I certainly felt back then, and still do now, that he was very insensitive and stupid to come into concentration camps where American citizens of Japanese ancestry were incarcerated and emasculated of all constitutional rights, and foist his "flag waving" bullshit tactics on the inmates. Talk about "chutzpa." He was the proverbial "goat" that lead the mindless, and unthinking "sheep" to slaughter.[28]

At this juncture in my research, I received a passel of letters from former Heart Mountain inmates that were embedded with nuggets of information pertaining to Ben Kuroki and the Wyoming stop on his 1944 camp tour. "Ben Kuroki's visit to Heart Mountain," wrote Kara Kondo, "may have occurred shortly before, or after my leaving camp. It's hard to recall, but I was not directly involved in any of the activities concerning his visit. . . . That we were aware of his accomplishments and proud of his heroism and acclaim, I recall. But, we were looking for 'positive' images of all kinds that might counteract the 'reasons' for our internment."[29]

From Rose Tsuneishi Yamashiro came this recollection:

I remember that I was 13 or so at the time he visited Heart Mt. I was tremendously proud of all the young men who were in the armed forces from our camp. Among them, of course, were my brothers serving in the South Pacific. Another young man was Ted Fujioka, our first student body president who was killed in Italy at age 18, so when I heard that Sgt. Kuroki would be visiting Heart Mt., I was very proud because we all had heard about the Nebraska farm boy who had flown so many missions in Europe. I remember being surprised to learn that he was born in Nebraska. I just did not realize there were many JA's outside of California. His brief story made a big impression on the student body to whom he spoke. He seemed to be such a mild mannered man to have gone on so many bombing missions. He was well received by the students but as I recall there was no big fanfare. He was treated very much like a celebrity, and I remember being very proud of him because he had survived so many bombing runs. I've often wondered what ever happened to him.[30]

Judge Lance Ito's parents, Jim and Toshi Ito, wrote to Mike Mackey at the height of the sensational O. J. Simpson murder trial to say that neither of them was still in Heart Mountain at the time of what they styled Kuroki's "recruiting mission."[31] Their letter to Mackey also told about a movie that another Heart Mountain internee, Eiichi Sakauye, had shot of Kuroki's visit. Finally, there was a letter from Ike Hatchimonji to Mike Mackey that indicated that a portion of the Sakauye film had been incorporated into a 1994 documentary video, *Something Strong Within*, shown in conjunction with the Japanese American National Museum's exhibit "America's Concentration Camps."[32] "My recollections about Kuroki and his visit," Hatchimonji ruminated,

> are quite fresh because I was in the Boy Scout drum and bugle corps and the big parade and ceremony held in his honor. He was considered a war hero because of his many missions as a tail gunner in the US Army Air Corps, including flights over the Ploesti oil fields in Rumania. Guy Robertson, the HM camp director[,] made a speech and introduced Kuroki. Looking back, I'm sure Kuroki's visit was intended as a promotional event to encourage Nisei to join the service. As an impressionable teen-ager [I thought] Kuroki was a hero even though I didn't realize the irony of being interned while a fellow Nisei made such a name for himself.[33]

I also was informed about the situation by two other Heart Mountain draft resisters, Tak Hoshizaki and Yosh Kuromiya, who said that they were in jail when Kuroki arrived at the camp. Hoshizaki conjectured, in a letter to Mike Mackey, that the purpose of Kuroki's visit was perhaps "to counter the draft resistance occurring in camp."[34] Kuromiya, in correspondence with me, was more expansive:

> It seems our cooperation with the evacuation effort, rather than to clear us of any suspicion of sinister intent, made it even more convenient for the government to question our loyalties. We were no longer Japanese American Citizens of the United States; we were merely "Evacuees." Obviously, Sergeant Kuroki's loyalty and patriotism was regarded as superior to ours and qualified him to act as role model to us, the disenfranchised.
>
> I can only imagine the coming of Sergeant Kuroki, resplendent in all his glittering medals, glorifying his overseas exploits and promoting the familiar JACL accommodationist line. No doubt the terms loyalty and heroism

were used a lot. What this had to do with evacuation, detention and the US Constitution, I don't know. Nor do I know what his real message was. Perhaps, "You too can join the Air Force and drop a few bombs on white folks in Europe." Ben Kuroki, in a word, was irrelevant.[35]

As one whose published writings over the years had squared in most particulars with the sentiment and line of argumentation enshrined in Yosh Kuromiya's letter,[36] it was very tempting for me to agree that probably Ben Kuroki was irrelevant. But to accept this evaluation involved, leastwise by implication, my also accepting that the 3,000 people who greeted him when he arrived at Heart Mountain and the more than 700 from that camp who did board the bus for their draft physical (385 of whom were accepted for induction, among whom 11 were killed in battle and another 52 wounded) were also irrelevant. Nor could I unstick from my mind the image and the memory of Ben Kuroki himself; in no way had my interaction with this human being given me occasion to conclude that he was, as some of his detractors then and now claimed, a "fool," "tool," "warmonger," or "dog." I did think that his perception on the draft resisters was grossly wide of the mark in 1944 and remained so fifty years later when I talked to him on tape about his experiences at Heart Mountain.

I also felt that, in spite of his being a free moral agent, much of what Ben Kuroki said and did during his home mission of 1944—his protestations to the contrary notwithstanding—was guided and goaded on by the War Department, the WRA, and the JACL. As Kuroki explained to me during our interview, his famous speech before the Commonwealth Club had not been written by him but for him by Staff Sergeant Bob Evans. "Hell," confessed Kuroki, "at that time I couldn't even write sentences, I don't think."[37] That speech was printed by the JACL and given mass circulation in print and in a dramatized radio program. When Kuroki came to Heart Mountain and the other two camps in 1944, he was shepherded around by the camp's administration and JACLers associated with the inmate government and newspaper. What he saw was filtered for him in such a fashion that it was extremely difficult for him to view the members of the Fair Play Committee as anything other than fascists, troublemakers, and traitors. Nor could he call upon his Japanese American background, having never lived in a Japanese American community, to help him achieve a profound perspective on the problem that the draft resisters posed for his sense of Americanism.

If people of Japanese ancestry were "strange" in Nebraska, Kuroki was estranged from them and their ways. In his interview with me, Kuroki made it clear how much he loved his family, even ending our interview by reading into the record a moving published eulogy that he had written about his father. Still, Kuroki told me that as a youngster he "was always . . . a little bit uncomfortable, especially whenever our family would go into North Platte or a place like that. Because when my parents met another one of the Japanese neighbors, they would converse very loudly in Japanese and bow and all that stuff. People would walk by and they would stare at them, and it was very uncomfortable for me." He also divulged to me that

> having grown up with the kids around Hershey, and going hunting and
> playing basketball, when the war broke out I felt terrible. I mean I hated being
> Japanese. But whatever it was, I had the right indoctrination, the right school-
> ing, and whatever democracy had done for me was so deep that there wasn't
> any doubt in my mind that I was going to defend the United States against
> Japan. And there had to be something like that in all internees who came out
> of those camps, because, man, they were treated badly.[38]

I sensed that Kuroki's fierce patriotism, whether expressed in his desire to risk his life as an aerial gunner on a bomber or in lecturing the FPC members at Heart Mountain about the inevitable outcome of the war, had a great deal to do with his socialization in Nebraska and his being courted by chauvinistic chaperons during his 1944 tour of duty in the United States. Surely it also must have had a lot to do with what Kuroki had experienced in the Army Air Corps, something that I had not inquired into in any detail. Although I have an aversion to reading, talking, or teaching about war, I knew that I could not be fair to Ben Kuroki or the cause that he represented at the camps unless my research was broadened to encompass his military service.

The complete details of my research in this area are not especially import-ant, but it did include reading a new history of the Army Air Corps during World War II (Geoffrey Perret's *Winged Victory*), a revisionist survey of US participation in that war (Michael C.C. Adams's *The Best War Ever*), and a remarkable and very personal book by a historian haunted by the death of his uncle in the last American bomber shot down over Germany in World War II (Thomas Childers, *Wings of Morning*).[39] I also supplemented my read-ing by talking at length to an uncle of mine who had been a P-38 pilot in the war and later suffered such severe amnesia attacks that it required forty-four shock treatments to unscramble his brain. I spoke, also, with my mother-in-law, who had lost her brother, an aviation machinist's mate, when his plane crashed in the Aleutian area. I even watched anew the 1949 film *Twelve O'Clock High*, reputedly the best motion picture made about the role of the Army Air Corps in World War II.

My combined reading, conversing, and viewing made me painfully aware of the courage it required and the toll it took on one's nerves to go on bombing missions. Flying, as Ben Kuroki did, in an unpressurized aircraft at over 30,000 feet with temperatures frequently dipping below minus 35 degrees Fahrenheit was certainly no picnic. Until mid-1944, the life expectancy of a bomber and crew was fifteen missions, and a flyer like Ben Kuroki had only one chance in three of surviving a tour of duty.

Sometimes the problem was oxygen deprivation, which could lead to blacking out and death. With such bitterly cold temperatures, sweat and blood would freeze and clog a flyer's oxygen hoses. There was, too, an ever-present danger of frostbite. The crew wore electrically heated flight suits, but if the electrical system shorted out or was damaged in combat, a crew member could freeze to death. To compensate for this contingency, the men wore layers of bulky clothes for warmth. But this clothing caused them to be even more cramped than they already were in their claustrophobic quarters; often, too, it prevented them from escaping a burning plane before it exploded. With good reason, the Germans referred to the American heavy bombers as "flying coffins."

The biggest problems of all was not, as might be expected, enemy fighter planes like the Germans' new Me 262 jets, but flak from ground-based enemy antiaircraft fire. When on bomb runs, the sky sometimes became so thick with flak, it was said, that you could walk on it. At such times, it seemed impossible to fly through this wall of flak unscathed. But somehow, defying the odds, Kuroki and his bomber team did and lived to tell about it.

Ben Kuroki's "team" on the bomber was ten men who had lived, trained, and done virtually everything else together. In the 1942 book that John Steinbeck was commissioned to write for the US Army Air Corps, he noted that "the ties between members of a bomber team are tighter than those of nearly any organization in the world" because "the men know one another as few men ever get acquainted, for they will be under fire together. They will play together after a victory. They will plan together and eat and sleep together on missions. And finally there is the chance that they may die together."[40]

What does all this have to do with Ben Kuroki, the resisters at Heart Mountain, and their differing views of loyalty and patriotism? I found a provisional answer to this question through reading a now all-too-neglected 1956 book authored by the late Morton Grodzins, *The Loyal and the Disloyal*. When writing this book, Grodzins was the chair of the political science department at the University of Chicago. But much of the book's insight derived from Grodzins's World War II years of employment with JERS, an experience that led to his controversial book about the JAI entitled *Americans Betrayed*.[41]

According to Grodzins, there is customarily a face-to-face group that serves "to define and to clarify abstract goals in terms of day-to-day activity." In a democratic state, groups such as these are the sources of life's principal joys as well as the objects of one's primary loyalties. The mere existence of such groups affords chances for sharp clashes between national and other loyalties. Paradoxically, however, these other group loyalties are also the most crucial foundation of democratic loyalty. "The welter of non-national loyalties," explains Grodzins, "makes a direct national loyalty a misnomer. It does not exist. Loyalties are to specific groups, specific goals, specific programs of action. . . . One fights for the joys of his or her pinochle club when he or she is said to fight for the country."[42]

Ben Kuroki's "pinochle club" during World War II—his primary reference group, if you will—was his bomber team. It is true that the Japanese American subculture was also an important reference group to him, but it remained largely a reference group of his imagination and not one deeply grounded in day-to-day activities. So his loyalties as an American were mediated and shaped far less by his ethnic subculture than by his interactions with his fellow bomber crew members. Moreover, his acceptance in that tight military subculture of ten, both as a crew member and as a real American, was perennially provisional, always subject to proving and reproving. For this reason, once his bomber's required twenty-five missions were done, Kuroki alone refrained from throwing his hat up into the air in a celebratory salute to survival. Instead, he decided to implore his superiors to allow him to fly on five more perilous missions (on the final one of which he almost lost his life).

When Ben Kuroki returned to the United States and was asked to go on still another mission, this time a home mission to Heart Mountain, Minidoka, and Topaz, he did not hesitate to discharge his duty as a good aerial gunner and American. When on this mission, he continued to reference his sense of loyalty to his bombing team and its objectives, which were to destroy the enemy, first in Europe and then in the Pacific. Although a shy man, he could unabashedly tell some 30,000 people of Japanese ancestry, two-thirds of whom were American citizens, that he fully planned, once his home mission was over, to fly on still more missions, this time in planes carrying bombs to be dropped on his ancestral country, including his Issei mother's hometown of Yokohama.

In the camps he visited, this message, as we have seen, was received well by some inmates, but not by others. Those who were receptive to Kuroki's message were those whose pinochle club was not a bomber team but Asian Americans whose national status was provisional like Kuroki's and constantly in need of validation, even if this should require the shedding of their blood. But there were also inmates at these camps, like the members of the Heart Mountain Fair Play Committee, whose loyalty to the United States was mediated by their participation in an organization whose position made it clear that, while they were willing to shed their blood for the nation, they would only do so once the United States started to treat them as citizens rather than prisoners and saboteurs. Given his brittle sense of loyalty and patriotism, when Ben Kuroki encountered these men and this message at Heart Mountain, he could only see in them what he most feared that others would see in him—not only an American who had the face of people living in a reviled enemy nation, but also someone whose loyalties squared with these people.

During his home mission in 1944, whether on the *Ginny Simms Show*, before the elite throng at the Commonwealth Club, or within the barbed-wire-girded confines of three American concentration camps, Kuroki reiterated the point that the war the United States was waging against fascism overseas was worthless unless intolerance was conquered at home. But Kuroki failed to see that the FPC members, whom he saw as draft dodgers rather than draft resisters, were his allies, and not his foes, in this two-front fight. These men in the FPC at Heart Mountain were deeply attached and fundamentally adjusted to American ways; nonetheless, they felt deeply that the Japanese American Incarceration was an affront to America as they conceived it should be. They risked being thought of as disloyal Americans precisely because of their impassioned Americanism. They, like Ben Kuroki, are courageous American heroes whose deeds, like his, should be both remembered and revered.[43]

NOTES

This article benefited greatly from the assorted services rendered to me by the following: Ben Kuroki, James Sakoda, Mike Mackey, Mits Koshiyama, George Nozawa, Frank Emi, and Yosh Kuromiya.

1. This 1994 film was directed by Robert A. Nakamura and produced by Karen L. Ishizuka, who also wrote its script.

2. Samuel Hynes, "So Many Men, So Many Wars: Fifty Years of Remembering World War II," *New York Times Book Review*, April 30, 1995, 12.

3. See Samuel Hynes, *Flights of Passage: Reflections of a World War II Aviator* (New York: Frederick C. Beil and the Naval Institute Press, 1988); and Studs Terkel, *"The Good War": An Oral History of World War II* (New York: Pantheon, 1985).

4. For a discussion by Sakoda of his JERS work, see "Reminiscences of a Participant Observer" and "The 'Residue': The Unresettled Minidokans, 1943–1945," both in *Views from Within: The Japanese American Evacuation and Resettlement Study*, ed. Yuji Ichioka, 219–45 and 247–84 (Los Angeles: Asian American Studies Center, University of California, Los Angeles, 1989), 219–84.

5. See Arthur A. Hansen, ed., *Japanese American World War II Evacuation Oral History Project*, pt. 3, *Analysts* (Munich, Germany: K. G. Saur, 1994), 342–457. This edited collection of selective interviews in the Japanese American Project of the Lawrence de Graff Center for Oral and Public History at California State University, Fullerton, includes four other titled parts: part 1, *Internees* (Westport, CT: Meckler, 1991); part 2, *Administrators* (Westport, CT: Meckler, 1991); part 4, *Resisters* (Munich: K. G. Saur, 1995); and part 5, *Guards and Townspeople* (Munich: K. G. Saur, 1993). Hereafter interviews in this collection will be cited by the appropriate titled part.

6. See James Sakoda to Dorothy Thomas, May 2, 1944, folder W1.32, Japanese American Evacuation and Resettlement Records, folder W1.32. Hereafter documents in this collection will be cited as JAERR.

7. Sakoda to Thomas, May 15, 1944, JAERR, folder W1.32.

8. See Bill Hosokawa, *Nisei: The Quiet Americans* (New York: Morrow, 1969), 226–27, 419–20. For the Kuroki biography, see Ralph Martin, *Boy from Nebraska: The Story of Ben Kuroki* (New York: Harper & Brothers, 1946).

9. James M. Sakoda, interview by Arthur A. Hansen, in Hansen, *Analysts*, 427–28.

10. Roger Daniels, *Concentration Camps USA: Japanese Americans and World War II* (New York: Holt, Rinehart and Winston, 1971); and William Minoru Hohri, *Repairing America: An Account of the Movement for Japanese-American Redress* (Pullman: Washington State University Press, 1988).

11. Daniels, *Concentration Camps USA*, 104–29. As Daniels explains (117n25), for his treatment of events at the Heart Mountain center he draws heavily upon Douglas W. Nelson, "Heart Mountain: The History of an American Concentration Camp" (master's thesis, University of Wyoming, 1970), which he supervised. Virtually unchanged, this thesis was published under the same title in book form (Madison: State Historical Society of Wisconsin, 1976).

12. Quoted in Hohri, *Repairing America*, 172–73.

13. James M. Omura, interview by Arthur A. Hansen, in Hansen, *Resisters*, 131–335.

14. This memoir is currently being edited for publication by the present author. See Arthur A. Hansen, ed., *Nisei Naysayer: The Memoir of Militant Japanese American Journalist Jimmie Omura* (Stanford, CA: Stanford University Press, 2018).

15. See James Sakoda, Journal, April 2, 1944, JAERR, folder R20.81.

16. See James Sakoda, Journal, April 2, 1944, JAERR, folder R20.81.

17. See James Sakoda, Journal, April 2, 1944, JAERR, folder R20.81.

18. Mike Mackey, "Heart Mountain Relocation Center: Both Sides of the Fence" (master's thesis, University of Wyoming, 1993); Jack Tono, interviewed by Jean Brainerd, December 1992, State of Wyoming Department of Commerce. Both of these sources, plus the reports and the newspaper articles, were supplied to me by Mike Mackey, one of the organizers of the 1995 Powell, Wyoming, conference where I presented an earlier version of this study.

19. Arthur A. Hansen to Jack Tono, November 19, 1944. This letter to Tono, regretfully, went unanswered.

20. "Ben Kuroki Opens World War II Exhibit," *Historical Newsletter* (Nebraska State Historical Society) 7 (January 1992): 1–3.

21. These two letters to Kuroki, dated August 28, 1994, and September 13, 1994, along with numerous other letters between us, are on file with the transcript of our October 17, 1994, interview in the archives of the Lawrence de Graff Center for Oral and Public History at California State University, Fullerton.

22. In addition to Hosokawa's *Nisei*, see Bill Hosokawa, *JACL in Quest of Justice: The History of the Japanese American Citizens League* (New York: Morrow, 1982); and Robert A. Wilson and Bill Hosokawa, *East to America: A History of the Japanese in the United States* (New York: Morrow, 1982).

23. Bill Hosokawa to Mike Mackey, September 24, 1994. Unless otherwise noted all correspondence cited in the remainder of this chapter is in the author's files.

24. Frank T. Inouye to Mike Mackey, September 29, 1994.

25. Mits Koshiyama to Arthur A. Hansen, October 28, 1994, in response to Arthur A. Hansen to Mits Koshiyama, October 23, 1994.

26. Arthur A. Hansen to George Nozawa, October 31, 1994.

27. George Nozawa to Arthur A. Hansen, December 9, 1994.

28. Frank Emi to Arthur A. Hansen, January 14, 1995, in response to Arthur A. Hansen to Frank Emi, November 19, 1994, and January 11, 1995.

29. Kara Kondo to Mike Mackey, January 5, 1995.

30. Rose Tsuneishi Yamashiro to Mike Mackey, January 5, 1995.

31. Jim and Toshi Ito to Mike Mackey, January 5, 1995.

32. Directed by Robert A. Nakamura, this documentary is based upon detainee-shot footage within the ten War Relocation Authority centers.

33. Ike Hatchimonji to Mike Mackey, January 8, 1995.

34. Tak Hoshizaki to Mike Mackey, January 22, 1995.

35. Yosh Kuromiya to Arthur A. Hansen, February 3, 1995, in response to Arthur A. Hansen to Yosh Kuromiya, January 25, 1995.

36. See, in particular, Arthur A. Hansen and David A. Hacker, "The Manzanar Riot: An Ethnic Perspective," *Amerasia Journal* 2 (Fall 1974): 112–57; and Arthur A. Hansen, "Cultural Politics in the Gila River Relocation Center 1942–43," *Arizona and the West* (Winter 1985): 327–62.

37. Ben Kuroki, interview by Arthur A. Hansen, October 17, 1994, O.H. 2385.

38. Ben Kuroki, interview by Arthur A. Hansen, October 17, 1994, O.H. 2385.

39. Geoffrey Perret, *Winged Victory: The Army Air Forces in World War II* (New York: Random House, 1993); Michael C. C. Adam's *The Best War Ever: America and World War II* (Baltimore: Johns Hopkins University Press, 1994); and Thomas Childers, *Wings of Morning: The Story of the Last American Bomber Shot Down over Germany in World War II* (Reading, MA: Addison Wesley, 1995).

40. John Steinbeck, *Bombs Away: The Story of a Bomber Team* (New York: Viking, 1942), 154–55.

41. Morton Grodzins, *Americans Betrayed: Politics and the Japanese Evacuation* (Chicago: University of Chicago Press, 1949). For the controversy over this book, see Peter T. Suzuki, "For the Sake of Inter-university Comity," in *Views from Within*, ed. Ichioka, 95–123.

42. Morton Grodzins, *The Loyal and Disloyal: Social Boundaries of Patriotism and Treason* (Chicago: University of Chicago Press, 1956), 28–29.

43. The initial version of this chapter was presented on May 20, 1995, for "Japanese American History: The Heart Mountain Experience," a conference held at

Northwest College in Powell, Wyoming. I am especially thankful to one conference organizer, Mike Mackey, not only for providing me lodging, transportation, and word-processing facilities during the conference, but also for abetting preparatory research for my presentation by putting me in touch with numerous key informants and sending me a variety of relevant primary and secondary sources.

8

PECULIAR ODYSSEY

Newsman Jimmie Omura's Removal from and Regeneration within Nikkei Society, History, and Memory

Following my participation in the symposium "Japanese American History: The Heart Mountain Experience," held May 19–21, 1995, at Powell, Wyoming, I motored over to Grand Junction, Colorado, to the family home of Dr. Gregg Omura. My reason for this trip was to secure temporary custody of the James Omura Papers from Dr. Omura, the executor of his late father's estate, so that I could arrange for their archival organization and, thereafter, aided by this rich collection of primary and secondary materials, edit the memoir that James "Jimmie" Matsumoto Omura had prepared between 1981 and his death in 1994. The timing of this Colorado trip coincided with the appearance of the fourth part (Resisters) of the five-part Japanese American World War II Evacuation Oral History Project, edited by me.[1] This volume consisted of tape-recorded interviews with selected Nikkei wartime resisters of note, including James Omura, conducted by members of the Japanese American Project of the California State University, Fullerton's Oral History Program.

This essay is from *Nikkei in the Pacific Northwest: Japanese Americans and Japanese Canadians in the Twentieth Century* edited by Louis Fiset and Gail M. Nomura (© 2005) and reprinted with permission of the University of Washington Press.

DOI: 10.5876/9781607328124.c008

Upon my return from Colorado to southern California I received a substantial California Civil Liberties Public Education Program grant from the California State Library to cover Rebecca Manley's preparation of a finding aid for the James Omura Papers (which were organized through four classes taught by my wife, Debra Gold Hansen, at the San José State University School of Library and Information Science) and sufficient release time for me from the Department of History at Fullerton to begin editing James Omura's memoir.[2]

Simultaneously with my editing of the Omura memoir, I capitalized upon my work in this capacity by serving as a historical consultant for two prize-winning films featuring Omura's World War II resistance role: Emiko and Chizu Omori's Rabbit in the Moon *(1999) and Frank Abe's* Conscience and the Constitution *(2000).[3] I also published two articles revolving around Omura's prewar, wartime, and postwar resistance activities. The first of these appeared in a 2003 volume of essays honoring Roger Daniels, the dean of Japanese American historical studies, and entitled* Remapping Asian American History. *The title of my piece in this festschrift was "Return to the Wars: Jimmie Omura's 1947 Crusade against the Japanese American Citizens League."[4] The second of my articles was initially presented as a paper at the May 2000 conference "The Nikkei Experience in the Pacific Northwest," sponsored by the University of Washington's Center for the Study of the Pacific Northwest. With a transformed title and a much broadened and deepened text, it appeared in print in 2005 as* Nikkei in the Pacific Northwest: Japanese Americans and Japanese Canadians in the Twentieth Century, *and it is that version which is reprinted here.[5]*

It galled many long-standing Japanese American Citizen League (JACL) members who read the "Millennium New Year's Edition" of the *Pacific Citizen*, the league's newspaper, to encounter "Influential JA Journalist: James Omura" in an issue commemorating outstanding twentieth-century Nisei.[6] Perhaps no other Nikkei name could so predictably have nettled Old Guard JACLers as Jimmie Omura, who was born on Bainbridge Island, Washington, in 1912 and who died in Denver, Colorado, in 1994.

Thus, JACL pioneer Fred Hirasuna wrote the *Pacific Citizen*: "Who named James Omura influential journalist of the past century? Omura . . . did not challenge evacuation by physically resisting evacuation [but avoided it] . . . by leaving the area [West Coast] in March of 1942. His main claim to fame seems to be that he supported the Heart Mountain draft resisters and castigated the JACL for not doing the same. His record pales when compared with that of Bill Hosokawa . . . [or] Larry Tajiri. . . . If any one person deserves the title of leading journalist, my choice would be Bill Hosokawa, and he would be the choice of the majority of JAs who actually experienced the evacuation and internment."[7]

Certainly a case could be made for Larry Tajiri, the paper's editor from 1942 to 1952.[8] Possibly Hirasuna's reason for ranking Hosokawa over Tajiri is tied to his rationale for depreciating Omura. While Seattle-born-and-bred Hosokawa was imprisoned at Washington's Puyallup Assembly Center and Wyoming's Heart Mountain Relocation Center, Tajiri did not "do time" in a concentration camp. Instead, he departed California on the final day of "voluntary evacuation" to "resettle" in Salt Lake City.

That same day, March 29, 1942, Omura left the Golden State for Denver, the other intermountain mecca for voluntary migrants. A Bay Area florist, Omura was publisher-editor of the Nisei magazine *Current Life*. If his 1930s sidekick Tajiri planned to convert the *Pacific Citizen* into a weekly,[9] Omura determined to resume publishing the politics and arts monthly he had founded two years before in San Francisco.

Likely Hosokawa's stellar *Denver Post* career from 1946 to 1992 made him Hirasuna's choice. Stridently anti-Japanese during wartime, the *Post* was afterward so liberalized as to embrace Hosokawa and, later, Tajiri.[10]

World War II–era Denver, with 325,000 residents, was a relatively favorable place for Nikkei. Located in the "free zone" near four War Relocation Authority (WRA) camps,[11] Denver attracted voluntary resettlers like Omura as well as those like Oregonian Nisei curfew resister Minoru Yasui, who resettled there from a WRA camp. Denver's wartime Nikkei population peaked at 5,000, even though the WRA clamped a 1943 moratorium on resettlement there.[12]

Colorado's 4,000 Japanese Americans was the largest such prewar population for non-Pacific Coast states, but only 700 lived in Denver. There a several-block transitional area around Larimer Street formed a Japantown. In Denver racism was not unremitting as it had been for prewar coastal Nikkei.

Likewise, Denver was a favorable place for Nisei journalism. As David Yoo observes, the expanded readership of Nikkei migrants to the intermountain region "breathed new life into the struggling English-language sections of three . . . papers outside the restricted zones: the *Rocky Nippon, Colorado Times*, and *Utah Nippo*."[13] The first two were published in Denver. The *Rocky Nippon* (later called the *Rocky Shimpo*) inaugurated its English-language section in October 1941, while the *Times* followed suit in August 1942.[14]

The *Rocky Shimpo* appealed more to WRA-camp inmates than did the *Times* (for which Omura wrote in late 1942), and it buttressed its masthead claim as the "largest circulated Nisei vernacular in the continental U.S.A." The *Times*, whose publisher-editor was veteran Issei Denverite Fred Kaihara, resonated more with resettlers in burgeoning midwestern cities, namely Chicago, which until mid-1947 lacked a vernacular newspaper with an English-language section. The early postwar addition of columns by Togo Tanaka, the prewar English-section editor of Los Angeles's *Rafu Shimpo* and one of Chicago's 20,000-plus resettlers, and Minoru Yasui helped the *Times* double its Denver rival's subscriber base.

Scattered evidence suggests that the two papers experienced a reversal in popularity from the wartime to the postwar years, probably because the Nikkei readership inside and outside of the Denver region changed from anti-JACL to pro-JACL. Indeed, Omura's shifting journalistic fortunes in Denver between 1942 and 1947, which led to his "banishment" from Nikkei life and letters until the 1980s, dramatize this transformed ideological climate in Colorado and throughout Japanese America.

This essay first treats this World War II and immediate postwar transformation in terms of the Omura-JACL battle. It then fast-forwards three decades to consider Omura's resurrected role as a Nikkei writer and outspoken JACL critic after testifying at the 1981 Seattle hearings of the Commission on Wartime Relocation and Internment of Civilians (CWRIC) and achieving community validation within the Seattle-originated National Council for Japanese American Redress (NCJAR).

By the time of Jimmie Omura's arrival in Denver on April 2, 1942, the JACL leadership saw him as their primary nemesis. Their mutual animosity began when a 1934 article in the Omura-edited *New World Daily News* of San Francisco—which seemingly impugned the integrity of a Placer County JACL leader—so provoked JACL founder Saburo Kido, a Nisei attorney for the rival pro-JACL *Hokubei Asahi*, that he threatened to sue Omura for slander.[15] Omura and Kido, later the JACL's wartime president, soon clashed directly when Kido interpreted Omura's editorials criticizing "nisei leadership" as attacking "JACL leadership."

When the JACL's 1934 national convention met in San Francisco, Omura was an established JACL critic. Omura's newspaper had him welcome incoming JACL president and *Japanese-American Courier* editor Jimmie Sakamoto to the city. The two Pacific Northwest Nisei had met four years earlier when Omura sought work on Sakamoto's paper. Then the JACL's founding father had patronized Omura, but now Sakamoto was reproachful. "He said, 'Why did they have to select you?'. . . . I felt so insulted that I turned around and walked away."[16]

Relations between Omura and the JACL came to a head in 1935 after the *New World Daily* and the *Hokubei* merged into the *New World Sun*. Both English-section editors, Howard Imazeki and Omura, managed a page. Omura wrote his own editorials, but Imazeki deferred to Saburo Kido's "Timely Topics" column. Before long, Kido confronted Omura: "I'm being embarrassed. . . . I write an editorial one way on the front page, and my friends say they flip the page and there's an exact opposite editorial on the second page."[17] In early 1936 Omura resigned.

Up until October 1940, when Omura began *Current Life*, journalism and the JACL figured little in his life. Larry Tajiri, the English-section editor of the *Japanese American News* and then staunchly anti-JACL, did get Omura to write editorial features. However, when Tajiri left for a New York post, Omura's writing was censured and then discontinued.[18]

Omura's *Current Life* editorials increasingly chastised the JACL: its leadership was feckless in not preparing Nisei for a probable United States and Japan clash, and its membership was reckless in partying at gala bashes instead of promoting social action. Moreover, the JACL's prolonged accommodation to Japanese imperialism and its flamboyant eleventh-hour American flag-waving bothered Omura. Finally, according to him, "shortly after or even before Pearl Harbor," JACL leaders fingered him as a potentially dangerous person.[19] While this accusation fell on deaf ears, the Omura-JACL war had heated up considerably.

The boiling point came in February of 1942 during meetings of the Bay Region Council for Unity (BRCU). Omura urged this progressive Nisei group's membership to form a coalition with the JACL *on an equal partnership basis* and pitched resistance to the prospective mass eviction policy. The BRCU chair, Larry Tajiri, unsuccessfully sought Omura's expulsion but argued successfully that the BRCU should affiliate as a "Sounding Board" with JACL. This meant BRCU would support JACL executive secretary Mike Masaoka's impassioned plea of "constructive cooperation" with the government for "future considerations."[20] Omura was outraged at Masaoka, felt that Tajiri had betrayed him, and was convinced he "didn't have a single supporter."[21]

Then, on February 23, Omura testified before the Tolan Committee. Following accommodating pro-JACL witnesses, Omura registered strong opposition to mass eviction and detention and then added: "It is a matter of public record that I have been consistently opposed to the Japanese American Citizens League. . . . I have felt that the leaders were leading the American-born along the wrong channels."[22]

In the March 1, 1942, issue of the *Pacific Citizen*, its editor, Evelyn Kirimura, scored Omura's testimony as a grand if worthless gesture by "a magazine with a circulation of 500 more or less" and lamented that "the tragedy of the whole thing is that simply because one puny publisher desired to make a show of himself, all the American citizens of Japanese ancestry are affected." Omura believed Saburo Kido had authored this rebuke. Five days later, at a San Francisco mass gathering, Masaoka named Omura the JACL's "Public Enemy Number One." His had been the sole voice raised against Nikkei cooperation with mass removal and confinement. When Omura left the meeting and brushed past Masaoka, the JACL executive secretary threatened, "We'll get you."[23]

Omura's wife and *Current Life* business manager, Fumiko Caryl Okuma, departed San Francisco on March 14, 1942. Seeking a "free zone" site for their magazine, she stopped in Salt Lake City before reaching Denver on March 18. In both places she found Masaoka at arranged meetings with public officials. Ruling out Salt Lake City as "enemy territory," she recommended Denver as the Omura wartime home. When *Current Life*'s publishing plans were dashed, Omura established the Pacific Coast Evacuee Employment Placement Bureau in April 1942 to give cost-free employment assistance to area resettlers; later that year his wife opened Caryl's Malt and Sandwich Shop.

Throughout 1942 discontent toward the JACL for "selling the Japanese community down the river" was widely shared within the Nikkei community, a situation Omura capitalized upon. Likely because Omura was one of Denver's few experienced Nisei journalists, the *Times*, on October 29, initiated his column, "The Passing Parade." It opened with an ominous entry: "The motto of the Japanese American Citizens League should be 'Let Well Enough Alone,' but if the report that a representative of the organization is to be sent out here to Denver for organizational purposes is correct, the JACL is still meddling where they are neither needed or wanted." Omura promised stiff opposition in Denver.[24]

By its November 17 issue, the *Times* had taken on JACL coloration. Prefacing Mike Masaoka's lead article was an editor's note explaining how its author "well put forth" the timeliness and urgent need for the JACL's current emergency conference in Salt Lake City. Masaoka's claim—that "when the supreme test came for Japanese Americans, the JACL met that challenge nobly, boldly, loyally"—must have been tough for Omura to swallow.

Although Omura's *Times* column appeared for the balance of 1942, he said nothing about the JACL. Mostly Omura commented on labor issues. Occasionally, as on November 24, he celebrated Nikkei community heroes such as Colorado governor Ralph Carr, who had welcomed Nikkei resettlers but then lost his next bid for elective office. At other times, as on December 10, Omura criticized the US government: "Here in one block [Larimer Street] can be found the evidence of . . . a history of which the nation should be ashamed but is not." By the end of 1942 the *Times* had metamorphosed into a JACL mouthpiece, and when editor-publisher Kaihara censored a couple of Omura's columns, Omura resigned.[25]

Earlier Omura had affiliated with the tri-weekly *Rocky Nippon*, so he retained an interpretive outlet. The prevailing tone of his column for this paper, begun on October 28, 1942, was established when he regretted that "in these times more Nisei are not alert to the grave situation on hand and willing to put their shoulders to the wheels crunching out the weeds of prejudice and racial maltreatment." On December 14 Omura took dead aim at the US government: "The great days of democracy, once an emblem of red-blooded Americans, have gone by the board and the nation is today ruled by the grip of dictatorship and fascism."

Omura came out smoking against the JACL in his 1943 columns. On January 4 he recapped his "war record" for readers, emphasizing his Tolan Committee testimony and invidiously comparing the JACL's performance against it. "Instead of looking at the evacuation from a broader standpoint," wrote Omura, "[national] J.A.C.L. leaders attempted to profit on the distress of US Japanese as individuals and as an organization. It was first J.A.C.L. and second, the cause." Omura then renewed his own pledge to that cause: "Perhaps the Evacuee Placement Bureau will drain me of every red cent I possess, but until that last cent is spent this work will be carried on. And even afterward."

In his February 3 column Omura vigorously opposed an all-Nisei combat team. But he feared the idea might appeal to many Nisei, for they "are too easily susceptible to the ingenuities of public officials and the trumped-up slogans of American patriotism." His February 8 column reiterated his opposition to the JACL's extension in Colorado and its capital and challenged the newly arrived JACL representatives to confront him in an open hearing on community issues.

Through the August 9, 1943, issue of the *Rocky Nippon*—renamed the *Rocky Shimpo* in April after Issei publisher Shiro Toda's removal to an alien internment camp for allegedly pro-Japan writings in the Japanese section— Omura filled his columns with his intensifying JACL feud. Shiro Toda's family likely approved of these JACL attacks because they believed its leaders behind his arrest.[26]

In 1943, however, Omura was fighting a losing campaign in Denver against the insurgent JACL. Mike Masaoka's brother, Joe Grant Masaoka, who had been driven out of California's Manzanar camp by the anti-JACL riot of December 1942,[27] was thereupon detailed to Denver to drum up JACL recruits. At a local meeting, the JACL field representative's responses to floor questions, as related in Omura's February 10 column, had been "vague, evasive and indirect." But even Omura conceded the audience had thought otherwise and warmly applauded Masaoka, especially after he read aloud his brother Mike's letter saying he had volunteered for the Nisei Combat Team.

A few weeks hence, on February 20 (?), Omura published an open letter in the *Rocky Nippon* delineating his ten key differences with the JACL. One point cut to the bone: "The League has failed to uphold freedom of the press, employing pressure on newspaper editors to curtail the expression of critics and to propagandize its own program." Although Omura enjoyed press freedom, he could not prevent the JACL's organizational wave from cresting in Denver. "Michael M. Masaoka, the high sachem of the J.A.C.L.," noted Omura in his March 12 (?) column, "is finally coming to Denver." Omura astutely predicted that "Mr. Big's" upcoming appearance at the Japanese Methodist Church would prove "an interesting test of strength in this area for the organization which he represents." But the results were not to Omura's liking. His March 19 column maintained that even Masaoka's presence could not override "the strong opposition which has taken root among the Nisei people of Colorado against the extension of the J.A.C.L. east of the Rockies." However, the same page provided readers with countervailing evidence: "J.A.C.L. Draws Capacity Audience," "Young Buddhists Hail Talk by J.A.C.L. National Secretary," "Ft. Lupton J.A.C.L Chapter Holds Monthly Meeting," and "Longmont Japanese Gather to Hear J.A.C.L. Talk."

Though surrounded, Omura refused to retreat. Instead, he took the offense. On March 29 the *Rocky Nippon* reported on a public talk that Omura had given the previous evening. The text of "Why I Oppose the JACL" occupied the entire subsequent issue. "I have watched for eleven years the gradual expansion of the J.A.C.L.," Omura declared, "[and] I have watched it clutching and grasping for power like the inexorable will of the octopus, relentlessly crushing out the honest criticisms of the ordinary man." After a tedious discussion of his employment service's trials and triumphs, Omura underscored the Nisei's need to resist the JACL's "egoistic," "narrow-minded," and "self-aggrandizing" leadership. "I do not want you to believe that I am alone in this fight," said Omura. "Look to the various relocation centers and you will find a great angered majority who have disowned the J.A.C.L."[28]

The April 2 *Rocky Nippon* was dedicated to Omura and his Pacific Coast Evacuee Placement Bureau, whose doors had just closed. Other Denver doors were slamming in Omura's face. In the April 10 issue of the *Times*, Kaz Oka of Poston, Arizona, denounced Omura. In "Why I Disagree with Mr. Omura," Oka dismissed Omura's recent lecture "on his favorite topic" as more of his rantings. He mocked Omura for devoting half his talk to his placement bureau. "I fail to see what it has to do with his discussion of the JACL and its alleged failings . . . UNLESS he is aware . . . that the JACL may 'invade' his territory and encroach upon his private enterprise by offering reasonably better services."

On May 14 Omura waved off Oka as just another JACL hireling who dealt in innuendo and propaganda, declaring that he had never charged a fee for his employment bureau services. On May 28 he returned to Oka in his new *Rocky Shimpo* column, "Nisei America: Know the Facts." Why, Omura agonized, had the JACL tapped such a nothing writer as Oka when their stable had so many capable writers, like "Mr. Tajiri himself, the editorial genius of the Pacific Citizen . . . to employ his prolific pen [in the JACL's defense]." What Nisei needed to know, explained Omura on June 28, was that Tajiri and his *Pacific Citizen* associates were suspected of alleged communistic leanings, and because of "this fact [it] may go badly for him and the J.A.C.L."[29]

In reality, things were going well for the JACL, leastwise in Denver, and Omura knew it. The main story in the June 4 issue of the *Rocky Shimpo* concerned the JACL district office's opening in downtown Denver to serve the organization's expanding needs in Colorado, Nebraska, and Wyoming. On July 7, the paper conveyed proof of the JACL's growing strength through a story about a meeting at which Joe Grant Masaoka informed potential members of the league's public relations efforts, new credit union, and legislative activities to ameliorate Nisei discrimination.

Omura tried putting a positive spin on his life in Denver. Usually he tried too hard, and it showed in embarrassing ways, as with the August 9, 1943, article "Caryl's Is Sold to Virginia Couple." This anonymous contribution was clearly Omura's handiwork. "In the Evacuation Period's most astounding transaction," it ran, "the widely-known Caryl's Malt & Sandwich Shop changed hands on August 2, going to the highest bidder. . . . The sale . . . is unquestionably the shrewdest deal put across by Miss Okuma." Four decades hence Omura recalled what this show of bravado had masked: "With all the problems we were having, we were going downhill financially." Moreover, the Okuma-Omura marriage was "deteriorating." Putting his anti-JACL campaign on hold, Omura took a gardening position and his wife became a "schoolgirl" and enrolled at Denver University.[30]

That 1943 winter Omura assumed a war industry trainee position that he later described as "killing me physically."[31] So when the *Rocky Shimpo* invited him back at the start of 1944 to be its English-section editor and public contact agent, he readily complied. Soon the draft issue exploded at Heart Mountain, and Omura launched the editorial series constituting arguably the most courageous and significant Nikkei journalistic writing ever produced. Omura relates this complex story in detail within his unpublished memoir, but its contours warrant coverage here.[32]

As noted, a year before he became the *Rocky Shimpo*'s editor, Omura contested the JACL-supported Nisei combat unit. He did so chiefly because it was to be segregated and, therefore, a symbol of racism. Omura's 1944 *Rocky Shimpo* appointment came on the heels of Secretary of War Henry Stimson's announcement about Nisei draft resumption. This was another policy Omura believed the JACL had urged upon the government. When it caused the Heart Mountain Fair Play Committee (FPC) to mushroom, Omura opened the *Rocky Shimpo* to the FPC for news releases. Then, on February 28, Omura wrote his first editorial about draft reinstitution and the reaction to it by those detained in WRA camps. His concern at this point was not Heart Mountain but the actions taken at the Granada, Colorado, and Minidoka, Idaho, centers. There draft resistance had been sporadic and punctuated with denunciations of democracy and avowals of expatriation to Japan. Whereas Omura believed the government should restore a large share of the Nisei's constitutional rights before asking them to sacrifice their lives in battle, he would not condone impulsive and irresponsible draft resistance.[33]

It quickly became plain to Omura that the FPC represented an organized draft resistance movement dedicated to the principle that citizen Japanese should do their duty as Americans, equally, but not before being treated equally by the US government.

Thereafter his editorials supported the FPC not as an organization but solely on the issue of restoration as a prelude to induction. That the *Heart Mountain Sentinel*, the camp newspaper, was staunchly pro-JACL (and, as such, censorious of the FPC for placing Japanese American loyalty and patriotism at risk) added fuel to Omura's fiery editorials. These gained members for the FPC and dramatically increased *Rocky Shimpo* sales in Heart Mountain and the other camps (where Omura believed the overwhelming majority of those detained there were opposed to the JACL).[34] But Omura's hard-hitting editorials also caused the government, facilitated by the WRA and the JACL, to force his resignation in late April of 1944, after which he was replaced by the actively pro-JACL Roy Takeno. Then, on May 10, the Grand Jurors of Wyoming secretly indicted him along with the seven FPC leaders. On July 20 Omura was arrested and jailed for unlawful conspiracy to counsel, aid, and abet violations of the draft. In early November, at their joint jury trial in Cheyenne, Wyoming, while the FPC leaders were found guilty and sentenced to federal imprisonment, Omura was acquitted.

But acquittal did not mean vindication for Omura insofar as the Japanese American community in the Denver region (and even beyond) was concerned. The community had cold-shouldered him at the time of his arrest and stymied the defense fund being raised for him. One solicitor was gang-beaten in a Denver alley at night, while the Fort Lupton JACL chapter president, threatening bodily harm, warned another solicitor against seeking donations in outlying agricultural areas. Also, when Omura sought employment after the courts cleared him, JACL Nisei harassed and hounded him so that he had "a hell of a time finding a job."[35] Eventually he settled into a landscape gardener job, but not before his impoverishment had so dampened his marriage as to bring about divorce in 1947.

During the last half of 1947 Omura did take another stab at editing the *Rocky Shimpo*. But his postwar editorial mission to expose and stop the JACL occurred when its leadership controlled the community, enjoyed the full support of the US government, and was promoting measures that resonated within their community and mainstream America. This story deserves extended treatment, but only one sidebar, Omura's clash of words and worldviews with Minoru Yasui will be broached here.[36]

It is ironic that Yasui and Omura, Pacific Northwest Nisei dissidents who alike championed constitutional and human rights, should have become mortal enemies in wartime and postwar Denver. Their interaction commenced while attorney Yasui was serving a jail sentence in Portland, Oregon, during 1942–43 for violating the army's curfew order so as to provoke a constitutional test case. Although Yasui was a member of JACL, its leadership opposed test cases by, to quote Mike Masaoka, "self-styled martyrs."[37] While in solitary confinement, Yasui took exception, by post, to Omura's published boast that his placement bureau "represent[s] the *ONLY* people of Japanese ancestry to demand equal consideration and treatment as citizens of the United States and to fight for these rights."[38]

Their next confrontation was in Denver on April 19, 1944, just before Omura's resignation as editor. While detained at the Minidoka camp, Yasui had altered his attitude toward Nikkei who chose the path of most resistance during wartime. Along with two local JACL leaders, Yasui came to the *Rocky Shimpo* office to confer with Omura about his Nisei draft position but left by snarling at him, "I'm going to see you go to prison one way or another."[39]

Yasui became a Denver resident in the fall of 1944 and began his law practice two years later. In addition, he promoted JACL fortunes as the local chapter's vice president and the national organization's regional representative. In the fall of 1947 he became a *Colorado Times* columnist, and through his "Denver Nisei-Grams" column Yasui next locked horns with Omura.

On May 16, 1947, Omura promised *Rocky Shimpo* readers in his resuscitated "Nisei America: Know the Facts" column to expect a "progressive type of journalism" that will "freely criticize wherever occasions demand." He further sounded a warning to the JACL leadership: "Those who have disagreed with us in the past and have been unpardonably guilty of working nefariously in the shadows may evince certain misgivings with our return to the Nisei journalistic wars. They have cause to feel uneasy."

Omura's special brand of "liberalism" pervaded his 1947 columns, roughly one-fifth of which criticized JACL leadership and policies.[40] On August 2, for example, Omura blasted the "selfish and arrogant" JACL leadership for denying "the right of any Nisei to hold views contrary to its own."

Min Yasui's initial *Colorado Times* column of September 23, 1947, boosted Denver: a liberal, progressive city that was "fair-minded toward minority groups." Thereafter, Yasui's columns were free of boosterism, except when spotlighting the JACL leadership.[41] "Despite acrimonious criticism to the contrary," declared Yasui on September 30, "[Mike] Masaoka has done an outstanding job in Washington D.C. He has been able to shove through a complete legislative program [naturalization rights for Issei; evacuations claims indemnification; and equality in deportation laws] halfway thru Congress in a single session."

A face-off between Omura and Yasui was catalyzed by Omura's strenuous objection to *Times* editor Fred Kaihara's statement that no discrimination of significance toward Nikkei existed in either wartime or present-day Denver. Wartime discrimination against Japanese Americans, fumed Omura, had been both "widespread" and "bitter," especially in employment, while postwar prejudice extended to public accommodations, education, and housing.

When Yasui charged that Omura's ravings about discrimination were "not borne out by facts," Omura denigrated Yasui as a "whipping boy" for Kaihara who was "not conscientious of the truth." Whereas the *Rocky Shimpo*'s policy "pointed up" instances of discrimination, observed Omura, the policy of the *Colorado Times* "pointed down" such behavior.

What differentiated his outlook from Omura's, bristled Yasui, was that "we have tried to DO something actual about discriminatory situations," while Omura had been "negatively fixated" on the fact of discrimination. There was probably a basis for a debate between them, Yasui pondered, "but we refuse to fight the wind, even as we found that butting our head against a stone wall during evacuation was fruitless."[42]

Omura's November 24 issue featured a city-commissioned report's finding that "racial prejudice in Denver was on the rise and had seeped into virtually every phase of community life." In this same edition, Omura took Yasui to task for calling him a do-nothing Cassandra while posturing as a constructive doer in the fight against discrimination.

On December 4, a small *Rocky Shimpo* item announced James Omura's resignation as editor, effective December 15. Personal finances figured heavily in Omura's decision. So also did fatigue. Throughout much of his editorship, Omura had operated the Omura Landscape Service, and this double duty exacted its price.[43]

Omura fired parting shots at the JACL, the *Colorado Times*, and Min Yasui. On December 3 he declared the JACL's liberal element its best reform hope. But it would have to occur, he wrote on December 9, before the JACL's fanatics destroyed the organization. Unfortunately, he remarked, these fanatics pervaded the top leadership, demanded other Nisei's unqualified allegiance, and were virtually immune to constructive criticism. Omura's December 12 editorial compared his newspaper's approach with that of the *Times*. Whereas the *Rocky Shimpo* was forthright about the inadequacy of the JACL leadership, the *Times* both defended that leadership and shielded it from criticism. A "vicious example" was Yasui's attributing to Omura the "patently false and absolutely untrue" allusion that none of Denver's leaders were any good at all. "We have labeled this statement," explained Omura, "a lie. Mr. Yasui has threatened to sue us unless we retract. We have refused to retract. The next move is Mr. Yasui's."

In the December 18 issue of the *Times*, Yasui responded to Omura's indictment of the *Rocky Shimpo*: The *Times* believed in objective reporting of the news and covering topics of interest to local Nisei residents, including discrimination, but also strove to encourage Nisei and place Nisei activities in "the best possible light." He admitted his having considered suing Omura but now felt this action pointless. It was quite enough for him that "a disturbing factor in Denver journalism is now gone."

Still, on December 29 Yasui revisited the issue most responsible for the bad blood with Omura—wartime Nisei draft resistance. What provoked Yasui's editorial was President Harry Truman's granting amnesty to the 315 convicted Japanese American draft violators. Although charitable toward those resisting "to register a legal protest against evacuation," especially under the extenuating circumstances, Yasui's commentary represented a stinging critique of the Fair Play Committee, Omura, and Nisei draft "evaders."

> When other Nisei boys were slugging against the enemy, reports of draft violation hit the morale of our Nisei GI's. On the home front, refusal to serve was construed by the public as out-right disloyalty. But now . . . we believe that this is the end of that sad and shameful story.
>
> A moral that we can safely draw . . . is that as citizens and as human beings, we must first fulfill our obligations to the nation and society before we can legally or socially expect that our complete rights will be granted to us.

Thus, by the close of 1947, a perceptive observer could conceivably have grasped the current power arrangements in Japanese Denver, glimpsed the contours of the emerging collective memory as to the Japanese American wartime experience (within both the Nikkei and mainstream American communities), and fathomed the likely trajectory of postwar Japanese American society and history.

Omura's retreat eliminated a formidable counterweight to the JACL's hegemonic hold over Japanese Denver's public life. The existence of a large, active JACL chapter, along with a favorable press to promote its agenda and social gospel, ensured that the organization would prevail. How the immediate Japanese American past would be configured within (and outside of) Denver's Nikkei community was also discernible. The basic lesson for Nikkei to learn from their wartime history, as adumbrated by Yasui, was that, unlike most other Americans, they needed to fulfill obligations like military service before their civil and human rights would be granted to them. This lesson's subtext was that the JACL's policy of "constructive cooperation" had been prudent and patriotic, while those who had advocated and/or practiced resistance on constitutional grounds were misguided, mischievous, or treasonable. The real Japanese American heroes had been those valiant Nisei who had answered their military duty call so that they could "go for broke" for America.

The *Pacific Citizen* disseminated this same JACL-shaped historical narrative throughout Japanese America. One of its two principal interpretive voices was Denver-based columnist Bill Hosokawa, with the other being its editor, Larry Tajiri, who moved to Denver after the *Pacific Citizen's* transfer in 1952 from Salt Lake City to Los Angeles. The *Pacific Citizen* was the unofficial voice of early postwar Japanese America. Because Mike Masaoka was a veritable one-man gang lobbying Congress for the JACL-crafted program covering Japanese American rights and benefits, he amplified the newspaper's version of Japanese American history within a strategic national center. During wartime Masaoka had strongly supported Nisei military service, viewing it as the best way of "proving" their loyalty. The all-Nisei 442nd Regimental Combat Team's first volunteer, Masaoka had served as a public relations officer and in that capacity was a very effective pitchman for the JACL rendition of Japanese American history.

For over three decades following his *Rocky Shimpo* resignation, Jimmie Omura disappeared from Japanese American society and was erased from Japanese American history. He remained a Denver resident but lived apart from the Nikkei community. In 1951 Omura got remarried, to another Nisei woman, and together they raised two boys. Omura operated a successful landscaping business until illness in the late 1970s forced him into retirement.

The JACL played a key role in expunging Jimmie Omura's name and memory from Japanese American history and consciousness. While he prospered in landscaping, the JACL thrived as an organization. Its expanding membership encompassed the Nisei elite, and outside of Japanese America it was viewed as that community's representative. This situation crystallized as early as 1948, as can be seen through one of Togo Tanaka's *Colorado Times* columns reprinted in the *Pacific Citizen* on September 25 that year.

Although Tanaka began his column pointing out how Japanese Americans had been transformed from a despised into an accepted, even respected American minority group, his primary motivation for writing it was to rejoice over the reversed estates of JACLers and anti-JACL resisters since camp days. Then "pressure boys" within such morally defiled places had intimidated and seduced the Nikkei majority into believing that JACL leaders were informers who had sold out their ethnic community for self-advancement and needed to be punished with beatings and banishment. Having accomplished this objective, resistance "messiahs" were themselves removed from the camps as "troublemakers." Still, as with Harry Yoshio Ueno, whose arrest had sparked the Manzanar Riot and driven Tanaka and his JACL cohorts out of the Manzanar camp, each of the other charismatic resistance leaders had been transformed into "a martyr to his glowing cause." However, explained Tanaka, posterity would vindicate neither Ueno nor his counterparts. Just three years after the war it was apparent that these individuals had not "contributed anything more than zero to securing the present position of Japanese Americans in U.S. life."

Having punctured the historical pretensions of camp resisters, Tanaka turned his pen to obliterating them, via Ueno, from the collective memory of Japanese and mainstream America: "This ex-fruit-stand clerk has disappeared into the obscurity and oblivion from which he reared his sallow head, and no one seems to care very much if at all. Thus, the story endeth."

Although Yasui and Tanaka were not literally conspiring to oust resisters from the Japanese American World War II story and to refigure the JACL's role in it, they worked in tandem toward those ends. While Tanaka was exorcising those who had resisted the WRA-JACL alliance's dismantling of the Nikkei community's traditional cultural arrangements, Yasui was extirpating those who had resisted that same alliance's compromising of Nisei citizenship rights.

Neither Yasui nor Tanaka presumed to write books about Japanese American history and its defining World War II experience. However, another prominent JACL leader, Bill Hosokawa, did tackle this task, authoring or coauthoring four interrelated publications: *Nisei* (1969), *East to America* (1980), *JACL in Quest of Justice* (1982), and *They Call Me Moses Masaoka* (1987).[44]

Setting aside these books' overall quality, what is instructive here is Hosokawa's erasure of resisters from the Japanese American wartime story. Nowhere appears the name of James Omura. This could hardly have been simply an oversight. Both Hosokawa and Omura had been born and raised in the Seattle area, figured significantly in the 1942 Tolan Committee hearings, were associated with Heart Mountain political developments, and resettled permanently in wartime Denver. Hosokawa does mention draft resisters in his last three books, but only perfunctorily and as a foil, variously, to discredit the purported revisionism of historians (like Roger Daniels),[45] to glorify the compassionate efforts of JACLers (like Minoru Yasui and Joe Grant Masaoka) to "save" them, and to highlight their meager number and lack of heroic merit relative to Nisei soldiers.[46] As for Harry Ueno and other militant anti-JACL resisters, Hosokawa is also silent, with the single exception of a reference in *Nisei* to Joe Kurihara, "perhaps the chief agitator in Manzanar."[47]

Between Hosokawa's *Nisei* in 1969 and his *East to America* in 1980, American society and culture, including the Nikkei community, underwent a tumultuous upheaval. As the mounting protests against the Vietnam War, racism, and sexism evinced, passivity and obedience to authority had ceased being admired. Historians were drawn to outspoken individuals and activist groups who had stood up for social justice and enlarged democratic rights. Moreover, they used this tradition of dissent to promote contemporary developments and personalities. Conversely, they subjected the past's sacred cows—whether individuals, institutions, movements, or events—to rigorous and skeptical scrutiny and, if necessary, strong criticism, and this legacy, too, was put into the service of present-day politics.

This development vis-à-vis Japanese American history was evident in seminal books by Roger Daniels and Michi Nishiura Weglyn.[48] Daniels's *Concentration Camps USA* appeared in 1971, and as Moses Richlin's foreword notes, Daniels "has given special attention to the resistance and protest of the evacuees, an aspect neglected or glossed over by others."[49] Daniels's acknowledgments discreetly intimated his break with the JACL interpretation: "The late Joe Grant Masaoka . . . would not have agreed with some of my strictures about the Japanese American power structure, but would, I am sure, have defended my right to make them."[50] Devoting considerable space to the Heart Mountain draft resistance movement and Omura's correlated role, Daniels contrasted his perspective with the WRA-JACL one:

> This account of the "loyal" Japanese American resistance . . . calls into question the stereotype of the Japanese American victim of oppression during World War II who met his fate with stoic resignation and responded only with superpatriotism. . . . The JACL-WRA view has dominated the writing of the evacuation's postwar history, thereby nicely illustrating E. H. Carr's dictum that history is written by the winners. . . . [But] there are those who will find more heroism in resistance than in patient resignation.[51]

Community historian Michi Weglyn used similarly bald terminology in her title and text for *Years of Infamy* (1976).[52] That book's dust jacket featured the Manzanar camp's controversial plaque blaming "hysteria, racism, and economic exploitation" for the ten WRA "concentration camps." As Raymond Okamura's review stated, Weglyn wrote "from the perspective of an outraged victim." She relied heavily on primary sources and "discarded preconceptions" such as benevolent administrative-inmate cooperation and invested her data with experiential meaning. Her selection of opening photographs coupled "WRA brutality" and the Nikkei response of "defiance and resistance" to such oppressive actions.[53] Weglyn was mute about the draft resistance movement at Heart Mountain, but for one chapter's epigraph she summoned Omura's Tolan Committee testimony: "Has the Gestapo come to America? Have we not risen in righteous anger at Hitler's mistreatment of the Jews? Then, is it not incongruous that citizen Americans of Japanese descent should be similarly mistreated and persecuted?"[54] Moreover, Weglyn provided copious, empathetic coverage to camp resisters in all of the WRA camps (including the Moab and Leupp isolation centers for "troublemakers" and the Tule Lake segregation center for "disloyals").[55] Even her dedication— "To Wayne M. Collins, Who Did More to Correct a Democracy's Mistake Than Any Other One Person"—conveyed the book's resistance motif. A civil rights lawyer and social crusader, Collins had been instrumental in closing the notorious Tule Lake stockade and also spent many postwar years restoring citizenship rights for nearly 5,000 Tuleans who had renounced them.[56]

Jimmie Omura was oblivious to this new resistance historiography. But as a 1980s retiree he began reflecting on his journalistic past, including his war against the JACL leadership. Plagued by a cardiac condition, Omura decided to write his memoirs and to emphasize the wartime years. Perhaps, in so doing, he could vindicate the Japanese American community and himself for the damage the US government and the JACL had inflicted on both.

His decision coincided with the Nikkei community's campaign to achieve redress and reparations for its wartime mistreatment. Aware that the congressional Commission on Wartime Relocation and Internment of Civilians (CWRIC) had scheduled hearings in ten US cities, Omura resolved to testify.[57] He chose to bypass Washington DC, where Mike Masaoka and Min Yasui (JACL's National Committee for Redress chair) testified, as well as his prewar journalism beats of Los Angeles and San Francisco and selected his "home town" of Seattle (where the hearings were sited at his high school alma mater). Seattle appealed also because it would allow Omura to visit people and places from his Bainbridge Island boyhood and do background research for his book.

Redress was rooted in Omura (and Seattle). As one redress leader, William Hohri, states unequivocally, "James Omura was the first Japanese-American to seek redress from the United States."[58] Indeed, on May 1, 1942, Omura had written to a Washington law firm seeking their representation, only to discover that the firm's start-up fee was more than he could afford.

Omura was among 150-plus individuals to speak at the three-day hearings.[59] Within a four-person panel addressing "economic loss and harassment," he was granted a five-minute presentation. Hugh Mitchell, chairing the proceedings, twice abruptly cut him off. Omura made two points: (1) CWRIC should broaden its inquiry to encompass "voluntary evacuees" like himself; and (2) he was speaking as "one of the chief targets of the JACL," which he had "fought . . . from start to finish." He requested the opportunity to submit a fuller report to the commission (which he subsequently did on October 16, 1981).[60]

Testifying in Seattle, too, were several Nikkei destined to play a significant role in Omura's remaining lifetime: Frank Abe, Lawson Inada, Chizu Omori, and Rita Takahashi. Yet the CWRIC testifier having by far the biggest future impact upon Omura was not any of these second- and third-generation Japanese Americans, but a fifth-generation Chinese American—Frank Chin.[61]

A California native, Chin came to Seattle in the mid-1960s and exploded on the Asian American and mainstream literary scene in the next decade as an innovative dramatist.[62] He was one of four editors—another being Sansei poet Inada—of a landmark Asian American literary anthology.[63] Chin's search for an Asian American literary and historical tradition led him to Nisei writers like Toshio Mori, whose earliest work Omura had published in *Current Life*.[64] But for Chin the most potent Nisei writer had been Seattle-reared John Okada. In his 1957 novel *No-No Boy*, which had been largely neglected, Okada modeled his protagonist on Jim Akutsu. He was a Seattle Nisei who, as a Minidoka camp draft resister, had corresponded with Omura in 1944 and who also testified at the Seattle CWRIC hearings.[65] Pronouncing *No-No Boy* the most significant prose ever produced by a Japanese American, Chin and Inada collaborated editorially to have it reprised as a self-published volume.

In the late 1970s, Chin got immersed in the redress movement. Abetted by onetime Sansei actor Frank Abe, Chin in 1978 conceived Seattle's Day of Remembrance and, under the aegis of the Seattle Evacuation Redress Committee, staged a Thanksgiving weekend evacuation reenactment. Although never a member, Chin played a key role in the May 1979 formation of the Seattle-based National Council for Japanese American Redress (NCJAR). Upon Michi Weglyn's urging, he convinced William Hohri of Chicago to assume NCJAR's leadership. Afterward NCJAR, to quote Hohri, "gravitated towards Chicago," but it retained a core of Seattle supporters, such as Chizu Omori and Frank Abe. They agreed with Hohri that CWRIC was a "cop-out" and had developed because of "the JACL's unwillingness to demand redress directly from the United States Congress." In spite of NCJAR's 1980 decision to seek judicial rather than legislative redress, Omori and Abe, like Hohri, decided to participate in the CWRIC hearings.[66]

Chin's Seattle CWRIC testimony indicted the JACL for its incriminating role in "the formulation of the infamous loyalty oath" administered at the camps in early 1943 and for its "intention to use the camps to modify Japanese American society, culture, history, and individual behavior." Concluded Chin: "The greatest damage . . . that the government inflicted on Japanese Americans was the imposition of the Japanese American Citizens League as the leaders of the Japanese Americans inside the camps."[67]

Such a position naturally commanded Omura's attention, and he asked Seattle redress activist Henry Miyatake to introduce him to Chin. Hearing Omura's name, Chin remarked, "Not *the* James Omura," to which Omura responded, "the very same." Chin and Lawson Inada then conversed, off tape, with this "long lost uncle" about his remembrance of things past, particularly the Heart Mountain draft resistance movement.[68]

Then Chin's "The Last Organized Resistance" appeared in the 1981 *Rafu Shimpo*'s holiday issue; it led to Chin being contacted in early 1982 by Frank Emi, a surviving Fair Play Committee leader,[69] and in that year Chin and Inada, along with allies, started collecting oral histories about this forgotten historical event.[70] As Chin later recalled, "Men who had never spoken of their resistance jail terms, appeared in broad daylight to meet James Omura."[71] These interviews also catalyzed, a decade later, two well-attended resisters' reunions and reader's theater presentations, in San Jose in May of 1992 and in Los Angeles in February of 1993.

The early 1980s activity had ramifications for Omura, who had been "reborn in Seattle."[72] Hohri invited him to speak in Chicago and there avail himself of research material amassed by NCJAR (for which he, along with other notable wartime resisters like Harry Ueno, became a substantial backer) for his in-progress memoir.[73] San Francisco and Los Angeles vernaculars commissioned Omura to write editorials,[74] while UCLA's Asian American Studies Center wooed his participation in conferences and panels and solicited him to review books for the *Amerasia Journal* (including Hosokawa's *JACL in Quest of Justice*).[75] Scholars elsewhere interviewed him for academic projects, documentary films, and museum collections. Radical historian Richard Drinnon included Omura within his *Keeper of Concentration Camps* dedication for being a Japanese American who had said "no."[76] Even in Colorado, a group calling itself "Making Waves" arranged speaking engagements for him in the Denver region.

Repeatedly, Omura returned to the Pacific Northwest. Hosted in Seattle by Chizu Omori and Frank Abe, among others, he sometimes had Jim Akutsu serve as his chauffeur. His most meaningful return occurred in March 1988 when he participated in the Association for Asian American Studies meeting at Pullman, Washington. Omura presented a paper, as did Frank Emi, at a panel moderated by Frank Chin. After mentioning that since Pearl Harbor the JACL had been "the voice of Japanese American opinion to the press and the voice of Japanese American history," Chin then mused: "I believe you will agree that Frank Emi of the Heart Mountain Fair Play Committee and James Omura of the *Rocky Shimpo* are honorable men. They have been written out of history. They should never have been forgotten."[77]

Meanwhile, Omura had been working diligently to ensure that the label script being prepared by the JACL- and military-dominated Advisory Committee for the Smithsonian Institution's National Museum's 1987 exhibit, "A More Perfect Union: Japanese Americans and the United States Constitution," would do the draft resisters justice. Upon traveling to Washington, DC, to see this exhibit, he was convinced that it pretty much did.[78]

Omura tried to set the record straight about another text that to him polluted the truth of the World War II Japanese American historical record—*They Call Me Moses Masaoka* (1987), written by Mike Masaoka with Bill Hosokawa. The opening salvo of Omura's *Rafu Shimpo* review presaged what would follow: "History indeed is infinitely the poorer and literature thereby greatly diminished by publication of this fabricated account of the historic Japanese American episode of World War II."[79] This review's damage was compounded by the finding in a 1990 JACL-commissioned report by researcher Deborah Lim that, at the JACL's March 1942 Special Emergency Meeting in San Francisco, Masaoka allegedly had recommended that "Japanese be branded and stamped and put under the supervision of the Federal government."[80]

In the late 1980s and early 1990s Omura received long-deferred public recognition and acclaim. Biographical encyclopedia and dictionary entries honored him while organizations feted him for his accomplishments.[81] Two tributes meant most to Omura. In 1989 the Asian American Journalists Association (AAJA), meeting in San Francisco, conferred its Lifetime Achievement Award upon him. Frank Abe, then a KIRO Radio reporter in Seattle and an AAJA board member, was instrumental in Omura's selection. Abe cited Omura's courageous journalistic World War II role upholding constitutional principles and contrasted his behavior with the JACL's capitulation to pragmatic accommodation. Not expecting an Asian American group to honor him during his lifetime, Omura doubted the award would change public opinion toward him. Then, in 1992, the National Coalition for Redress/Reparations (NCRR) recognized Omura in a Day of Remembrance candle-lighting ceremony, also in San Francisco, on the fiftieth anniversary of Executive Order 9066. Significant for Omura was the fact that he was the sole Japanese American among the honorees (civil rights lawyers Ernest Besig and Wayne Collins, crusading *Bainbridge Review* editors Walt and Millie Woodward, and the American Friends Service Committee). "I had no expectation that anyone would be thinking of me on the 50th Anniversary of the signing of Executive Order 9066," Omura wrote Michi Weglyn. "I was wrong"![82]

Meanwhile, the JACL was fighting to retain its righteous place in Japanese American history. But since the CWRIC hearings, and especially after the Civil Rights Act of 1988 enacting the commission's recommendations, it had been battling a defensive war. Having gained a US government apology, a growing number of Nikkei demanded a JACL one for its wartime leaders' community betrayal, a point driven home by the evidence in the Lim report (which the JACL attempted to suppress). In Omura's opinion, a rearguard JACL action to deflect criticism and restore its dignity was embracing "the glorification of the trio of failed Supreme Court challengers [Gordon

Hirabayashi, Fred Korematsu, and Minoru Yasui]." These test cases, argued Omura, had "no relevance to their [Japanese Americans'] sufferings and the tragedy of the Japanese American episode," but instead "sprang out of personal impulses." What really disturbed Omura was Denver's Mile Hi JACL chapter's fund-raising campaign for a city statue to honor Minoru Yasui, "unarguably the [Japanese American community's] number one informer, or in cultural terms, *inu*." The very idea to Omura was a desecration.[83]

Denver's Nikkei community disagreed with Omura, believing Yasui a deserving Nisei hero. From 1967 to 1983, he headed the city's commission on community relations, and from the 1970s to his death in 1986 he spearheaded the JACL's redress movement. Thus, he was much honored in Denver. In 1994, the year Omura died, Yasui's image was unveiled on a bronze plaque (sculpted by Ruth Asawa and relating the Japanese American historical narrative) in the Robert Peckham Federal Building. In 1999 this building was dedicated as Minoru Yasui Plaza, and prominent in its lobby was a replica of the Yasui bust in Sakura Square at the historic heart of Denver's Japantown. Finally, in 2000, Yasui was one of a very few Denver leaders granted Mayor's Millennial Awards for their extraordinary contributions to the city.[84]

Bill Hosokawa, another Pacific Northwest native and JACL leader, also had "monuments" created to his memory within his adopted city. Most came after Omura's death. In 1996 Hosokawa was inducted into the Denver Press Club's Media Hall of Fame. In 1999 the Japan America Society of Colorado and the Japanese Consulate recognized him as honorary consul general for Japan in Colorado. And in 2000 Hosokawa received the American Civil Liberties Union's Whitehead Award for "lifetime service on behalf of all who suffer inequality and injustice."[85]

But no similar city and state honors were forthcoming for Omura, before or after his death. He thus remains in the region where he lived from 1942 to 1994 as an unrecognized hero of Japanese American and US history. The same general situation still prevails throughout the nation, including the Pacific Northwest. But the winds are blowing in the other direction. In his *Rafu Shimpo* obituary for Omura, "Let Us Now Praise Famous Men," Frank Chin fittingly eulogized him: "He [Omura] had lived to see the resisters he championed begin to be restored to the community. After 40 years of silence and obscurity, Jimmie began to be rediscovered and his work recognized by

Asian America. . . . But Japanese America, Asian America never knew Jimmie well enough."[86]

Since Chin's obituary appeared, not only Japanese America and Asian America have come to know Omura quite well, but even the larger American community has been introduced to him. Chin deepened the first two audiences' awareness by including a long section on Omura and Heart Mountain draft resisters in his lead essay for a 1991 anthology of Chinese and Japanese American literature.[87] Moreover, Chin's 2002 documentary novel, *Born in the USA*, which valorizes the Heart Mountain draft resistance story and makes Omura a central interpretive voice for the authentic Japanese America legacy, promises to influence a large mainstream population.[88] Two documentary films—Emiko Omori's *Rabbit in the Moon* (1999) and Frank Abe's *Conscience and the Constitution* (2000)—have already reached this larger audience via national public television.[89] The first (coproduced by Omori's sister, Chizu) won major awards, including the American Historical Association award for the year's best historical documentary. Abe's film claimed top honors at film festivals and competitions, and in 2001 the AAJA recognized it as the year's best film for Unlimited Subject Matter in Television. Whereas *Rabbit in the Moon* was dedicated to Omura and praised camp resisters generally, including those challenging the Nisei draft, *Conscience and the Constitution* focused exclusively on the Heart Mountain draft resistance movement and Omura's support for it. Two 2001 books, *Resistance* and *Free to Die for Their Country*, both depict Omura within the larger draft resistance story so as to enhance his historical reputation.[90] William Hohri authored the first of these books, with essays by former Fair Play Committee members Mits Koshiyama, Yosh Kuromiya, and Frank Emi. According to Philip Tajitsu Nash's *Washington Journal* review of *Resistance*, "Hohri reminds us of the patriotism of those who chose incarceration, and a subsequent lifetime of ostracism, rather than see the Constitution undermined. . . . [and provides] sometimes gripping accounts of the human cost of standing up for justice."[91] *Free to Die for Their Country*, by University of North Carolina constitutional law professor Eric Muller, is more mainstream-oriented than Hohri's book. This is due to its prestigious publisher, the University of Chicago Press, and a foreword by Senator Daniel K. Inouye, an American as well as a Japanese American icon of patriotism, valor, and justice.

While it will take more time for Omura to gain the iconic stature achieved by Senator Inouye and now almost attained by the draft resisters of conscience, he seems destined to reach this lofty plateau. He had seen and written about fascism's darkening clouds in the prewar United States, he had testified, ominously, about the Gestapo coming to America during the war's early stages, and in the war's fullness he had waged a fearless editorial battle against lawless militarism and for civil, minority, and human rights. At the end of his life, Omura was reliving this past for his own purposes as well as the edification of posterity. "Jimmie," noted Frank Chin in his obituary, "was at work on his book when he was struck with a heart attack and died in Denver, at 6:35 a.m., June 20, 1994."[92] That book, his memoir, Omura had been laboring over for more than a decade. Perhaps when it is published, there will be a greater appreciation for why, at the turn of this new millennium, he was honored as Japanese America's (most) influential journalist of the twentieth century.[93]

NOTES

I extend my thanks to Louis Fiset and Gail Nomura for editorial assistance; Frank Abe, Frank Chin, and William Hohri for reviewing the manuscript; and Debra Gold Hansen, Rebecca Manley, Martha Nakagawa, Chizu and Emiko Omori, Wayne Omura, Rita Takahashi, Mary Kimoto Tomita, and Steve Yoda for facilitating my ongoing work on James Omura.

1. Arthur A. Hansen, ed., *Resisters*, pt. 4 of *Japanese American World War II Evacuation Oral History Project* (Munich, Germany: K. G. Saur, 1995).

2. The James Omura Papers were deposited at Stanford University's Green Library in 2017.

3. *Rabbit in the Moon*, directed by Emiko Omori, produced by Emiko and Chizu Omori (New Day Films, 1999), 60 mins; *Conscience and the Constitution*, directed by Frank Abe, produced and directed by Frank Abe and Shannon Gee (Resisters.com Productions, 2000), 60 mins.

4. Arthur A. Hansen, "Return to the Wars: Jimmie Omura's 1947 Crusade against the Japanese American Citizens League," in *Remapping Asian American History*, ed. Sucheng Chan, 127–50 (Walnut Creek, CA: AltaMira Press, 2003).

5. Louis Fiset and Gail Nomura, eds., *Nikkei in the Pacific Northwest: Japanese Americans and Japanese Canadians in the Twentieth Century* (Seattle: University of Washington Press, 2005).

6. Takeshi Nakayama, "Influential JA Journalist: James Omura," *Pacific Citizen*, January 1–13, 2000.

7. See Fred Hirasuna, "Letters to the Editor," *Pacific Citizen*, April [?], 2000.

8. For biographical information on Tajiri, see the entry by David Yoo in Brian Niiya, ed., *Encyclopedia of Japanese American History: An A–Z Reference from 1868 to the Present* (Los Angles: Japanese American National Museum, 2001), s.v. "Tajiri Larry (1914–1965) journalist" by David Yoo. See also Bill Hosokawa, "Larry Tajiri, A Better Choice," *Pacific Citizen*, February 11–17, 2000.

9. Bill Hosokawa, *JACL in Quest of Justice: The History of the Japanese American Citizens League* (New York: Morrow, 1982), 156–57, 178–79.

10. See Bill Hosokawa, *Out of the Frying Pan: Reflections of a Japanese American* (Niwot: University Press of Colorado, 1998), esp. chap. 8, "Hosokawa of the *Post*," 63–79.

11. Minidoka (Idaho), Heart Mountain (Wyoming), Topaz (Utah), and Amache (Colorado).

12. Russell Endo, "Japanese of Colorado: A Sociohistorical Portrait," *Journal of Social and Behavioral Sciences* 31 (Fall 1985): 100–110.

13. David K. Yoo, *Growing Up Nisei: Race, Generation, and Culture among Japanese Americans of California, 1924–49* (Urbana: University of Illinois Press, 2000), 129.

14. Yoo, *Growing Up Nisei*, 130.

15. James M. Omura, interview by Arthur A. Hansen, Hansen, *Resisters*, 209–11.

16. See Arthur A. Hansen, "Interview with James Matsumoto Omura," *Amerasia Journal* 13 (1986–87): 104.

17. Hansen, "Interview with James Matsumoto Omura," 104–5.

18. *World Biographical Hall of Fame* (Raleigh, NC: Historical Preservations of America, 1992), s.v. "James Matsumoto Omura."

19. Omura interview, *Resisters*, 254.

20. Omura interview, *Resisters*, 261; Jere Takahashi, *Nisei/Sansei: Shifting Japanese American Identities and Politics* (Philadelphia: Temple University Press), 95–96.

21. Omura interview, *Resisters*, 262.

22. US Congress, House Investigating National Defense Migration, *National Defense Migration, Part 29: San Francisco Hearings: Problem of Evacuation of Enemy Aliens and Others from Prohibited Military Zones*, 77th Cong., 2nd sess., February 21, 23, 1942 (Washington, DC: GPO, 1942), 11229–30.

23. Omura interview, *Resisters*, 263.

24. Omura became aware of the imminent JACL incursion in Denver shortly after moving there. See Omura's letters to A. Norman Depew, May 9 and May 22, 1942, James M. Omura Papers, Green Library, Stanford University. Hereafter material from this collection will be cited as Omura Papers, Stanford.

25. This point is discussed in James Omura, "Japanese American Journalism during World War II," *Frontiers of Asian American Studies: Writing, Research, and Commentary*, ed. Gail M. Nomura, Russell Endo, Stephen H. Sumida, and Russell

Leong, 72–73 (Pullman: Washington State University Press, 1989). "It was not until the fall of 1942," Omura writes, "that the *Colorado Times* transformed into a pro-JACL organ. . . . This policy switch resulted when the *Colorado Times* agreed to be subsidized by OWI [Office of War Information] and thus subject to its 'propaganda' releases. It was because the *Colorado Times* transformed into a pro-JACL organ that I discontinued writing for them."

26. Omura interview, *Resisters*, 284.

27. See Arthur A. Hansen and David A. Hacker, "The Manzanar Riot: An Ethnic Perspective," *Amerasia Journal* 2 (Fall 1974): 112–57.

28. For a profile of the JACL's predicament in the camps, see Niiya, *Encyclopedia of Japanese American History*, s.v. "Japanese American Citizens League," by Glen Kitiyama. "Within several of the camps," explains Kitiyama, "JACL leaders were the targets of threats and physical violence and had to be removed from the camps for their own protection. Because of the controversy surrounding the JACL, the wartime president of the organization, Saburo Kido [himself an assault victim at the Poston camp], estimated [in 1946] that the membership 'dwindled down to only about 10 active chapters and about 1,700 members.'"

29. See Omura's revealing letter to his brother, Kazushi Matsumoto, January 1, 1945, Omura Papers, Stanford: "The F.B.I. is shooting in the dark when it attempts to dress me in the garb of communism. I have been a militant foe of Nisei communism. . . . It wasn't much over a year ago that I attacked the editor of the Pacific Citizen for his left-wing affiliations. This prompted a threat of a libel suit from Lawrence Tajiri."

30. Omura interview, *Resisters*, 284.

31. Omura interview, *Resisters*, 27.

32. See Arthur A. Hansen, ed., *Nisei Naysayer: The Memoir of Militant Japanese American Journalist Jimmie Omura* (Stanford, CA: Stanford University Press, 2017).

33. This editorial, "Let Us Not Be Rash," is reproduced in Omura, "Japanese American Journalism," 78.

34. According to Omura, a contemporary FBI report noted that before Omura took over the *Rocky Shimpo*, it "had only about 500 subscribers at Heart Mountain," and that after he "took over and started the editorials, the number of subscribers zoomed to 1,200." Omura interview, *Resisters*, 287.

35. Omura interview, *Resisters*, 314.

36. See Hansen, "Return to the Wars."

37. See Minoru Yasui's interview in John Tateishi, *And Justice for All: An Oral History of the Japanese American Detention Camps* (New York: Random House, 1984), 80–82.

38. Minoru Yasui to James Omura, November 19, 1942, Omura Papers, Stanford.

39. Omura interview, *Resisters*, 301.

40. Omura praised the Committee for Industrial Organizations (CIO), urged Nisei to join unions, and called for the abolition of race, sex, and creed-based restrictions in union constitutions. He also lauded advances toward interracial progress and advocated legislation against racial discrimination. Furthermore, Omura decried the twin dangers to democracy of Communism and its magnification as a threat by the House Un-American Activities Committee.

41. Commonly, Yasui promoted minority rights and civic-minded, liberal organizations and individuals.

42. Yasui quotes are from his column in the *Colorado Times* on November 21, 1947.

43. See "Shimpo Editor to Assume Full Time Duty with Paper," *Rocky Shimpo*, October 30, 1947, and "The Facts and Mr. Tanaka," *Rocky Shimpo*, August 12, 1947.

44. Bill Hosokawa, *Nisei: The Quiet Americans* (New York: Morrow, 1969); Robert A. Wilson and Bill Hosokawa, *East to America: A History of the Japanese in the United States* (New York: Morrow, 1980); Hosokawa, *JACL in Quest of Justice*; and Mike Masaoka with Bill Hosokawa, *They Call Me Moses Masaoka: An American Saga* (New York: Morrow, 1987).

45. Hosokawa, *East to America*, 243–44; and Masaoka with Hosokawa, *They Call Me Moses Masaoka*, 179.

46. Hosokawa, *JACL in Quest of Justice*, 273–74.

47. See, esp., Masaoka with Hosokawa, *They Call Me Moses Masaoka*, 179. Quote from Hosokawa, *Nisei*, 361.

48. See Niiya, *Encyclopedia of Japanese American History*, s.v., "Daniels, Roger (1927–), *pioneering scholar on the history of Japanese Americans*," 148, and "Weglyn, Michi Nishiura (1926–1999), *Historian, Activist*," 411. Also influential were Gary Okihiro's articles on Nikkei; see, "Japanese Resistance in America's Concentration Camps: A Re-evaluation," *Amerasia Journal* 2 (Fall 1973): 20–34, and "Tule Lake under Martial Law: A Study of Japanese Resistance," *Journal of Ethnic Studies* 5 (Fall 1977): 71–86.

49. Moses Richlin, foreword to *Concentration Camps USA: Japanese Americans and World War II*, by Roger Daniels (New York: Holt, Rinehart and Winston, 1971), x.

50. Daniels, acknowledgments to *Concentration Camps USA*, vii–viii.

51. Daniels, *Concentration Camps USA*, 128–29.

52. Michi Weglyn, *Years of Infamy: The Untold Story of America's Concentration Camps* (New York: Morrow, 1976).

53. Raymond Okamura, "The Concentration Camp Experience from a Japanese American Perspective: A Bibliographical Essay and Review of Michi Weglyn's *Years of Infamy*," in *Counterpoint: Perspectives on Asian America*, ed. Emma Gee, 27–30 (Los Angeles: Asian American Studies Center, University of California, Los Angeles, 1976).

54. Weglyn, *Years of Infamy*, 67

55. See Weglyn, *Years of Infamy*, especially chaps. 9–12.

56. See Niiya, *Encyclopedia of Japanese American History*, s.v., "Collins, Wayne Mortimer (1900–1974), *attorney*," 140–41.

57. For the summary of the hearings, see Commission on Wartime Relocation and Internment of Civilians, *Personal Justice Denied: Report of the Commission on Wartime Relocation and Internment of Civilians* (Washington, DC: GPO, 1982).

58. William Hohri, *Repairing America: An Account of the Movement for Japanese-American Redress* (Pullman: Washington State University Press, 1988), 30.

59. See Yasuko I. Takezawa, *Breaking the Silence: Redress and Japanese American Ethnicity* (Ithaca, NY: Cornell University Press, 1995), 51.

60. See transcription of hearings held by the Commission on Wartime Relocation and Internment of Civilians, September 9, 1981, Seattle Central Community College, Seattle, Washington, and e-mail correspondence from Aiko Herzig-Yoshinaga to Arthur Hansen, May 15, 2001, Omura Papers, Stanford. The author thanks Herzig-Yoshinaga, a key research associate for the commission, who supplied both the transcription and the explanation for the context of Omura's panel testimony. See also "Written Submission by James M. Omura, Seattle Hearings, CWRIC," October 16, 1981, Omura Papers, Stanford.

61. For a biographical overview of Chin, see Shawn Wong, ed., *Asian American Literature: A Brief Introduction and Anthology* (New York: HarperCollins, 1996), 15–16.

62. According to Wong, *Asian American Literature*, 15, "Chin's *The Chickencoop Chinaman* was the first Asian American play performed on a legitimate New York stage when it was produced in 1972 by the American Place Theatre."

63. See Niiya, *Encyclopedia of Japanese American History*, s.v., "Inada, Lawson Fusao (1938–), *Poet, Writer*," by Emily Lawsin, 207–8; and Frank Chin, Jeffrey Paul Chan, Lawson Fusao Inada, and Shawn Wong, eds., *The Big Aiiieeeee! An Anthology of Asian-American Writers* (Washington, DC: Howard University Press, 1974).

64. See Niiya, *Encyclopedia of Japanese American History*, s.v., "Mori, Toshio (1910–1980), *writer*," 283–84. In 1985 the University of Washington Press republished, in its Asian American series, Mori's 1949 classic collection of short stories, *Yokohama, California*, with a new introduction by Lawson Inada. This edition also includes the original introduction by William Saroyan, a staunch supporter and contributor to Omura's *Current Life*.

65. For the context of this wartime contact between Akutsu and Omura, see Omura interview, *Resisters*, 300. As recalled by Omura in 1984, the situation forty years earlier was this: "Because he [Akutsu] was searching for an answer [about how to deal with the draft], he went to . . . Min Yasui [at Mindoka], feeling that, since he had violated a curfew, he was a champion of civil rights. He looked up to someone like that, see? Then he talked with Min. . . . He wrote me about this: 'I'm so disappointed.'"

66. See Hohri, *Repairing America*, 48–50, 87, and 83. Mitchell T. Maki, Harry H. L. Kitano, and S. Megan Berthold, in *Achieving the Impossible Dream: How Japanese Americans Obtained Redress* (Urbana: University of Illinois Press, 1999), 122, claim that NCJAR pursued redress via the courts partly because it "and William Hohri in particular were motivated by an intense dislike of the national JACL."

67. Hohri, *Repairing America*, 125–29.

68. See Frank Chin, "Let Us Now Praise Famous Men," *Rafu Shimpo*, June 25, 1994; this account in Chin's obituary of Omura was amplified by him in personal conversations with the author.

69. See Martha Nakagawa's entry "draft resisters" in *Encyclopedia of Japanese American History*, ed. Niiya, 153–54.

70. The Frank Chin Oral History Collection is in the Manuscripts, Archives, and Special Collections department at Washington State University.

71. Chin, "Let Us Now Praise Famous Men."

72. See Robert Sadamu Shimabukuro, *Born in Seattle: The Campaign for Japanese American Redress* (Seattle: University of Washington Press, 2001).

73. Omura and Ueno were both NCJAR *ronin*, signifying donations of at least $1,000.

74. In San Francisco, the *Hokubei Mainichi*, and in Los Angeles, the *Rafu Shimpo*.

75. For Omura's review of the Hosokawa volume see *Amerasia Journal* 11 (1984): 97–102; see also his review of Peter Irons, *Justice at War: The Story of the Japanese American Internment Cases* (New York: Oxford University Press, 1983), *Amerasia Journal* 10 (1983): 127–29.

76. Richard Drinnon, *Keeper of Concentration Camps: Dillon S. Myer and American Racism* (Berkeley: University of California Press, 1987).

77. Frank Chin, "Introduction to Frank Emi and James Omura," in *Frontiers of Asian American Studies: Writing, Research, and Commentary*, ed. Gail M. Nomura, Russell Endo, Stephen H. Sumida, and Russell C. Leong (Pullman: Washington State University Press, 1989), 39–40.

78. Omura's involvement in this process was encouraged and abetted by Aiko Herzig-Yoshinaga, a member of both NCJAR and the exhibition's advisory committee, and his efforts received a critical boost from historian Roger Daniels.

79. James Omura, "Debunking JACL Fallacies," *Rafu Shimpo*, April 11, 1989.

80. Deborah Lim, untitled report, 1991, 9. For an unabridged version of the Lim report, see Frank Abe's website, www.resisters.com.

81. See J. K. Yamamoto, "Wartime Journalist Recognized," *Hokubei Mainichi*, July 31, 1993, published when Omura was named to receive the Twentieth Century Award of Achievement by the International Biographical Association of Cambridge, England.

82. Jimmie Omura to Michi and Walter Weglyn, February 7, 1992, Omura Papers, Stanford.

83. See Jimmie Omura, "Yasui Statue Would Be Undeserved Honor," *Hokubei Mainichi*, June 15, 1980.

84. The information relative to Denver's honoring of Yasui was drawn chiefly from newspaper articles; see *Rocky Mountain News*, March 2, 1999; "11 Volunteers Will Receive Yasui Awards," *Denver Post*, December 5, 1999; and *Denver Post*, December 11, 2000.

85. For press accounts of Hosokawa's Denver honors, see the following: *Rocky Mountain News*, April 20, 1996, and August 20, 1998; *Denver Post*, December 13, 1998, February 9, 1999, February 14, 1999, and October 25, 1999; and *Rocky Mountain News*, September 28, 2000.

86. Chin, "Let Us Now Praise Famous Men."

87. Frank Chin, "Come All Ye Asian American Writers of the Real and the Fake," in *The Big Aiiieeeee!*, ed. Chin, Chan, Inada, and Wong, 52–92.

88. Frank Chin, *Born in the USA: A Story of Japanese America, 1889–1947* (Lanham, MD: Rowman & Littlefield, 2002).

89. For a joint review of *Rabbit in the Moon* and *Conscience and the Constitution*, see Naoko Shibusawa's review in *Journal of American History* 88 (December 2001): 1209–11.

90. William Hohri, *Resistance: Challenging America's Wartime Internment of Japanese-Americans* (Los Angeles: The Epistolarian, 2001); Eric L. Muller, *Free to Die for Their Country: The Story of the Japanese American Draft Resisters in World War II* (Chicago: University of Chicago Press, 2001).

91. Philip Tajitsu Nash, "William Minoru Hohri: Visionary, Writer and Activist for Resisters of Injustice," *Washington Journal*, August 17–23, 2001.

92. Chin, "Let Us Now Praise Famous Men."

93. See Arthur A. Hansen, ed., *Nisei Naysayer: The Memoir of Militant Japanese American Journalist Jimmie Omura* (Stanford, CA: Stanford University Press, 2017).

EPILOGUE

Since my 2008 retirement from California State University, Fullerton (CSUF), I have maintained currency in my specialized research area, that of World War II Japanese American historical studies. Such maintenance has been achieved mostly with those works focused on individual and group acts of resistance against oppression and illuminated typically by the research method of oral history.

The main vehicle by which I have kept abreast of such activities has been through my intensive editing for publication of the memoir penned by the late (and monumentally significant) dissident community newsman, James Matsumoto Omura (1912–94): *Nisei Naysayer: The Memoir of Militant Japanese American Journalist Jimmie Omura* (Stanford University Press, 2018).

A second means of my sustaining familiarity with wartime Nikkei resistance during my retirement years has been through service as an outside reader of manuscripts and manuscript proposals for university and commercial presses, especially the following four: the University of Illinois Press, the University Press of Colorado, the University of Washington Press, and Palgrave Macmillan.

DOI: 10.5876/9781607328124.c009

Being a paid historical consultant for the Japanese American National Museum (JANM) and a volunteer one for three other organizations—the National Park Service's Manzanar National Historic Site, the activist Manzanar Committee, and the Orange County Agricultural and Nikkei Heritage Museum at CSUF—has also returned me dividends in terms of staying attuned to Japanese American wartime resistance studies. The most consequential of these consultant-adviser roles has been that with JANM, for which I have acted as the lead scholar for multiple national conferences, such as that in 2013 held in Seattle, Washington, under the title "Speaking Up! Democracy, Justice, Dignity."

Finally, my ongoing authorship of entries for Seattle-based Densho's online encyclopedia edited by Brian Niiya, and book reviews for biannual special issues of the *Nichi Bei Weekly*, edited by Kenji Teguma and based in San Francisco, have aided me greatly in keeping my finger on the pulse of evolving Nikkei World War II resistance scholarship.

While all of the above strategic involvement has connected me with almost every genre of new Japanese American wartime resistance work (books, films, articles, museum exhibits, oral history projects, bibliographies, theses and dissertations, reviews, websites, etc.), for present purposes I will below limit myself only to the first of these genres, books, and then only to those volumes that I have both read since 2008 and judged to be unusually noteworthy.

Listed in no special order, the following volumes spring to mind: Mira Shimabukuro, *Relocating Authority: Japanese Americans Writing to Redress Mass Incarceration* (Denver: University Press of Colorado, 2015); Shirley Castelnuovo, *Soldiers of Conscience: Japanese American Military Resisters in World War II* (Westport, CT: Praeger, 2008); Matthew M. Briones, *Jim and Jap Crow: A Cultural History of 1940s Interracial America* (Princeton, NJ: Princeton University Press, 2012); Lorraine K. Bannai, *Enduring Conviction: Fred Korematsu and His Quest for Justice* (Seattle: University of Washington Press, 2015); Cherstin M. Lyon, *Prisons and Patriots: Japanese American Wartime Citizenship, Civil Disobedience, and Historical Memory* (Philadelphia: Temple University Press, 2012); Gordon Hirabayashi, with James A. Hirabayashi and Lane Ryo Hirabayashi, *A Principled Stand: The Story of Hirabayashi v. United States* (Seattle: University of Washington Press, 2013); Eileen H. Tamura, *In Defense of Justice: Joseph Kurihara and the Japanese American Struggle for Equality* (Urbana: University of Illinois Press, 2013); Alice Yang Murray, *Historical*

Memories of the Japanese American Internment and the Struggle for Redress (Stanford, CA: Stanford University Press, 2008); Roger Daniels, *The Japanese American Cases: The Rule of Law in Time of War* (Lawrence: University Press of Kansas, 2013); Linda Tamura, *Nisei Soldiers Break Their Silence: Coming Home to Hood River* (Seattle: University of Washington Press, 2012); John Howard, *Concentration Camps on the Home Front: Japanese Americans in the House of Jim Crow* (Chicago: University of Chicago Press, 2008); Takako Day, *Show Me the Way to Go Home: The Moral Dilemma of Kibei No No Boys in World War Two Incarceration Camps* (Middlebury, VT: Wren Song Press, 2014); Greg Robinson and Elena Tajima Creef, *Miné Okuba: Following Her Own Road* (Seattle: University of Washington Press, 2008); Ellen Wu, *The Color of Success: Asian Americans and the Origins of the Model Minority* (Princeton, NJ: Princeton University Press, 2014); Jasmine Alinder, *Moving Images: Photography and the Japanese American Incarceration* (Urbana: University of Illinois Press, 2009); Karen M. Inouye, *The Long Afterlife of Nikkei Wartime Incarceration* (Stanford, CA: Stanford University Press, 2016); and Charles Wollenberg, *Rebel Lawyer: Wayne Collins and the Defense of Japanese American Rights* (Berkeley, CA: Heyday, 2018).

Those who have already read or, in the future, have the opportunity to read a sampling of the above-noted books will likely be powerfully impressed, as I assuredly have been, by how their authors and editors have variously enhanced a field of Japanese American historical inquiry to which I was honored to be but a relatively early and very modest contributor.

Hopefully, in reflecting upon these volumes, readers will realize how World War II and postwar Japanese American community resistance already has reaped a bountiful harvest of achievements, with still more in the offing. Such actions as the following representative ones did not occur in a vacuum but rather were the byproduct of vigilant commitment to and struggle for constitutional principles, social justice, and human rights: the instituting in 1978 of an annual Day of Remembrance to observe and reflect upon the February 19, 1942, signing by President Franklin Roosevelt of Executive Order 9066, empowering the mass forced removal and incarceration of all Americans of Japanese ancestry on the West Coast; the conclusion of the 1983 report of the Commission on Wartime Relocation and Internment, *Personal Justice Denied*, maintaining that Executive Order 9066 was promulgated as a result of race prejudice, war hysteria, and a failure of political leadership;

the 1980s overturning of the World War II constitutional test case convictions of resisters Fred Korematsu (1983), Minoru Yasui (1984), and Gordon Hirabayashi (1987) through writs of coram nobis and their later selection as Presidential Medal of Freedom recipients; the August 10,1988, signing by President Ronald Reagan of the Civil Liberties Act of 1988, which granted redress of $20,000 and a formal presidential apology to every surviving US citizen or legal resident immigrant of Japanese ancestry incarcerated during World War II, along with provision for a public education fund so as to prevent future recurrences of displacement and detention for other Americans; the establishment of National Park Service–administered historic sites at two World War II War Relocation Authority centers, Manzanar (1992) and Minidoka (2001), and the prospect of still another, Tule Lake, achieving this same status; the May 11, 2002, Japanese American Citizens League's public apology to the Nisei draft resisters of conscience for demonizing their stand during World War II instead of defending them for exerting their constitutional rights as patriotic American citizens; and the December 7, 2011, awarding of a special Congressional Gold Medal to Japanese American veterans of the 442nd Regimental Combat Team, the 100th Infantry Battalion, and the Military Intelligence Service for their heroic World War II contribution.

INDEX